RADICAL PSYCHOANALYSIS

Only by the method of free-association could Sigmund Freud have demonstrated how human consciousness is formed by the repression of thoughts and feelings that we consider dangerous. Yet today most therapists ignore this truth about our psychic life. This book offers a critique of the many brands of contemporary psychoanalysis and psychotherapy that have forgotten Freud's revolutionary discovery.

Barnaby B. Barratt offers a fresh and compelling vision of the structure and function of the human psyche, building on the pioneering work of theorists such as André Green and Jean Laplanche, as well as contemporary deconstruction, feminism, and liberation philosophy. He explores how "drive" or desire operates dynamically between our biological body and our mental representations of ourselves, of others, and of the world we inhabit. This dynamic vision not only demonstrates how the only authentic freedom from our internal imprisonments comes through free-associative praxis, it also shows the extent to which other models of psychoanalysis (such as ego-psychology, object-relations, self-psychology, and interpersonal-relations) tend to stray disastrously from Freud's original and revolutionary insights. This is a vision that understands the central issues that imprison our psychic lives—the way in which the reflections of consciousness are based on the repression of our innermost desires, the way in which our erotic vitality is so often repudiated, and the way in which our socialization oppressively stifles our human spirit.

Radical Psychoanalysis restores to the discipline of psychoanalysis the revolutionary impetus that has so often been lost. It will be essential reading for psychoanalysts, psychoanalytic psychotherapists, mental health practitioners, as well as students and academics with an interest in the history of psychoanalysis.

Barnaby B. Barratt has practised psychoanalysis in Michigan and now in South Africa. He was Professor of Family Medicine and Psychiatry at Wayne State University, and is now Senior Research Associate at the University of Witwatersrand's Institute for Social and Economic Research. His previous work includes *Psychic Reality and Psychoanalytic Knowing* (Routledge, 1984), *Psychoanalysis and the Postmodern Impulse* (Routledge, 1993) and *What is Psychoanalysis? 100 Years after Freud's 'Secret Committee'* (Routledge, 2013).

"This brilliantly conceptualized and carefully constructed argument that psychoanalysis must return to Freud's most revolutionary method is not simply timely, but essential to the growth of psychoanalytical theory and practice."

Christopher Bollas, *from the Foreword*

"This book is full of passion, a *cri de coeur* by a committed psychoanalyst. Dr Barratt advocates a return to Freud different from Lacan's. He goes further—searching for roots that even Freud forgot because of his need for scientific respectability. Barratt reminds us that the cornerstone of psychoanalysis is Freud's method of free-association, which opens and exposes the repressed unconscious that is rooted in the flesh—the way of listening to our drives, which are virtually infinite vectors of freedom of thought. One should read this book!"

Marilia Aisenstein, *Paris Psychoanalytic Society*

"Free-association is the radical psychoanalytic clinical position that Dr Barratt faces head on and with subtle complexity of technique, philosophy and history. Skillful descriptions of Freud's theory building and metapsychology together with a constant gaze on the ethics of psychoanalysis are woven together in a rethought history that becomes the reader's constant companion. For Barratt interpretation must always be subordinated to the ongoing quest for a free-associative matrix. This is a tour-de-force!"

Dr Jonathan Sklar, *British Psychoanalytic Society*

"*Radical Psychoanalysis* underlines Freud's emphasis on the method of free-association as what is essential, central and defining for psychoanalysis. It is, as the author puts it, 'a method that uniquely discloses, and to a certain extent undoes, the repressiveness of human self-consciousness.' Dr Barratt rightly calls his text a manifesto which urges us to commit existentially to the method of free-association. Its liberatory intent succeeds—reading it moves us into the 'workplay' of lived experience at its center. Laplanche and Green to whom the book is dedicated would be pleased."

Dr Jonathan House, *American Psychoanalytic Association*

RADICAL PSYCHOANALYSIS

An essay on free-associative praxis

Barnaby B. Barratt

Routledge
Taylor & Francis Group
LONDON AND NEW YORK

First published 2016
by Routledge
2 Park Square, Milton Park, Abingdon, Oxon OX14 4RN

and by Routledge
711 Third Avenue, New York, NY 10017

Routledge is an imprint of the Taylor & Francis Group, an informa business

British Library Cataloguing in Publication Data
A catalogue record for this book is available from the British Library

Library of Congress Cataloging in Publication Data
Names: Barratt, Barnaby B., 1950– author.
Title: Radical psychoanalysis : an essay on free-associative praxis / Barnaby B. Barratt.
Description: 1 Edition. | New York : Routledge, 2016. | Includes bibliographical references.
Identifiers: LCCN 2015045895| ISBN 9781138954847 (hardback) | ISBN 9781138954854 (pbk.) | ISBN 9781315666723 (ebook)
Subjects: LCSH: Psychoanalysis. | Postmodernism—Psychological aspects. | Freud, Sigmund, 1856–1939.
Classification: LCC BF173 .B205 2016 | DDC 150.19/52—dc23
LC record available at http://lccn.loc.gov/2015045895

ISBN: 978-1-138-95484-7 (hbk)
ISBN: 978-1-138-95485-4 (pbk)
ISBN: 978-1-315-66672-3 (ebk)

Typeset in Bembo
by Florence Production, Stoodleigh, Devon, UK.

May all beings be happy and free; may these writings contribute to the happiness and freedom of all beings.

In appreciation of the contributions of André Green (1927–2012) and Jean Laplanche (1924–2012), whose scholarship and independence of thought should be a model for every genuine psychoanalyst.

CONTENTS

FOREWORD

This brilliantly conceptualized and carefully constructed argument that psychoanalysis must return to Freud's most revolutionary method—the free associating psychoanalys and the free listening psychoanalyst—is not simply timely, but essential to the growth of psychoanalytical theory and practice. Dr Barratt explores the place of this praxis in the history of ideas and methods, integrates the many sources of free association—biological, neuronal, hormonal—linked to the drives that generate representation, and challenges psychoanalysts to note that however tempting it is to use the freely associated as the material of interpretation, it is the act of free association itself that supersedes its epistemic yield.

Barratt does not simply call for a return to Freud, he returns to Freud's texts in German applying his own radical read to these texts, giving them an entirely new meaning, radiant with clinical implications for the future of psychoanalytical practice. He also returns us to those thinkers who have influenced his creative turn of thought: To André Green, Jean Laplanche, Luce Irigaray and Julia Kristeva. His review of their work, however, is not a removed scholarly exercise, but a passionate read that drives not simply his prose but shows the reader how he forges his own unique vision of clinical praxis.

For decades, many of us have followed Barratt's writings drawn by his remarkable idiom of thinking—reflecting his life in England, India, the United States, Thailand, and now South Africa—and his education in philosophy, psychoanalysis, and human sexuality.

This is a book of inestimable value. It is profound, moving, compelling, and illuminating.

Christopher Bollas
October 2015

1

INTRODUCTORY NOTE

> Das Jungsche Argument 'ad captandam benevolentiam' ruht auf der allzu optimistischen Voraussetzung, als hätte sich der Fortschritt der Menschheit, der Kultur, des Wissens, stets in ungebrochener Linie vollzogen. Als hätte es niemals Epigonen gegeben, Reaktionen und Restaurationen nach jeder Revolution, Geschlechter, die durch einen Rückschritt auf den Erwerb einer früheren Generation verzichtet hätten.
>
> The Jungian argument, which he makes 'in order to gain goodwill,' rests on the overly optimistic assumption that human progress in culture and in knowledge follows an unbroken line; yet after every revolution come the epigones—those who react against its advances, refusing its achievements and attempting to restore previous conditions.
>
> Sigmund Freud, 1914

The sentiments expressed in the above quotation set the mandate for this book. Writing a "history of the psychoanalytic movement" (when his discipline was barely two decades old), Sigmund Freud's 1914 commentary is directed against Carl Jung's claim to have "corrected" Freud's innovations and thus, by abandoning "unwelcome discoveries," to render the discipline more appealing to the "masses." He could equally have directed his remarks to Alfred Adler's revisionism. And, were he alive today, might he not offer similar injunctions against so many of the "corrected" versions of psychoanalysis contemporarily available? Evidently, Freud was acutely aware that, in certain respects, human "progress" can go backward, and specifically that his troubling revelations about the human condition might well be discarded or repudiated by those who might claim to be his successors. Today, the history of the psychoanalytic movement spans well over a century and touches, to greater or lesser degree, every continent north of Antarctica. The movement is now conspicuously heterogenous, boasting all sorts of "progressive developments," many of which are notably in conflict with each other (clinical and theoretical disagreements that are rarely articulated clearly or cleanly debated), and many of which treat Freud's innovations merely for their iconic value. In this context, does it not make sense to return to an assessment of Freud's most "unwelcome discoveries"?

There can surely be no question what Freud's most troubling revelation is—namely, that the "I" of self-consciousness is not the center of our psychic life, never the master of its own endeavors. Rather, the operation of self-consciousness is perennially self-deluding. The "I" that reflects on itself actively eliminates, evicts or excludes, meanings which are abhorrent to itself, yet which impact upon its own functioning. In a specific sense, we are condemned to live in a dream (often, a nightmare of a dream). Freud discovered this—and I believe he could only have discovered this—by diligent immersion in the method of free-association. It is this method that uniquely discloses, and to a certain extent undoes, the repressiveness of human self-consciousness.

This book is a *cri de coeur*—a plea for a return to Freud's originality, in the interests of a wisdom that has been, over the course of the past century, obfuscated and all but lost. There have been previous appeals for a return to these disciplinary origins, perhaps the most flamboyant of which is inscribed in the theorizing of Jacques Lacan and the Lacanians. As is now well known, the Lacanian enterprise systematically critiques the versions of "psychoanalysis" propounded by the ego psychologists, the Kleinians, the object relations and attachment theorists, the interpersonal and relational psychologists, and so on. But this book is not a Lacanian thesis, although I believe it owes much—in spirit, even if not to the letter—to the writings of distinguished "post-Lacanians" such as André Green, Jean Laplanche, Julia Kristeva, and Luce Irigaray.

The Lacanian plea for a return to Freud constituted a grand exercise in theory-building. The structural linguistics of Ferdinand de Saussure, the phonetic and morphological investigations of Roman Jakobson, the anthropological study of communication and exchange systems promulgated by Claude Lévi-Strauss and others, as well as a significant exposure to the surrealist movement, were all brought to bear on an effort to reread and thus elucidate the contemporary significance of Freudian theories. It would be absurd to hold opinions wholly for or wholly against this endeavor. As much as I have learnt from the Lacanian enterprise, I have also offered some criticisms of the Lacanian *oeuvre*. But in this book, I am not interested in the construction of grand theoretical edifices. Indeed, I shall argue that there are ways in which Freud himself, especially after 1914, somewhat betrayed the essence of his own most unwelcome discoveries by focusing on the elaboration of various objectivistic theories of the functioning of the "mental apparatus." The topographic depiction of mental spaces (which was formulated well before 1914), the elaboration of object-relations theories after 1914, the speculations of 1920, and the subsequent structural-functional conceptualizations (of ego, id and superego), all variously present Freud's discipline more as a series of objectivistic theoretical endeavors, and less as a radical innovation of method. In addition to Freud's major efforts—from 1914 to the end of the 1920s—to formulate an objectivistic model of the human psyche, we have to contend with the theoretical splintering of the psychoanalytic movement that began in the 1930s. Whether one considers this diversification in terms of the conflicts between the Vienna group (Anna Freud and what later became ego psychology), the London group (Melanie Klein and the movement that followed her), or the Budapest group (from Sándor Ferenczi, Sándor Radó, and many others, to Michael Balint and the eventual coherence of an "independent" group of object-relations theorists), or in terms of the conflicts between structural-functional or ego psychology, Kleinianism along with other object-relational formulations, and the social or interpersonal movement (which began in the United States), the debates are, at least initially, over models of the "mental apparatus" and not clinical practices.

What if we focus on method? This is a focus that permits us to sidestep many of the issues of grand theorizing, since the method was decisively practiced prior to 1914 (let alone the 1930s). Such a focus must comprise an exploration of the method of inquiry by which the "I" of self-consciousness comes to know, or at least to have some sort of intimation of meanings that are impacting it, yet are or have been in some way eliminated, evicted, or excluded from its purview—that is, we must ask how self-consciousness can possibly come to be aware of its own repressiveness. Thus, it is precisely the purpose of this book to explore the significance of the method of free-association as the uniquely derepressive process that thereby demonstrates the conditions of repression.[1]

The free-associative method that teaches us about the repressiveness of our self-consciousness is—as Freud stated unequivocally in 1914—"the cornerstone" on which rests the entire adventure of psychoanalytic inquiry. As Freud knew well, what this method teaches us concerns the unconsciousness of a psyche radically different from the ideas about an "unconscious" that had preoccupied philosophical speculation for many decades prior to his discoveries. Freud also knew (although more ambiguously or ambivalently) that a mode of inquiry in which self-consciousness divulges its own repressiveness makes "unwelcome discoveries" that are never going to be equivalent to all the findings that empirical experimentation in the behavioral and neurosciences might make about psychological and neurological mechanisms that are nonconscious. In short, the free-associative method is unique in its power to reveal the "repressed unconscious" (that is, the repressiveness of self-consciousness). That neither logical argumentation nor empirical research can address this "unconscious" should not bother the psychoanalytic practitioner one iota. This is the thesis to be argued herein.

Of course, this raises the central question as to what *is* this "unconscious," if indeed it is a living reality of our being-in-the-world and not a figment of the patient's imagination (that is to say, not an artifact of the method facilitated for the patient by the psychoanalyst). In this context, I will argue that free-associative method is not merely an epistemological procedure, designed to arrive at what Wilfred Bion might have called a *knowing about* the unconscious. Rather, it is an ontological and ethical process by which self-consciousness opens itself *experientially*

—erotically and existentially—to meanings that are *other* and also that are *otherwise* than those it owns, or could own, upon reflection.

As I intend to demonstrate, the notions of the *other* and the *otherwise* are essential to an understanding of the power of the free-associative method. As the process of free-associative discourse deconstructs the law and order of representationality (within which the reflectivity of self-consciousness is constituted), meanings that are other than those that self-consciousness represented to itself become available. These meanings that were previously repressed (or arguably, deeply suppressed) can be translated into the representational languages (thoughts and imagery) familiar to self-consciousness. In this respect, they are meanings of an *other* text. However, free-associative discourse is far more powerful than can be explained in terms of the operations of translatability (from repressed or suppressed ideas or wishes into those that can be self-consciously articulated). For the method also opens self-consciousness to impulses or pulsations from within us that are untranslatable in terms of the languages of representationality. Free-association opens self-consciousness to be able to listen to enigmatic messages, from within the depths and the ground of our being-in-the-world. This is a meaningfulness that is *otherwise* than that which can be represented—otherwise than textuality. Such messages are of our embodied experience—our libidinality, by another name—and this is why the unwelcome discoveries of free-associative discourse led Freud immediately to the troubling revelation the significance of our erotic embodiment in all of the everyday operations of our psychic life.

Because these early insights—adumbrated approximately between the mid-1890s and the advent of the First World War—have so regularly been "corrected," obfuscated or relinquished, in the subsequent history of the psychoanalytic movement, it is precisely the mandate of this book to focus on the free-associative method, and the erotically and existentially embodied discourse that comprise the liberatory potential of psychoanalytic inquiry.

2

WHAT IS RADICAL PSYCHOANALYSIS?

> . . . eine entscheidende Neuorientierung in Welt und Wissenschaft angebahnt ist . . .
>
> . . . a critical new direction in the world and in science is open to us . . .
>
> Sigmund Freud, 1915/1916–1917

This book explores and advocates psychoanalytic praxis as the healing science of human self-consciousness and our lived experience.[2] By a close examination of the method of free-associative thinking and speaking, I will explain why such praxis indeed comprises "a critical new direction in the world and in science." It will be argued that psychoanalysis, if championed as free-associative praxis, is more wild, more critical, more erotically corporeal, more mystical yet existentially pertinent, and more powerful as a critique of contemporary social, cultural, political, and economic arrangements, than has hitherto been fully realized.

Each of these salient terms (praxis, healing, science, self-consciousness, lived experience, the ideological constitution of a "world," and indeed "psychoanalysis") will require critical discussion in order for us to understand the uniquely radical features of psychoanalytic discourse in relation to *psyche*, the human bodymind (the "soul" of our aliveness). Indeed, at the heart of this book is an effort to show how psychoanalysis, in its radicality as free-associative praxis, challenges our conventional ideas about what it means to be human. Such is the purpose herein. In a sense, this chapter merely explicates what any lived experience of psychoanalytic discourse tells us—or should tell us, if the process is conducted authentically—about the human condition. Yet, it also argues for the prerogatives of psychoanalytic method or praxis, as contrasted with much of what today passes as "psychoanalysis" in the guise of "psychoanalytically informed" or "psychoanalytically oriented" theory and therapeutic practice. In the latter sense, this chapter is a manifesto for *radical psychoanalysis* or, at least, for a reradicalized approach to the discipline.

It might seem perplexing that a field of endeavor that has been in existence since some time in the 1890s should require a manifesto thirteen decades later. After all, the genre of a manifesto denotes a declarative argument that is to be made—a polemic, the issuance of which typically indicates a hope for some future eventuation, rather than an agonizing reappraisal of the significance of discoveries made over a century ago. Yet in a special sense, this manifesto is both revival and proclamation. In order to reactivate the revolutionary dimension of Freud's vision, it invokes Freud's seminal disclosure of an approach to the interiority of each human being that is *praxis*—as a method for understanding-by-changing the order of our lived experience. Thus, what is advocated here is radical psychoanalysis as a discipline significantly different from, and in some ways profoundly contrary to, from much of what is currently presented under the rubric of "psychoanalysis."

In this chapter, the notion of radicality has a threefold implication. Etymologically, it can simply mean to go to the roots of something, to address the heart and soul of the matter—and this is indeed what is intended here. However, in this sense, many fundamentalist religious movements would be classified as radical; whereas many supposedly leftist political initiatives (notably, the liberalism of social democratic organizations) would probably not. In the context of psychoanalysis, the radical rekindling of the discipline that is advanced in this book is grounded on the recognition that the free-associative method has a powerful potential for the critique of all modalities of fundamentalism, fascism, and fanaticism (indeed, all the ideologies and hegemonies of domination that infuse our intrapsychic, interpersonal, cultural, and socioeconomic lives). Moreover, this radicality involves an appreciation of the human condition that exceeds the palliative or reformist possibilities of liberalism, and that contests the seemingly limitless scansion of utopian imagination. The heart and soul of psychoanalysis is not only radical, but revolutionary. Thus, radicality here implies: (1) a return to the roots, which are those of method or praxis; (2) a leftist vision of change, which emerges from the discipline's contributions to the critique of ideology; and (3) the awareness of an anti-ideological momentum that is revolutionary.

What is revolutionary about psychoanalysis is to be discovered and rediscovered in every moment of the passage of free-associative thinking and speaking—namely, that the self-consciousness of our being-in-the-world is never identical with what it thinks and takes itself to be. Psychoanalytic experience, as the praxis of free-associative method, demonstrates that the living and lived experience of the human condition is dynamically nonidentical or interminably contradictorious. As Freud himself suggested several times (but nevertheless perhaps did not fully appreciate, as will be discussed subsequently), this discovery implies a revolution, a great blow to human narcissism, in a way analogous to that delivered by Nicolaus Copernicus. The Copernican revolution decentered our planet. After the publication of *De Revolutionibus Orbium Caelestium* in 1543, there could be no restoration of a comfortingly geocentric universe, or indeed of the conviction that the universe has any center anywhere (excepting perhaps as the alpha and omega, the absolute totality that we choose to ascribe to G, who actually now appears to be playing dice). The Freudian revolution decenters by unveiling the perpetually deferred and displaced condition of our psyche. The "I" of self-consciousness, our bodymind and our being-in-the-world is not, cannot become, identical with itself. After Freud's publication of *Die Traumdeutung* in the final days of 1899, or perhaps after the slew of papers that preceded it from 1896 onwards, there is actually no genuine return from this revolution. Thus, it should be of no surprise that Freud, toward the end of his life, judged the methods presented in *The Interpretation of Dreams* "the most valuable of all the discoveries it has been my good fortune to make."[3] With the awareness of free-associative praxis, there is no possible restoration of a center to our lived experience, for the human condition is shown to be inherently ruptured and contradictorious. Without such awareness, one lives in the illusions and delusions of centeredness.

Indeed, there is a fashionable history of theorizing that reverts to the illusions and delusions of mastery, by imagining or positing philosophically a temporal point, an absolute totality, or the possibility of complete harmony. This indulges our craving for the fallacious comfort of a subject that is not decentered. It can be shown that—both subtly within Freud's theorizing and blatantly in the theoretical edifices promulgated by his many successors—there are multiple and recurrent enterprises aimed at recentering the psyche. After the revolution comes the reluctance or resistance to accepting its profound and far-reaching implications. After the revolution, there surfaces a reactionary nostalgia for a return to the pre-revolutionary state! In the case of psychoanalysis, such reactionary enterprises elaborate monumental theoretical structures, intricate conceptual formulations, sometimes buttressed by experimental data, about the "mental apparatus" that effectively restore our sense that we are, in fact, or could be, centered. This is the nostalgia for certainties in a universe that is inherently uncertain—the universe that is the lived experience of our human condition.[4] We crave the restoration of some sense that, somewhere in the cacophony of events and processes are the "foundations" of being human, there might be, at the very least, either a "still small voice," a point of potential harmony within each individual, or an immutable transpersonal totality within which each of us is constituted (G, for example).

Freud's method of changeful inquiry itself cautions us to be suspicious of any faith in G. For that matter, it incisively impels us toward a critique of any metaphysical belief, from humanistic assertions about the agency of "I" to the Hegelian solution of *Absolute Knowledge*. It demands our critical disaffiliation from these systems, because psychoanalytic discourse exposes how desperately motivated we all are to believe in a center, or to hope for absolution in some totality. It is entirely understandable that Freud himself recurrently attempted to retreat from his own Copernican revolution—to believe, in effect, that his science could itself constitute a secure point from which to ascertain whatever might be "real, proper, right, true and pragmatically successful." As Jean Laplanche has so ably demonstrated, Freud repeatedly slides away from the radicality of his own discoveries, as if to reestablish a Ptolemaist universe. This occurs less in the writings between 1896 and 1914, but more emphatically after that date, when there is, as André Green suggests (and as I have argued elsewhere), some sort of shift or "caesura" in Freud's orientation to his discipline and to the world in which he lived. With the advent of the First World War and thereafter, Freud's productivity became less intimately connected to the revolutionary discovery of free-associative method. It became more imperiously attached to the masterful labors of speculative conceptualization and systematization of his theoretical structures (and it is to these enterprises of "re-centration" that so many activities that spuriously call themselves "psychoanalytic" today hold allegiance). Thus, what is more troubling than Freud's understandable ambiguity or vacillations—the vicissitudes by which the *oeuvre* bequeathed to us presents itself as far from monolithic—is that so many of the extant efforts of his successors have aimed consistently at recentering the human condition, as if the revolution of free-associative praxis could be undone. They have generated so many versions of what is called "psychoanalytic" theory and practice, which have in common the pursuit of an enticing illusion-delusion at the expense of a commitment to the scientificity of the free-associative method as well as to the healing of our lived experience that it entails (as will be discussed later in this chapter).

To survey all the theories and practices that today pass under the title of "psychoanalysis" or as being "psychoanalytically informed" or "psychoanalytically oriented" is to be confronted with an almost bewildering array of formulations about the human condition, about the nature of its torment and about the interventions that might alleviate it. Many of these formulations are actually in fundamental disagreement with each other, their basic assumptions diverging. This can be exemplified by even a brief comparison of the depictions of the human condition presented by Harry Stack Sullivan (1892–1949), Anna Freud (1895–1982), and Melanie Klein (1882–1960). These are three influential figures who, in the 1930s and 1940s, succeeded in taking "psychoanalysis" in quite discrepant directions. Additionally, the depiction of the human condition later advanced by Jacques Lacan (1901–1981) in his "return to Freud" that was propounded from the 1950s until the late 1970s, diverges in a sharply critical fashion from these three. However, I will postpone this sort of comparative critique until later. What must be indicated here is the extent to which all formulations of theory and practice since the 1930s, as well as much of Freud's own efforts, conspicuously after 1914 (to say nothing of the dissenting positions of Adler, Jung, and several others) typically have three effects in common.

First, the restoration of a center to psychic life. Consider, in this respect, such concepts as the following: The "self" that is, or can be, unified and that encounters an organized system of cultural forces (the lineage of Sullivan, and a diverse group of self-psychologists, interpersonalists, and so forth); the "conflict-free sphere" of the ego organization (the lineage of Anna Freud and Heinz Hartmann); and the archaic ego that already has "objects" that are activated by "drives" conceptualized as biological instincts (the lineage of Melanie Klein); or the transpersonal totality of language structures that precipitates the ego as a sort of "floating signifier" (the lineage of Jacques Lacan, which obviously involves a somewhat different mode of recentering, since it pertains not to the individual but to the matrix within which the individual is constituted). We can also notice here how readily the recentering of individual psychic life implies the acceptance of "reality" (or, in Lacan's case, of a transpersonal totality) as a predetermined given. We can also note how readily this recentering (with the possible exception of some relational or interpersonal depictions of a bourgeois "self") implies a static or anti-dialectical theorization of the relations between social entities.

Second, the reestablishment of a conventional relationship between theory and practice. Consider, in this respect, how typically "psychoanalysis" is identified as a theoretical set of conceptual structures, describing or even explaining how the mind functions in health and in sickness, which are then to be applied in the clinical encounter. Of course, it is claimed—with varying degrees of credibility—that these conceptual structures are derived from observations and inferences made in the clinical setting, as a sort of hermeneutic or metahermeneutic narrative or explanatory code (the "witch metapsychology," as Freud dubbed such conceptual edifices in his 1937 essay, *Die endliche und die unendliche Analyse*). However, this scarcely obviates what stands as a prioritization of epistemology in which theoretical structures have an objectifying and objectivistic hold over the being-in-the-world that is ostensibly their "object."

Third, the reassertion of therapeutic goals. Consider, in this respect, how much clinical practice commences with a theoretical distinction between normality and abnormality (even if this distinction is held as relative and culturally circumscribed, rather than absolute and contextually independent). That is, consider the extent to which the clinician engages in an essentially manipulative task (even if benignly so) that aims for results, the success or effectiveness of which is conceptualized as the client's progress toward more "mature" and "adaptive" functioning. The criteria of maturity and adaptation are predetermined, encoded in the theoretical structures by which the "mental apparatus" has been depicted. The implication is that "reality"—specifically, social and cultural reality—is not understood as the result of human productivity. Rather, it is treated as something inevitable and immutable, to be taken "as is" (in relation to which, the clinician claims expertise). Therapeutics thus readily inscribes itself as a mode of ideological transmission, by which the prevailing order is perpetuated.

The argument of this book is that the notion of praxis challenges these three assumptions. It is not, of course, that all the ideas of Harry Stack Sullivan, Anna Freud, Melanie Klein, and a multitude of others, including those of Jacques Lacan, are without value. No such sophomoric polemic is advanced here. Rather, I will argue that—in these various modes of recentering, in the prioritization of theory-building and effectiveness of therapeutic practice—the radicality of psychoanalysis, the crucial vitality of its heartbeat, has been occluded, obfuscated, or entirely lost. Hence, the revivalist trajectory of this manifesto.

Can we embark from the proclamation that psychoanalysis concerns *lived experience*? Can we provisionally define its discourse as the healing science of our lived experience and thus of human self-consciousness (quickly adding that the notion of healing cannot be equated with the illusions of harmonious recentering, let alone accommodation to an oppressive "reality" that is presumed to be immutable)? And can we succeed in demonstrating what Freud indicated on several occasions—namely, that *psychoanalysis is foremost a method*—which means, as I shall attempt to show, not a practice in the sense of an application of theory, even if it is a theory that has been modified by successive practices, but rather the *praxis* of understanding-by-changing the purview of self-consciousness, the domain of our lived experience?

In the memorial poem published just weeks after Freud's death in 1939, W.H. Auden emphasized Freud's discovery of the "technique of unsettlement." The tribute thus embraces a brilliant insight. It does so despite the fact that, strictly speaking and, as will be discussed, the processes of unsettlement comprise a method and *not* a technique, either in the traditional sense of *technē* or in the sense prescribed by contemporary technology. Freud's significance lies not with his metapsychological theories (a "speculative superstructure," which he himself suggested in his 1925 "Autobiographical Study," might readily be "sacrificed or exchanged without grief or disadvantage" and certainly without jeopardizing the viability of his discipline). Rather, it lies with his discovery of a method for the interrogation of self-consciousness.

If we approach psychoanalysis this way, emphasizing that it is foremost a method of working-and-playing with the lived experience of our self-consciousness (hereafter I shall use the term "workplay"), it is implied that the discipline is *not* primarily a theory or set of theories about psychopathology, *not* primarily a theory or set of theories about the functioning of the "mental apparatus," and *not* primarily a theory or set of theories about therapeutic practice. Such matters are, at best, derivative enterprises that cannot govern or direct the discourse of psychoanalysis. This is precisely because, as will be elaborated, psychoanalysis is praxis, rather than a practice governed as a theoretical application. Not infrequently these theory-building enterprises actually are formulations generated speculatively or as elaborations of prior conceptual structures or from nonpsychoanalytic "data," that should have no bearing whatsoever on the discourse of patient and psychoanalyst. As will be discussed, this is especially the case with Freud's writings from about 1914 onwards, when his theorizing became increasingly detached from lived experience with the method of free-association and he became more preoccupied with addressing conceptual issues that were raised by preceding structures of conceptualization.

Auden might well have written that Freud discovered *a unique method of unsettlement in Love* that addresses the fracturing of our lived experience. In recruiting the notion of "lived experience" throughout this book, with due regard to writers such as Simone de Beauvoir, my intention is to underscore the existential ground of psychoanalysis in the root sense of this term. It is not my intention to articulate this chapter in relation to those serious thinkers who are commonly associated, correctly or incorrectly, with existentialist philosophy or with the lineage of *Daseinsanalysis* (such as Ludwig Binswanger, Karl Jaspers, Paul Tillich, Martin Heidegger, Medard Boss, Jean-Paul Sartre, Maurice Merleau-Ponty, or

Ronald Laing). At this juncture, the term also serves variously to sidestep, finesse, or postpone discussion of the idea of the subject. Lived experience is the subject matter of psychoanalysis, even if its apparent "subject" (the "I" of self-consciousness) proves itself chimerical. This is strategically important because what is argued in this book is that the revolution instigated by free-associative discourse is precisely the discovery that the subjectivity of the human subject is incessantly formed in and through our subjection to what is *other*, and also, even more powerfully and precisely, *otherwise*. This implies that the ethicality of psychoanalytic discourse takes a certain sort of priority over epistemological or ontological considerations (as I intend to suggest). Indeed, differentiated from the mainstream of even the more sophisticated modes of existential philosophy and practice, psychoanalysis asserts the realism of the repressed (as an otherness that is otherwise) and, as I have elsewhere discussed, the "mythematic reality" of libidinality as a subtle energy system.[5] Thus, the term, lived experience, is deployed here as what Freud called a *Hilfvorstellung*, a helpful or provisional idea, which both serves to postpone—at least for the moment—the definitional complexities of the notion of subjectivity as well as, among other matters, discussion of the profound discordance between psychoanalysis and the epistemic assumptions of phenomenology in the tradition of Edmund Husserl.[6]

Lived experience is indeed what is at issue in the psychoanalytic understanding of self-consciousness, the temporal forum of all the thoughts, feelings, and actions that are, have been, or potentially could be, represented and thus acknowledged as "I" (even if, as Freud discussed in 1925, such acknowledgment occurs under the aegis of negation). However, in psychoanalysis, this is an "I" that in its truthfulness is destabilized. It is the "I" that, so to speak, liberates itself (*its-self*, in the sense bequeathed us by Georg Groddeck) by encountering its own dynamic formation in and through what is otherwise than itself (but within itself).[7] So, whatever else may claim to be derived from an immersion in the discourse of psychoanalysis (all the objectifying and objectivistic formulations of psychopathology, of theories of the "mental apparatus," and of therapeutics, laying claim to this title), I will insist that psychoanalysis is the healing science of lived experience that unsettles self-consciousness in the truthful and freeing kinesis that is Love.[8]

Psychoanalysis starts—if indeed the praxis of free-associative discourse can be said to start—with the lived experience of suffering. It "starts" with a self-consciousness that is aware of its suffering and that somehow has an intimation of the possibility that this suffering is not necessarily so. That is, we are only open to immersing ourselves in the praxis of free-associative discourse because we have some sense that all we think we are and take ourselves to be, all we take to be the reality of our "case," is not necessarily "all that is the case" (which is, in a different phrasing, an intimation of the nonidenticality of self-consciousness). Through psychoanalysis, it is found that the "cure" for our ailment, the cure of our inner suffering, is not that of alleviative comfort, not that of finding a palliative security that is illusory-delusory, but rather the method of unsettlement. As will be discussed, this is a cure not to be defined and assessed objectivistically by outcome or "results," but in terms of its effects on our "soul"—its effects in opening us to Love. By contrast with the pabulum of therapy, the movements of Love that animate psychoanalytic discourse, aiming toward truthfulness and freedom, cast the "I-ness" of self-consciousness into the fire.[9] To aspire to the authenticity of truthfulness (profoundly different from the pragmatic criteria of correctness, correspondence, coherence, or even consistency) implies that one must deconstruct the inauthentic. To aspire to be free, one must become aware of one's own imprisonment—an awareness of that which curtails the momentum of freeing.

Of course, psychoanalytic discourse often spawns insights out of the interpretation of preconscious ideas. As will be discussed later, these are at most, so to speak, byproducts of its momentum (and often resistances to this momentum). What this chapter will argue is that interpretation aimed at the development of insight is more central to psychoanalytically informed or psychoanalytically oriented therapeutics than to psychoanalysis per se. Such insights as are provided by psychoanalysis indeed do often articulate the "who, what, where, why and how" of the duplicities and illusions—delusions of our own self-consciousness—the very ideologies by which we defraud ourselves and in which we are imprisoned. But more significant than the arrival at "insightful interpretations," the free-associative method of psychoanalysis—as differentiated from therapeutics—is an ongoing disruptive disclosure of those forces of law and order by which self-consciousness deceives itself, and thus an opening to unthought and unthinkable realities that are otherwise.

We know from Theodor Adorno how easily the notion of authenticity can be ideologically co-opted. So it is imperative to appreciate the way in which the Love that moves psychoanalytic discourse is inherently processive, a journey without destination (neither goal-directed nor utopian). Rather, it is a movement against that which avoids Love, a deconstructive *via negativa* (to borrow, at least for the moment, from John Keats' 1817 letter, or from the writings of Søren Kierkegaard and Jacques Derrida, rather than from the longstanding traditions of apophatic theology). This is surely a concrete—one might even say pragmatic, in deference to John Dewey's 1934 essay on aesthetics—expression of humanity's "negative capability," which is the potential to revise and transcend our contexts, and thus break kinetically with the predetermination of limits.[10] Psychoanalytic discourse genuinely engages what Adorno would call a negatively dialectical process, and thus it does so without stipulation of the possibility of arrival at some harmonious but actually unobtainable state of authenticity. Indeed, the authenticity toward which radical psychoanalysis aims is that of the *truthfulness* of its own process as the critique of the inauthentic. The freedom to which it aspires is not a state of our being-in-the-world that can be specified, but rather an ongoing, deconstructive process of *freeing* ourselves from the ideological forces that both constitute who "I" am and that shackle all of us. The healing science of Love in psychoanalysis is thus not a celebration of those abilities that lie within the present limits of human self-consciousness, so much as an indictment of the pretensions of self-consciousness in its ambition to totalize itself. In short, the method of radical psychoanalysis unsettles the certainties, the self-possession of the "I"—disrupting all that self-consciousness takes to be the real, proper, right, true, and pragmatic, in order to open it to an awareness of its own being-in-the-world that is healing.

Even in such a brief abstract of this thesis, it can already be appreciated how far a psychoanalytic process might diverge from the ambitions of therapy as a procedure of palliative remediation or recentering. Psychoanalysis concerns neither maturation nor adaptation to preexisting conditions and predetermined limits. Nor does it even imply necessarily a spiritual process in which the patient finds that "still voice," which called the Prophet Eliyahu (Ilyāa or Eli'jah) out of his cave.[11] Free-associative method sets our lived experience on a journey of passion and action—a trajectory of unassuageable wildness. This is a journey for which the challenges of ethicality are primary, rather than subordinated, to the dictates of epistemological and ontological tenets (for indeed the movement of psychoanalytic discourse opens us to a dimension of life that is otherwise than the subject/object relation represented in the purview of the epistemological attitude). This radical acknowledgment that lived experience involves dynamics by which it is interminably decentered from itself must be grasped in terms of the revolutionary implications of Freud's discoveries.

3

FREUDIAN ROOTS I

. . . the fate of psychoanalysis is to disturb the peace of the world . . .
Sigmund Freud, 1911

The challenge of reading Freud is to comprehend the magnitude of his revolutionary contribution yet avoid falling into a "myth of the hero"—for example, by imagining that his ideas can be appraised without reference to their cultural and historical context, or that everything he wrote must be accepted without correction. A critical appraisal is warranted not least because Freud's specifically psychoanalytic *oeuvre*—an immense productivity of writing from the 1890s to 1939—is far from monolithic. Rather, the trajectory of his theorizing embraces numerous ambiguities and vacillations (as well as shifts from more revolutionary to more conservative or nostalgic suppositions). In this context, it is a matter of concern that so many of the diverse schools of contemporary "psychoanalysis" seem to be based not only on an inevitably selective reading of Freud (notably focused on his theorizing after 1914), but one that passes over, in an ideological gloss, some of the crucial issues about the human condition that are at stake. The intent of this chapter is not so much to contribute, in any detailed way, either to an understanding of the cultural-historical context in which psychoanalytic discourse came to be articulated, or to the monumental literature on Freud and Freudianism. Rather, I want merely to offer a depiction of these matters that is sufficient to develop an understanding of the revolutionary significance of the discovery of free-associative praxis, in the conviction that this discovery is what is at stake, in the most profound and far-reaching manner, for any reflection on the human condition.

This chapter and the next will set the stage for further discussion of free-associative praxis with three sketches. In the remainder of this chapter, Freud's intellectual milieu will be briefly described in order to sharpen our appreciation for the epistemic rupture that his discovery of free-associative praxis entails.[12] In the next chapter, the implication of Freud's discovery for the subversion of the masterdiscourse of the modern episteme will be briefly indicated. The trajectory of Freud's writings will then be sketched in order to indicate the conservative or nostalgic implications of his increasing preoccupation with speculative theory-building and the systematization of conceptual structures (shifts that actually served to occlude the unsettling impact of the discovery of free-associative praxis).

The idealization of Freud's labors, treating his originality as if it were without precedent or influence, and thus overestimating the ingenuity of the heroic individual—a tendency evident in Ernst Jones's hagiographic moments—is of no service to psychoanalytic scholarship.[13] However, although Freud did not "discover the unconscious"—inasmuch as such an unqualified claim would overlook, among other sequences, the lineage of 19th-century European philosophy since the zenith of Georg Hegel's 1807 *Phenomenology of Spirit*, and even prior to it—it is crucial to grasp the way in which his unconscious was uniquely discovered as both the *repressiveness of self-consciousness* and the ubiquitously relentless effusion of *libidinality in psychic life*. This unconscious, along with Freud's understanding of the effusive sexuality of the human condition, entails both an elaboration of, and far more significantly a radical break with, all previous notions.

To grasp this characterization of a discovery that is both advancement and revolutionary departure—both development and dramatic rupture—in relation to the preceding history of ideas requires an appreciation specifically of Freud's intellectual milieu, not only in Vienna itself but also, more generally, within the intellectual foment of Europe in the late 1800s. From one perspective, this period represented the flowering of the modern era (the masterdiscourse that Michel Foucault and others have described as the humanistic consequences of the European Enlightenment); its blossoming into giddy optimism that human rationality might master all.[14] Yet it is also the period in which a triple critique of absolute idealism and the apotheosis of reason installed by Hegel's philosophy gained influence.[15]

(1) Kierkegaard, for example in his 1843 *Either/Or* and his ironically titled 1846 *Concluding Unscientific Postscript*, mounted an attack on Hegelianism on the basis of individual selfhood or subjectivity, advocating the prioritization of passion over what he understood as Hegel's deterministic philosophy of "Thought."[16] Kierkegaard's interest in the limits of science with his adamancy that there are matters that empirical techniques cannot address (for example, in his *Concept of Anxiety*), and his thus contesting the epistemological primacy of science by questioning its claims to objectivity as actually based on the illusions of neutral facticity (for example, in *Repetition* or in his *Eighteen Upbuilding Discourses*), were all discussions somewhat familiar to the intelligentsia of Freud's milieu. Additionally, Kierkegaard's 1844 argument that truthfulness is only produced for the individual in action, as well as his ideas about seduction (distinguishing a psychology of motivation from that of manipulation—for example, in *Fear and Trembling* and in *Either/Or*), may well have had an impact on Freud's thinking, whether direct or indirect.[17]

(2) Freud's youthful environment was, willy-nilly, immersed in discussion of the social theories of Karl Marx, of Marxism and, of socialism in general. From his 1843 *Critique of Hegel's Philosophy of Right* to the three volumes of *Das Kapital*, the first of which was published in 1867, Marx's writings constituted a sustained assertion of materialist dialectics, positioned against Hegelian idealism. Although we know some about Freud's equivocal assessments of Marx ("an undeniable authority") and his general skepticism about the feasibility of the communist programme (for example, in his 1933 *Lectures*), how impactful Marx was on Freud, directly or indirectly, has yet to be fully assessed.[18] But for such an assessment, one would surely have to consider the humanistic tone of the 1844 *Manuscripts*. This is because Freud's materialist assumptions were much like those endorsed by the young Marx. For example, as he breaks with Hegel (in his 1844 essay "Critic of Hegel's Dialectic and Philosophy in General"), Marx insists on "the fact that man is a *corporeal*, actual, sentient, objective being with natural capacities means that he has *actual, sensuous objects* for his nature as objects of his life-expression, or that he can only *express* his life in actual sensuous objects." This is a viewpoint that Freud would surely have endorsed. One would also need to consider how strongly Freud would have concurred with the famous epigrammatic conclusion of Marx's 1845 *Theses on Feuerbach*: "Philosophers have hitherto only interpreted the world in various ways; the point is to change it."

(3) Better researched and documented is the influence on Freud's thinking—again direct and indirect—of the writings of his contemporary, Friedrich Nietzsche. Unlike the influence of Kierkegaard and Marx, here the impact is unquestionably direct, albeit ambiguous or ambivalent. Not only did they share a relationship with individuals such as Lou Andreas-Salomé (as recorded in her *Memoirs* and elsewhere), but Freud mentions several times the "very great pleasure" he took in reading Nietzsche's philosophy. Interestingly, in the 1914 "On the History of the Psychoanalytic Movement," Freud indicated that he occasionally felt the need to abstain from this pleasure in order not to be overly influenced by "any sort of anticipatory ideas," in relation to the findings of psychoanalysis, which "the philosopher" has already "recognized by intuition."[19] Indeed, much has been written subsequently about psychoanalysis in relation to Nietzsche's ideas—such as his death-of-god declaration, his doctrine of eternal recurrence, as well as his notions of power and the *Übermensch*—and it is not my purpose to review this literature.[20] Rather, I will merely note, very selectively, three aspects.

One would be Nietzsche's campaign against the self-deceptiveness of moralizing in the name of religion, and in general of moral systems (which, in the 1888 *Ecce Homo*, he called a "calamitous error") as indicative of cowardly self-dissimulation. The campaign was launched in 1881 with *The Dawn*, and vigorously pursued in the 1886 *Beyond Good and Evil*, the 1887 *On the Genealogy of Morals* and elsewhere. In this respect, there are some obvious points of convergence with Freud's attitudes (despite the important issue that repression is different and far stronger than an act of "bad faith").

A second point of convergence bears on the implications of Freud's discipline for the critique of domination (and hegemony). Nietzsche's excoriation of "slave morality" (located in a master/slave relationship similar to that described by Hegel in his *Phenomenology*) mounts a challenge to the values of the Judeo–Christian–Islamic tradition that had, according to his analysis, promoted hypocrisy, weakness, and nihilism. This challenge is mostly articulated in *Beyond Good and Evil* and in *On the Genealogy of Morals*. As is well known, Nietzsche is often read as favoring the morality of the master. That is, the values of exceptional people who follow their own precepts and thus might live according to Nietzsche's favorite directive (taken from the Greek poet, Pindar): "Become what you are!" We have it on the authority of Walter Kaufmann's influential text on Nietzsche that this is a partial misreading. While his endorsement of Pindar's aphorism stands, it is an error to assume that Nietzsche accepts or glorifies the position of the master. Here the connection to Freud's ideas is crucially significant but perhaps shrouded, inasmuch as the critique of domination inherent in Freud's labors is perhaps not sufficiently explicit. It is, however, inherent in what might be thought of as his method of "unmasking."

It is this idea of unmasking that comprises the most striking connection between Freud and Nietzsche, and suggests their common debt to Arthur Schopenhauer's *The World as Will and Representation* (first published in 1818, although Freud was probably more familiar with the expanded edition of 1844). Schopenhauer and Nietzsche both argued for the importance of unconscious forces and counseled against any overestimation of the power of the conscious mind. This is the third aspect of convergence, for Freud and Nietzsche share an attitude toward consciousness clearly indicated by the former's argument (for example, in his 1925 *Autobiographical Study*) that the repressiveness of self-consciousness constitutes the central tenet of psychoanalysis such that all other teachings are related to it. Thus, there is a sense in which Marx, Nietzsche, and Freud have in common a critique of the ideological functioning of consciousness—the way in which it misleads our comprehension of the world we inhabit. This is why Paul Ricoeur, in his 1965 essay, dubbed them the triumvirate of a hermeneutic "school of suspicion."

It is challenging to describe briefly the intellectual foment that characterized Vienna during Freud's first forty-four years—the latter half of the 19th century, which has been the focus of so much scholarship. This was a period characterized by heady optimism focused on cultural and scientific achievements, as well as a certain—personal and political—attitude of desperation. A single illustration of this paradox would be the way in which the Emperor Franz Josef authorized major renovations of the city (for example, demolishing parts of the old city to build the Ringstrasse as a "Christmas present" for the citizens of Vienna) even while his Hapsburg Empire was being eroded. The years of Freud's youth witnessed the so-called modernist reaction to the European Enlightenment—for example, the almost fashionable notion that irrationality might pervade matters of rationality and thus that the goals of mastery might be fallacious. Such a political, cultural, and intellectual climate facilitated a turn toward inner exploration to the point where, as one commentator expressed it, "self-examination defined Vienna 1900."[21] In this context, I propose to designate five areas of intellectual foment that both influenced Freud and in relation to which he made dramatic—radical and indeed revolutionary—innovations.

Ideas about science. It is well known that Freud, having abandoned plans for a career in law, rapidly became enamored with the spectacular progress made by the natural sciences. When he entered the University of Vienna, the Head of the Vienna Medical School was Carl Rokitansky, a pathologist (and amateur Schopenhauerian philosopher), who, with the help of his colleagues, initiated major changes in medicine, transforming it from a branch of natural philosophy into an empirical science. Freud was strongly influenced by the ideals of empirical investigation, and specifically the advances being made in neurology and experimental psychology. Not only did he work very productively for six years in the laboratory of the famous physiologist, Ernst Brücke, but he was surrounded by the scientific ambitions of pioneers such as Carl Claus in comparative anatomy, Hermann Nothnagel in internal medicine, Theodor Meynert in brain anatomy, as well as the experimentalism of the French physiologist, Claude Bernard. Also well known is how Freud was not only influenced by his studies of hypnotism under, or alongside, Jean Martin Charcot, Hippolyte Bernheim, and Pierre Janet, but he was a quite ardent student of the positivist psychology advanced by Hermann von Helmholtz's physiochemical theories, as well as the investigations of Emil Du Bois-Reymond, which were exemplary of the new "medical materialism."

However, although Freud "worshipped and admired" the anti-theological (and, in a sense, anti-philosophical) materialism of Ludwig Feuerbach, there was also another side both to his training and to the milieu in which his scientific interests were nurtured. Sitting alongside Husserl, Freud took no less than five courses in philosophy from Franz Brentano, whose doctrine of intentionality challenged Freud's identity as *ein geistiger Naturforscher* (an intellectual researcher into nature) and caused him, at least temporarily, to question his adherence to medical materialism. Freud's young adulthood was, after all, the period in which, under the influence of Schopenhauer's criticism of Kantian thinking and of Friedrich Schleiermacher's hermeneutics, many philosophers were intent on establishing the human sciences (*Geisteswissenschaften*) as separate from, and irreducible to, the sciences of nature (*Naturwissenschaften*). This ambition notably preoccupied Freud's contemporary in Berlin, Wilhelm Dilthey, as well as, in a somewhat different fashion, the Baden (Wilhelm Windelband, Heinrich Rickert, Ernst Troeltsch) and Marburg (Hermann Cohen, Paul Natorp, Ernst Cassirer) Schools of neo-Kantianism. It is also interesting to note the extent to which these movements impacted the writings of Hans Vaihinger (whom Frank Kermode dubbed the methodologist of narrativity), because Freud read and cited Vaihinger's *Philosophy of 'As If'* with some enthusiasm.

Although Freud's epoch spawned the logical positivism of Ernst Mach, the Vienna Circle (e.g. Moritz Schlick, Rudolph Carnap, Otto Neurath) and the unified science movement, it is not difficult to demonstrate the ambiguities in his writings about the status of psychoanalytic science. For example, whereas in 1913 he predicted the "destiny" of psychoanalysis as being "in opposition (*Gegensatz*)" or "in contrast to official science," by the time of his 1933 *Lectures* he seems to assume the coexistence of "two sciences, psychology . . . and natural history" (although here, interestingly, he does not mention the distinction made in post-Kantian hermeneutics between *Geisteswissenshaften* and *Naturwissenshaften*, which would have been familiar to him, but refers instead to natural history as *Naturkunde*). Yet a mere five years later, in his posthumously published *Outline*, Freud announced that psychoanalysis is "a natural science like any other." Perhaps if he had been more philosophically inclined (in the sense of professional philosophy), he might have pursued his own intimation that the psychoanalytic indictment of consciousness actually revolutionizes our ideas about what is, and is not, scientific. However, it was evidently beyond Freud to grasp fully how his own discipline might indeed subvert the traditional tenets of "official science" and indeed present itself as extraordinary science.

Ideas about the unconscious. Both traditionally and contemporarily, the term "unconscious" is used in multifarious ways to the point where it might well be argued that it is unserviceable. With a considerable measure of generalization, it can be suggested that there are three types of usage.[22]

(1) The term can refer to anything that lacks consciousness, although typically the reference is limited to the nonconscious properties of living beings. Here the definition of consciousness is obviously pivotal. Frequently, the definition is restricted to what Gerald Edelman calls "secondary consciousness," which is the distinctively human capacity to be reflectively aware of one's consciousness (conscious of being conscious, which I call self-consciousness), or to think about thinking. This is contrasted with "primary consciousness," which arguably characterizes the wakefulness necessary for the adaptive functioning of many, if not all, living beings (our feline and canine friends unquestionably enjoy consciousness, but it seems unlikely that they engage in reflectively thinking about their own thought processes).

(2) The concept of the unconscious is also used for any of a very considerable range of nonconscious or a-conscious processes that impact the functioning of consciousness (primary or secondary). Here, one might include not only all the natural mechanisms that are the substrate of psychic life, the networks of neural circuitry that makes thinking possible, but also the functions of implicit cognition, the deep structures of language, the devices of perception, memory, and information processing that we routinely use but without any actual or potential awareness of their functioning. In recent years, an impressively burgeoning field of empirical investigation has expanded our knowledge of these matters, and there have been many ambitious claims about a convergence of findings. That is, claims about the allegedly increasing visibility of a consilience between psychoanalysis and "hard science."[23] However, the promulgation of evidence for "the new unconscious," in a manner implying that empirical investigation is now vindicating the psychoanalytic "discovery of the unconscious," may prove foolish insofar as radically different usages of the term may be at issue.

(3) The first and second uses of the term "unconscious" are, in a sense, merely descriptive.[24] Freud occasionally slips into this way of using the term—for example, sometimes referring to any representations of the world that is not self-consciously represented but might possibly become so as "unconscious" (despite the fact that he developed the term "preconscious" for such contents). However, such lapses should not distract us from the third sense of the term, which is specifically psychoanalytic. This is the unconscious that results from the processes of repression—the processes by which self-consciousness dispels contents from its own domain of representationality. This is a crucial distinction for it indicates the dynamic contradictoriness of representational consciousness (secondary or self-consciousness), intimating an unconscious not in harmony with the domain that is or can come into the purview of reflective awareness.

Not only has empirical science since Freud provided much knowledge about the unconscious in the two descriptive senses of the term, but the unconscious as the harmonious natural substrate of consciousness was much discussed in the century of philosophical thinking that antedated Freud's psychoanalytic discoveries. Notable in this regard is Friedrich Schelling's *Naturphilosophie* and specifically his 1800 *System of Transcendental Idealism*, with which Freud had some familiarity. Schelling is credited with coining the term "unconsciousness," and his 1800 treatise is seen by some commentators as a precursor to Freud's *Interpretation of Dreams*. Notions of the unconscious are evident in the aesthetics of Schelling's contemporaries, Johann Goethe and Friedrich von Schiller. Also, the influence of Schopenhauer on Freud has already been mentioned. Thus, there can be no question that the idea of an unconscious, as the substrate of self-consciousness, was prevalent in the philosophies that preceded Freud. The influential publication of Eduard von Hartmann's development of Schelling's ideas in his 1869 *Philosophy of the Unconscious* attests to this prevalence.

What must be emphasized here is that—whereas the notion of an "unconscious" was fully familiar to philosophical thinking prior to Freud, and whereas "unconscious," nonconscious or a-conscious mechanisms and processes have been amply documented by empirical investigation subsequent to Freud—these usages of the term typically refer to a more or less harmonious substrate of reflective consciousness. This must be contrasted with the idea of the contents of psychic life that have been dynamically repressed from self-consciousness and yet that impact this domain in an actively ongoing, yet disguised, manner. Despite some slippages in his use of the term "unconscious," Freud clearly knew that the free-associative discovery of repression comprised a break with both philosophies of the unconscious and with empirical findings about nonconscious mechanisms.[25] As I mentioned earlier, in his 1914 essay on the achievements of his discipline, immediately after a paragraph in which he somewhat ambivalently distances his ideas from those of Schopenhauer and Nietzsche, Freud stated unequivocally that his teachings about repression are henceforth "the cornerstone on which rests the edifice" of psychoanalytic discipline (*Die Verdrängungslehre ist nun der Grundpfeiler, auf dem das Gebäude der Psychoanalyse ruht*).

The panorama of sexology. That Freud was a lone sexual pioneer in a supposedly "Victorian" era (with all the hypocritical stuffiness that this connotes: The hideous misogyny of the Magdalene asylums, the frequent abuse of children, and the persecution of homosexuality) is another aspect of the "myth of the hero" that actually obscures the revolutionary dimension of his discoveries about the significance of the sensuality or eroticism of our experiential embodiment in psychic life. Here I will mention three sexological developments that occurred around Freud, that clearly impacted his thinking, and that serve to underscore the way in which his discovery of libidinality implies a break with conventional thinking about human sexuality.

(1) Perhaps the most significant development concerns the attitude of sexual openness and self-examination. Peter Gay's study of middle-class culture from 1815 to 1914 aptly designates the period as "Schnitzler's Century". In so many ways, Arthur Schnitzler's life ran parallel to Freud's. As Austrian Jews, who graduated from the University of Vienna's Medical School (Schnitzler just four years later than Freud), each admired the work of the other and both were publicly excoriated for their interest in sexuality. From his late adolescence, Schnitzler kept meticulous notes on the quality of his and his partner's orgasms in multiple sexual relations, both casual and otherwise. As a famous author and dramatist, he was highly controversial for his frank explorations of sexuality. For example, his 1897 play "Round Dance" (*Reigen*) provides a serious examination of sexual hypocrisy by following the encounters of ten couples before and after sex. The play earned Schnitzler widespread and sometimes violent condemnation as a pornographer. Jones's biography records that Freud saw Schnitzler as his "double," writing to him on 14 May 1922, just two years after the first public performance of *Reigen*, to compliment him on his "deep grasp of the truths of the unconscious" and adding that "the impression has been borne in on me that you know through intuition—really from a delicate self-observation—everything that I have discovered in other people by laborious work." In different ways, Freud and Schnitzler exemplify a turn-of-the-century attitude of openness, combined with an abhorrence of hypocrisy. This seems to have characterized the *avant-garde* of their time, for they are not isolated instances of an innovative and path-breaking attitude of erotic self-consciousness and bodily awareness (here the work of Gustav Klimt, Oskar Kokoschka, and Egon Schiele might also be mentioned as further examples).

(2) Pertaining to matters of sexuality, another development in Freud's environment that surely influenced him was, of course, the establishment of sexology as a scientific discipline, marked by the 1886 publication of Richard von Krafft-Ebing's *Psychopathia Sexualis*, as well as the work of others such as Magnus Hirschfeld in Berlin and Havelock Ellis in London.

(3) Another highly important development impacting Freud came not only from the work of early sexologists but also from all the ethnographies as well as anthropological and historical speculation that followed from the European colonization of the Third World. These convergent scholarly endeavors focused interest on the issues of incest prohibition, producing a literature with which Freud

seems to have had considerable familiarity. As is well known, in 1861, the Swiss anthropologist, Johann Bachofan, published his *Mutterrecht*, which argued for an original human state of promiscuity later moving to monogamy and women-as-property (a theory that disputes the notion of the Aryan origin of religion, as Friedrich Engels noted in 1884). This publication was followed by John McLennan's 1865 *Primitive Marriage*, which suggested that the practice of bride-kidnapping functioned to ensure exogamy (the controversial book was reissued in 1876, under the less salacious title *Studies in Ancient History*). In 1875, Henry Maine published *The Early History of Institutions*, which again focused on the necessity of social arrangements forbidding incestuous relations. Following these publications, in 1891 the Finnish philosopher and sociologist, Edvard Westermarck, produced his theory of exogamy and incest taboo, suggesting that living in close proximity (rather than some "natural aversion" based perhaps on a genetic code) caused the avoidance of prohibited sexual relations. In 1898, Émile Durkheim wrote an influential review of anthropological findings on the incest taboo (as ably discussed in Claude Lévi-Strauss's 1949 essay), and Ellis weighed in on the controversial issues in his 1905 *opus magnum*. The central point here is not only that the origins and functions of the taboo were under active scholarly scrutiny in the last decades of the 19th century, but also that this considerable literature addressed these issues on an almost entirely sociological or biological level. That is, almost nothing was written about the impact of the taboo on the formation of the psychic life. Herein is a fundamental dimension of Freud's far-reaching originality. Contrary to all those commentators who were content to discuss this prohibition as if it were merely a "natural fact" with variable consequences in terms of sociocultural arrangements, Freud explores how each individual negotiates—for want of a more apt verb—the taboo and how this "negotiation" is integral to the formation of the repression barrier.

The panorama of aesthetics and spirituality. Raised in the Vienna of the university, the operetta, the salons, and the cafés, Freud was—as is well known—not only imbued with the ambitions of science, but was a serious student of the antiquities (reading both Greek and Latin literature), as well as being an avid reader of classic fiction (from François Rabelais to Fyodor Dostoyevsky), who was devoted to Shakespearean scholarship.[26] In this regard, Richard Sterba's *Reminiscences* emphasize Freud's stature as the epitome of a *gebildeter Mensch*, the epithet given to an individual of diverse intellectual interests and pronounced literary and philosophical sophistication. Vienna, in the latter 1800s and at the turn of the century, was seen as Europe's cultural center, imbued with a belief in innovation, a wealth of aesthetic creativity, and a richness of sensuality that was inflected with a profound awareness of the attendant processes of decline and death.[27] As mentioned previously, contextualized by the political weakening of the Habsburg Empire, this environment nurtured the modernist rejection of realism and the restrictiveness of enlightenment values.[28] It was a period that celebrated freedom of expression, radical experimentation, and aesthetic introspection—the aim to realize romantic aspirations empirically, shorn of their idealism and without theistic faith. In the literature, music, and art of Freud's Vienna, this momentum is well exemplified not only by writings such as Schnitzler's, but also by the music of Gustav Mahler or Arnold Schoenberg, and the art of Gustav Klimt or Egon Schiele.

Although Freud's education was markedly Eurocentric, the impact on his milieu of non-European ideas and in particular those coming from Asia should not be underestimated. The strong philological tradition in Germanic scholarship ensured that translations of many texts from the Sanātana Dharmic traditions of spiritual teaching were readily available (for example, the *Bhagavad Gita* and the *Upanishads*), including many from the Sanskrit and Pali literatures of Buddhist doctrine. To a lesser extent, translations from the Confucian and Taoic lineages were also available. Freud's awareness of Asian cosmologies and philosophies was perhaps overshadowed by the intensity of his studies of Greco-Roman and Hebraic traditions. It is, I believe, often underemphasized by commentators, probably in part because of Freud's conspicuous aversion to organized religions. Yet he cites the *Brihadaranyaka Upanishad* (in a 1921 footnote added to *Beyond the Pleasure Principle*), and had a statue of Vishnu (the creator god of lawfulness, time, and history) on his desk. As is documented in T.G. Vaidyanathan and Jeffrey Kripal's anthology, he offered the Swiss poet and Hindu enthusiast, Bruno Goetz, consultations. He had a lively correspondence both with Romain Rolland (about the oceanic feeling involved in some spiritual experiences) and with Girindrasekar Bose, founder of the Indian Psychoanalytic Society (about the specific qualities of the oedipal complex in Asian cultures). Additionally, it is known from Freud's diaries written during the years from 1929 to 1939 that he conversed with Yaekichi Yabe, a Japanese psychologist, about Buddhist philosophy. It must also be remembered how much Freud was influenced by Schopenhauer and Nietzsche, the former being deeply impressed by Vedantic and Buddhist literatures (he wrote "truth was recognized by the sages of India"). The latter recognized the atheistic trends in Buddhism as the only religion he could accept. Thus, while Freud was adamantly opposed to organized religion, his attitude toward what might be called "spirituality" is in fact less clear, although his connection to Kabbalist Judaism has been explored The point here is that the intelligentsia of *fin-de-siècle* Vienna knew much about "Hindu," yogic and Buddhist philosophies, as well as other non-Western (or marginalized Western) traditions, and that Freud himself perhaps embraced far greater openness to spiritual experience than is typically acknowledged.

Archeological perspectives. Finally, the attitudes toward history prevalent in Freud's environment should be particularly mentioned. In many ways, this was a period of optimistically progressive thinking, socially and politically. Not only because of the rise of socialist ideas and the decline of the Habsburg Empire, but also because of the expansion of empirical science, as well as the search for the deeper roots of the human condition and the florescence of cultural experimentation, the belief that humans might create and modify their world was prevalent. But this was not without a strong sense of the manner in which the past necessarily shapes the actual present and possible futures. Freud's "partiality for the prehistoric" (as he once told Max Schur) and his passion for Greco-Roman, Hebraic, and Egyptian antiquities are well known. He collected artifacts, told Stefan Zweig that he had "read more archeology than psychology," and befriended Emanuel Löwy, a professor of archeology in Rome. Freud lived at a particularly exciting time in the history of archeology. Emerging from the colonialist pillaging of Third World treasures and Napoleon's plundering of the Egyptian tombs in the early decades of the 19th century, the discipline became more rigorous and respectful. For example, Flinders Petrie, whose illustrious career as an Egyptologist was launched in the 1880s, pioneered systematic methodologies for excavation, including a system for dating layers based on ceramic artifacts. In this period also, Freud followed, and was quite enthralled by, Heinrich Schliemann's excavation of Hissarlik, the site of Troy, as well as the sites of Mycenae and Tiryns.

This enthusiasm for archeological endeavors contextualizes Freud's unique contributions to our understanding of the multiple temporalities of psychic life. To be considered here is not so much his dalliance with ideas about the influence of phylogeny and the individual's "ancestral heritage," but rather his radical understanding of life history as reworked and replayed through the free-associative process. This includes the commonplace proposition that the past might be "excavated" in a manner that would reduce its impact on the present, thus aligning Freud's labors with the oft-quoted aphorism of his contemporary, George Santayana, "those who cannot remember the past are condemned to repeat it." The proposition led him, not infrequently, to offer archeological allegories to depict the character of psychoanalytic inquiry, suggesting that, like the treasures of Pompeii, the ancient artifacts of memory might readily disintegrate into dust as soon as exposed to the light of conscious scrutiny.

The trope is somewhat misleading in that it suggests a static memory storage that Freud's own discoveries of the temporalities of psychic life call into question.[30] Free-associative discourse indeed discloses the way in which "past-futures" infuse the lived experiences of the present. However, what Freud discovers is far from a simple phenomenology of psychic temporality and indeed subverts the assumption that psychic life operates on a unilinear, equably flowing timeline (like Newtonian clocktime). This subversion is most powerfully illustrated by Freud's notion of *Nachträglichkeit*, which, as suggested by Laplanche, could be translated "afterwardsness" (*après-coup*). This is a process by which the past may—so to speak—be redone by the present, not merely in its impact upon the present, but in its very signification as past. All this remains to be discussed further. However, at this point it must be noted how Freud introduces radical notions of the multiple temporalities of psychic life, even while being attached to archeological imagery that actually does not match the radicality of his own discoveries.

We can now proceed to appreciate more fully the revolutionary character of psychoanalysis in relation to this understanding of Freud's intellectual milieu.

4

FREUDIAN ROOTS II

> . . . I claim my place alongside Copernicus . . .
>
> Sigmund Freud, 1917[31]

Clearly identifying—at least in his fantasies—with the conspicuously successful leadership of the prophet Moses and with the more ambiguously successful leadership of the strategist and political reformer Hannibal, Freud knew himself to be a remarkable helmsman for an innovative and extraordinary discipline. Nevertheless, although he occasionally grasped the comparison between his discoveries and those of Copernicus (as initiating a revolutionary "destruction of narcissistic illusion" and a great blow to the "self-love of mankind"), it is also the case that he could not but underestimate the radical and enigmatic character of this new science. Perhaps this is always the case with genuinely revolutionary changes in our vision of the human condition. While one is in the midst of the revolution, its significance cannot be assessed with equanimity. In Freud's case, it is clear that he was both aware that his method initiates "a critical new direction in the world and in science," and yet unable to appreciate the extent to which his discoveries might actually change our understanding of science itself. In this chapter, I want to emphasize Freud's vacillating awareness of his own participation in a profound process of epistemic rupture.

Free-associative method and epistemic rupture

In many respects, Freud endorsed the positivism of Auguste Comte, whose 1848 text he had probably read in the 1870s (very likely on the advice of Brentano). Later in his life, he may also have known of literature that qualified or countered the Comtean perspective, such as the early 20th-century writings on philosophy of science by his contemporary, Émile Meyerson, who influenced Thomas Kuhn. Freud was trained to believe, and indeed wanted to believe, in the continuous, unquenchable, and unified progress of—empirical—science. In some ways, he held to this vision, even while his own innovations (to say nothing of his contemporary, Albert Einstein) demonstrated the discontinuous character of the history of sciences. In other ways, however, Freud knew that his discoveries implied a discontinuity, a break with mainstream psychology and with normative science. "The destiny" of his discipline, he wrote in 1913, stands "in contrast to official science." Yet it was not until the last decade of Freud's life that Gaston Bachelard, himself a student of psychoanalysis, expounded the notion of an epistemological break (*rupture épistémologique*), which comprises a discontinuity in the advance of scientific methods and theories. A similar idea was later elaborated in Kuhn's popular text, *The Structure of Scientific Revolutions*, which was written under the influence of Alexandre Koyré. Bachelard demonstrated how science can accommodate a process of abrupt transformation in its fundamental ideas such that their significance in a new paradigm is radically different from their significance in its predecessor. The example most familiar today is of the concept of mass in Newtonian and Einsteinian physics.

It seems certain that had Bachelard's perspectives been available to him, Freud could have recognized the radical and enigmatic character of psychoanalytic discourse in this philosophical theorization. For example, in his 1934 *The New Scientific Spirit*, Bachelard discusses how theories that are dismissed as irrational are often precursor to a necessary shift in scientific perspective. Here we might note how, from the logical and rhetorical standpoint of conventional rationality, for the subject to cast itself into a free-associative process contravenes the rules of "making sense." As will be argued in this chapter, a process that does not hold the law and order of making sense in abeyance cannot disclose the truthfulness of the human subject.[32] Implicitly or explicitly, this is precisely Freud's consistent claim.

The epistemological break initiated by the free-associative method changes the meaning of fundamental ideas such that their psychoanalytic significance is radically different from their significance prior to, or outside of, psychoanalysis. Consider here the meaning of basic terms such as consciousness (and the unconscious as repressed), psychic temporality, and sexuality or sensuality, each of which is to be understood in relation to oedipal complexities (as will be discussed later). The unconscious prior to Freud was understood in a descriptive sense as the natural substrate (and/or the transcendental dimension) of consciousness. The pre-Freudian unconscious thus maintains the centrism of the human condition in its self-consciousness (as do most usages of the term since Freud). In contrast to this, Freud discovers an unconscious that is born of the repressiveness of self-consciousness—the processes by which the conscious subject is perpetually and dynamically deferred or dislocated from its own being-in-the-world. Prior to Freud, philosophy debated matters such as the relational (or presentist and endurantist) and the absolute (or eternalist and perdurantist) views of time, the nature of the time/motion connection, as well as questions about infinity and cyclicality. Indeed, the distinction between cosmological and phenomenological time would have been familiar to Freud, especially in those years from 1904 onwards, when Husserl was conducting his studies of internal time consciousness, and in the 1920s when Arthur Eddington popularized the theory of relativity and wrote about the model of a unidirectional and asymmetrical arrow of time. However, the implications of Freud's discovery of multiple temporalities in psychic life, and especially of the phenomena of *Nachträglichkeit* comprise a dramatic break with all preceding philosophical deliberations about the "time of the mind." Finally, we have noted how Freud's milieu was fully aware of the significance of sexuality in human functioning (as is evidenced by the notoriety of Schnitzler). Not only did this period witness an efflorescence of sexological research, but the classics of human sexual celebration (from Ovid's *Ars Amatoria* to Vātsyāyana's *Kama Sutra*) were well known to Vienna's intelligentsia. However, Freud's notion of libidinality as an energy system underpinning all our cognitive, affective, and motivational functioning—as well as his discovery of the way in which "infantile sexuality" is pervasively polymorphous throughout psychic life—radicalizes all previous perspectives on the role of sexuality in human experience.

These three inextricably connected discoveries, which are tied to the method of free-associative discourse, constitute an epistemological break within the science and philosophy of "mind." However, we must consider the possibility that Bachelard's notion of an epistemological break, which he applied in a circumscribed manner as relevant to the progress of science, does not fully account for the revolutionary impact of psychoanalytic findings. Perhaps the stronger notion of an *epistemic rupture* is warranted. For Freud's discoveries did not merely transform the science of the psyche in some limited sense. Rather, they revolutionized every aspect of our understanding of the human condition. In short, the discovery of psychoanalytic method upset a universe, exposing the dynamics of the subject "I" as perpetually decentered and thus unsettling the ground and horizon of discourse—not just the domain of science, but pervasively throughout everyday life.[33]

In this context, a "universe" is an episteme, implying an organized configuration of unexamined or even unexaminable assumptions and principles concerning the fundamental conditions of knowing and being. The episteme is a masterdiscourse, in the Foucauldian sense—incorporating other terms such as cosmology, root allegory, underlying paradigm, or tradition. It constitutes the metaphysical or epistemic conditions of experience, determining the possibility of particular epistemological or ontological theorizations, and governing the possibilities of experience—our ways of thinking, speaking, and acting in the world. The episteme establishes the universe in which we live, contributing such basic notions as those of substance, essence, identity, space, and time.

What might it imply to suggest that Freud's methodical discovery entails the subversion of the modern episteme? The triune discovery of the free-associative method (if one includes their convergence in the oedipal complex, these would be the four coordinates of Freud's discipline) ruptures the episteme that governed the universe of Western (or "North Atlantic") experience from medieval times, and it does so precisely by demonstrating the nonidenticality of the subject with itself, the repressiveness of self-consciousness in relation to its own being-in-the-world. As I discussed in *Psychoanalysis and the Postmodern Impulse*, the modern episteme can be characterized in terms of Newtonian physics, the mind/body dualism of René Descartes, the philosophies of Francis Bacon and Thomas Hobbes, the analytico-referential or "logical-empiricist" tradition of epistemology, and the rise of capitalism. Its origins have variously been discussed in terms of the ethos of the Judeo–Christian–Islamic tradition, the metaphysics of presence articulated in classical philosophy, and the hegemony of analytico-referential cognition associated with the development of capitalist socioeconomic formations.[34]

One way to appreciate how the Western masterdiscourse of the modern era is ruptured by the discoveries of free-associative method is to consider the episteme's motif of *mastery* as domination. In simplified terms, this masterdiscourse is committed to the notion of a privileged, self-certain subject that is identical with itself, operating with or within the unified authority of "reason"—the mediations of logic and rhetoric. It thus ascribes to itself the knowledge and power to interpret and thence to dominate the world as a unity that is "other." The motif is well exemplified in Bacon's writings, from the early essays to his 1620 revision of Aristotle's *Organon*, and especially dramatized in his passages on the "kingdom of man" and his "dominion over nature." From the medieval era until the crumbling of the modern episteme in the course of the 20th century (with Freud's discoveries as harbinger of these disruptions), mastery implies *man's* domination over what is other. The self-assured conquistadorial subject is *man*, which implicitly or explicitly means the white, Western, landowning, and later industrial capitalist (the man of today's corporate boardroom). *He* is to utilize his privileged access to knowledge and power, by means of "reason" or rationality of a certain sort, in order to exercise his mastery over nature, over women, over peoples of color, over children, over those who are "abnormal," and over the underclasses or subcultures of other men—the "bottom billions" who struggle in a hopeless effort to extract themselves from abject poverty and disease. Psychoanalysis deconstructs the motif of mastery in three ways: It challenges the identity of the subject, the hegemony of "rationality," and the ambitions of domination—that is, the assumed unity of the "other" that is supposedly to be controlled by the manipulations of knowledge and power.

Against the identity of the subject. The law of identity is one of the three classical laws of thought, articulated in Plato's *Theaetetus* and amplified in the writings of many philosophers, such as Thomas Aquinas and John Duns Scotus in the 13th century, Nicolaus Cusanus in the 15th century, John Locke and Gottfried von Leibniz in the 17th century, as well, of course, as Immanuel Kant and the post- or neo-Kantians. Freud's contemporary, the psychologist Wilhelm Wundt (who worked as Helmholtz's assistant and then in 1879 established the first formal laboratory for psychophysical research in Leipzig) elaborated an identity theory, as did his contemporary the Russian philosopher Afrikan Špir. The latter's writings had a significant impact on Vaihinger and Nietzsche, whom Freud read approvingly, as well as luminaries such as William James and Leo Tolstoy. In his

1873 "Thought and Reality" (*Denken und Wirklichkeit*), Špir maintained that identity is not only a fundamental law of knowledge, but also an ontological principle expressing the unconditioned essence of reality (and thus securing this essence from empirical, conditional, or temporalized realities). The principle of identity (that A is A and cannot be not-A) not only designates that entities have an atemporal essence ("everything that exists is both the same with itself and different from others" as Socrates suggests), but also secures the subject in the Cartesian formulation in which the "I" not only asserts its identity with itself, but also the identity of its reflective enunciations about its own being-in-the-world.

As has been discussed by several commentators, the effect of free-associative discourse—the implication of its disclosure of the repressiveness of self-consciousness—is a subversion of the Cartesian subject. Psychoanalysis exposes how the "I" of consciousness is never merely what it takes itself to be. Rather, it participates in a continual dynamic process of simultaneously concealing and revealing something that is other or otherwise than itself, yet is a dimension of its own being-in-the-world. Thus, the extent to which the "I" can ever be "the same with itself" is called into question, but so also is the meaning of *different* when the "I" asserts itself as "different from others." Psychoanalysis anticipates Derrida, as well as Gilles Deleuze and others, in demonstrating the vitality of the "I" as embodying a different or *différant* movement of difference.[35] The issue of what the "I" engages as other (as a hidden meaning that is descriptively unconscious) and as its otherwise (as the libidinality of repressed desire) will be explored in later chapters. At this juncture, what needs to be appreciated is the possibility (to be illustrated in the next chapter) that, through the passage of free-associative movement, the subject indicts its own self-certainty or self-assurance, undermining the foundation of what it takes to be real, proper, right, true, and pragmatic—that is, in the temporal and corporeal momentum of free-association, the "I" exposes itself as perpetually deferred or dislocated from itself. This comprises a revolutionary challenge to a universe or episteme founded on the identitarian thinking that had been—and in many ways still is—the foundation of rationality in Western or North Atlantic thought.

Against the hegemony of "rationality." It has already been noted that, in terms of the rules of the rationality of the conventional order (the logical and rhetorical lawfulness that dictates and regulates how to "make sense"), the subject's surrender to the flow of free-association, which holds the rules of "making sense" in abeyance, actively contravenes the law and order by which "sense" is constructed. In this respect, as he opened himself to free-associative discourse, Freud broke with the precepts of the European Enlightenment and the idealization of "reason," demonstrating how irrationality pervades constructions of the world that appear rational. Thus—even if he might have wished to evade all these implications of his labors—Freud called into question the ambitions of mastery.

As will be discussed later in this book, despite the fact that Freud frequently depicted his science as restoring the dominion of rationality over the irrational forces of our "drives," the very method by which the significance of these forces was divulged actually—indeed performatively—challenges the hegemony of rationality. The free-associative method attacks the foundational presumption that the truth of a psychic event can be determined by the maneuverings of logic and rhetoric. Rather, in a profound sense, the momentum of free-association departs from the rationality of such maneuvering. Against the constructions of logic and rhetoric, the passage of such discourse exhibits deconstructively the truthfulness of the subject, or of its subjects. In this respect, as Freud came close to realizing explicitly (for example in his 1937 paper on constructions), psychoanalytic truth diverges from conventional notions of correspondent, coherent, consistent, constructed, consensual, or pragmatic truth. Rather, the psychoanalytic method exhibits, or sets in motion, something that we can, at least provisionally, call the truthfulness of the subject-in-process (a term that can usefully be developed from Kristeva's writings).

In Bion's terminology, the truthfulness of psychoanalytic method is not a matter of *knowing about* a particular domain, but rather an experiential mode of knowing that decomposes—or *analyzes*—the subject's ideas about itself. This is significantly different from a procedure that aids the subject in arriving at some sort of logically and rhetorically accurate formulation about itself (as will be discussed further in subsequent chapters). Psychoanalytic truthfulness is thus deconstructive, deeply suspicious of the subject's constructions about itself, and operates as a retrogressive dismantling of the "truth" of whatever presents itself (and is present or presentable as a representation). As an aside, this is why Freud opposed the emphasis in Herbert Silberer's 1914 work on archaic symbolism, contested Jung's commitment to teleological interpretation, bluntly opposed the project of "psychosynthesis" (for example, in his 16 April 1909 letter to Jung and in his 1919 publication) and was clearly not impressed with Roberto Assagioli's aspirations in this direction.

If free-associative method challenges the assumption that arrival at a representational construction, even if immaculately crafted under the governance of logic and rhetoric, could ever capture the desirous exuberance of the repressed, then clearly Freud's discipline confronts the limits of rationality as representational. Indeed, it intimates how the systems of logic and rhetoric effectively sever us from an otherwise meaningfulness that is repressed.

Against the ambitions of domination. If the free-associative method deconstructs truthfully, it does so by disclosing or setting-in-motion the subject-in-process, rather than the subject-as-master or as-potential-master of what is other and otherwise (as will be demonstrated in subsequent chapters). In this respect, it not only participates in the break with the ontology of substance, which characterized classical epistemology as well as the modern episteme, and moves into an ontology of relations as a processive science. It also sabotages the goals of mastery as domination that characterized the modern episteme (and that still hold us in their vice-like grip).

I have suggested here that a commitment to free-associative method has implications that are anti-subjectivist, anti-foundationalist, and anti-hegemonic.

Freud's method challenges the epistemological or metaphysical assumption that to know the other entails the representational capacity to predict it, to control it, or at least to utilize knowledge of it for one's own purposes. It also challenges the ethical-political assumption that power resides in mastery over the other. Rather it implies the "power" (in a radically different sense) or truthfulness of an "auto-deconstructive" process that opens itself to the significance of what is other or otherwise than the edifices of representationality.

In this respect, psychoanalysis attacks the equation of *knowledge as power over* the other—the project of domination. As much as Freud may often have lapsed into describing his discipline as one in which a rational organization ("das Ich" or "the Ego") gains mastery over the rambunctious subterranean world of the unconscious ("das Es" or "the Id"), his commitment to the radicality of free-associative method belies the significance of these lapses. The imperial-colonialist analogies in which rationality annexes territory formerly in the grip of irrationality, or in which "culture" tames the forces of primitivism (or in which the Zuider Zee is drained, as Freud analogized in 1933), are ubiquitously misleading. This is because the very method to which Freud was loyal undermines the ambitions of mastery. It thus ruptures the keystone of the modern episteme and demonstrates the impossibility both of a centered universe and of a centered life of the psyche.

On reading Freud

Not only does Freud still have to be read (and the otiose belief that one can appreciate psychoanalysis without a serious engagement with this task has to be trenchantly refuted), but his writings have to be studied taking these considerations into account. Thus, the most consequential contemporary readings—or rereadings—of Freud, notably those by Laplanche and by Green, have been engaged with the awareness both of his role in an epistemic rupture and of his own difficulties appreciating his own positioning in that role. In the context of today's challenge to read Freud anew (and thus to comprehend what is and is not his discipline of psychoanalysis), these twin issues are cardinally significant.

Perhaps it seems paradoxical that an innovator cannot necessarily be expected to understand the full significance of his own innovations. Often an authentically original breakthrough that unsettles us gets rapidly buried by revisionism, initiating a process that Laplanche calls "going-astray" (*fourvoiement*, "wandering off the path" or "straying into error"). The originator is not immune from such deviations.

Freud knew that the free-associative discovery of the repressiveness of self-consciousness, of pluritemporality and polysexuality (and of their convergence in the universal complexities of oedipus) constituted a Copernican revolution that would forever decenter the human subject (or perhaps more accurately that would demonstrate the illusoriness of any appearance of a center). But he vacillated in this awareness, for it can be shown that he was never consistently able to appreciate his own radicality, nor to relinquish his own proclivities toward reactionary conservatism and nostalgia—that is, having discovered the decentered condition of psychic life, Freud repeatedly articulated theories that recenter. Such are theories of self-centering or even self-begetting; metapsychological depictions of the "mental apparatus" that make it appear as if the psyche could be centered. His writings need to be read with the focus of this understanding of the tension between revolutionary discovery and the revisionist "going-astray" of some of his theorizations.

In a series of essays from 1992 and 1993 (and later), Laplanche documents in detail his thesis that "if Freud is his own Copernicus, he is also his own Ptolemy." He understands Freud's discovery as that of an "internal other" (Laplanche does not use the term "otherwise," although he writes about similar distinctions), which is different from a centered-other or "other as center." The latter is, for example, implied by monadological theories of innate drives (a form of biological idealism), which will be discussed in later chapters. In this way, Laplanche's—in my opinion, superlative—reading of Freud's discovery emphasizes the repressed unconscious that interminably decenters the subject of self-consciousness. Its voicing, facilitated by the activity or functionality of the psychoanalyst, is only accessible free-associatively, for "it is overwhelmingly in relation to psychoanalytic *method* . . . that the originality of this new domain is ceaselessly affirmed."[36]

Approaching his highly sophisticated study of Freud's discipline in this way, Laplanche shows that "at almost every period" of Freud's writings, there is "an alternation between relapses into Ptolemaist and resurgences of the Copernican" vision. Laplanche sees this vacillation at many junctures, writing about two in particular (occurring in the mid-1890s and in the early 1920s).

Dating the free-associative discovery of repression in the early 1890s, Laplanche gives particular importance to the Freud's letter to Wilhelm Fliess of 21 September 1897, as exemplifying what is perhaps the earliest vacillation. In that communication, Freud announces that he no longer believes in his "neurotica" (his theory of the genesis of psychic conflict). In support of his own distinctive theory of general seduction, Laplanche sees this as Freud's retreat from an earlier view that repression occurs in response to the "implantation" or imposition of adult desires (transmitted as what Laplanche terms "enigmatic signifiers") into or upon the infant.[37] That is, Freud recoils from the recognition that the subject is, in its origination and structuration, irreparably decentered by otherwise forces, and he relapses back into an ipsocentrist (autocentrist or subject-centered) view of the psyche. Shortly thereafter—for instance, in the 1899 discussion of dreamwork—a resurgence of Freud's unsettling Copernican insight is evident.

Laplanche argues that such vacillations occur repeatedly. Another example would be Freud's 1923 naming *das Es* (which Strachey translated into the Latinate term *Id*). Freud attributed his choice of the term to Groddeck's *It* (which had in turn been influenced by Nietzsche), implying the recognition that "we are 'lived' by unknown and uncontrollable forces." Freud thus acknowledges the status of the repressed as what he had previously called an incessantly "strange invasion" within (*eine fremde Invasion*, in his 1917 essay, "A Difficulty in the Path of Psychoanalysis"). This clearly indicates Freud's ongoing insight into the foreignness of self-consciousness to itself, since Groddeck's "It" is an agency which lives us more than we live it. However, this "major reaffirmation" (as Laplanche describes it) of what I am calling otherwiseness is immediately offset by Freud's discussion of a substantively tripartite "mental apparatus" in which the "subject" is recentered on the Es/Id. The latter is depicted as the biologically based ground that is the beginning of personhood out of which the representational subject develops—seemingly without interference from enigmatic signifiers imposed on the infant from the external world.[38] In this way, Freud's structural-functional model ultimately renders psychoanalysis vulnerable to an integratively emergent theory of consciousness (such as the theories prevalent in much neuropsychoanalytic theorizing today, including those of "dual aspect monism"), and returns our thinking to a Ptolemaist universe.

Just as Laplanche sees the Copernican radicality of Freud's thinking continuing after its setback in 1897, he sees Freud's Ptolemaism as repeatedly asserting itself in what might be described as waves of conservatism or nostalgia for a universe in which the psyche can be centered (the structural-functional model being a major example of such a recentering). As much as I agree with Laplanche's reading, I also think there is a perspective on Freud's trajectory that supplements his insights. This is because the proclivity to retreat from the radicality of a decentered psyche is endemic to the very enterprise of metapsychological theory-building, and after 1914 Freud's commitment to this enterprise escalated. Specifically, the effort at recentering fuels the objectivistic mandate of the ambition to construct theoretical formulations that arrest (halt, censor, suppress, and obfuscate) the disocclusive momentum of opening to the voicing of what is otherwise, which is the psychoanalytic method. Freud's preoccupations with speculative theory-building are thus usually expressive of his Ptolemaist tendencies, and have discernible phases within the trajectory of his career.

The break that occurred in Freud's life in the years leading up to his fortieth birthday is well known. Between 1877 and the publication of his 1895 *Sketch* (the "Project" of a "psychology for neurologists"), Freud published over two hundred neurological papers. The advent of psychoanalysis, as the shift to free-associative method (and the relinquishing of all nonpsychoanalytic methods, such as hyponosis and suggestion), is various dated as occurring between 1892 and 1898. As is well known, Freud worked intensively and exhaustingly on his 1895 *Sketch* over a period of some weeks, only to abandon it unfinished, declining its publication (and indeed, at the end of his life, advocating that the manuscript be destroyed). How the ideas articulated in the *Sketch*, particularly those about repression, have echoes, in a modified or more blatantly allegorical form, throughout Freud's subsequent forty-four years of psychoanalytic writing has been a matter discussed not only by Laplanche but also by scholars such as David Rapaport, Karl Pribram, and Merton Gill (as well as by, in a different vein, some of the contemporary scholars enamoured with "neuropsychoanalysis"). However, as much as this shift is significant in terms of Freud's move into psychoanalytic discipline, and away from certain assumptions about neurological reductionism, there is another—perhaps less dramatic—shift in his thinking that occurs around 1914.

Similar to Green's idea that there is a "caesura" in Freud's writing about the time of the First World War, I have advocated a reading of what Freud in 1925 described as the "patchwork" of his "life's labors" (*das Stückwerk meiner Lebensarbeit*) that emphasizes an overarching shift toward conservatism during that war and thereafter. Here we do not need to hypothesize what factors induced a shift in the preponderance of his vacillations from more radical to more conservative—that is, recentering—theoretical constructions. Obviously, the pain of witnessing a horrific internecine war between European nations, his own deteriorating health, the approach of a sixtieth birthday, the decline of his clinical activities, and his dismay at the defection of prominent followers may all have played a role. There can be no question that, for all his humility (described by many commentators, for example, in Hendrik Ruitenbeek's *Freud as We Knew Him*), Freud identified himself as a leader who wanted to leave a legacy. Such a wish may have motivated the escalation of speculative theory-building in the dozen or so years subsequent to 1914. After all, as a sort of "thought-experiment," we might wonder how a legacy consisting solely of a method that, by Freud's own admission in lectures presented during the First World War, "brooks no audience and cannot be demonstrated" would have fared.

Freud's preoccupation with speculative and systematizing theoretical construction has at least several interconnected consequences. For example, there is a discernible shift from writing about *Ich* as the lived experience of "I" to discussion of "the ego" as an organization, defined objectivistically rather than experientially.[39] With this, there is a perhaps less obvious shift from the writing of an eminently practico-critical thinker to one who is more focused on speculation and systematization (and this especially affects the grounding of psychoanalytic method on libidinality and our experiential embodiment, as will be subsequently discussed). That is, there is a retrogressive turning away from psychoanalysis as praxis, toward the restoration of a more conventional relationship between objectivistic theoretical structures and practical application. Thus, overarchingly, there is a shift from the deconstructive praxis of free-associative discourse toward the establishment of "psychoanalysis" as an edifice of metapsychological theories. That is, without articulating it in this manner, after 1914 Freud presents his discipline as a hermeneutic or metahermeneutic framework (I will pass over this distinction, which Jürgen Habermas propounded in 1968) that guides the interpretive labors involved in a search for hidden meanings (a search which is, as I shall show in the next chapters, not the same as the free-associative voicing of the repressed).

After the 1895 *Sketch* and up to 1914 (the year in which Freud's paper "On Narcissism" was published), Freud occasionally referred to his theoretical speculations as mere "auxiliary notions" or *Hilfsvorstellungen* ("helpful ideas"), which Strachey mistranslates as "conceptual scaffolding," implying an intent to advance to a more elaborated theoretical edifice. In subsequent chapters, I shall show both how the notion of libidinal energies was indeed a helpful idea indissociably entwined with the free-associative method. I shall also suggest (as argued in my 2013 text) that the formulation of the topographic model, from his 1895 collaboration with Josef Breuer onwards, may have been a less than helpful idea, in as much as it requires that we consider representations as if spatial and substantial. At best, the model offers a sort of shorthand by which a retrospective account of what might have occurred in the course of a passage of free-associative discourse might be generated, and the model thus functions as a hermeneutic frame that is quite disconnected from the method by which it was allegedly produced.

The models of the "mental apparatus" with which Freud became preoccupied after 1914 betray an even greater disjuncture between praxis and theoretical speculation or systematization than is implied by the topography of conscious, preconscious, and unconscious localities. The papers on metapsychology, which he started writing around 1915, arise more out of Freud's efforts at conceptual elaboration than from further experience with psychoanalytic method. The essays that are the source of object-relational models, written during the First World War and the years thereafter (including the 1920 text, *Beyond the Pleasure Principle*), also offer a subtle recentering by depicting psychic life as if it were a stage on which the subject maneuvers its cast of self representations and object representations (of other people, things, ideas, and so forth). Finally, as mentioned above, Freud's last major metapsychological model, promulgated in his 1923 text and amplified in its 1926 sequel, initiates a highly problematic recentering of the subject both by its biological idealism in the monadological depiction of innate drive forces and by providing a model of the ego organization that invites the subsequent assertion of a conflict-free sphere of its functioning.

If the urge to retreat from the unsettling implications of Freud's discovery of the free-associative method is endemic to the enterprise of metapsychological theory-building, with which Freud himself became increasingly preoccupied after 1914, then an appreciation of his radicality is not to be achieved by renewed review of his theoretical constructions. All of these—in one way or another—move toward a resettling of the subject, the location of a center to psychic life. Instead, we must return to an examination of the method of unsettlement itself, aiming for an appreciation of free-associative discourse that may have been suppressed in the activities of metapsychological speculation and systematization.

5

SAMPLING FREE-ASSOCIATIVE DISCOURSE

> . . . Wissenshaft vom seelisch Unbewussten . . .
> . . . the scientific pursuit of the psyche's unconscious . . .
>
> Sigmund Freud, 1923

To have genuine insight into Freud's revolutionary discovery, which is the significance of free-associative method, one must enter psychoanalytic discourse. The essence of such access is to surrender to becoming a patient whose commitment is to think and speak aloud whatever "comes to mind," whose fate is invariably and necessarily to resist this mandate, and whose enunciations and expressions, which are both articulate and inarticulate, are presented to one who fulfills the functions of a psychoanalyst.[40] Such is the ongoing journey of psychoanalytic praxis.

Here I will sidestep critical discussion of Freud's so-called self-analysis, which is to some degree a hubristic myth (yet well discussed by Didier Anzieu and others), and will postpone the question whether, or to what extent, self-analysis is actually feasible for anyone (or to what extent this endeavor, like the clinical vignette, involves a seemingly slight but significant misunderstanding of the inner reality of psychoanalytic processes).[41] At this juncture I need not only suggest that there is a profound sense in which free-associative discourse occurs solely in the presence of the function of the psychoanalyst (here making a perhaps slight, but crucially significant, differentiation between the functionality and the personhood of the psychoanalyst); I also need to insist that what occurs between the patient and the psychoanalyst is ultimately relevant and comprehensible exclusively to their lived experience of these processes (by which I mean that all others are necessarily excluded). That is, I need to insist on the legitimacy of a science that cannot be genuinely grasped except by those who have immersed themselves in the power of its praxis. This is surely why, in his "new lectures" of 1933, Freud announced that his method can be genuinely known only to its participants.[42] And we should note that, in opposition to the prospects of "wild analysis," he had already, in the early 1920s, endorsed Max Eitingon's model of training, which stipulated that, to conduct a psychoanalytic treatment, the practitioner must have been psychoanalyzed. To genuinely grasp the discipline one must be in its process, and to become a psychoanalyst one must be psychoanalyzed (and in a sense one must remain in psychoanalysis).[43]

Actually, Freud had already advanced a related and even stronger opinion. Despite the regularity with which he wrote *about* psychoanalysis and, allegedly on the basis of his experiences with this method, theorized speculatively about the human condition, Freud was adamant on the privacy of this method. He perhaps anticipates Bion's writings of the early 1960s, discussing the dynamic difference between *knowing about* and the *experiential processes of knowing*—processes that are exclusively existential, in the sense this term is used herein. In 1915 (in the earlier set of "introductory lectures," published 1916–1917), Freud wrote that "the discourse of which psychoanalytic treatment consists brooks no audience and cannot be demonstrated." Thus, with the exclusion of all others, the method requires involves the couple's private and processive workplay—the free-associating and resisting patient in the presence of a psychoanalyst who functions as such.[44]

Obviously, this is an impediment for those who insist on the public conditions of science, just as there is a problem for those who argue that it is illegitimate for the "object" of a science to be indissociably tied to a unique method. Yet this is the situation of psychoanalysis. In the next chapter, I will discuss the tenet that the originality of the "new domain" opened to us by psychoanalysis—the exiled "domain" of the repressed unconscious and the libidinality of embodied experience—is indeed ineluctably bound to free-associative praxis. And subsequently, via a discussion of the functions of the psychoanalyst, I will defend the notion of a private science—the notion of a praxis or of a methodical understanding-by-changing, the scientificity of which is in the process itself. This is the ground on which Freud can assert that his science "brooks no audience and cannot be demonstrated," condemning the endeavors of all those who imagine that the process can occur in the presence of additional parties (observers, recording devices, and the like), and thus can be objectivistically rendered.

Nevertheless, the discipline has in fact been propagated by certain forms of nonpsychoanalytic reportage. Freud wrote about his "cases," offered dazzling analyses of cultural artifacts, such as jokes, that might illustrate the principles of repression, and tried to present examples of associative discourse. For better or for worse, the history of what is called the psychoanalytic movement has run on clinical vignettes.

For better: It is difficult to imagine how the history of Freud's discipline might have proceeded if it had been propagated solely as an esoteric science, passed down didactically and performatively from psychoanalyst to trainee (because surely such a wholly confidential transmission would have further aggravated all the narcissistic problems of orthodoxy, authoritarianism, and discipleship). Only in the realm of esoteric spiritual doctrines (such as tantric meditation, about which I have written elsewhere) can one imagine the "secret transmission" of processes and methods for the exploration of "other realities" occurring without recordable narratives about its procedures and accomplishments.

For worse: Vignettes are deadening and distortive, however vivid the language and the aesthetics of their inscription. This point needs to be emphasized. Whereas a vignette purporting to describe retrodictively a sequence of free-associations may succeed in providing us with hints as to how psychoanalytic discourse touches an incomprehensible dimension of life that is always in our midst, it does *not*, and cannot, represent the surfacing of repressed libidinality, the dynamics of the Freudian unconscious. It may give the illusion that something already actively immanifest can now be captured in manifest representation, but this does not make it so. Indeed, the illusion perpetuates the mistaken idea that psychoanalysis can be comprehended externally. To subscribe to this illusion is to abrogate the heart of Freud's discoveries about the repressed unconscious, about libidinality, and about the polytemporalities of the human condition (all of which will be discussed in due course). This is an error analogous to that noted in the *Lankāvatāra Sūtra* of the Mahāyāna texts (presented in English by Daisetz Suzuki), in which Gautama warns us not to mistake the finger pointing to the moon for the moon itself.

Although one can always render something preconscious into a conscious articulation of its meaning (inevitably with some loss in translation), this is radically different from the energetic significance of the repressed. The latter "energy" is what has aptly been called, notably by Laplanche, enigmatic messages, "designified" or "compromised signifiers"—the desirous impulses of libidinality, embodied erotic experience that cannot be captured in representations. Contrary to popular belief (as well as the acquiescence of all too many practitioners), the repressed is more challengingly complex than the notion of a text that is other than the text of consciousness and the preconscious.[45]

The psychoanalytic movement has been divided on this very issue and has, I believe, missed the fundamental issue (as did Freud himself). Some hold that the significance of free-associative discourse can be demonstrated, or at least illustrated, externally (and Freud himself clearly believed this to some extent, in that he provided copious examples of his own and his patients' free-associations to dream elements and other clinical material). Others hold that the significance of the streaming of free-associations is necessarily lost if one attempts to record it, report it, or examine it outside of the context of psychoanalytic participation (and Freud obviously believed this when he wrote that the process "brooks no audience and cannot be demonstrated").

So in this chapter, I shall offer a thesis that has not, to my knowledge, been previously articulated in the literature—namely, that free-associative discourse both can and cannot be demonstrated. To the extent that the method divulges *other* meanings that can be translated into the representational language of self-consciousness (meanings that were previously unconscious, in the descriptive sense of deeply preconscious, such as those that I shall later call the "root propositions"), it may be sampled and its significance discussed. But to the extent that the method opens self-consciousness to meanings that are *otherwise* than those that can be formulated representationally by self-consciousness (erotic messages of embodied experience that are untranslatable), there can be no demonstration of the significance of free-associative discourse, perhaps only the most tenuous of intimations, like the finger pointing to the moon.

Thus, in this chapter, I hope to show that, whereas the free-associative exposition of the dynamics of repression is indeed signifying or meaningful (in a radically specific sense), it is not merely equivalent to the unearthing or unveiling of another place, *terra incognita*, or "other text," the ethical and ontological coordinates of which are concordant with, and thus translatable into, those of conscious and preconscious representationality. Although Freud himself can be read as having made this error of exposition, there is actually no "otherwise text" that can be captured and integrated into the unfolding text of self-consciousness and its preconscious (or, for that matter, to which the text of self-consciousness could be assimilated). Indeed, as will be discussed in this chapter, there is no direct translatability between the narratives of self-consciousness (along with the preconscious realm that subtends it) and what is *otherwise than* representationality yet within its unfolding. As I argued in 1993, the repressed is *in* representationality but not *of* it, and is discordantly disruptive in relation to its law and order. Thus, we must appreciate the repressed not so much in terms of "word representations" but in terms of enigmatic and erotic "thing-presentations."[46] Freud wrote of these "presentations" in 1915, but the idea is anticipated as early as 1900 when Freud insisted that every text (for this cannot be true only of the textuality of the oneiric) has an "unfathomable navel" that is untranslatable into the languages of representationality. The potential distortions (and ideological impositions) that would be involved in any claim that there might be an *indirect* translatability (between the enigmatic messages of our repressed erotic embodied experience and the representational language of self-consciousness) need to be, and will be, discussed later. For, as Laplanche argued (for example, in his 1981 *Problématiques* and his 1993 "Short Treatise on the Unconscious"), "the reduction of the unconscious to a hidden *meaning* [is] a constant temptation, dragging Freud's discovery backwards towards a centuries-old hermeneutics."

The temptation to comprehend psychoanalysis as essentially an elucidation of hidden meanings bedevils every clinical vignette. It is one to which I have fallen in some previous writings and toward which I perhaps slide in what follows. Of course, hidden meanings come to light in every psychoanalytic experience, but to define the discipline—the field of psychoanalysis—in these terms is to miss the repressed unconscious and thus the unique radicality of free-associative praxis. Indeed, as I shall show, such a definition serves only to conflate psychoanalytic praxis with therapeutic practices that are applications of theories that purport to be psychoanalytically informed or psychoanalytically oriented. In short, the genre of the vignette leads to the errors mentioned earlier—those of defining "psychoanalysis" as a theory or set of theories about psychopathology, as a theory or set of theories about the functioning of the "mental apparatus," or as a theory or set of theories about therapeutic practices designed to render the patient more mature or better adapted to reality "as is."

Having emphasized all these problems with the genre of the clinical vignette, I am nonetheless going to offer descriptions of two sequences of psychoanalytic discourse. These will be followed by an attempt to indicate how, despite their claim to a certain sort of veracity (that is, their claim to describe more or less what actually happened in my workplay with two patients), they fail to convey adequately the unique dimension of free-associative praxis. That is, I am going to offer illustrations that may serve to convince the reader about the emergence of "other meanings," but can only offer the slightest intimation of the way in which the discourse empowers self-consciousness to listen to meanings that are "otherwise." My scanty justification for this strategy of exegesis is that perhaps no one would give credence to the moon, unless someone's finger had pointed to it.

Sample one[47]

What comes before and what comes after are always significant to what comes presently; the present being constituted by incessantly appearing "past-futures" as brilliantly discussed, for example, by Emmanuel Levinas (to whom I will return to later). So it is important to know that toward the end of a Friday session, I suggested to my patient, who was at the beginning of his second year of psychoanalysis, that perhaps his repeated forgetting to reimburse me for the previous month's appointments might indicate his reluctance to become aware of some feelings of hostility toward me. Here we need not pause to assess whether such an interpretation was warranted or even whether it was, if warranted, a "good enough" intervention. Rather, it needs to be noted that my patient responded with an immediate denial, followed by jocular "you're always harping on about our relationship, as if it has to do with absolutely everything, including the sinking of the *Titanic*" (the *Titanic* reference alluded to a joke previously shared which involved a riff on our common Jewish background).[48]

As he got onto the couch for Monday's session, this male patient announced that he had been "edgy" (a colloquialism for anxious) all weekend, since the Friday appointment, in fact. He then reflected that he could recall nothing about Friday's session, which puzzled him. He proceeded to recount how, over the weekend, his young son had been mad (that is, angry) at him. He had felt unable to cope with his son's anger, and at one point had retreated from the apparent hostility by taking himself off to a local bar for a few hours (from the standpoint of what Theodor Reik called the "third ear," it is not farfetched to note that I am a "bar/ratt"). As he told me about his weekend, he suddenly and unexpectedly ("I don't know why this is coming to mind now!") started thinking about the Rabbi who had tutored him for his Bar Mitzvah (again, we should note, another "bar"). He said that he had not thought about this Rabbi in years. He reported feeling sad as he told me how the tutoring was around the time of his father's illness (which was terminal). He recounted how he had become close to this Rabbi, but on one occasion had become angry at him over some disappointment that he now could not remember, and the Rabbi had subsequently distanced himself from their relationship. What next sprang into my patient's consciousness, as if abruptly and unbidden, was that he had had a dream the previous night—a fragment that he had forgotten on waking and only recalled at that moment. In the dream, he and I are walking in some luscious countryside and we are like "bosom buddies" (again, with the use of this rather unusual and richly connotative expression, it is not farfetched to note the proliferation of 'Bs' in my name, *B*arna*b*y *B* *B*arratt). In such luscious countryside, there is manifestly shared enjoyment (perhaps a homoerotic enjoyment of a landscape that might connote the feminine body).

Sample two[49]

The following sample also comes from the beginning of a session, but here with a female patient in her fourth year of psychoanalysis. During the previous session, I had remarked that she seemed to hint that she had some feelings of being frightened of penile–vaginal intercourse and that she seemed to imagine the penis to be a frightening weapon that might damage her. As with the previous sample, we do not need to pause here to assess whether my comment was justified, or whether it was a "good enough" interpretation. Rather, it needs to be noted that my patient responded with a murmur of what sounded like bemused assent, and gave me what I perceived as a winsome smile as she left the session.

As she got onto the couch the following day, she observed that I was "nicely dressed" (although I did not see myself as dressed particularly differently from most other days). She then announced that she wondered if psychoanalysis would soon draw to a close, as she felt she had "nothing much" to talk about. However, she immediately proceeded to describe how, since the previous session, she had been preoccupied with the tasks of taking care of her young sons. She once again indicated how much she reveled in such tasks (and it might be noted that previously I had frequently felt that she might wish me to be jealous of her ability to bear children). She briefly described what sounded to me like her dedication to these caregiving activities, and related how one of her sons had become involved in a squabble with another child in the neighborhood over the ownership of a prized toy (a squabble in which she had had to intervene). As she narrated the incident, it reminded her of an episode in her own childhood when she had actually taken her brother's bicycle and hidden it from him. She remembered how deeply ashamed she had felt when the "theft" was discovered. For reasons she said she felt "strange about," this made her recall fantasy—about which she said she felt much guilt—that she had had while her husband was serving at a noncombative post during the Vietnam War. She had imagined that he would be wounded and discharged as a paraplegic. She quickly added that she "would never have really wanted such a terrible thing to actually happen," but proceeded to imagine that, if he had been thus wounded, he would have been sent home early to her, and that she, because she "loved him so much," would have willingly devoted herself to a lifetime of taking care of him. Paraplegia, she then mused—as if in an aside—would mean that intercourse would no longer be an issue that could come so troublingly between them. Suddenly, as if abruptly and unbidden, my patient then found herself recalling her eldest son's bris and how she had, at the time, been "crazily worried" that his penis might fall off as she unwrapped the bandages around the circumcision. The patient then fell silent (appearing anxious to me), and eventually she reported feeling "utterly blank." I was preparing to offer a comment about the sequence of her thoughts, but had hardly uttered a word when my patient interrupted me. Evidently agitated, she told me she was alarmed to be seeing a vivid image—in her "mind's eye"—of herself as a little girl "smiling maliciously" while tugging ferociously on her pet dog's penis.

On the wiles of textual analysis

It is facile—indeed alluring—to offer interpretations of the sequences described in these two vignettes. However, what needs subsequently to be discussed and emphasized is the way in which such analyses actually miss the unique radicality of psychoanalytic praxis as the *kinesis* of libidinality that incessantly disrupts representationality yet itself eludes representation. Having stated this qualification, I will now offer a preliminary textual analysis of these two sequences.

Sample one: The thematic sequencing of my male patient's narratives exhibits a repeated contingency in which one person expresses anger toward another, and the latter quits the relationship. The contingency is transformed in the course of the sequence, both in terms of the actor/recipient relations and in terms of the timeframe in which the activity or affect is staged. At the end of the Friday session, I say something to my patient which could be heard as "You may be angry toward me." With hindsight, I could have improved this intervention by saying something like "You are apprehensive about expressing any anger toward me (yet you do so by the act of forgetting my payment), because you fear it will cause me to withdraw from you." In any event, the patient's immediate response to my actual remark was denial, accompanied by a jocular comment with a hostile subtext—namely, a jab at the putative self-aggrandizement involved in my taking myself to be so important to him. There is also perhaps an ominous—albeit framed as a joke—implication that our relationship could, suddenly and without warning, end in disaster, like the sinking of the *Titanic*. Possibly in response to my comment, the patient proceeds to forget the Friday session, and yet to experience anxiety throughout the weekend. However, he is curious about this and begins Monday's session with this curiosity.

The Monday series of narratives (son, Rabbi, and "bosom buddies") can readily be said to operate *as if* a sequence of manifest expressions of an underlying immanifest content, which we can speculate to be a descriptively "unconscious" response to my Friday remark such as: "If I become angry with the other, my psychoanalyst, he will abandon or reject me." Just for heuristic purposes, I will call this the "root proposition"—although perhaps, in acknowledging the multiplicity of interpretation, it should be designated *a*, rather than *the*, root proposition.[50] The story of weekend activities posits the son as angry and the patient, as the recipient of such anger, who then leaves his son at least for a few hours. The actions are staged in the recent past, but the contingencies of actor/recipient and action or affect are allegorically reversed with respect to those of the root proposition. The story of the Rabbi then posits the patient as angry and the Rabbi as the recipient of this anger, who then distances himself from the patient. However, the actions are now staged in the distant past, although the contingencies of actor/recipient and action or affect now allegorize those of the root proposition. The previous night's dream, suddenly surfacing after the telling of the son story and the Rabbi story, appears to abolish the contingencies of actor/recipient with respect to anger and abandonment or rejection. In a sense, the timeframe of the dream may have been the previous night, but its surfacing is in the immediate present of the psychoanalytic relationship (and it is well to note Green's thesis, in his various writings on temporality, that the time of a dream is that of the "pure present").

Sample two: The thematic sequencing of my female patient's narratives can also be "read" as exhibiting, by means of various allegories (condensations and displacements, or metaphors and metonyms, as well as, or including, reversals), a response to my comment in the preceding session. Here, it is *as if* there is a root proposition (equivalent to my male patient's "If I become angry with the other, my psychoanalyst, the other/he will abandon or reject me") along the lines of "(I fear that) I wish to damage the other's (my psychoanalyst's) penis." We may start by noting that, in the session prior to the one under consideration, the patient's immediate response to my interpretation (in which I mentioned that perhaps she feared intercourse because she perceived the penis as a frighteningly damaging weapon) is a murmur of bemused agreement, followed by her winsome smile. These expressions can, of course, be retrodictively understood as a denial of the root proposition. It is as if, by means of her affirmation of my "incorrect" interpretation, together with the charm of her demeanor as she left the session, she encourages her psychoanalyst to remain—colloquially speaking—"off track."[51]

The next session begins with my patient complimenting my attire, again as if catering to my narcissism might be a means by which to keep us both "off track." This is followed by some ideas about the ending of the treatment. One might readily conjecture that such thoughts express a wish (as if saying, "let us stop this treatment before further truths are disclosed") and/or a fear (as if saying, "let us not stop this treatment without further truths being disclosed"). To this, the patient then adds that she has "nothing much" to say, which can be comprehended as a resistance to further free-associating.[52] There follow a series of five narratives (caretaking her sons and resolving a dispute over a prized toy, the memory of stealing her brother's bicycle, a fantasy of caring for a paraplegic husband, "crazy worries" over her son's circumcision, and her recollection of attacking her pet dog's penis). It does not need perhaps to be detailed how this sequence might be allegorically organized, almost mythematically, around the root proposition in the following schematic way:

- I am a caregiver, not an aggressor; the hostility is between children, and it is about a toy, not a penis; moreover, it occurred not now but in the recent past (and, by the way, perhaps you, my male psychoanalyst, should be jealous of my enjoyment of children and my capacity to produce them).
- I did aggress against my brother; stealing not his penis but his bike; I was conflicted about the act; and anyway it happened long ago in my early adolescence (or late childhood).
- I am a caregiver, not an aggressor; the hostility occurred in Vietnam; paraplegia would have damaged my husband's penile capacity; although this is just a fantasy—the wish implied by which I now disavow; but if it had happened, I would not have to be confronted with his penis in intercourse; and anyway, the war happened many years ago (and my husband came home safely).
- I am a caregiver, not an aggressor; but I fantasized damaging my son's penis; although it was not really me that did it, rather it would have been an accident caused by someone else; and anyway, this is a fantasy for no damage actually occurred, and the scenario happened several years ago.
- I am horrified to recollect that I did aggress against my pet dog's penis; maybe I even enjoyed attacking it; but this happened a very long time ago, in my early childhood.

In this exercise, we can become overly focused on the differences between the thinking–speaking that is reported in such vignettes and the manner in which thinking–speaking is governed in ordinary conversation. Nonetheless, there does seem to be a difference, and it is instructive. Consider how we talk in a commonplace context that is not psychoanalytic:

> I meet a couple of friends for coffee and tell them that I am currently working hard on this essay; then I describe how a colleague recently told me that further attention to Freud's ideas is a waste of time, given the contemporary advances of neuroscience; I indicate to my friends how irritated I was over what I perceive as the colleague's arrogance, which I view as a sort of idiocy; and I proceed to tell them, with what I hear as both humor and affection in my own voice, that my dog, "Jazzie," also acts as if I am wasting my time and hers, because I am sitting at my desk and entertaining her less frequently than usual.

In this sort of everyday talk with friends over coffee (as contrasted with the thinking–speaking that occurs in psychoanalysis), there is a law and order to the thematic series of my narratives (the labor of writing an essay, my colleague's irritating judgment, the priorities expressed by Jazzie). It makes sense so readily that it requires little or no textual analysis. As the voice of this particular sequence, I am more or less confident that I know what I am talking about; nothing that "comes out of my mouth" surprises me; and I am reasonably certain as to how my stories will be received by my friends (that they will feel sympathetic or supportive, that they will appreciate the humor and affection of the final story, despite the fact that it also conveys a jibe against the arrogant idiocy of my colleague, and so forth). Although its underlying equation is never made explicit, I am quite conscious that I am making a hostile joke against my colleague (implying that his irritating opinion should be given less credence than that of my dog). In short, there seems to be little in this sequence that calls for exegetical explanation. However, this is *not* to suggest that what I have described is all that is occurring in the course of my brief monologue, and we might here speculate as to the character of the libidinality involved in my various attachments (to my friends, my colleague, and my dog), as to whatever "unconscious phantasies" are the substrate of my writing activities, as to the oral satisfactions of coffee and the multiple temporalities at stake in this conversation, and so forth.

However, this quotidian vignette contrasts somewhat with those describing events in the psychoanalysis of my two patients—although we can all too easily overstate the significance of this contrast. It is clear that, in the clinical setting that calls for free-associative thinking and speaking, the law and order of discourse—the rules that necessarily govern enunciation and exchange—are somewhat relaxed. Consequently, the sequence of narratives begs for a more sophisticated degree of textual analysis (the elucidation of meanings that are other than those immediately owned by self-consciousness). For example, it can readily be suggested that anxiety over the contingencies of anger and loss motivates my male patient's series of stories, or that anxiety over aggressive feelings toward men motivates my female patient's discourse. The danger here is that we mistake this sort of textual analysis, along with the interpretations that may be produced by it, for the otherwise change process that is unique to the praxis of psychoanalysis.

6

TEXTUAL ANALYSIS AND THE DOGMA OF INTERPRETATION

> . . . Acheronta movebo . . .
> . . . stirring up the underworld . . .
>
> Sigmund Freud, 1900/1927[53]

It is commonly thought that psychoanalysis operates in the following tripartite or triphasic manner:

> Patients talk (or have difficulty talking, instead expressing themselves nonverbally) and are listened to; interpretations are generated as to what underlies the manifest meanings of their talking (the underlying meanings that are supposedly "in" the unconscious, expressed through both the content and the style of the manifest enunciations); the patients assimilate or integrate these insights (in a process often called "working-through") and, now armed with these newly established representations of self-understanding (about the content and functioning of their psychic life), they proceed to conduct themselves with greater maturity and adaptivity.

There are a considerable number of variations in the theorization of the specifics caricatured in this sketch. For example: (1) differing opinions about the "rules" under which the patient is expected to talk and about the processes involved in listening; (2) divergent views as to what is being interpreted (reconstructed or correspondent memories, constructions that form a coherent narrative about the past, preconscious material, "unconscious phantasies," phenomena experienced in the here-and-now of transference and countertransference); (3) pivotal questions as to who formulates the interpretations (the psychoanalyst as an authority, the patient as a self-reflective participant, or both in some sort of interpersonal or intersubjective dialogue that is variously negotiative or cocreated); (4) how these interpretations come to be formulated; (5) how they are to be delivered and then worked-through; as well as (6) the criteria by which their therapeutic effectiveness is to be assessed; and finally (7) debates about the way in which these interpretative contributions bring about therapeutic transformations in the patient's functioning (which overlaps with the questions surrounding the processes or mechanisms of "working-through").

I am going to sidestep discussion of these seven variations in order to underscore their commonality. This involves how, in manifold ways, they all prioritize the epistemology of their therapeutic labors (in terms of the significance given to interpretations enunciated and exchanged in a relational context), they all reassert the conventional attitude of theory/practice in relation to the "beingness" of lived experience, and hence they all miss the radical significance of free-associative praxis.

On the fallacies of textual analysis

The almost bewildering variety of psychoanalytically informed and psychoanalytically oriented therapies (and the theories girding them) that today confronts the student of this discipline (or, more accurately perhaps, "these disciplines") should not beguile us into passing over the profound significance of their shared prioritization of the acts of interpretation. As is argued here, this commonality has less to do with their indebtedness to the path-breaking itinerary undertaken by Freud, and more to do with retreat, that is often almost clandestine, away from the revolutionary implications of his discoveries—an urgent need to recenter the human condition and to establish a locus of some sort of epistemological or ontological security. In a wide variety of fashions, all these therapies hold that the transformative significance of the labors undertaken by patient and practitioner lies in the impact of interpretations, rather than in free-associative praxis per se. Thus, in all these practices, the very mode of discourse that Freud held to be the *sine qua non* of his discipline is seen either as entirely unnecessary to the therapeutic procedure or as a mere adjunct—a preliminary, a "data gathering" phase, a confirmatory check for veracity, and so on—to the enunciation and exchange of interpretations.

As I itemized previously, the impact of interpretive labors may be conceptualized in a wide variety of ways according to different schools or lineages of what is called psychoanalysis.[54] For example, following the scheme discussed in John Austin's theory of speech acts, there are theories of therapeutic action that place more emphasis on the constative weight of interpretations and those that emphasize more the performative implications of interpretive labor as well as the relationship in which such labor occurs (especially its emotional qualities). The former theories present interpretation as a matter of equipping patients with correct (correspondent or, at least, coherent) formulations about their functioning (past and present), whereas the latter present interpretive labor as a matter of offering patients not so much understandings as the relational experience of being contained and understood, or even as a matter of dialogically instructing patients about their social and emotional conduct (in relation to its components that are not conscious). Other opinions emphasize both constative and performative aspects, presenting the act of interpretation as a matter of providing patients with formulations that restart a biologically determined course of development. Obviously, this summary is far from exhaustive.

Whatever the specifics of the conceptualization, what defines the therapeutic process in the many varieties of psychoanalytically informed and psychoanalytically oriented practice is some notion of the "unconscious" that is to be brought under the aegis of interpretation. Instead of "brought under the aegis," one is tempted to say *tamed* by a relationship aimed at the interpretive labors of understanding or gaining "insight" (because, from 1920 onwards, Freud himself wrote several times about "taming the drives," *Bändigung die Triebe*). It is evident that so much rides on the significance of this term, "unconscious." In the course of the past century, this has, of course, been the catchphrase that differentiates practices that claim to have developed out of Freud's initiatives from those psychological therapies that may involve a conversational relationship of some sort, but which hold no such allegiance. Yet even today, the term continues to be in need of critical examination, and indeed rescue from its usage by Freud's epigones. For what is troubling—and my purpose here is to challenge such errors—is that "psychoanalysts" now routinely invoke the term in a merely descriptive sense that refers to any psychic event or mechanism that is not in the purview (or potential purview) of self-consciousness. To be fair, as I indicated previously, Freud himself occasionally slides into this usage (that he also condemns at several points in his writings). However, the consequence of such a liberalization of terminology is that our methodical opening to the repressed dimension of psychic life—that is, the significance of free-associative praxis—is ideologically expunged.

The core commonality of all these ideas about the impact of interpretation (and of an interpretative relationship) involves assumptions about the "unconscious" as being a text, or like a text, other than that of self-consciousness. Therapy is then regarded as some sort of textual analysis by which this "other text" is brought into the domain of conscious reflection or preconscious apprehension (integrated into the functioning of the ego organization or assimilated to the self) by relational procedures of interpretation. In what Paul Ricoeur called the "hermeneutics of suspicion," it may well be theorized how the text of self-consciousness is designed to cover over this other text of what is descriptively "unconscious." It may well be that every individual is composed of multiple texts and the therapeutic enterprise is to interpret and revise these texts—or narratives. However, to be satisfied with this exegetical standpoint is to remain in the realm of therapeutics and to miss the radicality of psychoanalysis.[55]

The widespread yet crucial mistake here is to suppose that the unconscious that Freud discovered via free-associative discourse is merely a text in some way ontologically equivalent to the text of self-conscious and preconscious psychic life, and thus one that is potentially translatable, by means of an epistemology of interpretation, into the representationality of self-consciousness. This standpoint may account for therapy but misses the radical essence of psychoanalysis (as mentioned previously, there are, of course, therapeutic aspects to every psychoanalytic treatment, but that is not the issue here and will later be further addressed).[56] The thesis of this chapter is precisely that the discovery generated by free-associative praxis, which is the discovery of the repressiveness of self-consciousness that operates both in the clinical setting and in everyday life, implies that the unconscious, to which Freud's method opens us, is not some *other text*; rather, this unconscious is *otherwise than textuality*.[57] To go further with this argument, let us return to the clinical material described in the previous chapter, and discuss the dual error of confusing psychoanalysis with a form of textual analysis.

Most notably, what is involved are twin fallacies of spatialization and substantialization. As would be expected, it is evident that each segment of these associative sequences (indeed, each association) holds a quite readily specifiable logical and rhetorical relation to its predecessor. They are, after all, *associative*. The stream of contents in self-consciousness does not result from items being thrown randomly to the surface of psychic life (like some grotesque Vegas slot machine). There is indeed a flow to consciousness.[58] The relation between each element and that which precedes or succeeds it can be described in terms of condensation and displacement (as well as reversal). These operations are discussed at length in Freud's *Traumdeutung* as the transformations occurring in dreamwork (although, of course, it would be a mistake not to recognize that they determine the transformations of every condition of self-consciousness). As is now well known, metaphor and metonym are the linguistic categories deployed by Lacanian theory to describe these operations (in this instance, more under the influence of Roman Jakobson than of Ferdinand de Saussure). And we should note that some commentators would add reversal, as a third operation, differentiating it from condensation (metaphor) and displacement (metonym). Each association is a transformation (syntactically, semantically, and pragmatically) of that which surfaced immediately before it in what Freud called the concatenations (*Verkettungen*), the streaming path of thoughts (*Gedankengang*), or the chain of association (*Assoziationskette*). What is perhaps more relevant—from the standpoint of an interpretive therapeutics—is that the theme of each segment of the narration holds the same logical and rhetorical relation with the root proposition, as designated by my rudimentary textual analysis. In short, as I discussed in detail in my 1993 book, it is as if *each association in the concatenation simultaneously both reveals and conceals something other than itself*, which we can call its root (equivalent to the "latent dream thoughts"). What is crucial to note here is that the root (scheme, theme, motive, core conflict, or so-called "unconscious phantasy") is fully translatable into the various manifest associations (even if under the aegis of negation or reversal).

This character of simultaneously revealing and concealing something other, as if both pointing toward and pointing away from a meaning that I have defined as the root proposition, is important to understand because it intimates a type of opening; yet is not, in and of itself, the discovery of the repressed unconscious. It

is achieved in the transformation from one association to the next as if by "maneuvering" (by which I do *not* mean anything like a consciously intended manipulation) the positions of the actor, the recipient, the action or affect, and the timeframe to which the "scene" (to use what is surely one of Freud's favorite terms) refers. The audience for this process of revealing–concealing is both the patient and the psychoanalyst, as they share the task of listening to the free-associative chain. By this, I mean that we must firmly dispel any notion that the patient is self-consciously intending to direct some sort of striptease, as a dance of showing-and-hiding that intends to engage the psychoanalyst.[59]

This transformative maneuvering is well illustrated in both clinical vignettes. For example, when my male patient shifts from the story about his son to the story about his Rabbi, it is as if the shift both points a little more toward the root proposition and, at the same time, points a little more away from it. That is, the former narrative positions the son as he who is angry and the patient as he who quits the relationship, within the timeframe of the recent past; whereas the latter positions the patient as he who is angry and the Rabbi as he who quits the relationship, but now the timeframe is the distant past. In relation to the root proposition ("If I become angry with the other, my psychoanalyst, he will abandon or reject me"), the transformations from the one story to the next takes the patient closer (the son story reverses the positions of actor/recipient, whereas the Rabbi story does not), but simultaneously takes the patient further away (the son story is fresh from the weekend before a Monday session, whereas the Rabbi story refers to a time long ago and events barely remembered). Finally, we note that the suddenly recollected dream fragment abolishes entirely the contingency of action and affect, but is a scene that casts the *dramatis personae* in the presentness of the session, patient and psychoanalyst. It also introduces the idiom of enjoyment, rather than anger and rejection. Although the enjoyment only arrives in the manifest content of an oneiric construction—a dream—it presents the duo sharing harmoniously, and possibly homoerotically, the pleasures of a "third," the feminine aesthetics of beautiful countryside.

A textual analysis of this sort of maneuvering—the simultaneity of revealing and concealing in the passage of conscious thinking and speaking—is of such interest that it readily misleads us into believing that what I am calling the root proposition is an "other text" already formulated some place "in the patient's mind." I believe we must challenge this tempting conclusion and that we must do so despite the fact that Freud succumbed to it in both a minor and a major way. The minor way is exemplified by his suggestion in 1900 that a dream's "latent contents" (the thoughts that eventually emerge as one associates to each of a dream's manifest elements) are equivalent to, or at least indicate what were, the "latent dream thoughts" operative as a substratum in the formation of the manifest dream at the time of its construction (this has sometimes, rather misleadingly, been called Freud's "tally argument"). The major way is, of course, exemplified by the entire enterprise of speculative theorizing called the "first topography," which attributes regions to the psyche (conscious, preconscious, and unconscious). This is the model of the "mental apparatus" that offers us a spatial depiction of psychic events in terms of representations that occupy different areas of the psyche and that might move, or be moved, from one to another—for instance from the preconscious into self-consciousness. The trope of spatiality (if it is a trope, since indeed many practitioners seem to hold the model as if it might be literal) also misleads us into treating representations (thoughts, feelings, actions) as if they are substantial or material entities (since typically it is only physical things that migrate from one location to the next).

Despite promulgating this topographic model, Freud was relatively consistent in distinguishing between psychic and material reality.[60] In this respect, he acknowledges that a psychic event is not equivalent to a material thing (however, it may be noted that, as I shall argue, his theorizing of the bodymind's libidinality implies a radical departure from any sort of Cartesian dualism). In the next chapter, the problems engendered by a spatialization of the psyche and by the substantialization of representations will be further discussed. Here it merely needs to be emphasized how these spatial–substantial tropes reinforce the mistake of apprehending the repressed unconscious as if it were a text other than that of self-consciousness. That is, a text that must be understood in epistemological and ontological terms familiar to self-consciousness (the colonialist ambition is evident here, acting as if the geography of Mozambique can only be grasped via coordinates developed in Portugal).

The errors of spatialization and substantialization compound the dual fallacy of belief in root propositions as indicative of representations (schemes, themes, motives, and so forth) that are "in" the unconscious. Even if one accepts the topographic teachings as a useful heuristic (making allowances for their potentially misleading implications), one must still not mistake the root propositions that are constructed or reconstructed by textual analysis (or brought to the surface by some other means) for Freud's discovery of the repressed unconscious. As I have already indicated, this error seems widespread. All too many commentators assume that representations such as those which I am calling root propositions *are* the unconscious as discovered by Freud, or exist "in" this unconscious. Such assumptions are seriously wrong (and have done much damage to the appreciation of psychoanalysis).[61]

Representations such as the root propositions, if I become angry with the other, my psychoanalyst, he will abandon or reject me or I fear that I wish to damage the other's, my psychoanalyst's, penis, are not "in" the unconscious (indeed, at this juncture, it is not even wholly clear in what sense we might claim that the aggressive wishes intimated by these propositions are dimensions of the repressed unconscious, which is a matter to which we will return shortly). Such propositions may be, as Freud occasionally stated it, *descriptively unconscious* (or nonconscious)—they might be, so to speak, *deeply preconscious*—but their specification misses entirely the genuine significance of Freud's free-associative discovery of the way in which human self-consciousness represses something of itself from itself. By which I mean, the way in which self-consciousness represses from its domain of representationality—renders otherwise than that which can be represented—dimensions of its own being-in-the-world that nonetheless animate it. As shorthand for what must be further argued in this chapter, it might be said that, if it is, or can be, represented, it is not repressed. To express this differently: That which is repressed is otherwise than representationality (recall here the notion of enigmatic messages, "thing-presentations" or "unfathomable navels" presented as the traces of erotically embodied impulses). Again, the repressed unconscious is not a text other than that which is available, or which could be made available, representationally, to self-consciousness.[62] This issue is crucial of our understanding of the revolutionary significance of psychoanalytic praxis.

The commonplace but serious error of mistaking root propositions or core conflicts as they are sometimes called (again, schemes, themes, motives) for the repressed unconscious itself has generated much of the way in which psychoanalysis is confused with the procedures of psychoanalytically informed and psychoanalytically oriented therapy or, for that matter, other therapies that might privilege interpretation with the goal of accumulating "insight." the term "unconscious phantasy"—which has been, since Susan Isaacs's 1948 paper, such a powerful notion in some clinical lineages—has more recently contributed to the extent of this confusion, when its usage is accompanied by a certain disregard for the distinction between the preconscious, or what I am suggesting might be the deep preconscious and that which is repressed.[63] The vicissitudes of "psychoanalytic" theorizing since Freud—such that the term "unconscious" can refer to anything that is not conscious, including not only preconscious and deeply preconscious representations, but also nonconscious cognitive mechanisms such as the deep structures of language—must be confronted. It must be confronted if for no other reason than that, in this maelstrom of conceptualizations, the radicality of free-associative praxis is eclipsed or lost.

On the murmuring of what is otherwise than textuality

It is an acutely paradoxical commentary on the history of psychoanalysis that the notion of the repressed unconscious as being a text that is other than, yet hidden by, that of consciousness and the preconscious has held such sway over theorizing after Freud. Yet it is actually quite unsustainable. For example, it fails to explain why such a discovery should have required free-associative method, although indeed it explains why so many of those who claim to be Freud's successors have demoted or abandoned this method. If the individual is indeed composed of multiple texts, then it would seem that the relation between them is conceived as one of translatability, and the subject's relation to them could almost entirely be conceptualized in terms of attentionality (that of attending to one and not the other at various points in time and for various internally motivated or circumstantial reasons), as well as the conscious willingness to listen to and acknowledge oneself translatively. This is how Sartre read Freud's discovery, leading him—understandably—to condemn the Freudian unconscious as a matter of "bad faith" (*mauvaise foi*). By this, Sartre meant that all Freud had discovered was the individual's failure to "own up to" narratives that are being disowned by self-consciousness. In this Sartre merely assumed and reasserted prerogatives of an agency that Freud had already shown to be inherently and ineliminably duplicitous or contradictorious.

Those sorts of existential arguments rest on a failure to appreciate the radicality of the free-associative method and the way in which it opens us to an unconscious profoundly different from that envisaged by pre-Freudian philosophy (the unconscious exemplified by writers such as Schopenhauer). *Free-associative praxis opens us to an unconscious of energy rather than textuality*, and, more disturbingly, to an unconscious that, unlike that of Romantic philosophy (identified with thinkers such as Goethe, Schiller, and Samuel Taylor Coleridge), is far from the harmonious substrate of representational consciousness. Rather, the repressed unconscious is in a contradictorious relation with the self-consciousness it produces.

In the vignettes introduced in the previous chapter, there are perhaps three intimations of, so to speak, an anti-textual unconscious. That is, an energy that disrupts the law and order of what I have elsewhere called the narratological imperative.[64] Again, it is to be emphasized that these are intimative, rather than evidentiary. The caution about the limitations and distortions of this sort of depiction of free-associative discourse must again be emphasized. These three intimations can be mentioned now in the context of the first vignette, and their significance developed in the chapters that follow.

The vignettes aid us in raising a question: what impels the shift from one association to the next? Each vignette simultaneously reveals and conceals a meaning other than itself. That these shifts can be logically and rhetorically specified in relation to a narrative that I have called the root proposition does not address the impetus for such shifting. In these transitions, which disrupt the law and order of ordinary "making sense," something is intimated that seems extra-ordinarily and enigmatically otherwise than the syntactic, semantic, and pragmatic rules and regulations of the narratological imperative. This is not merely a matter of wish-fulfillment in a sense that might accommodate Brentano's notion of intentionality (which echoes through post-Husserlian phenomenology). Rather, it seems to be the obstreperous momentum of desire that shakes up, yet cannot be captured by, representationality.[65]

The vignette provides us with a second hint of a current deeper and different from the text of the root proposition, and from the mere transformation of representational forms from one to the next in the free-associative sequence. Here we might consider the thread of the *Bs*—the *bar* to which my patient fled from the anger of this son, the *Bar* Mitzvah for which the Rabbi tutored him, and the *B*osum *B*uddies walking in luscious countryside, one of whom appears to be *Bar*naby *B Bar*ratt. This is surely an example of, so to speak, an extraordinary and enigmatic energy that attaches itself to a signifier, the meaningfulness of which is entirely extraneous to the manifest text, and indeed to that other text that I have called the root proposition. Yet this very process hints at a momentum of energy that eludes textual analysis—an erotic bodilyness that pervades both the course of associative thinking–speaking and what has been called the "psychoanalytic field," the connectedness of patient and psychoanalyst.[66]

To take this further and offer a third suggestion as to what is intimated in the flow of associative discourse, let us note how the vignettes point to something extraordinary and enigmatic about what is routinely called transference. It is surely facile to specify my male patient's transference as simply as can be discussed in formulations such as "If I become angry with the other, my psychoanalyst, he will abandon or reject me," or for my female patient, "(I fear that) I wish to damage the other's (my psychoanalyst's) penis." To be sure such dimensions of the interpersonal relationship and the undertow they have for the patient are important, and their explication may be therapeutic. Yet our understanding of transference has to go deeper than that, and to be considered in a different register—namely, that of an intricately, intensely, and deeply shared flow of erotic sensibility.

With the male patient, for example, we have intimations of an otherwise current that wells up in the unseemly momentum from the *Titanic* to the Bosum Buddies, via the story of the son (and we need to remember how anticipation of a father's death is heralded by the vitality of a son) and the allusion to the actual death-of-the-father.[67] Here we must refrain from the temptations of textual analysis, in order to appreciate the currents of energy that are intimated. Despite being framed as a hostile jibe at his psychoanalyst ("you're always harping on about our relationship, as if it has to do with absolutely everything, including the sinking of the *Titanic*"), the watery deep calls upon the sensuality of union in the limitlessness of death.[68] "Bosum Buddies," with all its homoerotic resonance, casts the couple into a union that is slightly differently nuanced, with "luscious countryside" evocative of a certain sort of femininity and the maternal body (as a "third term"). The image also holds death perhaps in abeyance by the form of dreamwork which manifests an endless presentness (into which extraordinary and enigmatic messages have intruded).

One way to consider these murmurings of a meaningfulness that is otherwise than textuality is not only to consider the significance of "thing-presentations" that cannot be translated into the representationality of self-consciousness, but also to understand such murmurings as the "unfathomable navel" that animates the lived experience of the subject's discourse. As is well known, Freud said about dreams that each one has "at least one locus at which it is unfathomable, like a navel, a passage through which its meaningfulness is connected to the unknown" (and unknowable . . . *mindestens eine Stelle, an welcher er unergründlich ist, gleichsam einen Nabel, durch den er mit dem Unerkannten zusammenhängt*). The imagery of a navel also suggests quite graphically how this passage might point back, through the traces of erotic embodied experience, to an unknown and unknowable originary, an *arche* from which life began (requiring an *anarchic* method to appreciate). Such an insight cannot pertain exclusively to the textuality of dreams; it must surely be relevant to the entire discourse of self-consciousness. Moreover, Freud's analogy to the navel is profoundly illuminating, indeed brilliant. This umbilical scar intimates a connection of which we cannot speak—an erotically embodied, life-giving connection that antedates the formation of our subjectivity.[69]

Preliminary conclusion

Free-associative discourse is, of course, compliant with the rules and regulations of representationality. The passage from one association to the next "makes sense"—or, more precisely, can "be made sense of" retrodictively. But to rest with this reassurance is to miss the radicality of psychoanalysis. It is to miss the healing involved precisely in the "disassociative" dimension of free-association, wherein lies its derepressive impact (I will later return to this point). In short, to cling to the comforting supposition—that everything in psychic life can sooner or later be represented and thus understood—which is the fundamental dogma of interpretation, is to fail to appreciate the profound significance of free-associative discourse. Such dogma leads to a "model of the mind" that establishes the unconscious as if it were a place (and as if thoughts, feelings, and images were substantive entities that might populate it, or that might return to the domain of consciousness and the preconscious). Such models depict the unconscious as if it were a text hidden by, yet partially detectable or discernible through, the domain of representationality, and thus potentially translatable into conscious representation. Admittedly, Freud used such spatial and substantial allegories (from the elaboration of the topography to his 1925 discussion of the "mystic writing-pad"), but such heuristic usages in the promulgation of metapsychology have distracted us from the radicality of his own discoveries.

Yes! The passage of free-associative discourse is compliant with the law and order of representationality, but it also perpetually bears the mark—the wounding, if you will—of something otherwise than representation. The method opens us to the intimations of a seemingly chaotic or desirous energy that prohibits the fulmination or totalization of any and every effort to "make sense." Freud's revolution is thus to demonstrate, by this method, that we cannot "bend the heavens to our will"—*Flectere si nequeo superos*, as the first phrase in Freud's epigraph to his *Traumdeutung* tells us. For this is an energy that intervenes upon the transitions between representations, scarring their formation with its disruptive insistence and ineluctable persistence, and hinting perpetually at its erotic status as the brio of life itself. Thus, the experience of free-associative praxis opens us to the necessity of stirring up the underworld.

7

THE LESSONS OF THE METHOD

Psychic energy

> Wir können dem "Trieb" nicht ausweichen als einem Grenzbegriff zwischen psychologischer und biologischer. . . welch ausgiebige Vermittlung zwischen der Biologie und der Psychologie durch die Psychoanalyse hergestellt wird.
>
> We cannot avoid "drive" as a boundary notion for what mediates the psychological and the biological . . . psychoanalysis operates in a realm between psychology and biology.
>
> Sigmund Freud, 1913

It needs to be emphasized that, in now discussing exactly how the free-associative method of psychoanalysis uniquely "stirs up the underworld" and thus proceeds *beyond* a textual analysis that arrives at hidden meanings which can be captured representationally, there is no "pure" psychoanalytic treatment. This needs to be briefly discussed before proceeding to examine the implications of the method that is specifically psychoanalytic. Several different types of discourse invariably co-occur in the everyday workplay engaged together by the patient and the psychoanalyst. There are moments of friendly conversation as well as moments of educative and therapeutic dialogue. These are additional to, and must be differentiated from, the deconstructive momentum of free-associative thinking and speaking, which is—as argued throughout this chapter—the process that makes the discourse distinctively psychoanalytic. For the purpose of clarity, each of which I will call the *inevitable* (perhaps necessary, but not sufficient) *nonpsychoanalytic moments* in every psychoanalytic engagement should be briefly mentioned (although some of the issues raised here will be elaborated in later discussion of the position and function of the psychoanalyst).

On the relationship around free-association

Whatever else transpires, the patient and the psychoanalytic practitioner are embarked on a journey that necessarily and in the most profound sense involves a friendship—indeed, a unique mode of friendship that is professional and yet intensely intimate. In the psychoanalytic literature, the friendly character of the psychoanalytic partnership has perhaps been obfuscated by the somewhat antiseptic or even medicalized discussion of concepts such as the "treatment situation" and the "therapeutic alliance."[70]

Psychoanalysis involves an emotionally intimate relationship of two persons engaged in a "shared activity" and founded on a fundamental "bond of trust" (even if the bond is repeatedly challenged, questioned, provoked, and called into account). These are the twin hallmarks of friendship, as discussed extensively ever since Aristotle's *Nicomachean Ethics*. On the practitioner's side, the psychoanalyst trusts the patient to remain a more or less steadfast guardian of their relationship (to contribute significantly to the former's livelihood and to attend sessions on the condition that the psychoanalyst appropriately addresses his or her resistances to the free-associative method). On the patient's side, he or she more or less consistently trusts—whatever the vicissitudes of affection and animosity in the transference—that the psychoanalyst will facilitate a beneficial process with wisdom, equanimity, and love.

In common with ordinary friendships, psychoanalytic processes are *like* those of a familial relationship, *like* those of a romantic relation, yet proceed in neither direction. As will be later discussed, the psychoanalytic relationship—hovering inclusively between *eros*, *agape*, and *philia*—has to be scrupulously ethical and is destroyed whenever it becomes actually familial or actually romantic.[71] Unlike many ordinary friendships, the relationship is notably lopsided, not only because the patient's psychic life is addressed more explicitly than the practitioner's (for which privilege the patient pays a fee), but also because it is exclusively the psychoanalyst's responsibility to facilitate and maintain the ethicality of the relationship as one of openness of freedom, safety, and abstinent intimacy. Herein lies the unique professionalism of the psychoanalytic partnership. Although this friendship is not one of equality (in the way that many ordinary friendships need to be), there is actually no inherent reason why friends have to be equals.[72] Aligned with the ethicality of genuine friendship, as discussed in classic philosophy, the relationship between patient and practitioner involves virtue, utility, and pleasure. The virtue of the psychoanalytic partnership is its commitment to truthfulness. Its utility lies in its healing potential. And it is—even while embracing the hatred which inevitably surfaces in the course of its journey—a relationship that is, or should ultimately become, pleasurable.

These issues need to be stated strongly (and I will return to them in Chapter 11). Although the patient may never know more than a few of the details of the psychoanalyst's personal life, without a foundation of friendship, the relationship as a psychoanalytic process sooner or later deadlocks. The movement of free-association grinds to a halt and the partnership ends in a deadening and lamentable—indeed, heartrending—impasse.

The method of free-association is a process into which the patient surrenders, allowing—as Nietzsche would have it—the *it thinks me* to take priority over the *I think*. This is why many commentators have objected to the translated term "free-association" (*freie Assoziation* as Freud sometimes called it, starting in 1895) because it might be taken as suggesting that the conscious subject freely determines the course of the associative stream. Consequently, it has been argued that Freud's other expression, *freier Einfall*, expresses more accurately the way in which the patient has to *fall into* the process by which *it thinks me*.[73] As will be discussed, it is the principal task of the psychoanalyst to address the patient's fear of this process—to allay the power of his or her resistances to it. But one should never underestimate the sheer helplessness—the humiliation, anxiety, and fear—experienced by the patient's "ego" as free-association is engaged in the presence of the psychoanalyst. Without the foundation of friendship, no patient would ever proceed more than a few steps along the chain of free-associative thinking and speaking.

In considering the educative aspect of the psychoanalytic relationship, I emphatically do not mean to suggest that the practitioner offers his or her patients information about how to conduct their lives, but more restrictively that it falls to the psychoanalyst to educate each patient about the process of the treatment. This issue has become somewhat confused by the literature on child and adolescent therapy in which patient education may well have a more conspicuous role. However, here I am concerned solely with adult psychoanalysis, in which there are at least three specific topics on which the patient typically requires education.

(1) Much discussed is the issue as to how the psychoanalyst should deliver, and redeliver, the initial invitation to the patient to allow himself or herself to free-associate. That is, the issuance of what Freud designated, in his 1910 *Lectures*, the "fundamental rule" or basic principle of psychoanalysis (*psychoanalytischen Grundregel*). Although there is controversy as to how the patient is to be assisted toward this processive principle, it seems clear that some sort of direct instruction is required, because otherwise the patient would understandably proceed to engage the psychoanalyst in the narratives of ordinary conversation (I will return later to the questions surrounding how the fundamental rule is issued to the patient).

(2) The psychoanalyst is almost invariably required to instruct the patient as to the procedure for understanding dreams. This is the procedure to which Freud devoted much of his 1900 thesis—namely, that after the dream has been recounted, the patient associates to each separate element of its manifest content before any broader understanding of the dream is discussed. Without such instruction and for reasons both culturally and personally resistive, patients almost invariably attempt to understand dreams globally by elaborating and interpreting the manifest narrative. Such a narratological enterprise, as Freud discusses extensively, merely engages further processes of "secondary revision" that defensively deflect the patient away from the possible deeper significance of the dream's construction. Here the details and the possible variations in the manner in which the psychoanalyst educates the

patient on this issue do not need to be discussed; nor how he or she might intervene when the patient reverts to the more familiar practice of attempting to generate interpretations of the dream on the basis of a narratological amplification or gloss on its surface content (which patients typically do). Rather, it simply needs to be noted that it is only a very exceptional patient (usually one familiar with psychoanalytic writings) who will know how to break the dream into its elements and associate to each, without the practitioner's diligent education on the importance of adherence to this method.

(3) Another topic of education is the one most egregiously overlooked by many practitioners—namely, the importance of facilitating the patient's ability to listen to the "voicing" of embodied experience. An example of this would be the significance of listening to the "voicing" of momentary sensations as when the soft tissues "join in the conversation."[74] The expressiveness of the bodymind, in ways that are nonrepresentational or protorepresentational, is crucial for our understanding of the repressed character of unconscious communications, and will be discussed more fully in what follows.

This brings us to the aspect of *therapeutic procedures as a nonpsychoanalytic component of psychoanalysis*. As discussed in the previous chapter, the manifest contents of free-associative talk can be—and so some extent invariably will be—used as "data" for some sort of textual analysis.[75] Expression of the stream of consciousness provides evidence for the operation of root propositions and thus invites their formulation as interpretations. In this regard, there is always, at least to some degree, an arrival at hidden meanings—meanings that can be represented and that seem to lie *behind* or *beneath* the sequence of contents manifested in the stream of consciousness. It is the principal *technique* of therapy to formulate these underlying themes as interpretations, which are to be understood or assimilated as insights (as was discussed at the beginning of the previous chapter). Such a procedure may indeed generate a veracious understanding of the patient's functioning—insights that he or she may assimilate and subsequently deploy usefully. Of course, the criteria of what is useful is a matter for serious debate. In a sense, it becomes a technical issue (that can be differentiated from the method of psychoanalysis), and in this regard I have trenchantly maintained that such criteria are invariably steeped in ideology, subtly or blatantly conveying standards of what is assumed to be mature and adaptive. This sort of textual analysis and interpretive technique, with the goal of assimilated understanding that will subsequently govern more mature or adaptive functioning, is characteristic of therapies that are psychoanalytically informed or psychoanalytically oriented (and thus to be contrasted with "therapies" of behavioral manipulation).

Because such procedures occur, to greater or lesser extent, in every psychoanalytic treatment, it may be surprising that I will now argue that they are *not* the essential and unique process of psychoanalysis as such. Indeed, to equate psychoanalysis with this discursive momentum of therapeutic maneuvering—the generation, transmission, and assimilation of interpretive insights about the underlying propositions that motivate the sequence of elements in the stream of consciousness—is to commit the major error that has typified so much of the literature in this field, including some but not all of Freud's own writings.

The radically significant lesson of free-association is not so much that it provides evidence of representational schemes or themes (motives, root propositions, core conflicts, "unconscious phantasies") that are operative behind and beneath the manifest contents of consciousness and that can be usefully deployed (translated, interpreted, acknowledged, integrated) in the technical procedures of therapy. If this were all that psychoanalysis involves, then indeed other ways of inferring the operation of such root propositions could substitute for the procedure of free-associative expression. However, the unique significance of free-association as a *method*—as praxis—is that it opens the subject to a kinetic realm of its own being-in-the-world that is *beyond* that which can be represented, otherwise than textuality.

In this context, the importance of interpretation and insight in a psychoanalytic treatment is not so much the acquisition of knowledge *about* one's functioning (although this occurs, often dramatically). Rather, the role of the psychoanalyst's interpretations, of shared insights, and of his or her silences is foremost and essentially the ongoing facilitation of the patient's surrender to the free-associative process. For it is this process that not only discloses what representations might lie *behind* or *beneath* the manifest presentation of our self-consciousness, but also exposes—stirring the underworld—the realm of our being-in-the-world that is *beyond* representationality. This is the prime lesson of psychoanalysis that has, all too easily, been forgotten by thirteen decades of commentary and critique.

On the question of the (dis)associative copula

The impact of an otherwise force that is *beyond* representation, yet which disruptively influences the passage in consciousness from one representation to the next, is evident in the stirring that occurs *between* associative elements. This is the stirring exhibited and experienced through the psychoanalytic method, allowing to come forth, in Laplanche's words, "a *domain of being* (the 'processes of the soul')" to which "barely anything else" gives access. In free-associative discourse, the irruptions of the copula (the *between*, or "within" but not "of," representational transitions and transformations) point both to the operation of an energy that is otherwise than representation and thence to the repressiveness of self-consciousness. The salient issues may be considered in the following way.

In ordinary conversation or narration, the shifting of consciousness from one thought or feeling to the next is comparatively unproblematic, in as much as it *appears* to be fully explained in terms of specifiable logical and rhetorical operations. For example, I tell my friends "T-1" (I am working on an essay), "T-2" (a colleague told me the essay is a waste of time), "T-3" (my colleague is an arrogant idiot), and then "T-4" (my dog agrees with his judgment of my activities, although for far better reasons). There are definable rules of transformation—syntactic, semantic, pragmatic—that can account for this concatenation or chain of representations. Indeed, they produce the cogency of the story, thus implementing the narratological imperative. Following a track of philosophy that would include Ludwig Wittgenstein's *Philosophical Investigations* as much as Charles Sanders Peirce's semiotics, one can insist that the system of rules and regulations—by which, for instance, "T-2" follows "T-1"—fully determine the course of my enunciations, the possibility of my "making sense" conversationally and narratologically. In passing, we can note that "I" do not invent or create these rules and regulations. More accurately, they designate "me," determining the tracks of possible meaningfulness (in the sense of representational meaning) along which my subjectivity is constituted. By "fully determine," it is suggested that, in accounting for the copula (the contiguity of "T-1" *and then* "T-2"), we do not have to have recourse to any mode of explanation or understanding other than that provided by the law and order of representational discourse. This is also the case for the root propositions that textual analysis divulges, in as much as their relationship with the concatenation of manifest contents *can appear to be* fully explained by the rules and regulations of discourses which operate on several levels that are intertranslatable (for example, self-conscious, preconscious, deeply preconscious, or descriptively unconscious).

However, when we listen to the trajectory of free-associative discourse, we come to be suspicious of the claim made by the sciences of representationality to account *fully* for the copula, the relationship between one thought or feeling and that which is contiguous or continuous with it.

Every undergraduate textbook tells us—somewhat misleadingly—that there are *special* phenomena in consciousness that make evident the intrusion of the unconscious into the stream of conscious functioning. Such introductory texts rather naively nominate "aberrations" such as dreams, slips, jokes, and all the other demonstrably subversive eventualities, as having this privileged status. However, there is no reason to believe that suppressed or repressed ideas or forces are any less active in manifest contents that are not so ostensibly aberrant. Rather, through psychoanalysis we come to know or at least suspect that, in ordinary conversation or narration, the impact of such ideas or forces is merely camouflaged more successfully (efficaciously and efficiently). I will return later to this mistaken idea that some events in consciousness bespeak or betray this intrusiveness, whereas others supposedly do not. At this juncture we must use the evidence of free-associative chaining to dispel the ideological or scientistic myth that any enunciation that is self-consciousness can be explained sufficiently by the law and order of representationality.

To reiterate: The path of free-associative thoughts and feelings remarkably and compellingly suggests that self-consciousness displays, or might be motivated by, meanings that are other than conscious. In the preceding chapters, it was amply demonstrated how a textual analysis of the manifest contents of consciousness discloses the operation of root propositions, or allows us to infer the significance of these other-than-conscious meanings. It was also concluded that such textual analysis indicates meaningfulness that is, so to speak, deeply preconscious or decisively suppressed from consciousness (that is, descriptively unconscious). However, such analysis does not necessitate the postulate of a sort of meaningfulness that has been repressed from consciousness. Whatever is discerned by textual analysis is translatable into conscious representationality, and thus I would argue that its meanings are merely suppressed, even if deeply so. However, in addition to the matter of root propositions (schemes, themes, motives, and "unconscious phantasies"), the trajectory of free-association also suggests forces that impose themselves on consciousness disruptively, but are otherwise than the rule-bound sequence of representations that is still operative in the movement of this trajectory.

This can be understood as follows. It may be that a sequence of thoughts and feelings such as "T-1" (I am working on an essay) followed by "T-2" (a colleague told me the essay is a waste of time) *appears* fully rule-governed. However, consider now the shifting from "I am angry at the other" (as articulated by my psychoanalyst), to "My son was angry at me and I left," to "I was angry at my Rabbi and he left," to "We are Bosum Buddies." It is less easy to claim that such a sequence is "fully rule-governed." The application of such a claim to ordinary conversation or narration is easier, even if mistaken. Nevertheless, such a claim can be sustained by a *post hoc* or retrodictive textual analysis. However, the crucial issue here—the issue underscoring the distinctiveness of psychoanalytic processes from the procedures of therapy—is that there are intimations of something else animating this associative chain, something that eludes textuality. The movement of manifest thoughts and feelings intimates the pulsing of a *bar-bar-bar* or *b-b-b*, which hints, in an enigmatic and extraordinary fashion, at the tremors of deathfulness (*Titanic*, fathering, fatherhood) and of sexuality (from orgasmic death to homoerotic afterlife) *within* our representable or comprehensible system of meanings, yet not *of* the law and order of representational meaningfulness (untranslated and untranslatable).

Surely, claims Freud and every genuine psychoanalyst after him, here is a vibrationality otherwise than the rules and regulations of representational transformativity. Through psychoanalysis we open ourselves to the enigmatic and extraordinary meaningfulness of forces otherwise than textuality—forces that are infiltrating subversively the representational law and order of psychic life. Here is an animative source of meaningfulness that cannot be translated into the representable meanings by which we know how to "make sense." In this way, Freud claims that there must be an energy that discloses itself contradictoriously within representations and especially in the disruptions of the copula. This postulate both warrants our surrender to the free-associative method and is also the warrantable finding of this method. Thus, the experience of free-association requires that the copula which leads us from one thought or feeling to the next be reconsidered scientifically, because this method of opening, expressing, listening (and again opening, expressing, listening . . .) demonstrates that there is more to psychic life than the transitions and transformations of representational law and order. At issue is also some mode of psychic energy.

This conclusion is warranted by attention to the implications of what the chaining of free-associative discourse intimates about the copula, the link between one representation (or set of representations) and the next. That is, about the conditions of the transitional and transformative linking of one conscious thought or feeling with the next, the *between* of associative elements. This "between" or link invites into the discourse of consciousness not merely representations that are behind or beneath the manifest text (the root propositions), but also intimations of experiencing that is *beyond* representationality. Of course, in terms of the assumptions of logical-empiricist or positivist-naturalistic investigation, this "beyond" is a postulate, not amenable to direct proof (and its "conceptual status" will be discussed in the next chapter). But nevertheless it is the postulate that initiates the method that frees, at least to a degree, the subject from the repetition-compulsive governance of the "ego organization."

In sum, the passage of free-association is always governed by the rules and regulations of representation, but it is also animated by forces otherwise than representationality. As free-associative method, psychoanalysis exposes these otherwise forces of an unrepresentable meaningfulness that are wholly—or almost wholly—obscured by the manner in which ordinary conversation and narration appear to make "totally good sense." The method opens the subject of self-consciousness to this vibrationality of something otherwise that is like the pulsations of "psychic energy." As Derrida expressed it, free-associative discourse serves to illuminate that dimension of life "which can *only* uneasily be contained within logocentric closure."[76] In this context, "uneasy containment" points to the way in which this otherwise eventuates animatively and disruptively—*contradictoriously*—within self-consciousness, but is excluded by the law and order of its representational structuring. This is a notion of psychic energy, which is radically different from the notion of the unconscious as an "other text" that might be translated into the text of self-consciousness.

8

THE LESSONS OF THE METHOD

Theorizing praxis

> Ich würde mich sehr energisch dagegen sträuben, wenn jemand die Lehre von der Verdrängung und vom Widerstand zu den Voraussetzungen anstatt zu den Ergebnissen der Psychoanalyse rechnen wollte . . . die Lehre von der Verdrängung ist ein Erwerb der psychoanalytischen Arbeit, auf legitime Weise als theoretischer Extrakt aus unbestimmt vielen Erfahrungen gewonnen.
>
> I would emphatically oppose anyone who attempts to count the tenet of repression and resistance as merely a premise of psychoanalysis instead of its finding . . . the doctrine of repression is the result of psychoanalytic labor, achieved by a legitimate method, as a theoretical inference based on innumerable experiences.
>
> Sigmund Freud, 1914

The prime answer that the free-associative method offers to the question of the copula is that psychic life must be understood not only as a composition of representations (of others, of self, of affects, and actions) and their transitions and transformations; understanding the copula also requires our consideration of something otherwise than the law and order of representationality. That is, a special sort of energy. This energy is variously and disruptively invested in the linking of representations. That is, the enigmatic and exuberant "jumps"—disassociative and derepressive jumps—of association, as well as the aberrant signifiers that appear extraneously within the manifest text.[77] An example of the latter is the *bar-bar-bar* or b-b-b that intrudes into the discourse of the male patient discussed in previous chapters. It is this energy that perpetually decenters the subject of self-consciousness—the energy that instigates Freud's Copernican revolution.

A note on Freudian energetics

Throughout his life, Freud maintained that the psyche is a system of representations and energies. Although he intermittently suggested that psychic energy might be biological, his discipline opposes any effort to propound a purely cognitivist psychology that exclusively acknowledges representations and their biological substrate.[78] Indeed, the thrust of this chapter is to demonstrate how, without the notion of psychic energy, the discipline of psychoanalysis as praxis is abolished and the only significance of the term "unconscious" is to designate a variety of conditions (preconscious, descriptively unconscious, nonconscious, and so forth) none of which acknowledge Freud's discovery of the repressiveness of self-consciousness.[79]

Initially (in his correspondence with Fliess through the 1890s), Freud called this force that is otherwise-than-representationality an *Impuls*, which might have been translated as pulse, impulse, impulsion, momentum, or even as élan. It is certainly considered some form of energy. In "Draft K" of 1892, which he sent to Fliess, he wrote of "intensities" (*Intensitäten*) of "psychic energy" (*psychische Energie*). However, by the time of "Draft E" of 1894, he had started to use the notion of *Triebe* (in the plural). By 1899, with the writing of *Traumdeutung*, he shifted decisively to the notion of *Trieb* (singular), although the notion of *Energie* continues to run alongside its usage.

Trieb can appropriately be translated as "drive" (but, for reasons to be elaborated in the next chapter, it should *not* be translated as instinct, which the *Standard Edition* repeatedly uses). The term has interestingly ambivalent connotations. On the mechanistic side, it suggests the engine or power of the material apparatus, as in the German *Triebwerk*. On the existential side, it suggests the operation of desire, as related to the German *Wunsch* (wish, want, or will), *Lust* (pleasure, lust, or gusto), and *Gelüste* (as a sensuous or sensual longing). Herein the notions of drive and desire will be used to explicate the significance of *Trieb* for the discoveries of psychoanalysis.[80] As the chapter progresses (particularly in the next chapter), I shall also focus on drive-desire as *libidinality*, since it is this notion of subtle energies that is unarguably discovered by experience with the free-associative method.

As is well known, experience with the discourse of free-association compelled Freud to argue, from the very beginning of his psychoanalytic career, that drives must have a *source*, *object*, and *aim*, that variously impact the cogency and coherence of the representational system. Later, in the 1915 paper on *Triebschicksale* (the destiny or vicissitudes of drive-desire), he would add that they exert a variable *pressure* on the system. "This pressure," he wrote, is "the impulsiveness of drive-desire as a motoric moment, the sum of a force" or the degree to which drive-desire comprises a *demand for labor* on the part of the representational system. In short, the pressure of drive-desire is as an energetic force that compels, or "demands labor" on the part of, the representational system to instigate transformations of some sort within itself (e.g. from T-1 to T-2 to T-3 and so forth).

All these notions are tied to his experience with free-association, despite the fact that it is evident that Freud initially imagined—and continued to speculate intermittently—that this energy was physical, quasi-physical, or neuronal. This would imply that he had made a "discovery" much in the manner that, earlier in the 19th century, Michael Faraday and Joseph Henry had made discoveries about electric currents. Freud's struggle to establish a continuity between his adventures with free-association and his early career as a distinguished neuroscientific researcher (as exemplified by his productivity from 1877 to 1895) is clearly evident. For example, his protractedly conflictual and never fully completed writing of the 1895 *Entwurf* (his *Sketch* or "psychology for neurologists") indicates how difficult it was for him to recognize that the drive-desire of libidinal energies might be very real, and vitally significant, but not an *ostensible reality* that might be demonstrated empirically in the findings of neurological research.[81] The drive-desire or energies discovered by the free-associative method are otherwise that the law and order of representationality, but they are also not merely equivalent to anything that is demonstrably physical, such as the firing of synaptic connections (and this will be addressed in the next chapter).

Perhaps in conceding to this difficulty in acknowledging the realities touched by free-associative method, Freud allowed himself to become increasingly speculative about the nature of drives. It is well known that, as his writing drifted into a more conjectural mode, he began to attribute purpose to the drives in a manner that suggests—misleadingly—that they might have representable content. Initially, in articles ranging from the 1896 "Aetiology of Hysteria" to the 1910 paper on disturbances of vision, he argued that libidinality is counterposed to aggressive or quasi-aggressive forces that are born of libidinal frustration and the need for self-preservative or reality-testing functions (I will return to this later when discussing how drive-desire or Trieb is not equivalent to the biological operation of Instinkt). In subsequent, more speculative moments of theoretical construction, exemplified by his 1910 paper "Formulation of the Two Principles of Mental Functioning" and his 1914 "On Narcissism," he contrasted "sexual drives" and "ego drives" more explicitly. Finally, in his controversial 1920 essay, he propounded the existence of "life drives" (in which drive-desire forces are kinetically bound into representations that may be sexual or aggressive) and "death drives" (in which these forces tend to dissipate into inertia). As Laplanche has appropriately argued, these life and death drives are not really newly discovered drives as such, but rather the articulation of two distinct principles by which drive-desire may function in relation to the representations in which it is invested.[82]

All these issues require elaboration. However, before proceeding to examine the theorizing of drive-desire in relation to the three-plus-one inextricably connected implications of psychoanalytic method (the repressiveness of self-consciousness, the pluritemporality, and the polysexuality of psychic life, as well as the oedipal complexes), it is necessary to discuss further the significance of energy or drive-desire as what appears to be a theoretical notion.

Theorizing psychoanalytic method

If we were to summarize the argument thus far, it would be as follows. *Experiencing the method of free-associative praxis opens the participant's discourse to the disruptive "voicing" of otherwise forces that are between or beyond the law and order of representational transition and transformation, and that seem meaningful yet excluded or foreclosed from the system of representational meaning* (a system that includes conscious, preconscious, deeply preconscious, and descriptively unconscious ideas and images). Freud understands such forces as psychic energy, or drive-desire (*Trieb*).

Here we must ask what sort of "conceptual status" is to be attributed to this energetic notion, and later we will also ask what sort of reality it portends.[83] As I have already indicated, psychic energy is not amenable to the procedures of proof required of logical-empiricist, analytic-referential, or positivist-naturalistic science. Indeed, as Robert Galatzer-Levy and others have discussed, this unprovable condition is the ostensible reason that so many commentators after Freud have excised the idea of psychic energy from their lexicon (sometimes retaining the concept of drive-desire forces, but drastically corrupting the notion such that it merely designates either purely biological phenomena or motives that can be represented).[84] Freud's notion does not refer to any force that can be found within the neurons, nor merely to motives that could be represented generically (such as affection, envy, or rivalry). Yet this does *not* imply that the notion lacks truthfulness, is unjustified, fallacious, inconsequential, or scientifically illegitimate.[85] In this regard, three issues are pertinent.

(1) Foremost is the assumption that, if psychic energy is only privately, internally, and indirectly experienced (via what are sometimes clinically called "drive derivatives") and is neither observable nor directly reportable, it effectively does not exist within the annals of science. Yet Freud found the notion necessary to understand the eruptions and disruptions of the law and order of representationality that occur in free-associative discourse. That the "object" of psychoanalysis—namely, the repressed unconscious—may only be accessible through the method of free-association, surely should not be taken to imply that the status of its exploration must be condemned as unscientific (in the sense of *unwissenschaftlich*).

(2) To reject the notion of psychic energy as unjustifiable is to assume that, in order to be scientific, psychoanalysis must be objectivistic (and thus its method must potentially conform to the rules and regulations of logical-empiricist or positivist-naturalistic investigation). Yet psychic energy does not have the same status as a theoretical concept or construct that can be operationalized and arbitrated or modified in terms of publicly accessible "data" or facts, and that can then be applied to that domain of observables. The notion of psychic energy is not a theoretical construct in this sense (and below I will discuss its status in terms of the idea of science as praxis). Conspicuously, the conduct of psychoanalytic processes is not the conduct of an objectivistic science. Yet neither is it subjectivistic in the tradition of introspective disciplines, including Husserlian and post-Husserlian phenomenology, which assume the centering of the subject on itself.[86]

(3) These considerations would seem to imply that psychic energy is a mythematic notion required to understand psychoanalytic method (and indeed the human condition).[87] This is not a matter about which psychoanalysts need to be defensive—despite that, in the current cultural climate that celebrates the hegemony of "hard science," defensiveness might erroneously appear to be apt. As Leszek

Kolakowski, and others have shown, myth-making or allegorization is an ineliminable dimension of every scientific endeavor.[88] For example, this is conspicuous in the writings of several distinguished neuroscientists, such as Antonio Damasio and Joseph LeDoux, when they come to discuss how consciousness might emerge from brain mechanisms. They account for the consciousness/brain relationship in allegories (even if they do not acknowledge this). It seems as if they refuse to admit that the transition and translatability from cortical functions to the theatre of representation and reflectivity is a postulate that is not itself, and never could be, empirically testable, so they indulge in speculations that are, however compelling, acts of myth-making.[89]

As an aside, we might note that, as a mythematic reality discovered by psychoanalytic method, psychic energy (drive-desire or libidinality) has some notable parallels with ancient and widespread teachings about subtle energy systems. Depending on one's standpoint, this might or might not contribute to the credibility of the notion. Here we might consider a diverse set of doctrines such as those concerning *prānā* in the Sanātana Dharma lineages (Vedic, Jain, Buddhist), *chi* in Chinese and particularly Taoic teachings, *ki* in Japanese, *lom* in Thai, and others such as *mana* in some Oceanic cultures, *orenda* for some Native American groups, and *od* in ancient Germanic cultures. We might also consider certain threads in Kabbalist, Gnostic, and Sufi teachings, as well as more modern philosophical conjectures such as those expounded in Schopenhauer's writings (which Freud knew well), or by Karl von Reichenbach, by Henri-Louis Bergson, and by others. If we take the doctrine of *prānā* as a prime example of a notion now endorsed by many healing practitioners and others worldwide, we can note certain aspects of convergence with Freud's notion of psychic energy, drive-desire, or libidinality. For example, *prānā* is a subtle invisible energy that is a lifeforce pervading the entire universe, linking the individual's body and the mind, as well as weaving and circulating all around this bodymind. There are also certain points of divergence, as follows.

First, Freud assumes an endogenous/exogenous dichotomy, in which psychic energy may conjoin events within the individual field of eventualities, but that field is circumscribed within the person's bodymind. Although Freud toyed with the possibility of telepathy, as the mystical movement of thoughts between individuals, there is little additional evidence that he entertained the possibility of other modes of energetic connection.[90]

Second, Freud generally assumes that psychic energy operates as an enclosed economy that follows conservative principles of constancy that he and Breuer explicitly adopted between 1892 and 1895—that is, even before the psychoanalytic method had been fully discovered. As is well known, Freud vacillated and was challenged to maintain this assumption. In the next chapter, the way in which this assumption has to be relinquished in the context of the crucial distinction between drive-desire (*Trieb*) and biological *Instinkte* will be discussed.

Third, although Freud, especially later in his *oeuvre*, wrote of drives being "tamed" by the ego organization, there is little or no evidence that psychic energy can ultimately be aligned harmoniously with—or finally and fully captured within—the representational system of the ego. Indeed, what the free-associative method seems to suggest is the perpetually contradictorious relation between psychic energy and representationality. However, teachings about *prānā* typically hold out the hope of some ultimate condition of enlightenment or deliverance (*moksha*) in which the energies of the individual bodymind become harmoniously aligned with those of the universe. Ailments, in most if not all traditions that operate on these teachings, are held to be a matter of weakness or blockage in the flow of *prānā* between the *chakras* that are concentrated networks or plexuses of energy and through the *nādis*, which are the channels than run between them. This notion of obstruction seems significantly different from the experience of internal contradictoriness. Thus, health or healing, in these traditions, is usually considered to involve the free flow of *prānā* through the chakras and *nādis*, whereas the healing of psychoanalysis would seem to involve only the restarting of movement-with-contradictoriness, rather than the achievement of some endpoint of harmony—psychoanalysis being, as Freud argued fulsomely, *unendlich*, interminable.[91]

Given all these considerations, that psychic energy is a necessary but mythematic notion should not bother the psychoanalytic practitioner, and certainly not be an occasion for defensiveness about the notion. However, this leaves for discussion the status of psychic energy as a scientific notion that is not a concept or theoretical construct within an objectivistic framework of investigation. Psychic energy appears to be a theoretical concept, yet is not. This brings us to the idea of free-association as praxis—as a science neither objectivistic nor subjectivistic.

Science as praxis

Our comprehension of the significance of praxis for understanding the scientific status of psychoanalysis as neither an objectivistic nor a subjectivistic mode of inquiry is not only crucial to the proper appreciation of free-associative method, but also to the status of notions such as that of psychic energy. Discussion of the notion of praxis is made more complex by the fact that the term is often used as synonymous with "action" or "practice," and unfortunately has also recently been used merely as a trendy term for conventional practices.[92] Additionally, discussion of the notion in relation to psychoanalysis is made more complex by the fact that Plato distinguished praxis and revelatory speech (*lexis*). Yet the significance of the free-associative method is precisely that its action for change is that of a mode of speech exposing a realm of our being-in-the-world that is inaccessible by other means.

The Aristotelian usage of the term "praxis" is most significant for psychoanalysis, as is the way in which the term was developed after Hegel to indicate a distinctive mode of understanding-by-changing. Aristotle viewed the ethico–political domain of human affairs as constituted by both speech and praxis, the combination of which distinctively indicated that *praxis is a way of life open to free individuals* (and one might modify this to suggest that praxis is a way of life engaged in order to free individuals). Praxis is thus tied to the unique quality of humans as capable of narrating their lives (and thus by implication capable of deconstructing the extant narration of their lives). Its activities sustain the *bios politicos* and differentiates *bios* from *zōe*—the latter being the life enjoyed by species that lack the linguistic capabilities of humans.[93] It should be noted here how Aristotle dichotomizes praxis and *theoria*. Praxis includes *poiēsis*, which connotes "making" as a precursor of action, whereas theory implies the construction of knowledge for its own sake—a more abstract enterprise. These Aristotelian ideas were debated by philosophers from the period of medieval scholasticism to modern commentators from Locke to Schelling (and subsequently). Most importantly, Hegel, by presenting the truthfulness of theory and praxis as freedom, calls into question their dichotomization, and thus also the idea that praxis might merely be the application of theory. It is to Hegel's commentators, especially within the Marxist tradition, that we should now turn.

The philosopher of history and sociopolitical activitist August Cieszkowski was perhaps the first to give the notion of praxis its special significance as a mode of transformative or transmutative knowing that differs from the practicality of instrumentalist reason. Among other factors, it is probably Cieszkowski's 1838 text on history, along with Moshe Hess's idea that philosophy should not want to remain philosophical, that inspired Marx to reconfigure Hegel's *Geist* ("spirit") as sensuous human activity. Marx thus instigated a sort of metaphilosophical mode of thinking that is intimately tied to revolutionary transformation. This suggests a connection between theorizing and action that breaks with the instrumentalist assumption that theoretical concepts stand apart from action but can be applied to effect change (that is, it breaks with the conventional notion of practice). This break—indicating how praxis might entail a radically different mode of relationship between ideas and action—is subsequently developed in various ways by commentators from Antonio Labriola, György Lukács, Karl Korsch, Antonio Gramsci, and Mao Tse-tung, to the writings of the Frankfurt School (e.g. Theodor Adorno, Max Horkheimer, Herbert Marcuse, Walter Benjamin), the Yugoslav Group (e.g. Mihailo Marković), and others (e.g. Karel Kosík, Henri Lefebvre, Jean-Paul Sartre).

Although there are many variations, three ideas are strongly developed by these thinkers:

1 The logical-empiricist, analytic-referential, or positivist-naturalistic version of science falsely claims that facts "speak for themselves" and that the theories derived from such facts are value neutral. Against this position, these thinkers show how facts are always pretheorized or theoretically preconstituted, and thus serve ideological functions.
2 Abstract theoretical endeavors, which means philosophical or scientific endeavors that are distanced from the realities of human suffering, are to be rejected for their collusion in ideologically reproducing the *status quo*. Against such endeavors, the science of praxis calls for theorizing that serves the cause of transformative or transmutative action.
3 By the same token, practice, as techniques in which theoretical constructs that stand apart from real life situations are applied to them instrumentally, is to

be rejected. This implies the development of praxis that is an activity radically divergent from instrumental reason and the tradition of *technē*.

Perhaps most significant here is the way in which these three critical precepts (opposing conventional ideas about "data" or facts, about theory as an abstractive construction of correspondent or coherent models, and about practice as instrumentalist application) open the way to an entirely different relationship between thinking and change. Praxis is to be understood as a nonteleological method—that is, *not* merely as a technique that is implemented in order to achieve an end. Rather, the engagement of processes of knowing and being in praxis does not presume an endpoint, but starts with the unacceptable condition of what is the case in the present (this is why philosophers writing about praxis have fiercely debated the assumptions about potentiality and totality that seem to underlie this mode of engagement). What must be appreciated here is the possibility of praxis as an inherently and radically different epistemological and ontological mode in relation to our being-in-the-world, a mode of activity neither objectivistic nor subjectivistic. In relation to the former, it does not assume that the "object" of knowledge is "as is," nor is it an instrumentalist approach to changing the object. In relation to the latter, it does not allow the "subject" to be treated as a centered-point, nor does it merely deepen the subject's own apprehension of itself, again treating itself "as is," because instead it starts with the subject in need of transformation or transmutation. Rather, the practico-critical role of praxis in human affairs tends to involve methods of negatively dialectical thinking that comprise the breaking down, or transgressing, of whatever is hegemonic—creatively contravening or deconstructing the ideological frameworks of thinking that perpetuate the status quo, and thus facilitating the surfacing of hitherto undisclosed realms of our being-in-the-world. In a profound sense, this is what the psychoanalytic method of free-association does.

There are notions in Freud's early writings that *appear* as if they have the conceptual status of theoretical constructs, and indeed in his later, post-1914 speculative enterprises of metapsychological theory-building, they do have such a status. But this does not alter the reality that, as they emerged from and are intimately connected with his experience with free-associative praxis, they are moments of theorizing that are *not* to be comprehended as concepts within an objectivistic theoretical structure. I believe Freud had a sense of this when he occasionally refers to these moments of theorizing as *Hilfsvorstellungen*, meaning "helpful" or "auxiliary ideas." Unfortunately, in the *Standard Edition*, this is translated as "conceptual scaffolding," which gives the impression that such ideas are merely preliminary to the erection of a conceptual structure. However, this impression is mistaken. Rather, the functioning of these notions comprises theorizing moments that are highly provisional and auxiliary to praxis (and is thus quite distinct from the operation of theoretical concepts that are to be components in a metapsychological model of the "mental apparatus").

Hilfsvorstellungen are ideas intricately tied to the praxis of transformation and transmutation. They facilitate the ongoing commitment to understanding-by-changing and to the voicing of dimensions of our being-in-the-world that were previously recondite. Freud's notions associated with the repressiveness of self-consciousness, the pluritemporality and polysexuality of psychic life are inextricably tied to the method he discovered. For their understanding he needed to write about psychic energy, drive-desire or libidinality. For the purposes of this exposition, I refer to these *Hilfvorstellungen* as *notions-for-praxis*. Such theorizing may well be mythematic or allegorical, but it is inherent to the processes of psychoanalytic change (for which the grand metapsychological models of the "mental apparatus" are extraneous). As will be further discussed, the notion of psychic energy provides a way of understanding at least three practico-critical functions:

1 It provides a way of thinking about the paradoxical continuity *and* discontinuity between *psyche* and *bios* in relation to the dynamics of repression and the way in which the repressed surfaces "in" but not "of" the successive enunciations of representationality.
2 It also serves to depict how the performance of the incest taboo contributes to the formation of what Freud will call the "repression-barrier" (*Verdrängungs-schranke*) and this, as will be discussed in the next chapter, constitutes the essence of the oedipal complexities that confront every human.
3 The notion of psychic energy is a mythematic or allegorical notion that empowers Freud to describe the most radical aspect of the psychodynamics that he discovers. It is used to describe *both* how represented meanings can be repressed into the energies of our experiential embodiment (and become unrepresented) *and* how embodied energies meaningfully yet disruptively impact the cogency, coherence, and continuity of the reflections of our self-consciousness (and the system of representational law and order within which this reflectivity is constituted or established).

In sum, psychoanalysis needs the mythematic or allegorical notion-for-praxis of psychic energy both to understand the eventualities of the free-associative method and as a way for participants in the psychoanalytic experience to understand the significance of their commitment to this method.

9

THE LESSONS OF THE METHOD

Triebe and psychic reality

> . . . so muß man wohl sagen,
> daß die psychische Realität eine besondere Existenzform ist,
> welche mit der materiellen Realität nicht verwechselt werden soll.
> . . . it must be concluded that psychic reality is a particular form of existence, which is not to be confused with material reality.
>
> Sigmund Freud, 1900

Drive-desire may be comparatively unobtrusive, or even be eradicated in "computer talk" or texts that are disembodied, but there are sound reasons to know that its force operates within every human discourse, even if it is relatively successfully camouflaged in ordinary conversation or narration. Its significance is dramatically illuminated when free-associative praxis invites its manifestation and opens us to its vibrationality within us. This ongoing method thus amplifies the ground and horizons of awareness of our own being-in-the-world, without allowing us to recenter ourselves in the security of an arrival at fixed, firm, and veracious insights. In this chapter, three notions-for-praxis that are inextricably tied to experience with the free-associative method will be further examined. These are the notion of the repressiveness of self-consciousness, of the pluritemporality of psychic life (which will focus on the crucial notion of *Nachträglichkeit*), and of the significance of our polysexuality (or embodied erotic experience). As will also be discussed, these three converge interestingly on the notion of the oedipal complexities of psychic life. However, before proceeding, the mistaken notion that psychic energies or drive-desire (*Triebe*) are purely biological phenomena must be refuted.

On the crucial *Triebe*/*Instinkte* distinction

Earlier in this book, two mistaken theoretical tendencies that have been very prevalent since Freud were mentioned.

The first is the argument that the notion of drive energies can be clinically renounced as well as theoretically abandoned—the argument being that clinical practice does not require such ideas about energetics, nor does it require psychoanalytic theorizing to speculate about the biological substrate of psychic functions. This standpoint characterizes many of the theories that focus on the idea of the "self." For example, these include the lineage of Sullivan and the so-called Culturalist or "Familialist" School (Erich Fromm, Karen Horney, and many others), as well as a variety of self-psychologists, interpersonalists, relational psychologists, and so forth. Doing without the notion of psychic energy, this group of theorists typically also renounce the free-associative method or understand it merely as one method among several. Arguably, this group of theorists—despite their important contributions—also fails to grasp the full significance of the notion of the repressed unconscious.

A second theoretical tendency has been to retain the concept of drives, either in name only (as an oblique reference to the fact that psychic life must have a biological substrate) or as a shorthand for motives that can be represented (thus the sexuality of the drives is devalorized and "libido" comes to refer merely to a set of observable behaviors that might be considered as "sex acts"). This tendency is exemplified by the lineage of ego psychology (or structural-functional theory) that was initiated by Freud's daughter, along with Hartmann; it continues to the present with the students of Jacob Arlow, Charles Brenner, and their colleagues (for example, Dale Boesky, Fred Busch, Paul Gray, and others). This lineage typically asserts the goal of psychoanalysis as—more or less—the taming of drives by modifications in the organization of the ego and, although there are variations on this point, free-association becomes merely one method of "data gathering" in the application of objectivistic theoretical models. Despite the important contributions of this lineage to the description of ego mechanisms, there are major difficulties with its claim to theorize the originality of Freud's methodical discoveries—as has been discussed in my *Psychic Reality and Psychoanalytic Knowing*, as well as by several others.

The implications of radical psychoanalysis, as discussed thus far in this book, are conspicuously critical of both of the above tendencies.[94] Each of them involves a Ptolemaist retreat from Freud's radicality, by recentering psychic life on the subject as self, as the dialectic of "me-and-you," or as the ego organization. All of them misunderstand the significance of psychic energy as a notion-for-praxis, and thus none of them appreciates the free-associative method as the *sine qua non* of Freud's discoveries.

There is a third mode of revisionism that must now be addressed. It is a theoretical tendency that recenters the human condition on the drives by casting them simply as the biological source of all psychic life. This theoretical model establishes a form of biological idealism. It is conspicuously characteristic of much of the Kleinian lineage. Klein not only accepts the purely biological genesis of drives but, as is well known, characterizes them in terms of innate aggressivity and primal envy. Of course, in order for this standpoint to make sense, Klein has then also to posit the existence of an "archaic ego" that is also innate and operative from birth or even *in utero*. The difficult issue of the relationship between these rudimentary psychic structures and what we know to be their biological substrate (in neural circuitry, in innate reflexes, in hormonal and other neurophysiological phenomena) is simply sidestepped in almost all Kleinian commentary.

The way out of such a conundrum is through the distinction between *Triebe* and *Instinkte* (for reasons indicated below, I will continue to use the German terms, the singular for which is *Trieb* and *Instinkt*). This is a crucial distinction largely left implicit in Freud's writings and brilliantly explicated by Laplanche (in the course of his translation of Freud from German into French). Unfortunately, the distinction was disastrously overlooked for many years, in part because Strachey's English translation of Freud's writing used the terms "drive" and "instinct" more or less interchangeably.

Instinkte are genetically encoded, endogenous expressions of our biological constitution as it impacts behavior. Here one might review the entire literature of behavioral genetics.[95] However, I will selectively discuss a phenomenon that serves well the purpose of illustrating the psychoanalytically crucial distinction under discussion, the sucking reflex (later I will also discuss the physiological shifts that occur in puberty). The sucking reflex operates like the modal action patterns (or fixed action patterns) researched by ethologists and involves a specific neural network (with an innate releasing mechanism) that is activated by a particular stimulus from outside the organism known as a releaser (a sort of external–internal triggering).[96] The particular behavioral response of the sucking reflex is activated in the newborn by the stimulation of a nipple between the lips. It is clear that, although there are a very large number of *Instinkte* that impact the potentials of human behavior, Freud is quite uninterested in them and this would seem to be because, as we will see, their activation only bears indirectly on the lived experience of the individual. This issue needs to be carefully considered.

For example, it should be noted that Freud uses the term *Instinkte* rarely. It appears only five times in the *Gesammelte Werke* before the 1915 essay on the unconscious. In this essay, he wonders whether, *in addition to* drives (*Triebe*), there might be "inherited psychic formations, analogous to animal instincts" which somehow "provide a core for the psychical unconscious" (*Wenn es beim Menschen ererbte psychische Bildungen, etwas dem Instinkt der Tiere Analoges gibt, so macht dies den Kern des Unbewussten aus*). By contrast, the idea of *Triebe* appears early and often throughout Freud's thinking. In the singular and plural, the term appears over seventy times in the *Gesammelte Werke* prior to 1915. The frequency of this early usage is because, as the epitome of psychic energy, Freud needs the idea of the forces of drive-desire as a notion-for-praxis.

Laplanche (in association with Jean-Bertrand Pontalis) demonstrates how, in order to understand the way in which a *Trieb* is not an *Instinkt*, Freud's notion of *anlehnung* must be understood. This is a special form of attachment, better translated as *leaning-on*, "propped-upon" or even "following from" (and badly translated as "anaclisis" in the *Standard Edition*). The forces of *Trieb* are epigenetically acquired following the activation of an *Instinkt*. "Epigenesis" is here intended to convey *both* its biological meaning, as the development of an organism in a way that is not preformatist—that is, not strictly determined by the genetic code—*and* its philosophical significance as referring to the "jump" by which the "processes of the soul" emerge from material reality—that is, a qualitatively different domain of being arises, following from, or *leaning-on*, the realm of events that preceded it.

In terms of psychoanalytic thinking, the most felicitous example concerns the difference between the sucking reflex, which is an *Instinkt*, and the emergence of *Trieb* that is oral libidinal. Sucking may be a genetically encoded behavioral repertoire that is biologically automatic. However, the pleasure–unpleasure (*Lust–Unlust*) in the movements of drive-desire forces that develop following from, or *leaning-on*, the activity of sucking is neither automatic nor purely biological. Rather, it is the initiation of psychic life as a semiotic system. Thus, in his efforts to theorize the nature of psychic energy, Freud comes to call the sucking reflex an aspect of the self-preservative (*selbsterhaltungs*) *Instinkte*. The reflex has an "object"—the nipple, in the sense that physical contact with such a stimulating object triggers the reflex. However, this is not initially a psychic representation. It also has a "source" that is organic (*Organquelle*) or somatic (*somatische Quelle*), in the sense that the reflex is genetically encoded. *Trieb*, the eroticism of oral libidinality that leans on the activity of the sucking *Instinkt*, borrows, so to speak, its object and source from this *Instinkt*, and the dynamics of *Lust–Unlust* come to regulate the aim of this drive-desire. Note here the nonequivalence of the biological mechanism and the drive-desire that develops out of it (infused with enigmatic messages imposed on the organism from outside).

The putatively earliest *proto*-representations, into which drive-desire would be invested or bound, would be an undifferentiated "nipple-me-suck-pleasure" or "nipple-me-suck-unpleasure," in which the "me" does not yet imply a "self" but rather some sort of enactive image of the lips and oral cavity (this concords somewhat with the Piagetian account, as Peter Wolff discussed in his 1966 monograph). These are no longer equivalent to the activity of the reflext as such (the *Instinkt*). The capacity for representationality necessarily arises from the—always incomplete—emergence and binding of *Triebe* in these earliest imagistic or enactive representations. It must be emphasized again that "oral libido" (to give just one basic example) leans on the biological mechanism of the reflex but is not equivalent to this *Instinkt*, because, as I will discuss further, it is infused with the enigmatic messages imposed on it (implanted into the organism, so to speak) from the outside world, which means, first and foremost, the primary caretakers.

Here it may be noted that, contrary to Freud's conservative adherence to theorizing an enclosed economy of energy governed solely by the entropic principle of tension-reduction, pleasure (*Lust*) can be implicated in the arousal of *Trieb* as much as in its dissipation (this will be further discussed in what follows). What must be understood at this juncture is that, although the forces of *Trieb* are psychic energy, they do not actually operate in the manner of any known physical energy system. Rather, the energies of drive-desire are significatory, yet not representational. Although *leaning on* the mechanism of *Instinkte*, they are instigated by all sorts of messages that are imposed upon, or implanted into (as well as emerging from within) the suckling infant, in a way that is chaotic and incomprehensible to the infantile organism.[97] These are enigmatic messages, initially coming from the Caregiver (in terms of the emergence of oral libido, particularly those activated by the erotics of the breast)—that is, messages originating not only in the consciousness, but also and most crucially in the repressed unconscious of the adult world that surrounds the infant. This is akin to Louis Althusser's notion of interpellation, which is "a form of address that has conditioning effects on the child's nervous system."[98] In this sense, the psychic energy of the infant is "hailed into being" as the infant becomes a being-in-the-world.

Here we can understand how, in the emergence and differentiation of *Trieb* from *Instinkt*, psychic life is born in the processes of what Freud will, by 1915, posit in a metapsychological model as *primal repression*.[99] It is thus by primal repression that the earliest unconscious is formed around the enigmatic messages that are implanted in, or imposed upon, the infant by the caretaking world (for example, of crucial significance here are the incestuous-erotic feelings and fantasies of the breastfeeding Mother and other Caregivers). This is Laplanche's theorizing of the "fundamental anthropological situation" in which the psychic life of the infant arises in the context of a certain sort of *seduction* by the adult world. The implication of these being *enigmatic* messages is that they are not-yet-representational. Instead, they are what Freud would occasionally call imagistic "thing-presentations," as contrasted with word-representations (or other representations that are structured with the law and order we find in languages).[100]

We can now comprehend more fully the significance of psychic energy (*Trieb*, drive-desire, libidinality) in the formation of the human condition. Through the experience of free-association, we come to know that psychic energy is a force acting disruptively upon and within the inner theatre of representations (desire that is "in" but not "of" the law and order of representationality), but it is not equivalent to a material force. *Triebe* may lean on or follow from biological functions and mechanisms (such as neural circuitry or hormonal effusions), but they are not purely biological. Yet there is no reason to believe that they ever conform to the law and order we associate with the domain of brain events, nor with that of the representationality of psychic life. Rather, *Triebe* are an anarchic and momentous dimension of impulses and messages, a realm of energies that are dependent on, yet not intertranslatable with, the material operations of neurobiology.[101]

Thus, *Triebe* trace the elective condition of the connection between the corporeal and the psychical.[102]

To reiterate this critical issue. Whereas *Triebe* surface pervasively and contradictoriously within the representationality of psychic life, *Instinkte* do not directly affect psychic life, only impacting it via the promptings of *Trieb*—that is, biological operations only influence our inner theatre of representations via the movements of drive-desire forces or psychic energy. Brain functions and other anatomical or physiological mechanisms are not directly relevant to our lived experience, except insofar as the forces of *Triebe* lean on them or are propped upon them. Moreover, the processes of this *leaning on* are made chaotic by the infusion of otherwise messages from the outside. Thus, to say, as many textbooks do, that "drives are the psychical representatives of somatic excitation or arousal" is both correct and potentially misleading in two ways. First, because the forces of drive-desire are not representational in and of themselves (rather they signify disruptively within the representational world in a manner that is enigmatically *protorepresentational*), and second because they are only "representative" of organic or somatic functions and mechanisms in a manner that is radically modified by the messages coming from outside the organism.

In short (and this is a crucial point, as will later be elaborated), there is every reason, on the basis of psychoanalytic praxis, to assert that the operations of biology and of psychic representationality are not intertranslatable, precisely because *Triebe* (psychic energy, drive-desire, or libidinality) mediate these domains (in a manner that is, in a certain sense, elective). Of course, it is the case that the energies of drive-desire fuel every transformation of representations, but they do so excessively, disruptively—enigmatically and exuberantly—contradictoriously. And, of course, it is the case that organic or somatic activities "present the mind with demands," but only mediated by the momentum of the drive-desire—a momentum not exclusively regulated by biological functions and mechanisms. Thus, the relation between these domains is not one of translatability but, in Freud's terms, of the "failures of translation" involved in repression and in the formation of the psyche in which *Triebe* merely lean on *Instinkte* (neural circuits, reflexes, hormonal secretions, and so on) and are infused with messages imposed from outside the organism in its earliest years (and ongoing).

On the basis of the *Triebe/Instinkte* distinction, there are three further, inextricably connected sets of conclusions about drive-desire that may be found implicitly and explicitly stated in Freud's writings between 1896 and 1914. They follow from—indeed, are warranted by—the scientificity of free-associative method, and they converge on a specific interpretation of the role of oedipal complexities in psychic life. As has been previously indicated, they concern the character of repression in relation to the law and order of representationality, the multiple temporalities of psychic life, and the significance of our erotic embodiment (the reason that Freud expanded our definition of sexuality and characterizes psychic energy as libidinality).

Repression, '*Nachträglichkeit*' and our erotic embodiment

If the drive-desire forces of psychic energy (*Triebe*) are generated as a commotion of impulses and messages or "enigmatic signifiers" (which is Laplanche's preferred label), which come originally from outside us and which follow from, lean on, or are propped upon the endogenous operations of *Instinkte*, then the formation of the earliest representational world, as well as the unconscious that is split off from it, would seem to be adequately explained (without invoking an inherited "archaic ego" or implausible theoretical devices of that ilk).

The biological functions and operations of *Instinkte* do indeed, as Freud suggested, "provide a core for the psychical unconscious," but the unconscious itself involves *Trieb* rather than *Instinkte*, and *Triebe* are not purely biological. Out of the energy of the drive-desire, representations are formed, by means of encounters with the externality of the other in processes that have been much discussed in the literature.[103] The representational world binds psychic energy, but the latter always exceeds this binding, and this is demonstrated by the chaining of free-associative moments. As already mentioned, the earliest representations are probably formed as something like "nipple-me-suck-pleasure" or "nipple-me-suck-unpleasure" (initially not differentiating between the external nipple and the internal "me" of the lips or oral cavity). We have reason to believe that there is always an aspect that belongs to the outside other, an aspect that is "me" (at least in some inchoate sense) and an aspect of action and affect. This actually accords with many of the conclusions drawn by cognitive developmental psychologists, such as Jean Piaget (despite the fact that he foregoes the notion of *Trieb*).[104]

Thus, the inner theatre of representations is initially constructed using psychic energy by a process that Freud will call *primal repression* (*Urverdrängung*). However, this is a speculative notion (he writes, "we have reason to believe that there must be a "first phase of repression"). It is not something that he could claim to have been discovered through experience with free-associative discourse, yet such experience makes it the most plausible inference about the earliest formation of the human condition. We must note that Freud only developed the idea of primal repression in his 1915 metapsychological paper on "Repression" (*Verdrängung*)—that is, long after his discovery of the free-associative method.

Freud understood the repressiveness of consciousness as early as the 1890s and it is the epitome of a notion-for-praxis, intimately required to understand the lived experience of free-association. Freud understands this notion-for-praxis, which is one of the essential coordinates of his discipline, in terms of untranslatability. On 6 December 1896, he wrote to Fliess about "a failure of translation—that is what is known clinically as repression."[105] Later, as he moves away from praxis toward the more conjectural enterprise of constructing an objectivistic model of the "mental apparatus," he will distinguish this early notion from primal repression (the idea he developed only in 1915) by calling it "actual" or "real repression", *eigentliche Verdrängung*, which could also be rendered as "literal repression"). Strachey's English edition of Freud's writing refers to this as "repression proper" and contemporary textbooks often label it "secondary repression." It necessarily occurs later than primal repression in the individual's development. However, unlike primal repression, *eigentliche Verdrängung* is a notion necessitated by the discovery of free-associative praxis.[106]

In 1914, Freud wrote that "the doctrine of repression is the fundamental coordinate that guides the entire venture of psychoanalysis."[107] He indicates how this "quite certainly" came to him "independently" as a result of his experiences with free-association and not from "any other source" (such as the reading of Schopenhauer and Nietzsche). He also indicates that it is the theorizing "of a phenomenon which may be observed as often as one pleases if one undertakes" this method (he actually writes "an analysis of a neurotic without resorting to hypnosis"). Concerning this notion-for-praxis, *eigentliche Verdrängung* (a term derived from the early 19th-century writings of Johann Herbart), Freud definitely discovers a process radically different from any phenomenon of attentional focusing or of what he calls "gradations in the clarity of consciousness" (*Deutlichkeitsskala der Bewusstheit*). The latter are the result of the processes of suppression (*Unterdrückung*), condemnation (*Verurteilung*) and attentionality (*Aufmerksamkeit*), which account for meanings that are representable yet preconscious or deeply preconscious. Early in his writings about free-associative praxis, Freud adamantly distinquishes these from the repressed. He writes that the *eigentliche Verdrängung* actively impacts psychic life as if from beyond a topographic barrier (*Schranke*). For example, in discussing the case of Dora in 1905, he writes about the "barrier raised by repression" (*Die Schranke, welche die Verdrängung aufgerichtet hat*). It should be noted here that *eine Schranke* indicates a far stronger demarcation than would the idea of a border or some other type of boundary (which would be *eine Grenze*) which entities might cross without transmutation of the nature of their being.[108] Evidently, what is on the "nether side" of this barrier must be understood as radically different, in the status of its existence, from the representationality that preoccupies the familiar side of self-consciousness.

Although he does not make these links too explicitly, it is early in his experiences with psychoanalytic praxis (as early as the mid-1890s) that Freud grasps that the "repression-barrier" originates with the incest taboo, which is the essence of the complexities of oedipal conflict. The repression-barrier can thus be considered the internal demarcation of the individual's "encounter" with the primordial "no" of the incest taboo.[109] Thus, the significance of the incest taboo for the structuration of psychic life cannot be overestimated. This surely makes intuitive sense. The infant grows in a context of frequent intensely intimate contacts with the ministrations of his caregivers (the eroticism of these connections includes breast- or bottle-feeding, general skin sensuality as ably discussed by Anzieu and others, responsiveness to the configuration of the face and to familiar voices or sounds, and innumerable similar experiences). Speculatively, it is in this context, and in relation to such erotic experiences, that the infant undergoes the initial development of psychic life through processes of primal repression. But within the first five years or thereabouts, the child has to learn—although strictly speaking, the incest taboo is not simply a matter of learning—the limits of permissible erotic contact with his or her caregivers—that is, the child "encounters" the incest taboo and installs it internally.

Here we can understand a crucially important event (or set of events), the significance of which is not a matter of speculation, but rather more grounded in the evidence of free-associative experience. As the child "encounters" the incest taboo, along with the acquisition of language, the processes of *eigentliche Verdrängung* are initiated. However, this initiation cannot be a simple matter. Rather, it involves *Nachträglichkeit.* Freud developed this notion at the end of the 1890s, but it was relatively overlooked until its importance was discussed by Lacan.[110] The Strachey edition renders this notion as "deferred action," whereas Laplanche prefers "afterwardsness"—I shall retain the term in Freud's German. Briefly, *Nachträglichkeit* is the process whereby the subject revises past events and may even retroactively invest these events with a meaningfulness, efficacy, or pathogenic significance that they did not have at the time. This vitally significant notion is thus central to our understanding that the "time of the mind" is not a linear progression, or simple stratification of development, but is in the fullest sense pluritemporal.[111]

In the context of the initiation of *eigentliche Verdrängung* and the installation of the repression-barrier, the significance of *Nachträglichkeit* is schematically as follows (this may be schematic, but definitely not a fiction). It is *as if* the child looks back (so to speak) at his or her earliest erotic experiences with caregivers, of which his or her memory traces are prelinguistic, consisting largely of inchoate messages, protorepresentational signs, or enigmatic signifiers; he or she then "decides" (again, so to speak) that the eroticism of these experiences violates the incest taboo and that they must therefore be disqualified from accommodation in the domain of representationality; consequently, the repression-barrier is formed. Thus, the contours of this barrier reflect and refract the prohibition against incest in the structuration of each individual's psychic reality. Incest is, in a specific sense, unthinkable (or perhaps, more accurately, one can think it, but to entertain the enactment of such thoughts is to risk psychic annihilation.[112] Consequently, the repression-barrier comes to be the most significant limit to the individual's representational domain. Once it is established through the complexities of oedipal conflict, the individual's inner theatre of representations will develop in response to encounters with the external world, but circumscribed by the repressiveness of self-consciousness as demarcated by this barrier and the dynamics around it.

The question now arises, what lies "beyond" the repression-barrier—that is, what is the "nature" of the repressed? I have already suggested that the repressed is a domain of psychic energy, of the impulses, messages, and enigmatic signifiers of *Trieb.* However, this requires some further elaboration, since it has now been suggested that the repression-barrier forms as prelinguistic, inchoate meaningfulness becomes disallowed through the processes of *Nachträglichkeit.* Here I am going to suggest a thesis which most post-Freudians will dispute, and which embarks from the conclusion stated earlier: *That which is, or can be, representable, is not repressed, because the repressed is not an "other text" but a disruptively and contradictoriously meaningful domain of psychic reality that is otherwise than the law and order of representationality.*

This has several implications:

1. As already indicated, it implies that the "root propositions," which are inferred by a diligent procedure of textual analysis, are not equivalent to the repressed unconscious.
2. Concomitantly, however vigorously it may be suppressed (*unterdrückt*), much if not all that clinicians refer to as unconscious, including what is uncovered under the rubric of the Kleinian concept of "unconscious phantasy," is actually "deeply preconscious."
3. When something is repressed from the domain of representationality, within which self-consciousness is established, it becomes denatured, decomposed, or deconstituted as a representation; it becomes a seemingly senseless impulse of psychic energy, an enigmatic signifier or protorepresentation that is embodied as what Freud called a "thing-presentation" (*Sachvorstellung* or *Dingvorstellung*).

Freud wrote about "object-presentations" (*Objektvorstellungen*) in his early neuroscientific work on aphasia, but modified the notion, on the basis of his experiences with free-association, to "thing-presentation" in 1900, discussing it more extensively in his 1905 book on jokes and developing it metapsychologically in his 1915 essay on the unconscious. Freud's theorizing suggests that in the domain of consciousness, thing-presentations are combined with word-representations ("combined" but with a perpetual dynamic of contradictoriness), whereas "in the unconscious," there are only thing-presentations, which consist of impulses of psychic energy, not pertaining directly to images of things, but to remoter traces derived from them (*die Sachvorstellung, die in der Besetzung, wenn nicht der direkten Sacherinnerungsbilder, doch entfernterer und von ihnen abgeleiteter Erinnerungsspuren besteht*). I suggest that Freud's idea requires some modification in the light of theories of semiotics and symbolism that were unavailable to him. We can now assert that the domain of representationality, which includes everything preconscious or deeply preconscious and in which self-consciousness is constituted, is structured in the fashion of a language, whereas what is repressed consists of the impulsive and enigmatic meaningfulness of psychic energy movements, which Freud calls "thing-presentations," which are protorepresentational.[113] The proximity of thing-presentations to the unrepresentable beginnings of our emotional life seems evident, for, as Green writes, "affect is a movement waiting for a form." In the light of all that Freud discovered through his free-associative method, all this seems warranted.

If the existence of the repressed unconscious is of thing-presentations and these are impulses of psychic energy (castings, occupations, or investments, *Besetzungen*, which the Strachey edition renders as "cathexes"), then we arrive at an understanding of the repressiveness of self-consciousness quite different from that which is commonly taught under the rubric of psychoanalysis. We know that this realm of psychic energy persists and insists itself into the domain of representationality (the repressed is only found "in" but not "of" the systemic law and order of representationality). It insists itself excessively, which means that the transformations of representation never fully capture the meaningfulness of this energy, as is abundantly demonstrated by experience with free-associative discourse. We also know that this realm of psychic energy is, in the words of Freud's 1901 text, "timeless" (*das Unbewusste ist überhaupt zeitlos*), which means that it fails to conform to the unlinear model of temporality that characterizes cosmological (T1 . . . T2 . . . T3 . . .), narratological (beginning/middle/end), and phenomenological (past/*now*/future) time. Thus, Freud characterizes the repressed unconscious as having no sense of death as an ending (or as a condition of not-being), and as subverting the fundamentals of logical and rhetorical operations (defying the laws of identity and noncontradiction such that *A* can be different from *A* and can indeed be not-*A*).

The implication of this is not only that the repressed comprises an exuberant energy that is both invested in and overflows the representations and transformations of representation that occur in the domain of self-consciousness, preconsciousness, and deep preconsciousness. It is also implied that, when a representation is repressed, it loses its character as a representation. It becomes, as suggested earlier, denatured, decomposed, or de-constituted, transmuting into a "thing" that is unthinkable and henceforth unthought—a seemingly senseless impulse of psychic energy, a protospasm, an enigmatic signifier that now lives on as erotic embodied experience. This is the repressiveness of self-consciousness. The significance of repressed thing-presentations being erotically embodied but not representational is precisely what Freud will call *sexuality* or libidinality, using the term in a manner to be discussed in the next chapter. The way in which the free-associative method opens our being-in-the-world to an expression of the voicing of the repressed as unrepresentable yet animatively active in the concatenation of associations is perhaps well illustrated by the pulsing of *bar-bar-bar* or *b-b-b* in my first patient's speaking. This is an enigmatic and extraordinary "voicing" of embodied, erotic tremors coming from within. And surely these psychic energies hint, but only hint, at a meaningfulness of—so to speak—the heart, the skin, the throat, the abdomen, the pelvis, the genitals, the rectum-anus, and our entire sensual being—that is, a meaningfulness of the seemingly senseless, the unrepresentable.

In sum, we arrive at three conclusions about *eigentliche Verdrängung*, the repressiveness of self-consciousness that Freud discovered through the free-associative method:

1 That the repressed is not representational, rather it is like a denatured representation or protorepresentation, existing as an impulse of energy or *Trieb* that is enigmatically active and excessively meaningful in that it is, or has been, shaped or moulded by lived experience. Additionally, it persists and insists itself upon the inner theatre of representationality ("in" but not "of" this domain),

subverting the latter's law and order (disruptively and exuberantly existing as if "timeless," unconstrained by the rules of logic and rhetoric, as an endless libidinal lifeforce).

2 The dynamics of the repressiveness of the representational domain are formed around the individual's "encounter" with the incest taboo, by processes involving *Nachträglichkeit*. Thus, recognition of the Oedipus complex (which is to be understood as a set of narratives around this "encounter") becomes, in Freud's words, "the shibboleth that distinguishes the adherents of psychoanalysis from its opponents."

3 Perhaps the most interesting way to understand the significance of repression (*eigentliche Verdrängung*) in psychic life is that, unlike conscious, preconscious, and deeply preconscious material which is always structured as language or like a language, the repressed exists only as "thing-presentations" and the unrepresentable beginnings of our emotional life.[114]

These are sparks or traces of psychic energy (as indicated above, *Trieb* that is enigmatically active and meaningful in that it is, or has been, shaped or moulded by lived experience from outside the organism). But most importantly, while they depend upon neurological functions and mechanisms (but are ontologically different from the latter and not intertranslatable), these impulses are stored pervasively as embodied erotic experience, in all the tissues and organs of our being-in-the-world. And so we come to the tenet that *sexuality* or *libidinality*, understood as embodied erotic experience, is of paramount significance in every movement of psychic life.

A note on the threefold character of psychic reality

Writing, in the last section of the *Interpretation of Dreams* in the final weeks of 1899, that "it must be concluded that psychic reality is a particular form of existence, which is not to be confused with material reality," Freud was perhaps unable to grasp fully the complex and radical challenge posed by his discovery of free-associative discourse. That there might be "two forms of existence" is scarcely a novel idea in a culture which had for several hundred years contemplated the distinction between mind and body. The problem posed by Freud's discipline, however, is of a different order, for the free-associative method exhibits how psychic reality comprises two ingredients: Representations and psychic energy, libidinality or drive-desire.

To reiterate. The relationship between representationality and psychic energy is contradictorious: Representations and their transformations requiring the infusion of psychic energy which Freud called *Besetzung* (casting, occupying, investing, or "cathecting"), yet this energy always exceeding the limits of representationality, subverting the possibility that these formations could ever capture "all that is the case," despite their pretensions to do so. The idea that "drives" might ever be fully "tamed" by the formulation of rational constructions, correspondent, and coherent accounts of the inner or outer worlds, is misbegotten (psychoanalysis stands against the Hegelian dream that "absolute knowledge" might ever be attainable). Freud's method is therefore a process that is inherently interminable (*unendlich*). The psychic energy of thing-presentations may be invested in, or conjoin with, what Freud calls "word-representations," but in no sense are these two forms of existence ontologically equivalent, and in no sense are they intertranslatable.

Moreover, as discussed above, although it has been a common error to believe that the forces of "drives" are purely biological, this standpoint is nonetheless mistaken. Drive-desire follows from, leans on, or is propped upon, biological functions and mechanisms, but with such an infusion of enigmatic signifiers that there is no path of translatability from the material reality of neural circuitry to the swirling momentum of drive-desire energies (that are never to be understood as purely biological phenomena).

Thus, the significance of Freud's findings is that reality is not simply divided between mental representations and corporeal events, because psychic energy mediates these domains. The physical events of neural circuitry cannot be translated into the kinesis of drive-desire energies, which in turn cannot be translated into the transformations of representationality. Thus, although one may adhere to a philosophy of empirical reductionism, knowing that there is no representational or drive-desire activity without the participation of the neurological system, one cannot accept the standpoint of logical reductionism which would imply translatability between these domains.

It is beyond the scope of this book to explore the philosophical complications that psychoanalysis instigates, although such exploration is urgently needed, because, despite the plethora of literature on the philosophy of psychoanalysis, this challenge has yet to be met satisfactorily. It is perhaps sufficient to note, by way of conclusion to this chapter, that the extant approaches to the "mind/body" problem do not accommodate psychoanalytic discoveries. Three such approaches should be briefly mentioned:

1 Emergentism holds that "higher-level" organizations, such as consciousness, emerge from "simpler" or "lower-level" organizations, such as brain mechanisms, and that the novelty of the former is neither predictable nor reducible to the latter.[115] However, despite its logically anti-reductionist implications, emergentism scarcely allows for the complexity of relationship that pertains either between neural circuitry and psychic energy or drive-desire, or between the latter and the inner theatre of representationality.
2 Double-aspect monism (sometimes called dual-aspect monism) can take many forms, including the famous version discussed by Jung and Wolfgang Pauli. Originating with a particular reading of Baruch Spinoza, it is often the approach adopted in contemporary neuropsychoanalysis.[116] All versions of this standpoint argue that there are entities that are neither mental nor material, but can present themselves under either aspect. The aspects are ontologically inseparable, but conceptually irreducible. Thus, there is an objective and a subjective approach to understanding the "mind-brain" and they are assumed

to be complementary and consilient or convergent. While this standpoint may be enticing, it is not psychoanalytic in that it skips over the difference between *Trieb* and *Instinkt*, and typically assumes some sort of translatability between explanations concerning subjective "mind" states and those concerning objective "brain" states.

3 Neutral monism has various forms, but all argue that reality is ultimately all of one kind, and that it is intrinsically neither mental nor material. Spinoza, who is also interpreted as influential on this doctrine, held that this ultimate reality is singular, whereas most subsequent theorists have opted for pluralism. The doctrine is both anti-reductionist and noneliminativist (meaning that both mental and material are considered).[117] Mental events are held to depend on material events. Neither the psychic-representational nor the corporeal-neural are to be excluded. Both are grounded in an ultimate reality that differs from each of them. However, the question of translatability remains and, in a strange way, psychoanalysis makes this question more acute by suggesting that "neutrality" is not what pertains between these domains. For all we know, *Triebe* might be some mode of "ultimate reality," which is certainly what is suggested by the ancient doctrines of subtle energy systems (*prāna* and so forth). But Freud's discoveries imply that, whatever the double—or threefold—character of reality, "neutrality" and intertranslatability are mistaken assumptions.

This brief and perhaps unfairly sketchy survey does serve to indicate why philosophical resolutions to these issues do not appear to be on the horizon. In sum, Freud's findings concerning psychic reality would seem to raise philosophical problems, which are both vexing and onerous, and which would seem to be urgently in need of attention.

10

ON THE PARAMOUNT SIGNIFICANCE OF OUR PSYCHOSEXUALITIES

> Keine der Aufstellungen der Psychoanalyse hat so hartnäckigen Unglauben und so erbitterten Widerstand gefunden, wie diese von der überragenden ätiologischen Bedeutung des Sexuallebens.
> Nothing in psychoanalysis has met with such stubborn disbelief
> and such fierce resistance as our discovery of
> the paramount significance of sexual life.
>
> Freud, 1923

The idea of the unconscious has endured in the various versions of psychoanalysis and psychodynamic psychology that have been promulgated since the 1930s. Indeed, the term has become employed in so many ways as to become almost meaningless. In the course of this diversified usage—or perhaps one should say, one of the reasons for this diversified usage is that—the unique way in which Freud discovered the unconscious, as the repressiveness of the constitution of the representationality that produces self-consciousness, has been resisted and almost forgotten.[118] However, the resisting of Freud's discovery of the paramountcy of sexuality or psychosexuality in our lives has taken a course somewhat similar and somewhat different. There is a triple irony to the way in which this discovery has been treated.

1 As Freud predicted, of all the findings of free-associative praxis, his ideas about sexuality provoked more excitability and excoriation in the public sphere than any other. As discussed elsewhere, this bivalent reaction accords with the paradoxical processes of "sexification" that increasingly characterized North American culture through the 20th century (and thence influenced many other parts of the world, as much via Hollywood as by the expansionist politics of the United States).[119] Beneath both the excitability and the excoriation, which Freud subsumes under the term "fierce resistance," there is fearfulness. The

spread of Freud's discipline, which became a fashionable topic of conversation on the part of the mid-20th-century intelligentsia of Europe and the Americas, may have ridden on a cultural wave in which people were becoming more willing to discuss sexuality openly, but one should not conclude that the reality of people's anxieties and fear of their sexuality ever diminished more than a degree or two.

2 Most reactions to Freud's emphasis on the significance of sexuality or psychosexuality were based on considerable misunderstandings—both generally in the culture and specifically in the professional community—many of which actually underestimated the radicality of his discoveries. This will be elaborated in what follows.

3 The predominant misunderstanding, shared both by lay people and those who claimed expertise in psychoanalysis, is to confuse sexuality or psychosexuality with observable "sex acts," or erroneously to equate the motives for such acts, which are matters of representation available for textual analysis, with the pervasive *drivenness* of libidinality as the lifeforce that suffuses our experiential embodiment (rendering the entirety of our bodymind an expression of the erotic). That is, "sexuality" is still taken to be a concept that defines a category of behaviors, as contrasted with psychosexuality or libidinality, which underlies both those behaviors and all others. Psychosexuality or libidinality is thus a wider, and more interior, notion than sexuality (which gets equated with sex acts), and serves to refer to a force that intrudes upon and fuels every aspect of psychic life.

As I have already suggested (at the beginning of the previous chapter, where the avoidance of drive-desire as a notion-for-praxis was discussed), contemporary practitioners, who nominally subscribe to Freud's discipline, increasingly tend to demote the role of sexuality (and psychosexuality) in psychic life, seeing it as just one aspect of psychic life among many, even if it is often the least "adaptive" one. The significance of sexuality is thus eclipsed by the emphasis on ego functions, on attachment and object-relations, on the self and its interactions, and on whatever is observable about "sex acts." In all such directions of theoretical "progress," the *Trieb/Instinkt* distinction is ignored. As previously discussed, theory proceeds either in the direction of assuming that "drives" are purely biological (in different ways, both the lineage of ego psychology and that of Kleinianism do this), or in the direction of rescinding the notion altogether (for example, Sullivan insists on calling it the "lust dynamism," which notably lacks the flesh and blood of erotic embodiment, and later interpersonalists and relational psychologists will revoke the term entirely). As Green has ably argued, these sorts of "reformist" vision may eventually rob psychoanalysis of its creative potential.[120] Additionally, they serve to reestablish an ideological tenet that Freud was intent on disabusing—namely, the idea that the concept of sexual normalcy is justifiable.

In this chapter, I will begin by addressing the fallacious notion of "sexual normalcy," then argue for the polysexuality of the human condition, discuss the conditions of libidinality or "psychosexuality" (a discussion that follows more or less seamlessly from the previous chapter's elaboration of *Trieb* as a notion-for-praxis), and finally briefly review the three universal junctures in the personal history of libidinality (the events of primal repression, the "encounter" with the incest taboo, and the biphasic maturation of human sexuality resulting from the advent of puberty).[121]

Against sexual normalcy

It seems odd to many commentators that, at the end of his life, Freud should assert that only a couple of his writings would have lasting value: The 1900 *Interpretation of Dreams* and the 1905 *Three Essays on the Theory of Sexuality*. The former presents the discovery of the repressiveness of self-consciousness as indicated by dreams (or, more precisely, by the psychoanalytic interrogation of dreams as the *via regia* of his discipline). The latter warrants further consideration as the earliest and most explicit elaboration of Freud's notion of libidinality.

Reading the 1905 text can still be an exhilarating experience—assuming it is read with an understanding of its context and of what it intends to achieve. Divided into three sections, yet clearly integrated as a single endeavor, Freud starts with an extensive discussion of "perversions," which we would now more aptly call *paraphilias*, and which he calls "sexual aberrations" (*sexuellen Abirrungen*). The second essay then focuses on the characteristics and vicissitudes of infantile sexuality, while the final essay discusses the transformations of puberty that inaugurate the adult sexual repertoire. From a conventional standpoint without the benefit of experience with the psychoanalytic method, it might seem strange to begin a book (which is unquestionably a single thesis, despite the modesty of its title as "three essays") with an exposition of the "abnormal" or "aberrant." However, this strategy is not only adopted in order to render his dissertation a response to the 1886 publication of Krafft-Ebing's famous *Psychopathia Sexualis*. It is also Freud's way of challenging the assumption that sexuality is ever, or can ever be, normal; indeed, with psychoanalytic insight, the "aberrant" proves to be normative and "normal." This is because, as Joyce McDougall succinctly expressed it ninety years later, "human sexuality is inherently traumatic" and, we might add, *inherently perverse* or paraphilic. In short, from a Freudian standpoint, *we are all queer*, even if we do know it or admit it to ourselves.

In many respects, the history of psychoanalytic commentary since Freud's early writings can be characterized as a sustained effort to reassert the cultural ideal of sexual normativity—that is, to uphold penile–vaginal intercourse, as the sex act engaged by a high percentage of the adult population and lauded culturally as the epitome of "having sex," as if it were the standard of normalcy. This is, in a sense, the reassertion of an evolutionary, if not a teleological and theological, definition of sexuality (in which procreation defines what "sex" is really about). However, the thrust of Freud's 1905 publication is precisely to suggest that, at least for the human species, the concept of "normal sexuality" has no scientific status and that reproduction cannot be the defining feature of our scientific comprehension of human erotics. Rather, the notion of "normality" may serve to function primarily as a pivotal aspect of a perniciously oppressive ideology. Although it is supported by deep cultural prejudices, within the professional community it is also perpetuated by means of the refusal to acknowledge the crucial psychoanalytic distinction between sexuality as merely the category of behaviors that are popularly designated as "sex acts" (for example, fucking but not eating or shitting) and sexuality as the pervasiveness of psychosexuality throughout our psychic life.[122]

This is the significance of the textual positioning of the second 1905 essay. Having presented, in the first essay, a thorough-going exposition of clinical "perversions" that more or less squelches any conjecture that there is somewhere to be found a sexuality that is uncontaminated by perversity, Freud then discusses the ontogenesis of our adult repertoire in terms of the vicissitudes of these "infantile sexualities." The latter explains how all adult sexuality is infused with the erotic fantasies of childhood. Here one may question what status "normal sex" actually has—at least provisionally taking this term to refer to penile–vaginal fucking. For even if this particular "sex act" is statistically normative, through psychoanalysis it is discovered and demonstrated how the act is invariably animated by the "perversity" of infantile and childhood fantasies. In relation to Freud's theorizing, which is unquestionably tied to his experience with free-associative interrogation (because psychosexuality or libidinality is, after all, the quintessential notion-for-praxis), several issues may be noted.

Freud certainly does not underestimate the importance of puberty as effecting dramatic changes in the individual that will inaugurate his or her repertoire of adult sexual activities. This is why the last of his three essays is devoted to this topic. Freud clearly understands the significance of hormonal and anatomical changes—innately programmed activations of *Instinkt* occurring at the onset of puberty—is that they instigate a new outlet for the individual's *drive-desire* expressions, which have been already been shaped through infantile and childhood experiences. Puberty is forcefully significant but, contrary to popular prejudice, it is not the beginning of our sexual lives. Puberty activates new functions and mechanisms of *Instinkt* (such as anatomical and neurohormonal changes), which will necessarily modify, at least superficially, the expression of drive-desire that have already been dynamically (and conflictually) configured in the course of childhood. This is the remarkable consequence of the distinctively biphasic development of human sexuality—that is, the long period of drive-desire activity that emerges and is expressed, leaning on the *Instinkte* of infancy and the oedipal complex, prior to the biological maturation of adult sexual capacities. As Laplanche states it, humans are "subject to the greatest of paradoxes—*acquired* drive sexuality *precedes* innate instinctual sexuality." By this, Laplanche means not the *Instinkte* of infancy and early childhood, but the physical changes of puberty, "such that when it surges forth, adaptive instinctual sexuality finds its place 'occupied' [read *invested* or even 'cathected'] by the infantile drives, already and always present within the unconscious."[123] It is noteworthy that, as will be discussed shortly, when Laplanche refers here to the "unconscious," he is indicating the way in which the sexuality of drive-desire (which I prefer to call psychosexuality or libidinality) is foremost a matter of *fantasy* that can attach itself to a wide variety of physical functions and their corresponding childhood activities (cuddling, sucking, biting, stroking, burrowing, pissing, shitting, looking or being looked at, genital fondling, as well as smacking, poking, pinching, tickling, rough-housing, etc., etc.).[124] These fantasies persist after puberty and attach themselves even to those adult "sex acts" that are to be treated as paradigmatically "normal." In short, puberty brings to the fore new phenomena of *Instinkte*, which already shaped drive-desire forces will then lean on (I will return to the issues of puberty later).

This point can be elaborated. There are all sorts of physical activities, which we know empirically involve specific organic phenomena (and thus are matters of *Instinkt*), which erotic *drive-desire* fantasies come to lean on or be propped upon in the course of childhood experiences. These same fantasies obviously persist post-pubertally, and may or may not be behaviorally enacted to various degrees during adulthood. If enacted (for example, enjoyment in pissing on one's partner or being pissed on), the label of perversion is immediately invoked by those professionals who see their role as the standard-bearers of the prevailing cultural norms and prejudices. But the more salient point here is that such fantasies persist influentially, even if not explicitly enacted. With arousal, even the most "normal adult" (presumably, we might joke, one who confines his activities exclusively to penile–vaginal intercourse in the missionary position) engages unconsciously in these sorts of fantasizing.[125] To put it colloquially, at least in fantasy, one is never just in bed with one's ostensible partner (due to oedipal complexities that will later be elaborated), one is probably never just enjoying the pleasure of the penis and vagina in concert, and one never self-pleasures (masturbates) without the activation of fantasy (often a conscious fantasy, but always one that is descriptively unconscious).

Thus, in addition to the "evidence" for the *Trieb/Instinkt* distinction that is experienced through the method of free-association, here is a different type of evidence for the significance of the distinction in understanding human functioning. Of what advantage can it be, in evolutionary terms, that whenever humans engage in a "mature sex act" (that is, fucking) the act is infused with fantasies that serve the aims of drive-desire, but typically have no connection to the purposes of reproduction? "Perversion" does not seem to be characteristic of the copulation engaged by subhuman species. Indeed, it appears to be an inherently human characteristic. Polemically, we might add that one finds little or no evidence that animals, even those closest to our species, engage in perverse fantasies (oral, anal, bisexual, voyeuristic, exhibitionistic, and so forth) while they copulate. Yet fantasy is indeed a normative feature of our adult sex lives, unquestionably associated with the distinctively biphasic maturation of our sexuality. Surely this can be most plausibly explained by the fact that the contours of our psychosexuality, the embodied erotics of our *drive-desire* history, are always already established before the onset of the *Instinktive* biological changes (anatomical and hormonal) of puberty.

This is the basis of what sexologists call our "sexual patterning." The point is that it is repetitively and compulsively set in place before we ever embark on the "mature sexual activity" of fucking. The latter is the only activity necessary for our evolutionary destiny. It is also the only sexuality—the ideological paradigm of a "normal sex act"—that is, theologically, supposed to define how we consecrate our romantic capabilities and implement our capacity for marital attachments.

Against Freud's 1905 thesis, post-Freudians and anti-Freudians alike have been in a rush to reestablish the idea—that is, the culturally prevalent ideal—or sexual normalcy.[126] But this can only be achieved if the distinction between *Trieb* and *Instinkt* is ablated and sexuality comes to be understood as a purely instinctual matter.[127] "Drives" are now treated as simple expressions of biological functions and mechanisms. Intercourse becomes an entirely "natural act," preformatively determined by innate propensities. For those who find they cannot enjoy penile–vaginal intercourse, but perhaps enjoy oral or anal activities with a partner of the same gender (to focus for a moment on just the eminent example of homosexuality), an explanation as to how this too may be a variant of "natural" must be found (since it is no longer acceptable to designate homosexuals as abnormal). The explanation is supposedly to be found in the chromosomes or in the hormonal bathing that occurs *in utero*. In this way, clinical discourse succeeds in treating sexuality either as an entirely biological propensity (not worthy of interrogation) or as merely one motive among many.[128] To the extent that psychoanalytically oriented clinicians still recognize the significance of Freud's findings about psychosexuality, they often write of "sexual maturation" as a sequence in which infantile gratifications progressively drop out of the individual's repertoire of enjoyments (which actually means that the possibility of such gratifications becomes ever more deeply buried by suppression and repression). Thus, the clinical community comes to subscribe to what Gayle Rubin humorously characterized as the "teleology of the missionary position." Such is this community's conformity to the prevailing ideology.

It is evident that there are major ideological pressures in our culture to keep secure the nonscientific tenet that there is such a thing as sexual normalcy, and thus to reject Freud's discovery that there is not. The tenet is additionally supported by centuries-old religious orthodoxy in the Abrahamic tradition that upholds the purpose of sex as reproduction and condemns the immorality of its enjoyment in other modes or for other purposes. Again, his 1905 insight is that the most apparently "normal" variants of sexual expression are actually always infused—unconsciously—with what is disparaged as perversity. That is, "normal sex," whatever its claims to statistical normativity (a very high percentage of the adult population try penile–vaginal intercourse, even if they later turn to homosexuality, to abstinence, or to other variations), is as perverse in its inherent operation as what is condemned as "abnormality." In a culture that is increasingly both sexually obsessed and sexually phobic (in other words, a culture in which the "sexual revolution" has not diminished our underlying fears of sexuality), the precept that some modes of sexual expression are "proper, right, and true," whereas others are not, has to be strenuously defended.[129] The scientificity of Freud's free-associative exploration of our psychosexualities has to be ignored or preemptively repudiated. Yet in colloquial terms, the psychoanalytic method shows how "we are all queer," and thus goes beyond the idea of our innate bisexuality, which has been discussed from Fliess's correspondence with Freud (at which time it was a quite progressive notion) to the more contemporary writings of Christian David and many others.[130] In more scientific terminology, *we are actually all inherently polysexual* ("queer"), and it is regrettable that Freud did not use this term (instead writing of "constitutional bisexuality" and "polymorphous perversity"). Moreoever, the less suppressed and repressed is our functioning, the more we are aware and able to celebrate this polysexuality.[131]

Sexuality as psychosexuality or libidinality

In the course of Freud's discoveries, various notions-for-praxis converge: Psychic energy, *Trieb* or drive-desire, and psychosexuality or libido (the term *libidinality* is used as a generic for libidinal processes). As I have indicated, *Triebe* account for the conjuncture of, as well as the disjuncture between, *psyche* and *bios*. The capricious forces of psychosexual drive-desire mediate, often disruptively and never as a matter of a simple or direct translation, how the law and order of representationality, the warp and woof of our "ego organization," respond to corporeal requirements (these drive-desire forces also influence, again often disruptively, how the organism responds to the requirements of the external world). The dynamics of repressiveness and the repression barrier thus come between organization and organicity. Psychosexuality is the pervasive *drivenness* of libidinality as the desirous lifeforce that suffuses our experiential embodiment, rendering the entirety of our bodymind an expression of the erotic (I will return to this point in what follows). In psychoanalytic praxis, libidinality is the inevitable but variable or elective link between the psychical and the corporeal (as well as between the being-in-the-world of the patient and that of the psychoanalyst). Yet to refer to it as "elective" is not to suggest that it is chosen by an agent, but rather to emphasize how it is acquired through lived experience (initiated from outside the organism by an entity so radically "other" that it is experienced as "otherwise" and, in this sense, the link is always capricious). Green's reflections help us understand how there are three conditions by which Freud can assert the paramountcy of libidinality. Here I will elaborate Green's thesis with some modifications.

First, libidinality is always coupled or entangled with antagonistic or oppositional forces of self-preservation. These forces operate, so to speak, from two "sides" of the realm of the drive-desire. On one side, there are the self-preservative functions of the *Instinkte*. We can learn much about these from the investigations of evolutionary biology or ethology and from neuroscience (although great care has to be taken in how we learn from these fields).[132] *Instinkte*, from the sucking reflex and other inborn mechanisms to the hormonal and anatomical changes of puberty, are innately programmed and have clear evolutionary significance; they protect and perpetuate the species (here I think we can legitimately include the incest taboo as such an *Instinkt* for it certainly operates on our psychic life as if it were such (but this is an issue to be discussed further). Libidinality is *Trieb* not *Instinkt* and, as has now been much discussed, this energy follows from, leans on, or is propped upon the functions and mechanisms of our biology; in Green's terminology, it is "metabiological." However, the critical issue is that *Trieb* or libidinality is far from equivalent to the functions and mechanisms that it follows from or leans on. Libidinality indeed is in a complexly nonidentical relationship with the neurobiology on which it depends. Biology and libidinality are not intertranslatable; rather, they are, so to speak, different realms of discourse.[133]

On the other side of drive-desire, as it were, is the law and order of representationality. We can learn much about this domain from the disciplines of textual analysis (logic, rhetoric, pragmatics) and from cognitivist psychology (again, provided great care is taken as to how we learn from these fields). Representationality is acquired under the mandate of self-preservation; it permits the organism to grapple with the environment it inhabits. Yet, as I have almost exhaustively suggested, the entire adventure of psychoanalysis, as steered by its unique method of free-associative discourse, discovers and demonstrates how, although libidinality is to be found animatively "in" but not "of" the structures and transformations of representationality, it is not equivalent to them. Rather, libidinality always overflows its capture—its binding or "cathexes"—within the law and order of representationality, and indeed holds a contradictorious relation within this domain of ego organization. Representationality and libidinality are not intertranslatable; they are different realms of discourse.

Second, libidinality is thus essentially transgressive of the law and order of representationality—of our "ego organization"—within which it surfaces disruptively. The most plausible understanding of the origins of libidinality is that it is generated from what Laplanche calls the "fundamental anthropological situation," in which unconscious messages from the adult world of caregivers, experienced by the infant as coming from outside in an otherwise fashion (a fashion that he or she cannot possibly, in any way, comprehend), shape the processes of leaning on the infant's repertoire of *Instinkte*. Out of such origins, libidinality does not observe boundaries, rules, or etiquette. As mentioned when I compared libidinality with the doctrines of *prānā*, it is not even clear whether libidinality conforms to the endogenous/exogenous distinction. In short, what psychoanalysis discovers through the free-associative method is the animative dimension of lawlessness and anarchic disorderliness—the brio of life itself—that is ineluctably within us.

Third, libidinality is a constant in psychic life, even if only capriciously so (for it follows both the principles of lifefulness and deathfulness). Not only is its momentum inexorable, libidinality is relentless, passionate, unpredictably fluctuating, phantasmagoric, and, in a specific sense, treacherous (also to be considered here is the notion of *aphanisis*, as the fading of desire, the deathfulness inherent in every instantiation of "I"). As Green states it, without the Freudian notion of libido, psychoanalysis disappears, for this notion-for-praxis "is alone capable of accounting for variations, transformations, extensions, coverings-up, fixations, regressions, time-lags, enmeshing and unravellings" that are exposed in free-associative discourse.[134]

As is well known, to the extent that libidinality can be said to be principled, Freud suggested that its desirous movements are to be understood in terms of the lifefulness principle of *lust/unlust* (pleasure/unpleasure), although he also suggests that "the real essence of sexual arousal"—or psychosexual momentum—"is unknown to us." Of course, Freud tried to argue that psychic energy operates as if in a closed system, following a homeostatic or tension-reduction model. This argument was a mistake (not least because it cannot possibly be correct), and its precepts have to be relinquished. However, before we can discuss further what may be conjectured about the "principles" of libidinality, more must be said about three critical junctures that occur in every human's odyssey of *lust/unlust*.

A note on three universal catastrophes

I have discussed how libidinality is an incessantly swirling force that leans on biological functions and mechanisms, and is known to us through the method of free-association precisely because it animates, constantly and yet disruptively, the law and order of representational transformation. Here, by way of a partial recap, three catastrophes that occur in every human's psychosexual odyssey must be briefly noted.[135] These are major turning-points in the relation between *Trieb* and *Instinkt* that occur in each individual's formation.

(1) *The "fundamental anthropological situation."* As previously mentioned, this is Laplanche's term specifying his conjectures about the genesis of libidinality in infancy. The situation refers to the earliest Caregiver–Infant interactions. Libidinality is generated not only from processes that follow from, lean on, or are propped upon the infantile *Instinkt* (such as the sucking reflex and innumerable others), but also from the implantation or imposition upon the infant of incomprehensible messages, "enigmatic signifiers" or subtle impulses from the unconscious of the adult world. The prime example pertains to the mother's erotically incestuous feelings as she offers her breasts to the suckling infant. These feelings—which seem to be profoundly forbidden for us to talk about—are accompanied by unconscious fantasies that are inflictably communicated to the infant, in a manner that Laplanche polemically calls a "seduction." There is little or no conscious intent involved in this seduction, since the adult is almost entirely unconscious of the material he or she imposes on the infant.[136] However, in terms of the infant's lived experience, such messages are incomprehensible. They will henceforth comprise the thing-presentations, impulses and feelings, or affects that are the inchoate and unrepresentable of the core of the unconscious as formed by primal repression (*Urverdrängung*).

(2) *The "encounter" with the incest taboo*. As previously indicated, it is no accident that Freud started to write about the oedipus complex in the closing years of the 1890s, just as he became more committed to his experiments with the free-associative method. The complex or complexity of oedipal conflict brings together the three cardinal findings of the method he discovered: The repressiveness of self-consciousness, the pluritemporality, and the polysexuality of psychic life. To understand this is, in Freud's words, the "shibboleth" of his discipline.[137]

Freud tended to write about the complex in terms of familial constellations—and thus he became embroiled in discussions as to whether the complex might not operate in cultures where the prevailing family pattern was not that of the patriarchal European nuclear group that had been its ideal, if not always its tradition.[138] This has somewhat misled subsequent scholarly attention to the complex, for its essence is not in any particular pattern of child-raising, but rather in the child's inevitable "encounter" with the incest taboo.[139] It surely is entirely understandable that, for every child, whose infancy necessarily involves intimate physical contact with caregivers, whether blood relatives or not, this realization (that it is precisely with these individuals that the most intimate sensual connections are most forbidden) is, in one way or another, traumatic. This is the universal tragedy or trauma that Freud calls oedipal.

It is as if the "encounter" with the incest taboo prompts the child to review and revise the events of his or her infancy, by processes of *Nachträglichkeit* and then of amnesia. It is *as if* the child recognizes the erotic or psychosexual implications of birth, of suckling, and of countless other infantile experiences, and then (through the revisioning of afterwardsness or *Nachträglichkeit*) "decides" on the horror of their unacceptable implication, and represses whatever memory traces he or she has of these experiences. This, then, is the way in which the complexity of oedipal conflict initiates and instigates the processes of actual or real repression (*eigentliche Verdrängung*) that we know well from experience with free-association (and it is also why we seem to have so few memories prior to the sixth year of life).

As I have reviewed previously, there are very few plausible explanations of the power and ubiquity of the incest taboo. Lacan's effort to understand it as encoded in what might be considered the deep structures of language has some merit, particularly since there is both developmental and anthropological evidence linking the advent of symbolic systems with social fatherhood (via phallocentricity and triangulated cognition). However, the alternate explanation that the taboo is somehow encoded genetically perhaps has equal or greater plausibility. This would imply that the taboo is inherently "natural" (in the manner so many theorists have supposed), even if there are significant variations culturally in its interpretation and implementation. This "natural" explanation implies that the taboo is an innate biological mechanism—like a modal action pattern that is triggered at some point in our development. The plausibility of this, from a psychoanalytic standpoint, is evident, *especially because the incest taboo acts as an Instinkt that demands a reconfiguration of libidinal drive-desire*. This is Freud's finding, and it explains why "encounter" is not an accurate characterization of the processes that the child endures. The finding is compellingly supported by clinical evidence for the reality of the taboo for, although it can be overridden, to violate this taboo in the most acute manner (genital intercourse between mother and son, or between father and daughter) is to invite, if not physical disaster, the inescapable prospect of psychic annihilation ("castration," death, or deathfulness).

(3) *The changes of puberty.* As is well known, the pubertal releasing of hormones to the gonads, and the consequent growth of the brain, bones, muscle, blood, skin, hair, breasts, and sexual organs, comprises a dramatic shift in the biological attributes of the individual. To give a specific example, the increased production of estradiol and of androgens can be viewed as an *Instinkt* that elevates the individual's capacity for sexual arousal.

Here what is salient—and, as mentioned previously, well elaborated by Laplanche—is that, as the biological functions and mechanisms change to permit adult sexual and reproductive activities, the individual's libidinality has already been crafted by the prior history of lived experience. In short, as adult sex acts become feasible and the propensity for biological arousal increases, these biological changes are—as it were—met by already formed psychosexual patterns of drive-desire proclivities. This is a unique feature of our species, arising not only out of the distinction between *Trieb* and *Instinkt*, but also as a consequence of our biphasic maturation, which implies a protracted period of acculturation before the biological accoutrements of reproduction develop. Thus, when adult sexuality becomes potentiated, infantile psychosexuality is always already there to fuse with the changes of puberty, and indeed to direct unconsciously our reactions to this acquisition of an adult physicality.

Puberty is a catastrophe not so much because the transformations of our physical being are dramatic, but more because the triggering of new patterns of *Instinkte* demand a reconfiguration of the repertoire of *Triebe*. Infantile libidinality now comes to lean on physical phenomena that are capable of new forms of sexual activity. In short, the changes of puberty are transformations of *Instinkte* that compel a limited reconfiguration of the forces of libidinal drive-desire. This, then, is the third psychosexual catastrophe of being human.

Libidinality, the erotic body, life and death

If libidinality leans on the functions and mechanisms of our biology, yet is a swirling realm of energy impulses (incomprehensible messages, enigmatic signifiers, thing-presentations, traces, and unrepresentable feelings or proto-emotions and proto-representations), then what occurs, so to speak, "across the repression barrier" is, in Freud's words, a "failure of translation." In relation to the law and order of representationality, these energy impulses or incomprehensible messages are untranslatable, either because they were always untranslatable (*Urverdrängung*) or because they have been rendered so (*eigentliche Verdrängung*).[140] All efforts at retranslation are never more than partially successful—that is, the attempt to capture in representations the meaning of the untranslatable can never fully succeed, as the interminability of free-association intimates.

Since libidinality always leans on biological functions and mechanisms (but is not wholly determined by them), it seems legitimate to ask how or even where its traces reside. I think it is a serious mistake to assume that they can only be stored within the nervous system (in the same way that we usually assume that representational memories are somehow stored in the cortex). Although this is not an issue that can be extensively discussed in this book, the field of somatic psychology offers various unusual answers to this question—answers that involve the entirety of the bodymind, as contrasted with assumptions that all traces of the experiences of our personal history must reside "in the head."

As I discussed in *The Emergence of Somatic Psychology and Bodymind Therapy*, this lineage began to flourish in the latter part of the 20th century, influenced by psychoanalytic discoveries (including the early work of Wilhelm Reich and his successors) and somatic psychodynamics (as well as other traditions of bodywork, Asian spiritual teachings, and shamanic or transpersonal psychologies).[141] It currently embraces a wide range of doctrines and practices, many of which focus on the way that traces of trauma and other psychic conflicts are held in the soft tissues (as well as cells, organs, and so forth) of our experiential embodiment. That is, to express this minimalistically, it is as if (and perhaps "as if" is too weak a qualifier here) imagistic and emotionally charged traces are found, not only in the neural circuitry of the brain, but also coming from the connective tissues of the skin, ligaments, fascia, tendons, synovial membranes, and so forth, as well as the musculature, blood vessels and, of course, the peripheral nervous system. Most of the healing practices of these traditions of somatic psychology are empirically based—that is, what they find through extensive experience with healing practices is often far more advanced than the theorization of these practices.

The profound significance of the practices of somatic psychology and bodymind healing is that they discover meaningfulness outside what is conventionally understood as the "mind." They find that addressing—by touch or even by verbal intervention—the tissues of the body, as well as other aspects such as posture, the rhythms of breathing, and patterns of movement, often brings new, and sometimes surprising, thoughts, images and emotions into consciousness and that such methods release psychic conflict, with or without insight. The yoga tradition, with its emphasis on awareness of both the breath and the flow of energy or *prānā* within the body also contributes ancient wisdom with similar implications.[142] This has to be understood not only as a vindication of Freud's subversion of the Cartesian mind/body dichotomy, but also as having radical implications for the healing praxis of the free-associative method.

Psychic energy and "thing-presentations" are to be found not only in the representationality of what is conventionally understood as the "mind," but are also active outside it, in what is usually called the "body." That libidinality pervades our erotic embodiment, and is in this sense a reality and not just a mythematic conjecture, has far-reaching implications for the way in which we consider the method of free-association. Although some of the bodymind methods to which I am referring probably only address preconscious and deeply preconscious material (for example, Eugene Gendlin's practice of "focusing," which is derived from a phenomenological and Rogerian approach to therapy), other approaches within this lineage clearly have a derepressive impact. In short, psychoanalytic practitioners can learn from the empirical evidence generated by this tradition.[143]

Obviously, addressing the voicing of our erotic embodiment by any means of physical contact cannot be assimilated to psychoanalytic praxis, which depends so crucially on an understanding of the way in which the repression barrier reflects and refracts the incest taboo. In this regard, it must be said that many of the practitioners or somatic psychology are strikingly naive about the processes of transference and countertransference.[144] However, in my praxis of psychoanalytic treatment, I have found that free-association is, if not engaged as a "mental technique" (as in a mere exercise in uncensorious story-telling), powerfully facilitative of the patient's capacity to listen to the voicing of his or her erotic embodiment. As I have discussed elsewhere, sometimes a slight adaptation of the free-associative method is necessary to facilitate this healing process.[145] The adaptation involves both a slight focusing on particular physical sensations that attempt to "join the conversation" (a focusing that is, after all, no different from asking a patient "what comes to mind about that" when they mention a particular image, feeling, or thought), and sometimes a minimal use of imagery or visualization (imagining the breath moving in and out of the location of the intrusive sensation) that serves to distract the patient's reflective and representational capacities from generating a story about the sensation.

The crucial point here is that somatic psychology has developed ways of listening to our erotic embodiment that originate, at least in rudimentary form, in psychoanalytic praxis—for example, in Freud's listening to sensations that appear to wish to "join in the conversation." This way of listening to the voicing of embodied experience has mostly disappeared in contemporary versions of the discipline, which have become very focused on what is "in the head" and that thus overemphasize representational introspection or narratological reflection. It is a way of listening that urgently needs to be reinstated—namely, that, unlike the therapeutic techniques of introspection, reflection, and narration, the free-associative method opens us to the nonrepresentational voicing of embodied experience that cannot be translated into the languages of representationality. It allows them more explicitly to "join the conversation," even if their messaging is untranslated and, significantly, never-to-be-translated.

Here, then, is one of the most profound and radical implications of the free-associative method. It not only provides material that can be assimilated to the "I" by representational reflection, it opens the "I" to the untranslatable impulses of the libidinal forces that are "in" but not "of" the law and order of the "mind." Thus, psychoanalysis does not merely facilitate advances in the purview of reflective consciousness—that is, insights and all that go with them—it opens the "I" to a different mode of consciousness, which is an awareness of its own embodied erotic experiencing that is unrepresentable—the pre-subject/object or pre-naturalistic awareness of the voicing of our aliveness, the founding of our lived experience. This awareness opens new possibilities of freedom that will be discussed at the end of this book.

The free-associative discovery of ability to become aware of this source of our aliveness, the libidinality of our erotic embodiment, of course raises complex questions about our human condition. In a sense, whereas the functions and mechanisms of *Instinkte* serve to secure the organism's physical needs, the momentum of *Trieb* as libidinality assures and amplifies our capacity for pleasure and enjoyment (even for transcendence as some commentators suggest). In the course of his theorizing, Freud is clear that libidinality operates on the lifefulness principle of pleasure/unpleasure (*lust/unlust*), as well as on the deathfulness principle, and that it is animated by life experiences and never wholly determined by its physical sources. Somewhat related to this principle are his threefold assumptions about a closed energy economy, the principle of constancy as regulating the functioning of the "mental apparatus," and the idea that pleasure necessarily involves tension reduction. Although these issues cannot be explored in full herein, I have suggested that Freud's theory needs to be relieved of these assumptions.[146] Indeed, much of his grand metapsychological speculations, his construction of an objectivistic theory of the "mental apparatus," can and should be set aside in order to focus on the radicality of psychoanalysis as praxis.

However, it can be claimed that Freud's ideas about pleasure and enjoyment, although not comprehensively treated in his writings, emerge intricately from his experience with the free-associative method and our ability, through this method, to become aware of the aliveness of our erotic embodiment. As such, his ideas about pleasure and enjoyment are close to what I am calling a notion-for-praxis. In the context of this approach to psychoanalytic method, it does not seem feasible to try—as Freud did in his metapsychological speculations—to specify conjecturally rules and regulations that might be followed by an energy that is inherently transgressive.[147] However, three points may be noted:

1 Pleasure may come from an indiscernibly wide range of movements of libidinal energy, and may involve tension-reduction or tension-accumulation—for example, as we all know, sexual arousal may be as pleasurable as sexual release or gratification.
2 Pleasure may also come from experiences that are physically painful; this is a conundrum—the "economic problem of masochism"—with which Freud struggled throughout his metapsychological theory-building career.
3 The relationship between libidinality and the aggressivity that may be derived from it has been a subject of longstanding speculation; here I will only note what is, sadly, well known—namely, that there can be pleasure in hating, in hostility, and in hurting the other.[148]

This brings us finally to the questions about life and death that Freud notably raised in 1920. Without going into a detailed exegesis of what, if anything, lies "beyond the pleasure principle," I am inclined to agree with Laplanche that what Freud came to call *Lebenstrieb* and *Todestrieb* are not so much new drives, or even reformulation of the drives about which he had already written extensively. Rather, life and death must be subsumed under psychosexuality. This contrasting pair of "drives" are actually better understood as the divergent ways in which *Triebe* move or operate. Freud's text has allowed from considerable latitude in its interpretation, which seems to be because, as Gunnar Karlsson and others have commented, the essay invites two seemingly conflicting interpretations of the notion of *Todestrieb*: One as the binding of energy involved in the compulsion to repeat; the other (emphasized more conspicuously) as the dissipation of energy as a return to conditions of inertia. Here I believe that Laplanche's perspective integrates both directions of interpretation by understanding lifefulness and deathfulness as coexisting features of psychic energy. The lifefulness principle involves the *binding* of libidinality (according to pleasure/unpleasure), whereas the deathfulness principle involves the *unbinding* of this energy from the representations in which it had been invested.

I have already suggested that the realm of psychic energy has two domains, so to speak, on either side of it, both of which function in ways that serves the goals of self-preservation. This scheme can now be augmented as follows:

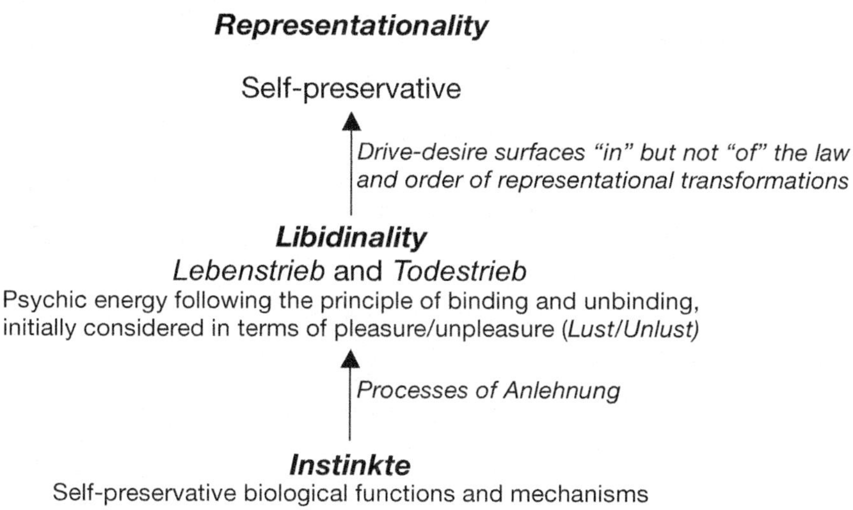

This implies that *Lebenstrieb* and *Todestrieb* are contrasting features of the *Trieb* of libidinality or psychic energy. Again, it must be noted here how Freud introduced these drives in his 1920 text. His ideas owe much to Sabina Spielrein's 1912 paper in which she discusses creation and destruction as partnered in every act of becoming. Freud's text is one of the most controversial of his writings—

one that has given rise not only to outright repudiation as "metaphysical speculation," but also to a range of dubious reinterpretations.

In terms of *Lebenstrieb*, similarities have been noted between Freud's libidinality and Schopenhauer's "will-to-live," as well as Bergson's 1907 notion of *élan vital*. These are both instructive and potentially misleading. *Lebenstrieb* is misunderstood if merely taken to be a vital force, the *lifeforce* or *prānā*, that mystically acts upon physical reality. It might be more usefully interpreted in the manner similar to that suggested by Deleuze's 1966 text, as a force indiscernibly connecting the material and psychic domains. *Lebenstrieb* can thus be understood as the directionality of libidinal movement that *binds* with representations (which Freud explicitly stated in his 1938 *Abriss*). It is the direction of psychosexual momentum that is assimilative and unifying—the force of an untranslatable meaningfulness that nevertheless persists and insists itself upon the domain of representations and their transformations, albeit in a way that always overflows the capacity of their meaningfulness—that is, a force moving toward a retranslation that will never fully succeed.

In terms of *Todestrieb*, there have been several interpretations that I view as more or less illegitimate. These would include Paul Federn's *mortido* and Edoardo Weiss' *destrudo*—both developed in the 1930s as the cathexis of representations of death and destructive activities respectively. It would also include the miscellaneous uses of the term *thanatos*, which first appears in some 1916 abstracts by Leonard Blumgart, but became common parlance again in the 1930s, as a reinterpretation of Freud's ideas and as a shorthand for self-destructive tendencies. Finally, the Kleinian reinterpretation of *Todestrieb* as indicative of innate aggressivity, destructiveness, and primal envy has to be mentioned, although in many respects—as interesting as the hypothesis of primal aggression may or may not be—to call Klein's ideas a reinterpretation is stretching the concept. Related to these revisions of the 1930s and 1940s—although only indirectly connected to *Todestrieb*—is Jones's most interesting idea that individuals fear the fading of their desire (*aphanisis*), which we might interpret as loss of libidinality or a sense of the lifeforce, and which Jones offered, in his 1927 and 1929 papers, as an alternative to Freud's emphasis on the castration complex.

Against these variations, *Todestrieb* has to be understood as the unbinding directionality of libidinal movement that overflows and unbinds itself from representation. It is the direction of psychosexual momentum that is dissolutive—the force of a meaningfulness that defies translation, dissipating its messaging as if in a movement of returning toward previous conditions of meaninglessness—that is, a force moving toward—to use a neologism that Laplanche deploys—a detranslation.

Here I think we must grasp the crucial point that, in psychic life, *libidinality sponsors the lived experiences of presence and absence*. Consider here the "I" that Western metaphysics, even before Descartes, takes as the secure point at which the subject—in what, if you will, is a brandishing of the lifeforce—asserts its identity and its knowledge of its own existence. Here is, surely, a binding of libidinal forces in the establishment of an "ego." By contrast, consider how this same "I," when interrogated free-associatively, finds itself dispossessed, perpetually deferred and dislocated, its security shattered. Here, we might say, is the overflow or unbinding of libidinal forces in the free-associative momentum in which—to borrow Kolakowski's imagery of metaphysical horror—the "ego" comes to feel as if it were entering, or finding in its most fundamental composition, a black hole.[149] This is the inherent deathfulness of the "I" that will be discussed further in the final chapter, for it is germane to our understanding of all that is accomplished by the psychoanalytic method.

Between birth and puberty, our psychosexualities, the shaping of our libidinal momentum and flow, are crafted in the deepest interiority of our humanity. Libidinality is not pre-programmed in the manner of our biological functions and mechanisms, not glued to particular aspects of our embodiment, and not at all connected to the difference between the sexes (except insofar as the sexes evoke different communications from the adult world). Our libidinality is indissociably connected to fantasy, precisely because of the way the unconscious is formed through primal and actual repression. Its directionality can be both deathful and life-giving or life-affirming. In this regard, I believe we would do well to rehabilitate the insights of Sabina Spielrein, which she discussed with Freud almost a decade before his 1920 publication of *Beyond the Pleasure Principle*. In her 1912 paper, Spielrein argues that libidinality has both attributes, the momentum toward death and toward life. Her argument is insightful, although far from theoretically elaborated. After dutiful acknowledgment of the ideas about death in papers by Stekel and Otto Gross, as well as an extended quotation from Jung's 1912 paper, Spielrein marshals much clinical, mythological, and literary evidence. Not only does she demonstrate that "without destruction, coming into being is impossible," but intimates how within our psychosexuality itself, life-affirming and deathful directions are always operative. This, then, is an essential aspect of the fundamental lessons about psychosexuality that may be drawn from our experiences with the free-associative method. As will be discussed, it has profound implications for the freeing process that are the radicality of the psychoanalytic method.

11

THE NECESSITY OF THE PSYCHOANALYST

> . . . das Schicksal der Psychoanalyse,
> sich in einen Gegensatz zur offiziellen Wissenschaft zu stellen . . .
> . . . the destiny of psychoanalysis—to stand in contrast to official science . . .
>
> Sigmund Freud, 1913

As the healing science of self-consciousness, psychoanalysis is—as Freud famously told Jung—a cure "effected by love." In the letter of 6 December 1906, containing these words, Freud was specifically referring to the "transference cure" characteristic of a certain class of patients, who seem to get better simply because they love and feel loved by their clinician. Perhaps it is impermissible to read too much into Freud's statement, yet there is a wider and deeper sense in which Freud might have meant these words.[150] That is, not as the chimera of change based on transferential feelings, but as the Love that is involved when our being-in-the-world opens to the process of its own truthfulness, in a radical way that is often turbulent and discomforting.[151]

This is not the type of "love" favored by the "I" of self-consciousness, nor by what Freud later called our "ego organization." As Freud made clear in his 1914 essay, "On Narcissism," our ego prefers not the cure of psychoanalytic Love, but the intoxicating reverie that occurs when we "fall in love," as well as all the illusionary–delusionary palliatives of gratifying attachments with family, friends, fans, and even professionals; love of that sort can, at least for a while, make us feel whole and harmoniously at one with ourselves as well as with the world around us. Yet, as psychoanalysis concretely demonstrates, the truth of the human condition is such that we are never fully integrated, never entirely unified within ourselves, and thus, ultimately, love by attachment is an illusion or delusion (by which I simply mean that, however gratifying, it cannot fulfill the promise that we consciously or unconsciously assume it to proffer). It fails us, if for no other reason than that we are irrevocably fractured within ourselves, despite our longings for harmony and wholeness. Our self-consciousness perpetually holds at bay rampant desires that are intolerable, unthinkable. This is not only because even the most apparently civilized individuals harbor fantasies of violence, domination, and exploitation. Rather, it is because—as was demonstrated by Freud and has been discussed herein as the Oedipality of the incest taboo—our most intensely sensual longings, our most flagrant and fiery erotic connections, are deeply forbidden to us.

The Love for which the psychoanalyst optimally stands—while obviously it must be admitted that we all repeatedly fall far short of this ideal—is that of facilitating the patient's opening to the truthfulness of his or her own being-in-the-world. Such a process of opening entails a freeing of the patient from his or her imprisonment in repetition-compulsivity.

In this regard, consider the dispute that has raged (in one of its earliest iterations, between Freud and Sándor Ferenczi, who had Otto Rank's support) as to whether therapeutic change involves "insight" (*Einsicht*) or some other aspect of the relationship such as its tenderness or empathy.[152] Obviously, both are involved. In this sense, the debate may have always been, and continues to be, overblown. However, it is also misconceived in another sense. The force of insight and the force of relational factors (the "something more" than interpretation) are doubtless both significant agents of change in therapy. Moreover, as indicated previously, there are therapeutic aspects in every psychoanalytic treatment, so interpretation and insight, as well as relational factors, are indeed implicated in the changes effected in psychoanalysis. However, contrasted with therapy, the essential and distinctive feature of psychoanalytic processes is a different sort of change—that occurs solely within the course of the free-associative method.

This is the "third alternative," so little considered in the current literature. In its everyday journey, psychoanalysis may involve insight, empathy, and tenderness. These are its therapeutic aspects (as discussed in previous chapters). But the central message of this book is that *only free-associative discourse opens the patient's discourse to what is otherwise than that which can be translated into a text.* It is, therefore, central to the differentiation of an authentically psychoanalytic process from that of therapy.

In this context, we can consider the position of the psychoanalyst as having three dimensions or levels:

1 as friend to the truthfulness of the patient's being-in-the-world;
2 as interlocutor who receives and frustrates, thus becoming the "object" of the patient's transferences in at least a double sense;
3 as the one who listens free-associatively with the patient to the erotic messages or "thing-presentations" of the repressed.

It is this third dimension that decisively differentiates a psychoanalytic process from that of a psychoanalytically informed or psychoanalytically oriented therapy (and is the dimension that Laplanche might have referred to as a *seduction*, as will be mentioned shortly). In the facilitation of this process, we can consider the labor or function of the psychoanalyst to be ultimately singular—the psychoanalyst is the conduit of Love expressed as the discourse that empowers the patient to dissolve or relinquish his or her resistances to an ongoing immersion in the truthfulness of free-association. Additionally, we can consider how the implementation of this function depends crucially on what should be called the "ethical stance" of the psychoanalyst. I will address each of these aspects in turn.

The psychoanalyst as friend (and foe)

As was mentioned previously, the relationship around free-association can only begin with friendship. This is a special mode of friendliness that must endure throughout the treatment, despite the fact that the patient will inevitably come to hate and exasperate the psychoanalyst in various ways and at various phases of the journey they undertake together. That the psychoanalyst befriends the patient reliably and congruously is the foundation of any possibility of psychoanalytic treatment. As has been discussed, at certain junctures of every psychoanalysis, the practitioner necessarily acts as an educator and also therapeutically as an empathic textual exegete, using techniques of interpretation. These educative and therapeutic moments are quite a limited aspect of the treatment (although they do not always appear so), whereas the underlying processes of friendship are not so limited.

The conditions of psychoanalytic friendship are surely unique, for the psychoanalyst needs authentically and consistently to be a friend to the patient, although not one that is necessarily friendly to the patient's "ego organization." This characteristic of the practitioner must be tangible, in a profound way, even while the patient may be varyingly friendly or unfriendly.[153] The patient, after all, recognizes the process of free-association as a threat to his or her subjective sense of security—the self-certainty or self-assurance of subjectivity. At some level, the subject immediately recognizes the process of free-association as undermining the repetition-compulsivity that constitutes the foundation—the cornerstone—of what it takes to be "real, proper, right, true and pragmatic." It is only in the context of the psychoanalyst's friendship that this subject will allow itself to be thus undermined.

This unique quality of the friendship offered to the patient by the psychoanalyst is perhaps emphasized by my assertion that, whereas the psychoanalyst's educative and therapeutic commentary may often actually obstruct the movement of the psychoanalytic process, the befriending of the patient by the psychoanalyst never does.[154] Indeed, its authenticity and consistency as well as what one might call its palpability are essential to the process. With qualifications, one might assert that the friendship of the psychoanalyst is less a matter of *doing* and more one of *being*, for the two necessary activities of the practitioner (setting and securing the "frame" of the treatment, interpreting resistances to free-association) are conveyed less by anything he or she states, and more performatively by how he or she *is* in relation to the patient.

The character of the psychoanalytic friendship notably shifts in the course of the treatment. Although it may start as an alliance between the professional and the patient's "ego"—exemplified by a very reasonable decision that, since the patient knows that he or she is suffering and the psychoanalyst offers some sort of hope for some sort of relief, it is a "good idea" to commit to a treatment relationship.[155] However, soon—usually within the initial months of treatment—this rationale crumbles as the patient is facilitated, or seduced, to move deeply into the distinctive method of unsettlement. The patient can only allow him- or herself to submit to this facilitation if he or she feels appreciably and concretely the friendship—that is, the ultimate goodwill—of the psychoanalyst. This is because, as the transference becomes more intense and/or more manifest (and irrespective of its "positive" or "negative" quality), the psychoanalyst increasingly appears as foe to the patient's sense of security (self-certainty and self-assurance)—that is, in a certain sense, the patient becomes a little more mad. In short, the psychoanalyst's befriending of the patient does not imply that he or she performs anything other than the function of unsettling the patient's *status quo*.

The psychoanalyst as interlocutor (and dual "object" of transferences)

As is well known, a principal position of the psychoanalyst is to serve as the "object" of the patient's transferences.[156] The literature on this topic is voluminous, but for the purposes of this book most of the extant debates can be bypassed. For example, in this context, it is not germane to debate how much the patient experiences the psychoanalyst "realistically" (as opposed to these experiences being determined by the problematic history of previous relationships), nor to discuss the extent to which transference is provoked by the practitioner (it thus being a cocreated rather than a unilateral production). What I think is unquestionably correct is that the psychoanalytic situation, because of the way in which the practitioner sets and secures the frame of the relationship (adhering to boundaried principles of ethical, moral, or judgmental neutrality, of emotional engagement with physical abstinence, and of lopsidedness), accentuates, makes more evident, and "gathers in" the patient's transferential experiences.[157]

What is most significant for the purposes of this book is the extent to which transference is within the domain of representationality (despite the fact that the relationship is pervasively an embodied encounter, albeit one that abstains from physical contact). That is, the extent to which transference is a matter of the patient's representations of the psychoanalyst (realistic or not, reciprocated or not) that are presumed to be animated by unconscious or deeply preconscious wishes and that are transformed in the course of the treatment. In this sense, while transferential processes may become more manifest through the praxis of free-association, there are other methods by which these processes may be identified and discussed; the elucidation of transference, at least in one sense of the term, is not the sole prerogative of this praxis.

The position of the psychoanalyst as a receiver of the patient's experiences and of the practitioner as a person cannot be disentangled from the patient's experiences of the treatment as a process. We owe to the Lacanian literature the recognition that there is a duality to these experiences. There are, so to speak, two dimensions of transference (that seem to be inextricably connected). We have learned to distinguish, at least theoretically, transferential experiences as the desire and demand for the psychoanalyst as *other* (as an "object representation" within the patient's inner theatre of representational discourse, denoted by the lower case 'o') from experiences as the desire and demand for the psychoanalyst as the grand *Other* (denoted by the upper case 'O') in relation to the constitution of representational discourse.[158] These warrant separate consideration. However, in both cases, what must be emphasized is that addressing transferences in the course of radical psychoanalysis is *not* so much a matter of arriving at interpretations as to what these phenomena are about; rather, it is a matter of free-associating to these phenomena until they dissolve.

The psychoanalyst as other

It is very familiar to every psychoanalytically informed or psychoanalytically oriented therapist how the patient performs multiple transferential scenarios in the course of treatment, most of which are attributable to historical conflicts with maternal or paternal figures and also with the relationships perceived between these figures (epitomized by the fantasies of the "primal scene") This is not to discount the salience of sibling transferences. The psychoanalyst's position is to be the "other" with whom the patient works through and plays out (workplays) his or her experiences with such scenarios. The psychoanalyst must willingly and with equanimity receive these experiences (and often, by interpretation, he or she has to make it evident to the patient that these experiences are thus received), as the patient eventually comes to deconstruct them free-associatively. In my opinion, the function of being such a receiver is foremost a matter of appreciating the significance of the patient's desires and demands, as well as maintaining a compassionately neutral and graciously abstinent stance in relation to their articulation (and thus allowing these scenarios to be worked through and played out free associatively). It is *not* so much that of actively offering the patient interpretations of these experiences, even though the psychoanalyst acts as a sort of unsettling, ironical, or disruptive voice in relation to the patient's sense of conviction about the treatment relationship. Thus, more meaningful than interpretation is often the silence of the practitioner, which prompts the patient to free associate further to his or her experience of *wanting* something from the psychoanalyst.

Transferences are routinely associated with three tropes: The maternal, the paternal, and those derived from "primal scenes." Obviously, specifying a triad such as this is highly schematic, because these are tropes rather than three categories of actual historical relationships (so the particular significance of the specific impact of siblings, grandparents, other caretakers, and the extended milieu of the individual's childhood may appear omitted). Given that these are tropes, it is also well to remember that transferences are never singular, that they are in-mixed more often than not, and that psychoanalysis typically reveals complex patterns in which one mode of transference hides another—that is, one mode serves to defend against the more acute emergence of another.

In the course of the treatment, the patient's transferences are usually initially expressed in a somewhat "genteel" form. For example: *I like feeling comforted by you; I found yesterday's session jarring, as if I were being prodded out of my relaxed state; I like the strong color tones of your consulting room; I need your guidance how to do things out there in the world; I would like to have that statue on your desk; I sometimes wonder about who else lies on this couch; I am curious where you go on vacation; I think it might be nice to be part of your family.* Inevitably, as the free-associative process grips the patient more deeply, transferences come to be expressed in more "raw"—that is, as erotically embodied "unconscious phantasy"—forms. For example: *I would like to nestle with you on the couch; I want to bite and burrow into you; To hell with you, leave me in peace; I think about sucking your nipple, your clitoris, your penis; I want to rape you anally; I want to feel you inside me; I have an imaging of stabbing your genitals viciously; I bet your spouse doesn't fuck as well as I do; I want to have a baby with you.* This small sampling of the intensity and diversity of the patient's transference experience perhaps gives some sense of the unrestrained depths of relational candor that are usually to be attained in the course of the treatment. Although in general transferences can be elucidated by methods other than free-association, it seems unlikely that the rawness of their depths could ever be accessed without commitment to this unique method.

The desire and demand of the patient's transferences are often compensatory, always conflictual. Patients want, *with* and *from* the psychoanalyst, experiences that they believe (in what might be considered a positive sense) that they have not had or have not had enough of, as well as (in what might be considered a negative sense) those that they have had in such a way that the experiences need remedy or rectification (such as the reenactment of traumatic relations). In all cases, the repetition is compulsive, needs to be understood, but most importantly needs to be unlocked through further free-associative workplay.

The psychoanalyst as grand Other

There is surely also a sense in which the desire and demand of the patient for the psychoanalyst to express something behind, beneath, or beyond the concrete wants and wishes conveyed by the "little other" or "object" transferences (the concrete longings to cuddle, suck, bite, stroke, burrow, piss, shit, look or be looked at, masturbate, as well as smack, poke, pinch, tickle, rough-house, fuck, etc.). There is a sense in which the patient, articulating his or her desires and demands within the realm of representational discourse, requires the psychoanalyst to speak from a superordinate position (that of a master-signifier). It is as if—behind, beneath, or beyond the concrete wants and wishes—the patient is always expressing longings such as: *Speak to me / Do something for me / Listen to me in such a way . . . that I may know that I am alive, that I am not mad . . . that I may know that I am desired . . . that I may know that I can speak unscathed in truthfulness . . . that I might genuinely become the author of my own enunciations.*

Here we must understand how the patient positions the psychoanalyst as what Lacan called the "subject-supposed-to-know," the locus of the master-signifier.[159] As the patient enters into the psychoanalytic process, he or she comes to realize how the claim of self-consciousness to be author of its own representational meanings is a chimerical conceit. It is an illusion–delusion by which the "I" believes itself, like Humpty Dumpty, to be the author of its own intentions, the director of its own inner theatre of representations. However, the possibilities of meaning are actually already established by the representational system to which the "I" is subjected—condemned merely to trace pathways of "intention" already determined by this system. The subject of self-consciousness does not, and cannot, create itself, but rather is the creation of a system of meanings that it has not itself generated. Representationally, "I" am called into being by enunciations that come from elsewhere.[160]

With this realization, which characterizes the structuralist movement throughout the human sciences of the past century, the pretension of the "I think" is found to be hollow; rather, "it thinks me." The "I" of the subject of self-consciousness is disabused of its illusion–delusion of mastery over its meanings, discovering itself to be little more than an enunciatory figment of the law and order of the representational system—the law and order of a big-Other that is *(phallo)logocentric.*[161] However, for the system to be lawful and ordered—for representations to be able to make sense and thus to make a world—it is still presumed, metaphysically, to have an identitarian center or authorial source. This is, in Lacan's terminology, the *phallus*, the symbolic center of the system's authorial authority—the power to designate presences and differences, to name, to say no, and to render a universe of binary oppositions. Equally, it might be suggested that, in the mythology of Sanātana Dharma, this is Shiva's lingam, the grand Other that is the absolute and primordial mark by which it became possible for form to be enunciated out of formlessness.[162] In the Abrahamic tradition, this is surely the beginning *Word* that is with God and is God. In the Hegelian discourse of the modern era, this is the image of "Absolute Knowledge."[163]

Here is, once again, the longing for a center (an ultimate starting-point, an absolute totality, or what Jean Baudrillard called the "fatal illusion of the end"). The relevance of this big-Other or master-signifier to the patient's quotidian experience of transference is as follows. To some extent, and in the course of a profound journey, patients come to realize that the representational meanings by which their self and their world have been articulated, are not actually authored by the "I" of their self-consciousness. They come to realize that they have been formed by a cacophony of voices that have—at both early infantile and oedipal levels—called them into their being-in-the-world. They come to realize that they are not, in any authentic sense, the authoritative masters of the discourse that has established the experiences by which they have lived. Despite these unsettling realizations, the longing for a center nevertheless persists. In this persistence, the patient typically requires, at least to some extent, that the psychoanalyst be "the one who knows," the grand subject who is in the position of the phallus and is thus masterful author of his or her own meanings (and thus the person who might restore to the patient the illusionary–delusionary status of being the one who knows). This is the transference of the grand Other (the capitalized big-Other).

Yet truthfully, no one has the phallus, and our belief that we can speak from this (mythical or at least somewhat mythical) position of authority is at best a dismal, even if tyrannical, pretense.[164] Rather, as human beings, *we are all castrated*—the capacity to make meaning comes to us from elsewhere, and we are merely the enunciatory subject of a power that comes from others and from the grand Other. Indeed, this is the profoundly important significance of the notion of castration–none of us are masters the meanings by which we live. If we ever appear able to express what Lacan calls "full speech" (*parole pleine*), the appearance is no more than momentary, evaporating with the next free-associative instantiation. Truthfully, we are all castrates, who try almost incessantly, and by a variety of ruses, to avoid the acceptance of our own castration; this is the human condition and the truthfulness of our being-in-the-world.[165] The psychoanalyst is as decentered as the rest of humanity. His or her experience with the method of unsettlement certainly does not render him or her the master of his or her destiny, the author of his or her lived experiences. So the patient's determination to locate a center, and thus to elevate the psychoanalyst to the position of mastery, must be interrogated free associatively, deconstructed as much as the patient's initial belief in the propriety of his or her own self-consciousness.[166] Indeed, in this sense, the position of the psychoanalyst is not only one of seduction, facilitating the opening of the patient's unconscious, but one that is ironical to itself, accepting of its own ongoing deferral and displacement.

Although Lacan may have yearned to be "the master" in Freud's wake, it is surely a trap to imagine that psychoanalysis is the transmission of mastery from the psychoanalyst to the patient (who is now to be considered willy-nilly an acolyte or psychoanalyst-in-training, and whose Lacanian treatment will terminate in a flash of *satori*-like enlightenment). Rather, if a commitment to the free-associative method is maintained—if the abyss of a perennially decentered psyche is to be faced in the spirit of truthfulness—then surely the myth of mastery must itself be deconstructed, and this implies the ongoing interrogation of the patient's transference to the psychoanalyst as the locus of the master-signifier, the big-Other or "one who knows."

The psychoanalyst as facilitator of listening to the untranslatable

In large measure, the patient's various experiences of transference (and the psychoanalyst's various countertransferences) are potentially representable, even if their operation is deeply preconscious or is, in Kleinian terms, an "unconscious phantasy." Addressing these transferences is the métier of a successful psychoanalytically informed or psychoanalytically oriented therapy. To a limited extent, such labor may even be accomplished without the method of free association. Interpretation, as the formulation of insights, as well as empathy or tenderness in the therapeutic relationship (thus making it a different sort of relationship from any that the patient may have previously experienced) may be sufficient to transform patterns of transference in ways that are considered more adaptive and mature (this is unquestionably correct for the "other" transferences, but more debatable in relation to those pertaining to the grand "Other"). However, if this is done without an unflinching commitment to the free-associative method, it is very implausible, perhaps impossible, that the work will move into the depths of embodied "phantasy" that I described above as the "raw" forms of "other" transferences. Without free association, invariably therapy remains more or less "genteel" and ultimately superficial.

However, unlike therapy, psychoanalytic processes do not only open up the patient's expression of transference experiences that are representationally translatable. The psychoanalytic method also opens the patient to what is alive, but representationally untranslatable, within his or her lived experience—the sheer *kinesis* and voluptuousness of his or her being-in-the-world. What the praxis of free association accesses, in a way that no other method can, is the "voicing" of fleshly libidinal impulses as they intrude disruptively on the law and order of representational discourse, as if attempting to "join in the conversation." That is, the method uniquely opens the subject's capacity to listen to the erotic expressiveness of the bodymind in ways that are *otherwise* than representationality and, indeed, to do so without subscribing to the imperialist ambition that such messages be able to be subjugated to, or captivated within, the law and order of representation.

To the extent that this expressiveness occurs specifically in the context of the psychoanalytic relationship, this might be considered an untranslatable otherwise experience of transferential processes. In this sense, the psychoanalysis recreates what Laplanche calls the "fundamental anthropological situation."[167] This is the universal experience of the human baby, in which the helpless infant is subjected to countless implanted or imposed messages from the unconscious of caretakers—messages that are enigmatic or incomprehensible to the infant and that comprise the earliest form of the repressed unconscious. As is now well known, Laplanche terms this subjection a *seduction*, and in this sense the psychoanalyst seduces the patient into an awareness of the enigmatic signifiers or thing-presentations that comprise the wellspring or brio of his or her unconscious—the enigmatic expressions of incomprehensible desire from within the depths of our erotic embodiment.

Thus, to catch on to psychoanalysis, it is crucial to understand the incomparable and distinctive power—the extraordinary and enigmatic caliber that must be appreciated *sui generis*—of its processes as an ontological and ethical opening to the messages or enigmatic signifiers, the thing-presentations (or protorepresentations) of the repressed. Above all else and unlike all other methods of inquiry into the human psyche, the method of psychoanalysis involves listening to these incomprehensible messages, enigmatic signifiers, thing-presentations, traces, and unrepresentable feelings or proto-emotions, that occur insistently and persistently within our lived experiences. Thus, above all else and unlike all other methods of healing, the psychoanalytic relationship is an embodied erotic encounter made sacred by its abstinence with respect to physical contact.[168]

Although the meaning of these experiences is otherwise than that which can be represented, and is thus, in a sense, esoteric, the experiences themselves may often be quite concrete. For example: The onset of a headache, the tightening of a muscle, a feeling of heat or of chill, a sudden localized twitch, a sucking movement of the mouth, a slight engorgement of the genitals (labia and clitoral gland, testicles and penis, as well as nipples), an ache in a joint, the tensing of the anal sphincter, irritability of a patch of skin, a cramp or minor pain, sudden blinking or flickering of the eyes, an unwarranted sensation of urinary urgency, a shortening or acceleration of the breath, nausea, unexpected sweating, "pins and needles" or the numbing of a particular muscle group, an unusual feeling in the back of the throat, the rumbling or gurgling of the abdomen, the quivering of the lips, an unanticipated moment of flatulence, a flushing or itchiness of the skin, sudden postural rigidity, a hiccup or burp, the clamping of the jaw, a sniffy (sneezy or runny) nose, the emission of a yawn or sigh, a watering of the eyes (when tears do not seem apposite), a flexing of a limb, an anal irritation, a change in the timbre (color or rhythm) of the voice, a feeling of deadness or fatigue throughout the body, the moistening of the vaginal canal or the exuding of a drop of pre-ejaculate (even when nothing "sexual" is being expressed in the stream of consciousness).

All of these are quite commonplace experiences, but rarely in everyday life are they attended to as meaningful. Indeed, in many treatments that are nominally psychoanalytic, their significance is often obscured in the haste to "make sense" interpretively. That is, the possibility that our bodymind can express itself meaningfully, yet not "make sense" by the criteria inscribed in the law and order of representationality, is effectively excluded or preempted. In psychoanalytic praxis, the patient must often be encouraged to notice the extent to which he or she is *not* relaxing on the couch, to attend to these sorts of enigmatic experiences, to breathe into them and to free associate.[169]

In this context, the psychoanalyst's labor must sometimes include active education of the patient in relation to this procedure, but yet more significant is the facilitation of the patient's ongoing commitment to the free-associative process (that is, the addressing of resistances) as well as of the patient's capacity to listen to the expressiveness of the bodymind. In performing this labor, the psychoanalyst's position is manifested, to a great extent, by a contemplative silence, accompanied by his or her constant and acute awareness of the erotically embodied nature of the relationship with the patient. That is, the psychoanalyst not only listens with an evenly suspended or "free-floating" attention, all the while free associating silently, but ensures that the inner expressiveness of his or her own bodymind is included in the multiple channels of his or her attention. When this procedure is followed, the psychoanalyst inevitably becomes aware of the very alive, proto-emotional, voluptuous, and unrepresentable dimensionalities of the psychoanalytic relationship.

It cannot be overemphasized how important it is for the psychoanalyst to be self-consciously ready to accept—in a different terminology, for the psychoanalyst to become resonant—incomprehensible messages flowing throughout the treatment. He or she must also be alert to the patient's anticipation of a certain sort of erotic intrusiveness coming (traumatically or at least almost traumatically) from the psychoanalyst himself or herself. These are messages of which the psychoanalyst may feel—indeed, will very likely feel—entirely innocent. For example, it is as if the patient will "know" that the sudden cramp or twitch was "caused" by the personage of the psychoanalyst. This, I believe, testifies to the plausibility of Laplanche's ideas as to how the earliest enigmatic signifiers (the thing-presentations that become the unconscious precipitated by primal repression) are implanted or imposed upon the infant from outside. Thus, it is as if the patient's bodymind poses to the psychoanalyst a profound and characteristically anguished question: *What do you want of me*? (to which the psychoanalyst can only respond seductively but with irony, and thus typically with a certain quality of silence). This is the workplaying of what I am calling the otherwise aspect of the transference.

The psychoanalyst and patient are in a flesh-and-blood encounter, a libidinally alive and highly charged relationship that is comprehensible to neither of them. Yet it is solely the psychoanalyst who has to take ethical responsibility for the way in which the strange occurrences experienced by the patient are to be addressed.[170] This responsibility is implemented by the psychoanalyst's facilitation of the patient's free-associative journey—that is, for the most part, by the interpretation of resistances to free-association—but also by the psychoanalyst's unique mode of silence, which constitutes *both* an acceptance of the patient's messaging *and* a refusal to posture by acting as if such untranslatable meaningfulness can or should be translated into representational meaning. Thus, in the context of this dimension of the psychoanalytic relationship (behind, beneath, and beyond the complexities of other and Other transferences), the psychoanalyst's refusal to know is more significant and has more healing potential, than his or her ability to formulate and have the patient assimilate knowledgable interpretations or insights.

The psychoanalyst is, in Laplanche's words, "the guardian of the enigma." This vital but frequently overlooked position of the practitioner enables us to understand precisely why the myth of mastery—the ultimate vacuity of the capitalized Other, which is as much a "black hole" as the "I" of consciousness—must be deconstructed in the course of psychoanalysis. For if the psychoanalyst hides behind, or clings to, the fantasy of correspondent or coherent knowledge—that is, of being the subject-suppose-to-know—he or she will effectively exclude or preempt the potential of the free-associative process to access the enigmatic and extraordinary voicing of the embodied experience of the repressed.

The function and the ethical stance of the psychoanalyst

In the context of the radical approach to psychoanalysis being explored in this book, the distinctive labor or function of the practitioner is threefold:

1. The psychoanalyst must interpret the patient's resistances to free-association, and thus empower the patient to listen more fully not only to his or her textuality but also to the voicings of his or her erotically experiential embodiment.
2. The psychoanalyst must receive, silently but if necessary interpretively, the patient's demands that are articulated representationally—that is, an exploration of the way in which the patient was formed oedipally by interpellation.
3. The psychoanalyst must also receive, silently and rarely interpretively, the demands coming from the voicing of the patient's experiential embodiment—that is, the enigmatic, untranslatable messages or thing-presentations coming from what Laplanche called the "fundamental anthropological situation." This is an exploration of the way in which the patient was formed by implantations or impositions that cannot be represented.[171] Only if this third dimension is performed can psychoanalysis fulfill its de-repressive potential.

These considerations enable us to appreciate how self-analysis is ultimately impossible, and why the presence of an interlocutor—indeed, the special presence of the psychoanalyst's participation in this asymmetrical or lopsided "dialogical monologue"—is fundamentally necessary to the initiation and maintenance of a genuinely psychoanalytic process.[172] The practitioner who made a practice—as legend has it—of talking into a recording device for fifty minutes a day and then listening to his own productions, might achieve insights of therapeutic value into his or her fantasies, relationships, and sense of personal identity. However, precisely because this procedure lacks the presence of an interlocutor, it is questionable whether this practitioner can actually be free associating, and certainly the sense in which transferences (as other or as Other) can be worked through and played out seems, to say the least, dubious. This is not psychoanalysis, and probably not even anything like an adequate mimicry of free-associative processes.

The psychoanalyst is necessary as a presence, literally and figuratively.[173] Contrary to so much of the thinking in the psychoanalytic literature, the crucial feature of the psychoanalyst's presence is not his or her epistemological functioning, but rather is ontological and ethical. The labor of the psychoanalyst is a matter of his or her *being*—as a friend, as receptive to the multilayered fluctuations of the other and Other transferences, and as a silent witness to the erotic vicissitudes, the dynamics, of the untranslatable otherwise. Foremost, this is an ethical task that Viviane Chetrit-Vatine (and others such as Kristeva and Irigaray) might characterize as a feminine-maternal way of caring for, or taking responsibility for, the patient.[174]

The psychoanalyst, who—as someone who has been fully in psychoanalysis—is aware that all appearances of a center to psychic life are to be interrogated, must be one to whom everything is strange, but nothing is alien; everything is to be approached as familiarly unfamiliar or unfamiliarly familiar. Indeed, the psychoanalyst is in the ethical and ironical task of being the one who perpetually knows how little he or she knows—knowing that the strangeness within each of us will never be other than strange, yet insisting that this is not a motive or reason for being alienated from it. Psychoanalysis is a labor of enstrangement (of defamiliarizing the familiar)—that is, it unsettles that which was, or might be, settled. Thus, the psychoanalyst's labor is essentially the ethical task of facing what is other and otherwise in the mode of the caress, as ably explicated by Levinas.[175] Levinas's philosophical writings have much to teach us about the ethicality of taking responsibility for what is "other." As he expounds the issue, the caress is the way in which I approach the other as we come face-to-face. It is an ethical stance of passionate nonindifference in the face of unknowability; it is an asymmetrical approach to the other that takes responsibility for the encounter despite the other's being unknown and perhaps unknowable. The caress aims not to compensate, correct or repair, but to allow suffering to free itself of itself by opening to its inherent meaningfulness.

Obviously, the psychoanalyst's caress of the patient—the specificity of the practitioner's caring—is relationally discursive, rather than physically engaged, but it is passionate nonetheless. The psychoanalyst is an engaged, passionate presence in a process that is libidinally charged, but physically abstinent and indeed faceless.[176] The faceless proximity of the psychoanalytic situation is intensely intimate, freeing yet safe, for only under such conditions can the otherness and the otherwiseness of the repressed be given voice and listened to in a manner that is liberatory. Not only must the psychoanalyst labor to facilitate the patient's relinquishing of his or her resistances to free-associative praxis, the mode of the caress is ultimately how one comes to listen, think, and speak, as a psychoanalyst.

12

RESISTING PRAXIS

Notes on clinical and theoretical retreats

> Wie schafft man den Widerstand weg? . . . deuten, erraten und es mitteilen . . . aber sondern dem Ich an, welchesunser Mitarbeiter ist, und dies, selbst wenn sie nicht bewußt sein sollte.
> How do we dissolve resistance? Interpreting, guessing, communicating . . .
> but now on the side of the "I" which is our ally
> (even if it does not know it).
>
> Sigmund Freud, 1917

Our "ego organization"—committed to its own security and sense of its own probity—dreads the discourse of free-association, sensing the profound and unsettling challenge of listening to the intimations of any meaningfulness that is otherwise than that which can be captured representationally.[177] The course of every psychoanalytic treatment might most aptly be chronicled in terms of the vicissitudes of the patient's—and the practitioner's—resistances to free-associative praxis. What is far less acknowledged is the extent to which the history of the psychoanalytic movement can be charted in terms of multiple series of theoretical retreats from the significance of the free-associative method. In this chapter, I will offer some preliminary notes both on some of the clinical implications of resistance and on the way in which major trends in psychoanalytic theorizing since 1914 (and particularly in the 1930s and thereafter) have constituted a covert effort to avoid the implications of free-associative discourse.

On addressing resistances in psychoanalytic treatment

The clinical literature on resistances is voluminous. Here I will offer just a few comments on their interpretation in psychoanalysis—advancing what is, in the context of contemporary thinking, a maverick view of the topic. There has been much attention in the literature to the content of resistances (as distinguished from their processive significance). Freud is partially responsible for this emphasis, writing in 1926 about the distinctions between five sources or types of resistance, without clarifying what implications such distinctions hold for the interpretive activities of the psychoanalyst.[178] One distinction, which Freud did not particularly develop, is between resistances that are mostly intrapsychic (the patient stops free-associating because he or she does not want to experience a particular set of thoughts or feelings) and those that are mostly interpersonal (the patient stops free-associating because he or she does not want to speak aloud to the psychoanalyst whatever is being thought or felt). In the clinical setting, this is often a useful distinction.

In terms of the content of resistances, it is obvious that, at least descriptively, there are different sorts of resistance which may appear at different times in the treatment. For example: Resistances to the psychoanalytic setting (keeping appointments, paying fees, and so on), resistances to experiencing and talking about transference feelings and fantasies, resistances to uncovering thoughts and wishes that are conflictual, and so forth. However, in a profound sense, there is ultimately only one resistance, which is the patient's—and the psychoanalyst's—resistance to associating freely and to listening compassionately, appreciatively, and gracefully to what is thus expressed, whether intrapsychically or interpersonally located.[179]

In a sense, every psychoanalytic treatment begins with the "fundamental rule" and thereafter proceeds by addressing the inevitability of resistance to its ongoing adherence. The psychoanalyst's initial task is to inform the patient of the necessity and desirability of free association as the essential activity and process of healing. This educative aspect often pivots around the way in which this "fundamental rule" is communicated. After that, the principal responsibility of the practitioner is—as indicated in the previous chapter—the interpretation of the patient's resistances to ongoing free association. Thus, consideration of this topic may be divided into the delivery of the "fundamental rule" and the resistances in adhering to it that are subsequently manifested by the patient.

The "fundamental rule" and the reasons for it may be communicated in a variety of ways, and often the communication has to be varied and repeated with variations. It may be noted that early psychoanalysts were accustomed to issue Freud's *Grundregel* as an imperative (the patient's compliance with which constituted the condition for ongoing treatment). However, at least since the 1930s and 1940s, it has generally been found that the preferable way of presenting the "rule" is more invitational or solicitous. After all, it is a rule that the psychoanalyst knows in advance is bound to be broken frequently by the patient, so the authoritarian injunction is inevitably perjorative.[180] To some extent, this shift is a benign result of the discipline's greater attention to the experience of the "ego" in treatment.

In a parallel fashion, early psychoanalysts seem to have been somewhat inclined to issue orders to their patients, requiring them to overcome their resistances to free-association (e.g. "Your sex life and your bowel movements are important, you have to tell me about them" or "Stop being silent, it will jeopardize your treatment"). Against this approach, it is now more commonly recognized that understanding the reason for resistances is a preferable approach to their compliant relinquishment or dissolution (e.g. discussing the patient's conviction that talking about sexuality and bowel movements will result in excruciating humiliation, or addressing the anxiety that prompts the patient to fall into silence). Thus, it is now acknowledged that facilitating a patient's empathic understanding and thus the gentle resolution of his or her resistances around a particular issue is a central dimension of the healing impact of psychoanalytic treatment.[181] In large measure, this facilitative mode of interpreting resistances is the key to the psychoanalyst's craft.

Although the clinical literature often limits the notion of resistance to those ostensible breaks in the patient's free-associative participation in the treatment (missed appointments, unpaid fees, coming to sessions inebriated, falling into silence, and so forth), it is more useful to consider how every thought, feeling, wish, and action performs resistively in relation to other possibilities and thus serves the patient's "ego organization" protectively. Resistance as an outright refusal to free-associate (missed sessions, silent sessions) is actually easier for the practitioner to address than the subtle resistances enacted by the patient. Three examples of these subtle resistances will suffice. One would be the patient whose "associations" remain steadfastly on the level of "chatter" (as Kierkegaard might have expressed it, *parole vide* in Lacanian terms), such that there seems to be an almost complete lack of emotional significance to the material. What passes as "free association" devolves into a string of clichés, and the patient chatters in this platitudinous manner to avoid the emotional significance of genuine free association.[182] Another example would be the patient whose "associations" make too much "good sense" narratologically and conversationally—that is, the patient who engages in what might be called *faux association*.[183] A final example would be the patient who consistently undoes, from moment to moment, whatever associative thoughts and feelings he has expressed.[184] Many more examples could be given, but this is not the place for a detailed discussion of such a complex clinical topic. Rather, what must be emphasized is that it is the psychoanalyst's foremost function to address such resistances to free association in a way that dissolves the commitment of the "I" to their perpetuation. Since resistances are ubiquitous in every psychoanalytic treatment, this is a moment-to-moment labor that must be engaged judiciously.

On the resistances of psychoanalytic theorizing

The "I" of self-consciousness, and indeed our entire "ego organization," resists free-associative praxis ultimately for a single, despotic reason—because free-association is uniquely the praxis by which the subject finds itself decentered from itself, and its claims to mastery are thus irrevocably subverted. The troubling revelation of this method is that the living and lived experience of the human condition is dynamically nonidentical, interminably contradictorious, and inherently erotic. Moreover, the representational appeal for a center to psychic life that is outside itself (G, for example, or the big-Other, the master-signifier or the "Laws" of science) is consistently found to be instable, if not illusional and delusional, and thus not a center in which the "I" of self-consciousness might take permanent refuge. Thus, a diligent immersion in the praxis of free-association experientially vindicates Freud's Copernican revolution: "I" do not hold the authority of authorship my own thoughts and feelings; "I" am not the center of "my" psychic life, nor can I have representational access to such a "center." This is the unwelcome discovery—indeed, the vertiginous experience—of Freud's method by which self-consciousness interrogates itself. It is the discovery of the repressed unconscious, which is inherently a processive critique of the phantasm of centeredness in the constitution of each individual psyche as much as in religious belief and other ideologies.[185]

The emphasis of the clinical literature is on the patient's resistances to the treatment—but the psychoanalyst also resists his or her own free associations as he or she listens to the patient's utterances with what Freud characterized as "evenly suspended" or "free-floating" attention. As I have suggested elsewhere, the foremost resistance of practitioners is manifested as the compulsion to position themselves as epistemological agents for whom the patient is an "object" of investigation and manipulation.[186] This quasi-centering tendency is unfortunately supported by the formal structure of clinical training at psychoanalytic institutes and elsewhere, in which patient material is "objectively" discussed in case conferences, in supervisory consultations, and in the professional literature. Free-association becomes "data" which, along with other assessment material such as the patient's history, is conceptualized by the practitioner, using his or her selected theoretical model of the "mental apparatus" (in order to formulate interpretations that might be therapeutically useful to the patient). In all of this, the practitioner remains spuriously centered in his or her epistemological position.

Just as it is unsurprising that every individual resists psychoanalytic praxis, it is not surprising to find that the efforts of theory-building promulgated by the psychoanalytic community in the wake of Freud's methodical discovery have been significantly directed toward a recentering of the human subject. Indeed, despite the diversity of forms that these efforts have taken, this ideological motive is the fundamental common factor. For such a recentering to be achieved, the discourse of free association must be abandoned or recast—for example, as a mere "data-gathering" procedure in the application of an objectivistic model of the "mental apparatus," suitable for the task of ideologically domesticating the errant or "abnormal" subject. In Chapter 2, I suggested that every theoretical retreat from the psychoanalytic method has three intrinsic purposes: To restore a center to psychic life; to reestablish a conventional relationship between theory and practice, in which the latter is performed mostly as an application of the former; and to reassert therapeutic goals over psychoanalytic ones. These are the ideological motives of the speculative theory-building and systematization of conceptual structures that can be found in Freud's writings, especially after 1914, and that characterize the development of the psychoanalytic movement, both around Freud's leadership and conspicuously with the diversification of the discipline that became particularly evident in the late 1930s and 1940s.

This book has exposed the inherent radicality of psychoanalytic praxis as Freud described his discipline, particularly during the span of his career between approximately 1886 until 1914. As I have argued, during and after World War I, he conspicuously shifted away from this radicality, although he continued to develop the discipline until his death in 1939. As is well known, even during the most productive phases of Freud's career, there was dissent from the radicality of his ideas. In 1911, Adler's followers left the *International Psychoanalytic Association* (hereafter IPA), which Freud had founded just a couple of years earlier.[187] As is well known, they objected to Freud's emphasis on sexuality and argued for the indivisibility of the individual's personality. In 1914, Jung finally resigned the IPA, after years of debate with Freud over—among other matters—his presentation of an unconscious in harmonious alignment with consciousness. Rank left the organization in 1924, disagreeing with Freud over the significance of oedipal complexes in the structuration of psychic life. From about 1910 through the 1920s, there were also less publicized differences between Freud and figures such as Wilhelm Stekel, Girindrasekhar Bose, Franz Alexander, and others.[188]

It is perhaps an error to consider these various disagreements and differences to be scientific "deviations" from a monolithic corpus of Freudian ideas. The notion of defection is perhaps more apt. The process of affiliation with the movement was initially quite loose. The resignations that occurred between the founding of the IPA and Freud's death in 1939 were often based as much on personal–political disaffection as on lucidly elaborated divergences from some clearly articulated IPA standard that might define the discipline's scientific status.[189] As is well known, Freud's imaginative hero was Hannibal, one of the great commanders in military history, and Freud wanted to build a sociopolitical "movement," perhaps almost as much as he wanted to develop a science.[190] In those early years, to be in his ranks or out of them was, to a significant degree, a statement of acquiescent allegiance or disgruntled perfidy in relation to the leader's authority. As I have argued, Freud's *oeuvre* is far from monolithic, so what it might mean, scientifically, to agree or disagree with his tenets was not necessarily obvious. What it would mean to be a "Freudian" if you read Freud's writings from the mid-1890s to 1914, or if you focused on the theoretical speculations that preoccupied him between 1915 and 1920, or if you studied his texts from the mid-1920s, might be quite discrepant. However, although very different stylistically and substantively, the major defections of Adler, Jung, and Rank have a fundamental similarity—namely, a resistance to the possibility that the human subject might be interminably and inescapably caught in the contradictoriness of its own formation.

In addition to the drama of the well-publicized dissent occurring in the two decades after the founding of the IPA, it is important to understand the theoretical developments that occurred in Freud's wake. Many versions of what is currently called "psychoanalysis" or "psychoanalytically informed" and "psychoanalytically oriented" therapy developed at some ideological distance from their disciplinary roots. This occurred conspicuously in the 1930s and 1940s, with the development of self/relational perspectives, of the ego psychological or structural–functional model, and with the emergence of Kleinianism as a distinctive standpoint. However, it has continued in almost every decade thereafter—for example, with the emergence of an independent school of object-relations in the 1950s and 1960s, the development of self-psychology in the 1970s, the expansion of interpersonal-relational and intersubjective perspectives in the 1980s and thereafter. Today, theories and practices passing under the "psychoanalytic" banner are diverse, often quite discordant with respect to the basic assumptions on which they operate, and tendentious in their connection—or lack thereof—with Freud's radical discoveries.

However, I argue here that they all have one crucial feature in common—namely, to restore a center to psychic life, even at the expense of initiating an ideological refashioning of "psychoanalysis" (and with this, to understand clinical practice as an application of theory, and to value goals of adaptation and maturation over the liberatory truthfulness of the human condition).[191] Here I will briefly elaborate this argument in relation to the three most significant developments of clinical thinking after Freud.

The ideology of the self/relational tradition. What I am calling the self/relational tradition encompasses several arguably distinct developments that have burgeoned especially since the 1970s in North America. Although they have clear precursors in European philosophy and in what has been called the "third school of Viennese psychotherapy," they flourished as a distinctively North American movement, occurring more or less entirely outside the European ambience of the early IPA and characterized by the ideology of individual integrity, self-reliance, and achievement.

Historically, Adler's "Individual Psychology" stands at the head of the "third school of Viennese psychotherapy" with its emphasis on the unity of the human personality—an individual self that is always connected to, and develops within, his or her social or interpersonal world. With that axiom came the repudiation of psychoanalytic discoveries around sexuality and Adler's counteracting emphasis on the individual's "will to power."[192] Although Adler is often listed as a proponent of "depth psychology," less well known is the connection between his school and the proponents of a "height psychology" that was specifically critical of Freud's focus on the unconscious aspects of psychic life. For example, Viktor Frankl, whose 1946 book on "logotherapy" (as the human search for "meaning") became notably popular in the United States, was a member of the Adler's group for a few years. He had also joined the fascist movement in 1934 and was affiliated with the Göring Institute. In a 1937 issue of that Institute's journal, he published a paper extolling "height psychology" and emphasizing the central importance of an individual having a mission in life.[193] The assumption of an integrated or potentially integrated self, whose activities are directed toward "higher" ideals than those arising from embodied desire, is evident.

Alongside these developments in Europe, social or interpersonal versions of "psychoanalysis" were already germinating on the far side of the Atlantic. It is beyond the scope of this book to explore the significance of the ideologies of individualism, self-reliance, and self-interest that have variously permeated North American culture since the days of the frontier, or to discuss the development of notions of selfhood through the modern era.[194] What is pertinent here is the manner in which "psychoanalysis" became modified through its assimilation to such ideologies.

To a certain extent, "psychoanalytic" perspectives took hold in the United States almost independently of their initiation in Europe and almost dissociated from the movement that Freud spearheaded.[195] For example, *Psychoanalytic Review* was launched in New York just four years after Freud's 1909 visit to the USA, and was intended to be "free of sectarian bias" (which in practice initially meant that it published papers by clinicians, such as Jung, who by that time had broken with the IPA). The eminent psychodynamic psychiatrist, William Alanson White, began publishing papers in the *Psychoanalytic Review* in 1914, and was a founder of the journal *Psychiatry* in 1937. He then severed his connections with the psychoanalytic mainstream to collaborate with Harry Stack Sullivan, Erich Fromm, Clara Thompson, Frieda Fromm-Reichmann, and others, in order to establish in 1946 the institute named for him. Along with the Washington School of Psychiatry—and the influence of Ferenczi, Rank, Karen Horney, Otto Allen Will, Edith Weigert, Bruno Bettelheim, and many others—these developments were indicative of a shift in the notion of "psychoanalysis" as a discipline focused on intrapsychic conflict to one that addresses interaction between the individual and his or her social and cultural environment.

Such a shift is epitomized by the highly influential writings of Sullivan and Rank (in the latter phase of his career). In two major books and a series of minor texts, as well as through his work with the Washington School from 1936 to 1947, Sullivan argued that the individual must be understood in terms of the network of relationships in which he or she is entwined. "Interpersonal psychoanalysis" thus starts with the individual's "self-system" that is formed through a complex of interlocking "me–you" relationships. The unconscious is merely considered as the arena of perceptions not receiving sufficient attention, and sexuality is reduced to the motivational impact of the "lust dynamism."[196] This sort of shift in thinking was buttressed by Rank's publication of *Will Therapy*, which was translated into English in 1936, two years after his relocation to New York. As with Sullivan, Rank's influence on the development of therapy in the United States can scarcely be overestimated, as he had a major impact on figures such as Carl Rogers, Rollo May, Paul Goodman, Fritz Perls, Ernest Becker, and Stanislav Grof. Here again, the emphasis on the individual's aspirations and potential self-integration (with therapy or not), as well as the deprecation of the sexuality of our embodiment, is evident.

Concordant with the sociology of Charles Horton Cooley's 1902 notion of the "looking-glass self" (a self that develops from the perceptions of others) together with George Herbert Mead's notion of the formation of the self as a social process arising from the individual's symbolic interactions, and supported by later developments such as Alfred Schütz's social phenomenology, the ideological assumption of an individual self, that is actually or potentially integrated but that develops interactively through its social milieu, became central to the ideological canon of North American social sciences. Within the mental health industry, many contemporary variants of "psychoanalysis" have been drawn into this ideology. Here one might consider the focus on matters of identity exemplified by Erik Erikson, the elaboration of self-psychology by Heinz Kohut, the development of "relational psychoanalysis" by Stephen Mitchell, Jay Greenberg, Lewis Aron, and many others, the intersubjective theories of George Atwood and Robert Stolorow, as well as many versions of attachment theory and "infant psychoanalysis"—for example, the perspectives of Daniel Stern, Joseph Lichtenberg, or Beatrice Beebe.

There are, of course, many significant differences of theory and therapeutic technique between all the various practitioners mentioned above. For example, both in terms of their theoretical model and their practices, some might be said to emphasize the motivational strivings of the self—for example, Erikson and Kohut; others might be said to emphasize more the impact of the milieu—for example, Will and Bettelheim; many strive to maintain an interactional or coconstructivist approach—for example, Lewis or Stolorow. However, despite the many variations within what I am designating as the self/relational tradition, there is an often unacknowledged commonality that should by now be evident. It is assumed that self-consciousness is no longer irremediably fractured. Rather, psychic life is assumed to be centered (or is to be therapeutically reformed to be centered), on the self, on the system within which the self operates, or on the mutuality or reciprocity of the interaction or discourse between them. "Psychoanalysis" no longer starts with the repressiveness of self-consciousness, but with the assumption that self-consciousness can integrate itself. Accordingly, there is, as if by fiat, nothing otherwise than the textuality of self-consciousness (the representations of the self and its others). The notion of drive-desire or psychic energy either disappears or is treated as more or less inconsequential; repressiveness is no longer the cornerstone of the discipline. The expressiveness of the erotic energies of our embodiment is downplayed or discarded (the body merely treated as the machine designated to do the mind's bidding). In line with this retreat from Freud's unsettling contributions, the method of free-association is abandoned. Instead, techniques of conversational dialogue between the two persons in the consulting room are championed. Such techniques must invariably be underpinned by notions of therapeutic success—values such as adaptation, maturation, and the harmonious integration of the individual. Directly or indirectly, the clinician functions as spokesperson for such values, and thus all too readily becomes an agent in the ideological transmission of the social and cultural system, the *status quo*. Above all, the potential consonance of the individual's internal world, and thus his or her potential orderliness or concinnity in relation to the external world of social relations, is assumed. In short, the revolutionary dimension of Freud's discipline is rescinded, psychic life is comfortably recentered. Thus, in terms of the radicality expounded in this book, the self/relational lineage is not psychoanalysis.

The ideology of ego psychological tradition. With the exception of Kohutian self-psychology and some aspects of more recent interpersonal-relational school (notably in its affiliation with attachment theories), the developments of the self/relational tradition have occurred largely outside the political orbit of the IPA. This is not the case with the ego psychological tradition, which was politically empowered by the leadership of Anna Freud, and which for many years constituted the orthodoxy of American psychoanalysis (largely due to its hegemonical influence within the American Psychoanalytic Association).

Although inspired by Freud's 1923 and 1926 writings, ego psychology—as a differentiated lineage within the psychoanalytic movement—is initiated by Anna Freud's 1936 publication of *The Ego and the Mechanisms of Defense* and expounded in her subsequent writings. However, certain aspects of her ideas had perhaps been anticipated by the minor surge of interest in ego functions that appeared in the psychoanalytic literature earlier in that decade. For example, there was Robert Wälder's 1930 essay on the ego's "multiple functioning" (which was republished in 1936 and became very influential), Hermann Nunberg's 1931 essay on the "synthetic function of the ego" (elaborated in his book a year later), Sterba's 1934 paper on the "fate of the ego in analytic therapy" (the material of which had been presented as early as 1928) and, also in 1934, Paul Federn's essay on the awakening of the ego in dreams (which contained a section headed "Postulates to serve as a Basis for an Ego Psychology"). Additionally, just a year after Anna Freud's major work, Hartmann presented his seminal 1937 paper further advocating a disciplinary focus on the functioning of the ego organization. This was elaborated in his magisterial 1939 book, *Ego Psychology and the Problem of Adaptation*, which asserted that there is a "conflict-free sphere" of this organization's operation. This assertion, which is the crucial theoretical act of recentering that characterizes the ego psychological lineage, was immediately well received by many practitioners in the official movement.[197] Significantly, in the same year, Hartmann published his paper, "Psychoanalysis and the Concept of Health," which attempted to reassert the concept of normality and establish its definition, and which foreshadowed the emphasis in Anna Freud's later writings on the maturational psychology of "normal development."[198]

With the ascendance of the Nazis, Anna Freud, accompanying her father, relocated to London where, over the subsequent decades, the group she trained and led has elaborated her work on developmental ego psychology. This brought her group into conflict with the Kleinians, who had established themselves in London some years previously.[199] As is well known, out of the conflict between Kleinian and ego psychological standpoints, there emerged a fertile—hybrid—British lineage of independent object relational theorists such as Donald Winnicott, W. R. D. Fairbairn, Michael Balint, Paula Heimann (in the later part of her career), and their many successors.[200] However, it is in the United States that the ego psychological tradition achieved its greatest power and influence. This was the result of the diaspora, in which theorists such as Hartmann, Rapaport, Ernst Kris, Rudolph Loewenstein, Edith Jacobson, René Spitz, and Margaret Mahler immigrated to the USA between 1938 and 1940.[201] These émigrés trained a second generation of ego psychologists—names such as Arlow and Brenner—who came to dominate, theoretically and politically, the American Psychoanalytic

Association.[202] This generation has, in turn, influenced many contemporary practitioners (for example, Boesky, Busch, Gray, and many others who have focused their attention on "technique"); these developments were also greatly aided by the systematizing work of Rapaport and his followers.

The most acerbic and well-known critique of the ego psychological tradition comes from Lacan, who understood the conflict-free sphere of the ego organization as an ideological concept that ultimately comprises a repudiation of psychoanalysis in the name of the therapeutic virtues of adaptation.[203] Although Lacan does not necessarily develop his reasons for this conclusion in an explicit or focused manner, my 1984 book elaborates some aspects of this critique. I have argued that those theorists who misguidedly link psychoanalysis with a phenomenological or subjectivistic inquiry, and those who assume that, to be valid, its procedures of investigation must be objectivistic, are both attempting to refashion Freud's discipline to conform to epistemological assumptions that its praxis actually transgresses.[204] In short, against the architectonics of subject/object epistemology, the free-associative method elucidates an instable "subject" that is continually shifting as its certainties progressively implode, its coordinates undermined. Moreover, this subject supposedly confronts an "object"—the unconscious—that is never really external but intrudes disruptively on the being of this subjectivity. The lineage of ego psychology exemplifies this latter error.

From its inception, this tradition has insisted on the importance of a certain sort of partitioning of the ego organization whereby one quasi-autonomous domain of its programming is able to observe and subsequently regulate the operation of other domains. The assertion allegedly secures the epistemological possibility of objectivity in the interpretations and insights generated by psychoanalytic procedures. This is exemplified by Sterba's 1934 argument that "therapeutic ego-dissociation" must occur for a successful treatment process, because the ego must observe itself and then, by means of what Nunberg called its "synthetic function," bring what it observes under its control in an adaptive manner.[205] This sort of thinking is preeminently elaborated by Hartmann's concept of the "conflict-free sphere" of ego functioning. Since 1923, this model of the "mental apparatus" had specified that the ego organization confronts managerially both its own internal "id unconscious" and the frustrating factors of external reality, as well as the differentiated stipulations of the ego-ideal and superego. The model thus posits an organization inherently wracked by the conflictual demands of these forces. However, with the positing of a "conflict-free" sphere of functioning, it becomes the task of treatment to expand the influence of this sphere and the task of what is "conflict-free" to take charge of those aspects of the ego organization that are, so to speak, "conflict-ridden."[206] In brief, there are at least three problems with this sort of theorizing.

First, as I have already indicated, the ego psychological model is a refashioning of Freud's discipline into an epistemological framework that it does not fit. It imports the natural attitude to posit an ego organization as a stable subject that confronts as "objects" not only external reality (as a pregiven world of self-subsistent facticity), but also its own "unconscious" (as the biologized impulses of the "id"), as a thing-in-itself (or more precisely, "things-in-themselves"). It also confronts the forces of its ego-ideal and superego (but that is a matter that can be set aside at this juncture). This implies that the ego organization operates somewhat independently of its "unconscious" and its task is to know *about* the unconscious by objectivistic procedures in order to control the unconscious domain by manipulative measures. It is evident that such a model of therapeutic action entirely disallows the free-associative discovery of the way in which the otherwiseness of the repressed perpetually disrupts the law and order of the representational system—the finding that the unconscious is always "in" but not "of" the representationality and reflectivity of self-consciousness.

Second, ego psychology invites the unfortunate notion of "health" conceived as the stases of inner alienation. The goal of treatment easily becomes that of training the patient in the use of those "higher cognitive skills" by which he or she self-observes objectivistically, self-interprets rationally, and then self-regulates by means of the assimilated or "worked-through" interpretations, thus gaining control over what is being treated throughout as a quasi-private domain of "objects." Identification with the practitioner—and thence assimilation of the formulations about the patient that the practitioner offers—thus inevitably becomes the fundamental *modi operandi* of the treatment. This is far from a freeing of the patient's dynamics—a momentum that proceeds from the stases of alienation to the kinesis of estrangement.[207] It invokes the ghost of the "well analyzed" patients who, equipped with a veritable armamentarium of "valid insights" about their own functioning, find themselves strangled by their own intelligence. If the goal of the treatment is for the patient's conflict-free sphere to be enlarged (and to gain precedence or even mastery over conflict-ridden functioning) and to become increasingly capable at "self-analytic" functioning (which is a currently fashionable axiom), then one can appropriately envisage the endpoint as a patient who is constantly checking and doublechecking himself or herself. This is, in a sense, the epitome of self-alienation. When patients are assisted to achieve a more objective relationship with themselves, then they ultimately become an object for themselves. Their internalized epistemological positioning now distances themselves from their own being, from the being of their own truthfulness as a *subject-in-process*. There are some interesting reasons why Lacan dubbed the ego a "paranoid construct" and no doubt, if called upon to "heal" itself, it can become increasingly paranoid—at least in the colloquial sense of the term.

Third, it must be emphasized that the above considerations do not imply that the ego psychological approach to the "mental apparatus" cannot be a basis on which successful—that is, effective—psychotherapy can be conducted. The techniques associated with this tradition can, after all, assist the ego organization of patients to develop patterns of compromise formation (between id, reality, ego-ideal, and superego) that are more adaptive and mature. Tellingly, in the voluminous literature of the ego psychological lineage, startlingly little critical attention has been given to the social and cultural context within which adaptation and maturation are to be assessed. Rather, the *status quo* is assumed, which surely means that it is effectively endorsed. This is evident in the efforts of Hartmann and Anna Freud to discuss "health" or "normality" as if such concepts might be scientifically established without consideration of contradictions—endemic relations of exploitation and oppression—in the sociocultural and interpersonal arrangements that constitute the individual's milieu. The thrust of the ego psychological tradition positions the clinician as arbiter of the patient's healthy, normal, or "conflict-free" functioning—depicting treatment as inevitably tied to an objectivistic procedure in which the ego organization accommodates to "reality" by gaining conflict-free mastery over its unconscious.

To render this program coherent, fanciful concepts such as "sublimation" must be elaborated.[208] This is a term used rather sparingly by Freud (and rarely in more than a casual, descriptive sense) to denote the transformation of activities and interests that are initially "drive-infused" into those that appear less so—that is, the "drive" changes its character. For example, in Freud's 1910 essay, he shows how Leonardo da Vinci turned his sexual interests (which then "atrophy") into a craving for knowledge and an unquenchable passion for research. To give a less inspiring example, one might imagine an individual with a childhood obsession over bowel movements achieving productive citizenship as a sanitation engineer.

The point at which the individual sublimates his problematic "drives" and his "conflict-free" sphere of ego functioning achieves a predominant role in the conduct of his or her life is the juncture at which therapy ends successfully. The spurious objectivism of therapeutic procedures in the ego psychological mode has achieved a transformation of the individual in a way that is judged positively. The criteria for what is judged sublimated and what is "conflict-free" functioning—criteria that determine at what point the individual's conduct is no longer in need of therapeutic remedy—come from a double source—namely, the milieu and its ideological transmission by the mental health practitioner. These are the criteria of "adaptation" and "maturation" to Western or North Atlantic cultures that advance by the alienation of labor and the exploitations of capital—a culture in which "love" devolves all too readily into oppressive relationships, "play" becomes the scheduling of sporting events, and our erotic embodiment is treated as a machine that operates merely to serve the mind as master.[209] That the judgments of "health" and "normality" are contextualized by a social milieu that is transparently, ubiquitously and disastrously "unhealthy" is a fact that must be consistently ignored, for it is the task of the ego psychologist to render the "mental apparatus" of the suffering individual into one that is "well adapted" and "psychologically mature."

All too readily, the therapist in the ego psychological tradition unwittingly becomes one of those purveyors of conventional morality and of the prevailing ideological canon (whom Nietzsche excoriated in his *The Gay Science*). The slide into practice as ideological transmission depends on a double movement in which Freud's discipline is refashioned as the epistemology of an objectivistic theoretical model and the method of free-association is forgotten (or reduced to a mere "data-gathering" phase of the therapeutic procedure). Psychic life is now recentered on the objectivity of a conflict-free sphere and, in this sense, however effective a therapy the practices derived from this model may produce, ego psychology is not psychoanalysis.

The ideology of the Kleinian tradition. There is perhaps no more politically powerful deviation from Freud's discipline than that of Kleinianism. If one were to count the affiliations of today's membership of the IPA, this doctrine would probably claim the most adherents. Only Lacanianism, the proponents of which practice almost entirely outside of the IPA's enclosure (Lacan having been effectively expelled from membership in 1963), can rival the popularity of Kleinian thinking. Kleinianism may be considered as it was practiced prior to the founder's death in 1960 and as it is now by the so-called "contemporary Kleinians."

Hanna Segal designates three phases to Klein's theoretical contributions. The first, in which she pioneered the investigation and treatment of babies and young children, dates from Klein's earliest publications in the 1920s to her 1932 *Psychoanalysis of Children*. As is well known, this led her to assert that oedipal conflicts and the formation of the superego could be detected in the earliest years of life. Although she claimed continued allegiance to Freud's movement, these assertions actually modify, in a manner that has practical consequences, Freud's theory of both oedipal complexities and the superego. The second phase is characterized by Klein's brilliant theorization of the depressive position, notably in the 1935 paper "Contribution to the Psychogenesis of Manic Depressive States" and its 1940 sequel "Mourning and its Relation to Manic Depressive States." In the final phase, Klein developed her (also brilliant) theory of the paranoid-schizoid position. This phase is notable both for her masterful 1946 paper, "Notes on some Schizoid Mechanisms," and for the impressive and influential 1957 book, *Envy and Gratitude*. The processes comprising this position are held to be less mature, both functionally and developmentally, than those of the depressive position, despite the fact that the latter was theorized in the previous phase of Klein's theoretical elaborations. In this last phase of her very substantial contributions, Klein seems to progressively soften what she herself understood to be the tragic aspect of her depiction of the human condition. For example, in the 1957 book, "real relationships" are credited with greater significance than previously (and thus Klein departs from a stance of absolute idealism), reparative motivations are more emphasized and the infant is now endowed with a spontaneous capacity for care, concern, and feelings of love (described in her posthumously published 1964 essay). This softening evolves further in the writings of her successors, the neo-Kleinians and the so-called "independent" object-relational theorists (perhaps most notably Winnicott).

These three phases of this theoretical trajectory still constitute the foundation of Kleinianism, the central motif of which depicts how our adult functioning typically oscillates between "primitive" paranoid-schizoid anxieties and the more organized depressive–reparative position. The latter is characterized by guilt over destructive-aggressive impulses and remorseful sadness. Both of these are associated with the activation of compensatory restorative processes designed to mitigate the effects of our innate greed, hatred, envy, and destructive rage. Klein's basic tenets were propounded by a distinguished group of followers such as Segal, Isaacs, Heimann (in the earlier phase of her career), Joan Riviere, Roger Money-Kyrle, and Herbert Rosenfeld.[210] There followed a second generation of Kleinians—the "contemporary" group—that includes such luminaries as Michael Feldman, Jean-Michel Quinodoz, Edna O'Shaughnessy, Ignes Sodre, Donald Meltzer, John Steiner, Ron Britton, Horacio Etchegoyen, Elias Barros, Irma Brenman-Pick, Elizabeth Spillius, and many others.[211] However, I think it is fair to say that much of the work done by this group has amplified matters of diagnosis and technique, rather than modifying the basic tenets of Klein's theorizing.

To adopt a Kleinian stance, it seems as if one must accept the premise that psychic life begins with a neonate who is wracked by an innate aggressivity and at the mercy of an endowment of archaic "phantasies."[212] This concept of a primordially destructive *Instinkt* (for there is little or no credence given in Klein's work to the possibility of a distinction between *Trieb* and a force that is biological) is pivotal to the entire theoretical edifice.[213] This is the hallmark of Klein's somewhat anomalous reading of Freud's 1920 notion of *Todestreib* that she also believed to have been empirically demonstrated in her work with babies and very young children. However, the testimony of neonate observation is notably ambiguous and, without a doubt, it lacks validity as the evidentiary basis for a theoretical framework concerning the origins of psychic life.[214]

However, if one adopts the speculative tenet of constitutional aggressivity in psychic life, then one has to posit an "archaic ego" as the organization that enables mental development to proceed from an unintegrated condition (chaotically disorganized around destructive impulses and persecutory phantasies), into a tenuously more integrated condition that is regretful and reparative toward whatever damage it believes it has caused. Thus, one arrives at the conjecture of an innate ego organization accompanied by an innate repertoire of frightening aggressive "unconscious phantasies" (directed toward "objects" that are somehow known prior to experience with them). There is, in this sense, no accounting for the beginnings of psychic life—rather, the psyche is just there, from the beginning, equipped with drive, objects, and an inchoate organization. Skeptically, one might say that this is as plausible as the idea that there is a pre-birth soul equipped with ideas and motives. Indeed, several commentators, even ones sympathetic to Kleinianism such as Donald Meltzer or Fred Alford, have suggested that this doctrine is indeed fundamentally infused with Christian theology. The prelapsarian state is abrogated and life, as we know it, begins with the "Fall" (now portrayed in terms of our inherent destructiveness, rather than our lascivious proclivities) and, if we are fortunate, we restore ourselves to a gracious condition of guilt through care. This is Klein's tragic and moralizing—albeit salvific—"take" on human nature. It starts not from experience with the free-associative method, but from a series of assumptions about psychic life. This is, according to Kleinianism, a life in which each individual's aggressivity cannot be avoided or assuaged. It can only be contained by the accomplishments of depressive-reparative functioning, which allows humans to harbor within themselves a restorative hope (which, as Hegel and Nietzsche both indicated, is always a dimension of tragedy).

There is no question that this model provides a powerful moral code by which to conduct therapy. There can be little question that the aim to engage a process that moves the patient from an aggressivized and less integrated condition to one that is sadder, wiser, and more integrated has powerful potential for healing. From a Freudian standpoint, there are several lines of criticism concerning Kleinian precepts. For the purposes of this book, three issues must be mentioned.

First, there is the Kleinian positing of innate destructive forces accompanied by an archaic ego organization, which is entirely speculative. The evidence for this in the empirical observation of infants is spurious, and the idea that it might be inferred from the memories and the psychic constitution of adults is based on a disproven theory of memory and development (that ignores Freud's finding of *Nachträglichkeit*). Such speculation does not provide a coherent account of the emergence of psychic life from its biological substrate. This is because it erases the crucial distinction between biological mechanisms or *Instinkte* and the energies of *Trieb*. Instead, it appeals to the "innate."

Second, having developed a theoretical model that prioritizes speculative assumptions over method, Kleinianism essentially has no need of free-associative processes. Rather, the clinician knows in advance that the issue is one of helping the patient shift from paranoid-schizoid to depressive-reparative functioning. Thus, the only purpose served by any semblance of free-association is to alert the practitioner to the manifestation and valorization of the shifting between paranoid-schizoid and depressive-reparative functioning. In an effort to keep their discipline connected to Freud's, Kleinians typically advocate attention to two types of process as substitutive for the method of free-association. They claim that spontaneous play engaged by young children as well as the interplay of transference and counter-transference in the adult treatment situation are equivalent to the process of free-association. Interestingly, a parallel assertion is made by Jungians and others who argue that the techniques of active imagination might substitute for free-association.[215] Such claims are fallacious.

These three processes or modes of discourse (young children's play, the back-and-forth of transference–countertransference in a dialogic relationship, and the productions of active imagination) are all crafted in accordance with what I have called the narratological imperative and, as such, they preserve the centrality of the enunciatory subject. Thus, like the processes Freud described in 1900 as the "secondary revision" of the manifest dream (the means by which the ego organization "cleans up" the dream in order to have it appear a little more in conformity with the law and order of story-telling, and thus to hide further its repressed inspiration), these three modes of discourse are designed to "make sense." Thus, they may elucidate a text other than that which self-consciousness initially owns; but, even if they thus expand the purview of representational consciousness, there is no way that they invite the voice of that which is otherwise than textuality. In short, such discourse constructs, rather than deconstructs, and thus misses the repressed dimension of psychic life.

Third, with Kleinianism, the criticism that therapy all too readily devolves into transmission of ideology is again pertinent. Whereas the self/relational lineage assumes the potential consonance of the individual's representational world (and thus his or her harmonious integration with externality), and whereas the ego psychological lineage assumes the qualities involved in the possibility of "conflict-free" functioning (supported by scientistic criteria of adaptation and maturation), Kleinianism inscribes in the conduct of the clinician some unexaminable suppositions about the quality of maturation involved in the shift from paranoid-schizoid to depressive-reparative functioning.

Although rendered in a more tragic coloration than the robustly optimistic "happy self" and "conflict-free" egotism of the North American vision, the Kleinian practitioner transmits moral values about integration (which is the hallmark of the depressive-reparative position), and does so with seemingly little interrogation of the social and cultural milieu in which such values are invariably located. Perhaps because the Kleinian depiction of the human condition is tragic, its ideological implications seem less blatant than those of the self/relational and ego psychological therapeutic traditions and certainly less tied to the image of the "good citizen." Yet proclaiming the innate tragedy of the human condition nevertheless transmits an ideology both in which the status quo of "reality" is presumed, and in which the individual struggles almost endlessly with his or her constitutional endowment. Perhaps it is no surprise that Kleinian therapy is notoriously protracted and that, at the 1949 Congress of the IPA, when Klein was challenged to discuss the criteria for successfully ending a therapeutic treatment, she floundered.

In sum, Kleinianism is a most powerful mode of therapy, resting on the threefold conviction: (1) that infants are born with rudimentary but unintegrated egos, with object representations; (2) that they suffer horrendous anxieties (due to innate phantasies, the endowment of the death instinct, which is taken to mean inherent destructive-aggressive drives, as well as the terrifying experiences of birth trauma or quotidian frustrations such as hunger); and (3) that they deal with these anxieties and experiences by phantasies involving splitting, projection, and introjection (and hence the clinical emphasis on projective identification), with the attendant fears of retributive persecution. Although each of these three tenets may be more assumptive than empirically vindicated, and thus comprise the ideological core of Kleinian doctrine, they provide the basis for powerful techniques of treatment—despite, or perhaps in part because of, the subtlety of their mode of ideological transmission. Yet, for all that, Kleinianism is a retreat from psychoanalysis, if the latter is defined radically in terms of its Copernican revolution. In this tradition, the individual is recentered on his or her innate constitution. This is a recentering which may be framed in terms of its biologization of unconscious instincts as innate aggressivity (which is how Laplanche pitches his critique of Kleinianism) or in terms of its appeal to an innate endowment of psychic life as unconscious phantasies, structures of an archaic ego, and objects that allegedly operate prior to our earliest actual experiences. These two ways of describing how Kleinian theory recenters the psyche are not, of course, exclusive. However, the conclusion cannot be avoided that, in this recentering, Kleinianism departs from psychoanalysis.

Concluding note

The images of an integrated self in harmony with its milieu, of a conflict-free sphere of the ego organization, and of an individual whose inner functioning might be more or less consistently established in the depressive-reparative position, comprise diverse efforts to retreat theoretically from the free-associative discovery that psychic life, indeed the universe, has no center. Powerful modes of therapy can be, and varyingly have been, generated on the basis of a theoretical reassertion of a center to our psychic lives. Indeed, the mission of these three theoretical revisions—the self/relational, the ego psychological, and the Kleinian—as disparate as they may seem, and indeed in many respects are, is to retreat from Freud's troubling revelations and unwelcome discoveries about the human condition. Yet, only at the cost of a retreat from science, into ideologies that require the untranslatable within us to be subordinated to that which can be translated, can one dispense with the free-associative method and cling to a theoretical framework that promises—spuriously—a return to the security of what appears to be real, proper, right, true, and pragmatic. These three traditions of retreat are indeed monuments of theory-building, ideological edifices that may contribute mightily to the procedures of therapy. Yet their shortcoming as science rests with their refusal of a diligent immersion in, an existential commitment to, the interrogations of free-associative discourse.

Freud's method requires that we face the abyss that is inscribed deeply and pervasively within each of us.[216] Our self-consciousness is interminably nonidentical with the subjectivities or agencies that produce and reproduce its meanings; moreover, there is no other center in which to take refuge. Against the intolerable vertigo—indeed, the terror—of this unending yet strangely healing "encounter" with the abyss, these theorizations are to be understood as efforts to reestablish the security of a center. Of necessity, the ideological impetus of such theoretical counter-revolutionary movements (of theory-building and the attendant modifications of clinical conduct) requires that the method of free-associative interrogation be relinquished.

13

WHAT IS FREEING ABOUT FREE-ASSOCIATIVE PRAXIS?

> What is the contribution of Freud's discovery? Is it tautologous—or simply a reaffirmation of something that has been substantially forgotten—to say that is primarily . . . 'analysis,' primarily, as Freud insists, a method? . . . We must never cease to emphasize the unprecedented, revolutionary and, at the same time, scientific character of the Freudian method. Even if this method appears to be something acquired once and for all, it must be continuously reconquered against the ever-recurring facile temptations . . . The 'revolution' brought about by the Freudian method is constantly on the wane: a 'permanent revolution' is essential.
>
> Jean Laplanche, 1992

> What I think we are doing in analysis is to enable the people who come to us to increase their feeling of freedom . . . to liberate the forces which are present in themselves to enjoy life, not as scared people looking for all sorts of safety . . . We don't have to say what they will find out . . . In other words, analysis should improve what the patient already has, or give him the possibility of finding that life is worth living.
>
> André Green, 1995

If psychoanalysis is, first and foremost, a psychology of repression, as Freud announced in 1901—that is, a method of psychological inquiry that discloses the dynamics "between the cohesive 'I' and the repressed which is split off from it," as he later elaborated—then we must also understand it to be the revolutionary discovery of the derepressive praxis of free-associative discourse. This is the essence of the psychoanalytic method, its *sine qua non*. To engage in free association is to subvert the illusions and delusions of mastery—to expose how *the living and lived experience of the human condition is dynamically nonidentical, interminably contradictorious, and inherently erotic*. The profound implication of this is that psychic life has no authentic center, only the ideological appearances of centeredness, and there is no extrinsic center to which it might appeal for the alleviation of its intrinsic suffering. This exposition justifies an ongoing existential commitment to the praxis of free-associative discourse, as a genuine process of healing. Although today this is typically forgotten—obscured beneath a welter of clinical and theoretical preoccupations—*psychoanalysis is a project of liberation*. It is to be understood as the process of emancipating the human spirit on both personal and political levels, even though the truthfulness of its liberatory momentum does not, and cannot, ever arrive at some fixed and final state of freedom.

In this context, the intent of this manifesto has been both to return psychoanalysis to what could be called its "root method," its taproot, which is Freud's discovery of the free-associative method as he presented it between the mid 1890s and 1914, and to demonstrate the contemporary relevance of free-associative praxis for the project of both personal and political emancipation.[217] To grasp this relevance, it has been necessary to clear away much of what currently passes under the banner of psychoanalysis—speculative theory-building, the systematization of conceptual structures, and specifically the technicalities of its therapeutic manifestations. Having done so, I shall—in this final chapter—conclude the book with a few notes as to what it might mean to insist that psychoanalysis is fundamentally a project of liberation.

Against the ambition of "results"

In a concretely experiential sense, there is no pure psychoanalysis. As indicated previously, every psychoanalysis includes therapeutic aspects (and no doubt a few therapies that are "psychoanalytically informed" or "psychoanalytically oriented" can sometimes include moments of a genuinely psychoanalytic process). From the standpoint of minimalistic theorizing adopted in this book, the therapeutic enterprise depends on the binding and rebinding (more precisely, the compulsively repetitious rebinding) of drive-desire energies into conventional configurations of representationality.[218] This sort of change procedure, dependent on the repetitious enunciation and assimilation of interpretations, can be engineered by the clinician as the practical application of a theoretical model that details how the "mental apparatus" functions. Such models of psychic functioning, which specify certain techniques of maneuvering to bring about the patient's transformation, might be self/relational, ego psychological, Kleinian, or something different (such as a derivative-hybrid of these major theoretical formulations). In a certain respect, these variations perhaps matter less than the fact that each model stipulates what sorts of result should be achieved in the course of therapy. In short, the mandate of such therapies is specifically to achieve "results," whereas psychoanalysis has no such mandate (which is why, as mentioned earlier, the application of the term "treatment" to psychoanalysis is understandably controversial).

In the face of suffering, the liberal humanitarian response is that we must *do something*! This is the imperative of therapy, the pledge undertaken by every clinician as he or she confronts the patient. The discontented individual must be changed into a "good citizen" (who is seemingly content with his or her fate within the extant milieu). Neurotically or psychotically unhappy patients must be transformed into ones who are "reasonably (un)happy" with the prevailing conditions of their "reality" (and who, being "normal," must "know their place" within this reality). This is the condition that Freud, in his 1893 essay on the psychotherapy of hysteria, famously called our "common misfortune" (*gemeines Unglück*). Even if what can be achieved is merely palliative, the imperative of therapy is to *do something* for the patient's unhappiness—therapy inevitably has goals, the achievement of which is to be measured in terms of "results."

As I have said, there are therapeutic moments in every psychoanalysis, but they are not germane to the distinctive radicality of its method. Moreover, there is no simplistic attack on the prerogatives of therapy to be launched here. The goal to alleviate pain, for example, is not to be begrudged, whereas the goal to produce a "good citizen" must urgently—psychoanalytically—be called into question and deconstructed.[219] What must be understood here is that the alleviation of pain is not the same as a remedy for human suffering and, against the conservatively quietist goals of therapy, a freeing of the subject from suffering is the unique aim of psychoanalysis. The point to be emphasized here is that there can frequently be a very serious catch—indeed, a pitfall—to the mandate to *do something*, and to the requirement that the success of an activity implies an arrival at the sorts of result anticipated as the goal of the enterprise. As radical commentators, including Slavoj Žižek (in his analysis of the connections between the levels of subjective, objective and systemic violence that are endemic in our sociocultural relations), have argued, successful results in alleviating a problem at one level often entrench or exacerbate the self-same problematic dynamics at another level.[220] I argue here that this is certainly true of any therapy (whether psychoanalytically informed, psychoanalytically oriented, or of some other kind) that is not committed foremost to the free-associative processes of psychoanalysis.

Successful therapeutic results typically entail the exchange of one mode of alienation for another—sometimes with reckless disregard for what is worsened or lost in the procedure. For example, the patient's alienation in his or her symptoms is transformed into the patient's alienation in his or her insights and "self-analytic functioning"—as Freud hinted darkly at the end of his life in his paper on "Constructions." Perhaps rather than embarking with the therapeutic goal of achieving results (that is, with the *techniques* of *doing something* supposedly to alleviate the patient's unhappiness) it is fundamentally preferable to engage a *method* by which the reasons for this unhappiness are to be unpacked, disclosed and exposed (without ever formulating a repacking as the goal of closure).[221] As Laplanche has elaborated, psychoanalysis has "aims" in that free-associative process necessarily has certain sorts of effect on the subject—but these effects emerge from the process itself, and are quite unlike the "goals" which are proposed, so to speak, "from the outside."[222] This is why it must be argued that psychoanalytic processes necessarily have profoundly significant effects, but do not necessarily produce "results" (and certainly are not to be engaged with any goal of achieving a preconceived endpoint or benchmark of effectiveness).[223]

In order to sharpen the contrast I am making between the practical results of applying a technique (as in the gains and goals of therapy) and the effects of psychoanalytic processes as praxis, let us consider the three main ways in which our prevailing culture treats the "body."[224] There is the idealized body purveyed by the media; the body of athletes and fashion models. If athletes do their job right, then games are won; if models are successful, more products are sold. There is the idealized body of the unit of labor in the market of a capitalist economy. If miners, farmers, factory workers, or secretaries do their job right, then surplus value is created and profit accrues to the owners of the enterprise. Finally, there is the idealized body of medicine (which, at least in the allopathic tradition, is somewhat like a cadaver that is not yet dead); the body as a complex system of anatomical and physiological structures and mechanisms. If physicians do their job right, then the broken limb will be repaired, the course of the viral infection arrested, and the patient will continue to live, hopefully pain-free. Even if these accounts seem cynical, no one would begrudge the results of this third example. It is often, but I believe questionably, judged to be the closest parallel to the practices of therapy in the field of "mental health." However, the contrast with psychoanalysis is that the method of free-association does not have the goal of producing an individual who is successful by the criteria of the media or the marketplace, nor even one who is necessarily devoted to the prolongation of a pain-free "life." Against such goals, psychoanalysis instigates a mode of listening—of treating our embodiment in terms of the "voicing" of its wisdom. That is, treating it as the "home" of our lived experience—a home to the inherent meaningfulness to which we are called to attend. This is quite different from the body as a unit functioning in a particular sociocultural system (that establishes the values purveyed by the media, the labor market, and the medical model).

We must now consider this analogy to the treatment of the "mind." It is obvious that the question of what one considers a "normal mind" is integrally contextualized by its sociocultural and historical circumstances. Moreover, it cannot be said that the normal mind is one that does not suffer, since palpably all humans suffer and are aware of their suffering to varying degrees (and with varying ideological and possibly anti-ideological modes of awareness). The question of "abnormal" suffering raises complex issues about the distinctions and the interactions between subjective, objective, and systemic suffering (questions which parallel Žižek's discussion of these three levels of violence, mentioned above). Surely one must ask in what ideological sense is an individual who claims not to suffer subjectively—the ideal of a happy, "good citizen"—but who is oblivious to the systemic exploitation and oppression in which he or she participates, to be considered "normal"? And if this individual was previously unhappy, yet transformed to his or her present state by therapeutic procedures, in what sense are the results of that therapy to be counted as a success? Even if such individuals consider themselves to be helpless bystanders who supposedly "do nothing" (which in itself is a pernicious sort of myth), is this to be considered "normal"? Conversely, is the individual who is victim of systemic exploitation and oppression, and who protests his or her fate with violence, to be considered "abnormal"?

My point here is not to raise questions in what might be considered a sophomoric manner, but to point to the ultimate truth on which they pivot—namely, that what we call "normality" is a hegemonic performance, a mere benchmark of normativity (in a sociocultural context that could appropriately be designated "sick," exploitative, oppressive, homicidal, ecocidal, and so forth). This is a truth that Foucault and others have advanced, but that remains far too little discussed within the field of therapy. The point is that, whereas therapeutic procedures may aspire to results comparable to those measurables imposed on the labors of the professional athlete, fashion model, miner, farmer, factory-worker, secretary, or physician, psychoanalysis has no such measure of results (nor should it).[225] Rather, it necessarily has effects.

On the effects of free-associative praxis

Therapy is about relationships and, if conducted under the aegis of a psychoanalytically informed or psychoanalytically oriented model, it may teach the patient much about his or her relationships (whether conceived interpersonally as the actuality of external interactions or intrapsychically as the connections between internal representations). The goal of therapeutic maneuvers is to reform such relationships in accordance with conventional principles. Such principles are implied by a model of allegedly harmonious and supposedly integrated relations subjectivistically and intersubjectively, or a model of an objectivistic or adaptive encounter between the conflict-free ego and its "objects" (which would include its representations of its self, of other people, material goods or things, and abstract ideas), or a model of coming-to-terms with our innate aggressivity toward those whom we might "love" and thus falling into, or maturing into, a depressive-reparative attitude toward life, or some other model, derivative or hybrid.

In short, the therapeutic goal is to *settle* the subject into a more adaptive or mature dispensation. This would be a revision of the patient's system of representations—a binding and rebinding of drive-desire energies—that palliates, *if only on the level of appearances*, the pain of his or her suffering. Such goals inevitably both imply and require the ideology of a Ptolmaist recentering of psychic life. Their implementation, the results by which success is measured, necessitates the maneuvering practices of technique, rather than the praxis of a method. By contrast, psychoanalysis has no goals and no technique, only the aim and the effects of *unsettling* the subject, the dispossessing of that which is censorious.

An existential commitment to free-associative praxis invariably moves the patient both to face his or her interpersonal and intrapsychic relations (including the circularity of relations with the self, which always entails relations with "objects"), and then to listen further both to the voicing of his or her erotic embodiment and to the liveliness and the deathfulness that is the heart of our being.

In this sense, an authentic psychoanalytic process compels the patient to face and to listen to the *reality*, or what Freud called the "real causes," of his or her suffering, in spite of the resistances of the patient's "I" to this deconstructive and processive encounter.[226] The aim of the treatment is not to practice what the psychoanalyst, in some theoretical sense, already "knows about." Rather, it is to engage an ethical and existential praxis that opens and moves the patient and the psychoanalyst into the unknown—a spontaneity of experiential knowing that contrasts with the "knowing about" the "mental apparatus" that is the claim of therapy.

Psychoanalysis faces what does not change—in psychotherapy, in psychoanalysis, or in any other procedure or process—which is the truth of suffering and what the poet might have called the "will to change" suffering.[227] What psychoanalytic experience concretely demonstrates is that both suffering and the will to change suffering persist, in some sense, ineradicably throughout our lived experience. This is because both are entailed by the nonidenticality of the subject, the Copernican reality of psychic life. However, what psychoanalysis also concretely demonstrates is that suffering occurs in two radically divergent modes: The paralysis of repetition-compulsivity, which is the rule of egotism that complies with the law and order of representationality (which I dub the static condition of *alienation*); and by contrast the kinesis involved in transgressing repetition-compulsivity in a way that remobilizes the dynamics of nonidenticality (which I dub the "ecstatic," gracious or joyful, condition of *estrangement*). The character of psychoanalytic healing involves an ethical and existential movement of the subject from the staleness of alienation into the dynamic spontaneity of estrangement.

The perpetual contradictoriness between the logical and rhetorical "making sense" of representationality and the exuberant excess of libidinal energies or desire (desire itself being a mobility that is not in itself desirable, at least to our ego organization) cannot be altered. There is no resolution to this contradictoriness, especially not in terms of the further repression (and suppression) of desire (although permutations of such tactics are the mandate of therapeutic transformation). However, the derepressive praxis of psychoanalytic healing is an ethical and existential opening—by dismantling—the representationality of self-consciousness, not only to other texts, but also to the brio of life that is otherwise than textuality. It initiates these effects by destroying the apodicticity of the "I"—deconstructing free associatively all that self-consciousness takes to be real, proper, right, true, and pragmatic. Such a process of deconstructive opening implies the empowerment of a capacity—that is enigmatic, extraordinary, and even somewhat esoteric—for listening to the untranslatable or otherwise voicing of that which the structuration of self-consciousness represses. So there is a sense in which it is precisely the "disassociative" dimension of free-associative praxis that is actually its most powerful and profound contribution to our ability to listen to the voicing of the repressed unconscious. The repressed surfaces "in" but not "of" representational transformations as the expressive and exuberant excesses of our embodied erotic experience. In this way, the lived experience of the "I" of self-consciousness is always found to be exceeded, but not by anything subjectively or objectively ascertainable. Thus, in the stases of alienation, the meaningfulness of what is otherwise than representationality is almost entirely blocked, whereas the kinesis of estrangement opens representationality to the voicing of that which is otherwise than its possible texts. This is the key to psychoanalytic healing, to its truthfulness and to the significance of asserting that freeing the subject from suffering is the unique aim of psychoanalysis and that such freeing involves a shifting of the subject of self-consciousness from the stases of alienation into the mobilization of estrangement.

Freedom as the process of freeing

Much of this argument hinges on our understanding of the psychoanalytic discovery of psychic energies or libidinality—an elucidation of the pluritemporality and polysexuality of our psychic life. It is facile for us to know, objectivistically, that our lived experiences depend on the operation of neural circuitry and countless other anatomical and physiological mechanisms. And it is equally facile for us to know, subjectivistically, that these same experiences involve a theatre of representations, referring literally and figuratively to ourselves and to matters other than ourselves. Although we have great difficulty thinking outside of the dualism that Descartes so ably articulated—difficulty in thinking of ourselves holistically as a bodymind—we have evidence of the fallacy of such "this-or-that," either/or depictions of psychic life. However, psychoanalytic experience, as well perhaps as other modes of disruptively nonordinary experience, makes these issues yet more complex. Free-associative experience challenges the principles of sufficient reason and absolute knowledge. These principles lead us to assume mistakenly that everything in the psyche would be known if a complete account of neural circuitry could be added to a complete account of the law and order of representationality. Against the hegemony of such logic and rhetoric, the free-associative method of psychoanalysis demonstrates *in vivo* what I call the libidinal copula, the way in which drive-desire energies must be assumed mythematically to mediate the realms of biology and representationality—and to do so in a manner that is perpetually nonidentical or dynamic.

Psychic energy is manifested by the way in which something otherwise than representationality intrudes upon and disrupts the law and order of this system in the transformative chaining of thoughts and feelings. Libidinality is always "in" but not "of" the law and order of the representations and transformations between them, through which it emerges exuberantly and disruptively. Lididinal energy as a sort of non-thetic intentionality is never to be fully captured by representational formulations. Their nonidenticality persists, however cleverly we modify our representations of self and other. But such energy is also not identical with the physical operations of our biology. Inscribing enigmatic messages, *Triebe* are not equivalent to a physical mechanism or force, despite the fact that such energies "lean on," are propped upon, or follow from physically evident operations (which we generically called *Instinkte*, to include reflexes, modal action patterns, neural networks, hormonal infusions, and so forth). Thus, libidinality does not merely conjoin the realms of the objectively physical and the subjectively mental. Rather, this psychic energy is dynamically different from both biology and representationality in the "information" it conveys between them, thus "conjoining" them in a double dynamic of nonidenticality. This is the irrevocable contradictoriness of the human condition.

Psychoanalysis thus runs counter to the oldest philosophical assumptions of the greco-occidental world, which entails the theorization of differences in terms of the putative invariability of identity. Free-associative discourse undermines identity discourse and the depiction of the universe in terms of binary oppositions.[228] Libidinality deviates from the physicality of *Instinkte* on which it depends. Yet it drives self-consciousness, as the "I" of the representational subject, rendering it perpetually different—*différant*—from itself. This psychic energy always "breaks out from within" us, voicing an aliveness from which the repetition-compulsivity of our "ego organization" constantly tries to alienate us, locking us into stale patterns of established meaning. The method of psychoanalysis unlocks—that is, it transgresses and deconstructs the stale configurations of repetitiousness, and thus transmutes alienation into the brio of dynamic mobility. In this condition of free-associative kinesis, our estrangement from our libidinality is never resolved—there is no final solution or endpoint of arrival. However, in the dynamic of estranged mobilization, we are refreshed by our openness to the aliveness within us, the voicing of our embodied erotic experience.

In the Western or North Atlantic philosophical tradition, much has been written about freedom (mostly by philosophers whose labors were funded by those whose entrepreneurial activities involved the enslavement of others). Yet as Kolakowski wrote in 1988, "among questions that have sustained the life of European philosophy for two and a half millennia not a single one has ever been solved to our general satisfaction; all of them remain either controversial or invalidated by philosophical decree." Yet I believe that, in large measure because of Freud's discovery of free-associative praxis, we are today at a strange and interesting juncture in our philosophical ability to think about freedom and, for that matter, in our capacity to think freely. Put simply, "freedom" has become a grievously overworked term, almost drained of substantive significance, and all too frequently drenched in ideological hype (the "free world" and so forth). Yet it still retains an allure that bespeaks its fundamental and ongoing significance for the human condition. Writing between 1817 and 1830, Hegel had already warned of this evacuation of meaningfulness. In his *Philosophy of Mind*, he grieved the notion of liberty, writing that there is no idea "in common currency with so little appreciation of its meaning," and no idea so "indefinite, ambiguous, and open to the greatest misconceptions (to which therefore it actually falls a victim)."

Today, if we follow the distinction, popularized by commentators such as Erich Fromm and Isaiah Berlin, between negative freedom or "freedom from" and positive freedom or "freedom for," then it is clear that we have a strong *sense* of the former (even if we cannot always elaborate and justify it philosophically), even while the latter often seems to elude entirely our philosophical reflection and comprehension. That is, we know—*as if in our bones*—what it might mean to escape the structuralized violence of oppressive sociocultural, political, and economic arrangements—to be free from exploitive conditions, from racism, from sexism, from wage slavery, from colonialist or imperialist oppression, and so forth. But, except in the utopian imagination, we seem to become less articulate realistically when called to specify what our sense of "freedom for" might be about, or on what dimensions of our lived experience it might be grounded. We strive for "freedom from" without being able to articulate what a possible world free of exploitation and oppression could feasibly look like (let alone how to move toward it). Freedom is significant to us, but only under conditions of negativity.[229] Another way to consider this is that we can easily say what freedoms are, in localized contexts and in the plural, but become confused when challenged to define freedom itself.

Why might this be? In North Atlantic philosophy, the notion of freedom has been articulated in two modalities, the separation of which became disconcertingly evident in the course of the 20th century. The first of these concerns the putative free-will of the subject, the ability of the "I-know-is" to imagine that it governs its next cognitive production ("I know I am free because I will choose my next thought and stipulate what I mean by it," thus spoke Humpty Dumpty). In such philosophy, the apparent prerogatives of the thinking subject reigned, for example from Descartes to Husserl. It is compelling, even if philosophically of limited value, to feel that one might harbor, without compulsion or constraint, one's own private thoughts, even while imprisoned, even while tortured, or even as one sees the gas extruding from the chamber's ceiling. Historically, in Western scholarship, the authority of the "I-know-is" was peculiarly buttressed by the ascendance of empiricist and logical-analytic epistemologies, insofar as they issue into scientific practices with the power to counter dogma and our indoctrination into belief systems deemed to be irrational. Thus, the "freedom" of the subject, within the limits of its rational governance—its obedience to determinacy and necessity—remained inviolable throughout the modern era—which is to say, from 15th-century Europe to the end of the 20th century. But clearly, in the past hundred years, the metaphysical supremacy of the subject has crumbled. Philosophy has reached the limit of the ontology of subjectivity, and this crumbling has much to do with the advent of psychoanalysis. The thinking subject is now shown to be subjected to structures over which it has no authority. For example, there are ideological forces that secure the reproduction of oppressive social conditions and that limit our capacity to think outside their parameters; there are cognitive-affective programs or procedures that are nonconscious; there are deep linguistic structures of transformation that are recondite, and so forth. The science of psychic life has to let go the dream of an ontology of a substance or quasi-substance. Rather, it has to be processive and relational, as is required by the mythematics of libidinality. Moreover, as the 20th century progressed, it also became clear—again in large measure due to the advent of psychoanalysis—that the dichotomy of rational and irrational procedures is no longer as secure, or as ideologically unfettered, as previously imagined.

The development of Western discourse on the philosophical freedom of free will—a discourse which has now almost entirely expended itself—occurred quite separately from that of the second modality of thinking about freedom, which addresses the moral–legal–political sphere. It is surely significant that John Stuart Mill's seminal 1859 text, *On Liberty*, which continues to inform liberal and neoliberal notions of freedom, announces from the start that free will cannot be discussed, only civil liberties; Mill was, of course, influenced by David Hume's dismissal of freedom as an indefensibly theological notion (in the 1748 *Enquiry Concerning Human Understanding*). To condense history grossly, we might assert that the liberal and neoliberal notions of moral, legal, and political freedoms culminate, exactly two hundred years after Hume, in the 1948 *Universal Declaration of Human Rights*, with all its subsequent codicils and covenants. The significance of this document cannot be overestimated, if for no other reason that it stands as the only discourse claiming universal applicability, other than those of the various fundamentalisms that currently compete for the governance of the world stage of global capitalism—evangelical Islam, evangelical Christianity, American Imperialism, the proclamations of various commissars, the politburos, the Chinese state council, and so forth.

Perhaps we must accept that, in the moral–legal–political sphere, we cannot specify how a utopian state of freedom could operate as a practical system of sociocultural arrangements; we do not know what it would be like to live free-associatively in terms of this public sphere.[230] However, we can know the characteristics of systems of domination, exploitation, and oppression. So the apparent choice of our action is to support those discourses that are anti-patriarchal, anti-capitalist, anti-colonial, anti-imperialist, anti-sexist, and anti-racist—wherever they appear.

There is a parallel in our private domain. We now know that the discourse of our thinking, feeling, and acting can never be free in the sense of lacking determinants. The possibilities of ordinary discourse—conversationally and narratologically—are tightly determined by the law and order of the representational system, in order for this mode of communication to make sense. However, free-associative discourse transgresses the rules and regulations of ordinary sense-making, and in this respect it is, so to speak, less tightly controlled systemically (but controlled nevertheless). Thus, free-associative discourse both is and is not determined by the law and order of representationality. The happenstances of the copula that transforms one instance of thinking and feeling into the next may be capricious but are never aleatory in that they are necessarily regulated by the law and order of representationality. Ordinary discourse permits little disruption of this sequencing by which matters make sense. It is, so to speak, tightly governed by repetition-compulsivity that keeps the subject locked in stases of alienation. But the praxis of free-associative discourse libidinizes the copula, ethically opening discourse to the voicing of the untranslatable, that which is otherwise than representationality.

In this process of freeing, self-consciousness remains estranged from itself, but is no longer so firmly bound to repetition-compulsivity.

Free-association is thus a process of freeing, but is not to be understood as arriving at some definitive state of freedom. The interrogation of self-consciousness entailed by this method does not eventuate in a utopian dream, but rather comprises a deconstruction of the system and structures of censorship in the here-and-now. In sum, what psychoanalytic experience teaches is that it is futile to hope for freedom. But it is profoundly significant to commit ourselves existentially to the process of freeing. This is the essential act of healing that unleashes the truthfulness of the human subject-in-process, against the ideological constitution of the world.

The subject-in-process: Relationships, embodied desire, and death

The journey of psychoanalysis is to surrender to the truthfulness of the subject-in-process and thus indeed to come to enjoy—to find the joy in—the strangeness of ourselves to ourselves. This alleviates our alienation in the repetition-compulsivity of a representational system that can only allow meaningfulness to be inscribed as texts that are merely the other of the apparently authorial one. The psychoanalytic method exposes and sets-in-motion the subject-in-process. In so doing, it finds the authorial "I" to be empty, forever deferred and displaced from itself, despite its identitarian appearances. Thus, in every private moment of its flow, the free-associative method of psychoanalysis demonstrates the perpetual decentering of self-consciousness, which can only be theoretically or conceptually recentered by abandoning the scientificity of this method in favor of ideological embellishments (scientistic, theological, or blatantly politic). This is the troubling revelation of Freud's Copernican revolution. It is his unwelcome discovery that only free-associative praxis invites the voicing of that which is otherwise—that which cannot be translated into the law and order of representationality—and thus the journey of free-associative praxis is the uniquely scientific and healing interrogation of our psychic life. In this respect, three "topics" are regularly traversed in every psychoanalytic journey: Relationships, embodied desire, and death.

In every psychoanalysis, there is, of course, endless talk about relationships. Patients necessarily chatter about their relations with various aspects of their selves, other people, things, and ideas—both as external actualities and as internal representations. Of crucial significance in this talk is the effect of transference and countertransference interventions that prompt the deconstruction of these configurations of relating to self and others that are repetitiously patterned (preconsciously or unconsciously in the descriptive sense). To a certain extent, this is a dialogic dimension of the treatment. However, the free-associative method opens the patient's discourse beyond that which can be accommodated by dialogue (for which the negotiation of meaningful agreement is always held to be a realizable and beneficial goal). It opens the subject to a more radical realization of the otherness of the other—an other that cannot be assimilated to the "for me." It is thus a journey in which patients take ethical responsibility in relation to the manner in which they "face" the radical otherness of the other. That is, the method opens the subject to become passionately engaged with the unknown and potentially unknowable differences presented by the other with whom the patient is, so to speak, "face-to-face" (even if on the couch). This involves processes that have been so valuably discussed by Levinas. In this way, the journey moves the patient behind, beneath, or beyond the common mode of functioning in which every other is treated in terms of the "for me." This is the ethicality of the—figurative—caress that is, sooner or later, shared between the patient and the psychoanalyst. The caress is the realization of a genuine, albeit asymmetrical, encounter of the self with unknown and possibly unknowable otherness. Often, perhaps rather misleadingly, this has been called the "resolution" or "dissolution of the transference."[231] It must be emphasized again here that the caress does not compensate or correct and, most importantly, no longer insists on assimilating the other to the self-owned system of representations. Rather, it allows the suffering of a different mode of difference—*différance*—to free itself by opening itself to the otherness of this profoundly other mode of meaningfulness.

Could this opening to the other be achieved by any method apart from free-association? It seems unlikely, almost certainly impossible. When therapy—that is, a treatment not existentially committed to the ongoing pursuit of free-associative discourse—transforms the patient's relationships into those that are, by some criteria, "better," it usually does so by providing the individual's self (to use just one term) with seemingly new experiences and apparently valuable insights into the patterns by which he or she treats self and others. Thus, we are all familiar with patients who emerge from a successful therapy knowing that, for example, "I am treating (and/or avoiding treating) John like my father" or "I enjoy (and/or flee from) Mary's mothering me" or "My envy of the Jones family prompts me to want to help them out (and/or enjoy their misfortunes)" or similar useful instances of "psychological mindedness." But, however sophisticated such insights might seem, this is not psychoanalysis (or rather, it is "psychoanalysis" that aborts the commitment to free-associative praxis, and thus goes no further than therapy). In contrast with these stases of a successful therapeutic conclusion, free-associative discourse ultimately requires the subject to go beyond the application of supposedly more "adaptive" or "mature" patterns of relationship. The method, as an ongoing deconstructive momentum, eventually faces the patient with an other otherness—the radical plurality of the unknown, of an otherwise other that cannot be translated into the familiar patterns of representational relationship. This otherness operates behind, beneath, or beyond the purview of dialogue, touching as it does on the untranslatable repressed that is within each of us. This untranslatable unknown demands Love and not just the love-and-hate that sustains common discourse and ordinary relationships.

What free-associative praxis touches, by opening our discourse to its voicing, is *within but behind, beneath, beyond*, or "through yet against" the theatre of representationality—the extraordinary force of Love, erotic embodiment, and deathfulness.[232] Following Freud, we have named this psychic energy, libidinality. Palpable yet ineffable, we might have called it *spirit*, if there were not sound reasons to avoid this term.[233] The palpability testifies to the erotic embodiment of libidinality as desire; the ineffability intimates how such desire always overflows, exuberantly and ecstatically, our ego organization's striving to capture it representationally. What else can these enigmatic prepositions (*within yet behind*, and so forth) possibly or impossibly entail or portend? Why should "I" be concerned to become acquainted with a meaningfulness of my being that can never be fully translated into the language of "making sense"? Surely the answer is—if an answer is feasible—because the embodied and erotic otherwiseness of libidinality shows itself, via psychoanalytic praxis, to be the source of both our suffering and of our joy. The psychoanalytic method reveals libidinality as the essential gift to our humanity. It is a gifting that comes from an otherwise or unfathomable "elsewhere" (neither a creation of the subject, nor a phenomenon of the object or of the ascertainably material world). It comes bearing past–future temporalities that defy the structured chronological or narratological time of our personal and collective identities. It comes as the sensuality of impulses that occurs as movements of pure expenditure.[234]

Against repetition-compulsivity, the method of free-association libidinizes the copula (the transformation from one formation of thinking and feeling into the next). That is, it opens thinking and feeling to the libidinal energies that animate the successive transformations of thought and feeling. In short, the method "keeps thinking erotic"—it divulges the erotic sources of self-consciousness.[235] Sooner or later, free association reverts to our embodied experience, empowering us to listen to the voicing of what Freud called "thing-presentations" that cannot be represented, the unfathomable passages that connect us to the unknown and unknowable.[236] That is, if an ongoing commitment to free-associative praxis is maintained, thinking and feeling not only become more evidently libidinized, but the operations of self-consciousness move toward their own "unplumbable navel."

Thus, despite—or rather, it should be insisted, because of—the strictures of abstinence, which are essential to any engagement in a psychoanalytic process, the encounter between the patient and the psychoanalyst is profoundly erotic for both participants. Without any of the physicality of touching, it is nevertheless a pervasively and profoundly embodied experience. Opening discourse to the libidinality within the ego organization's structures and transformations of structure, the free-associative process appears to "make thinking erotic"—but more precisely, it discloses or unmasks the erotic nature of our thinking and feeling that is always already there. The method divulges the erotic basis of being human. Thus, to become aware of the gifting of libidinality is not equivalent to the accrual of insights, but is an opening to the meaningfulness of that which is otherwise—the meaningfulness of the energies, the "thing-presentations," by which desire moves within us. This is surely why it is reported that Freud emphasized to the practitioners in the Vienna Psychoanalytic Society that the effect of their labors is "to follow the libido into its hideouts."[237] Psychoanalysis takes the patient beyond all the permutations of relationships between self and other, empowering the patient to listen—in a manner that the free-associative method effects singularly—to the voicing of his or her erotic embodiment.

Being an issue of pure expenditure, this voicing—the kinesis of libidinality within us—is a matter of life and death. As Laplanche has indicated, Freud's speculations of 1920 must be read not as the promulgation of additional notions of "drive" or *Triebe* (*Lebenstrieb* versus *Todestrieb*), but rather as the recognition that libidinality moves under two principles. The principle of "lifefulness" (as I believe it should be called) indicates the movement by which libidinal energes attach themselves to representations (the moment of a binding of energy), whereas the principle of "deathfulness" indicates the movement by which libidinal energies detach themselves from representions (the moment of unbinding, which Freud understood as analogous to dissipative effects of entropy). Under the principle of "lifefulness," libidinality is creative, but only under the constraints of the law and order of representationality. Under the principle of "deathfulness," libidinality is "destructive" in the dissolutive, rather than the active-aggressive, sense, opening the way for a more anarchic mode of creativity.[238]

The operation of these principles can be understood in the following way. Every representational act of establishment—the instantiation of a thought or feeling in consciousness—involves simultaneously a moment of both presencing and unpresencing or absencing, the inherent lifefulness and deathfulness of our being-in-the-world. As mentioned previously, it is the force of libidinality that sponsors our lived experiences of presence and absence, by binding and unbinding itself in relation to representational formations. The capacity to open self-consciousness to what is otherwise than the repetitious transformations of textuality inheres to the momentum of unbinding (which is invariably accompanied by yet another rebinding). The secret of free-associative movement against repetition-compulsivity thus lies in the "destruction" of our ego organization's foundational *modus operandi*, its commitment to the repetitiousness of binding. This movement entails the deconstruction of the ego organization's rigidity, its imprisonment in the compulsive operations of repetition. Thus, the liveliness of life is implicated by these principles of libidinal momentum—principles of lifefulness and deathfulness that, in and of themselves, will never be divulged to the subject, but to which the "I" of self-consciousness is ineluctably subjected.

In this way, free-association facilitates for the subject an intimation of a profound paradox that is at the heart of our human condition: The life of the subject, as a locus of representational enunciation and exchange, is secured by repetition-compulsivity, but the liveliness of this life comes from its readiness, so to speak, to cast itself into the deathfulness that inheres to every representational formation and thus to face the unfathomable within us. The praxis of free-association is that of deathfulness; it leads the subject to face the abyss that is within.

The effects of the free-associative method are not on the side of interpretation and the arrival at representational meanings (which is the preponderant goal of therapeutic maneuvering), but rather on the side of unbinding and the opening of discourse to the voicing of what is otherwise than representation.[239] It will be remembered how emphatic Freud was in asserting that his discipline is not a synthesis, neither an integration nor the aspiration toward a spurious harmony, but rather *analysis*. His method veers toward undoing, decomposing, deconstituting. In his essay on resistance, Derrida points out that Freud cannot mean *analysis* in the common logical sense, but rather in an etymological sense that embraces two motifs: The *archeological–analogical* as a momentum that appears to turn or return toward the arche–originary (toward the animative but unfathomable navel), and the *philolytic* as a movement of dissociation or unbinding (a momentum that is *an-archic*).[240]

Although unbinding may always be followed by rebinding, to focus on the idea that there can be no analysis without synthesis misses the crucial character of Freud's discovery. As he indicated, the ethical responsibility of his discipline is *analytic*, and it is not for the practitioner of psychoanalysis to prescribe ideologies of synthesis and integration. In this sense, psychoanalysis is hyperbolic, outrageously committed to the ethicality of deconstruction and never to any moralizing ideology of construction. This emphasis on unbinding—on the deconstructive momentum of the psychoanalytic method—is both healing and scientific, precisely because it is linked to the reality that our psyche is both pluritemporal and polysexual, which is the reality that psychoanalytic praxis itself discovers. Derrida suggests how the character of deconstruction takes psychoanalysis beyond the transcendental or schematic commitments of philosophy—behind, beneath, or beyond any speculative theorizing or conceptual systematization—and thus beyond the great formulations of the Western lineage, inscribed in the writings of Kant, Hegel, Husserl, and Heidegger.

If this commitment to life through the embrace of deathfulness in the unbinding momentum of free-associative discourse—the negativity of *mokṣa* or *nirvāṇa*—does it not "make sense" that our ego organization would resist its momentum? Does it not "make sense" that the "I" would prefer instead to refuse the existential commitment to the addressing of suffering that it has itself determined, in order to devote itself to the ideological devices of recentering (exemplified by speculation, systematization, and the wiles of palliation)? The history of psychoanalysis has charted, all too stridently, the course of Ptolemaist revisioning—desperately attempting to recenter the subject against the unwelcome discovery of free-associative praxis as the process that reveals troublingly the perpetually dynamic decentering of human self-consciousness. Against the comforting falsity of the ideologies of centration, psychoanalysis pursues a processive freeing of the truthfulness of our being-in-the-world.

To commit existentially to the method of free-association is to jump erotically into Heraclitus' river, the liveliness of life itself, without clinging to the banks of interpretive rectitude. Swimming, floating, cascading in this river, free-associative praxis embraces the inherent deathfulness of the subject of self-consciousness—the *mysterium tremendum* at the heart of our being-in-the-world. This process of embracing, which follows from the caress of the radical otherness of the other, resonates deeply within our erotic embodiment in all its otherwiseness, its pluritemporality and polysexuality. It thus comprises a freeing of the truthfulness of human self-consciousness as our dynamically nonidentical, interminably contradictorious, and inherently erotic subject-in-process.

Many will say that this book—a manifesto for radical psychoanalysis—sets psychoanalysis back a hundred years. To this I respond that it is an effort to help us rethink the essentials of a discipline that has, despite all its alleged advances, gone astray. Against the ideological recenterings of the human psyche that are the common motive of the alleged "advances" that have been made since 1914, psychoanalysis must stand by the method of free-associative praxis, for this is the key to its scientificity, its truthfulness, and its potential as a liberatory healing the human condition.

NOTES

1 There is no question that, in the past hundred years, Freud's praxis of free association has been marginalized or suppressed by the mainstream "psychoanalytic" community. In this book, I survey this aspect of the discipline's history only indirectly, and shall not engage in a comprehensive review of the relevant literature. Rather, the book's intent is to vigorously counter this marginalization or suppression in a comparatively novel manner. Suffice it to indicate here how much I appreciate the writings of those who have attempted to restore this method to its rightful place as the *sine qua non* of psychoanalysis. Here I must mention, perhaps foremost, Christopher Bollas's important writings—especially his 2002 *Free-Association*, his 2007 *The Freudian Moment*, his 2009 *The Evocative Object World*, and his 2009 *The Infinite Question*. This is not to imply unqualified agreement with his perspectives (a *homage* that he himself would, I believe, not wish for). However, more than any living writer whose work I know, Bollas has consistently, explicitly and lyrically presented the case for the unique significance of free association. My appreciation for the writings of André Green and Jean Laplanche is evident from my dedication of this book. In addition, special mention should be expressed for the books authored by Anton Kris in 1996 and Marita Torsti-Hagman in 2003. Jean-Luc Donnet's 2005 *The Analyzing Situation* has also made a landmark contribution, as have several other French authors in a post-Lacanian vein. I apologize if this tribute omits other contributions of which I am either unfamiliar or have erroneously failed to mention.

2 Most obviously, this text is the sequel to my 2013 book, *What is Psychoanalysis?* It also amplifies and modifies some of the ideas initially presented in my 1984 *Psychic Reality and Psychoanalytic Knowing* and my 1993 *Psychoanalysis and the Postmodern Impulse: Knowing and Being since Freud's Psychology*. This is not to discount the relevance of intervening publications on meditation, sexuality, and somatic psychology. Throughout this book, I will use the term "self-consciousness" to denote the reflectivity of consciousness. That is, so to speak, the consciousness of being conscious—the "I think" or "I feel" that knows it is thinking and feeling, even if its reflections on its own thoughts and feelings are, in a sense, a matter of dream and delusion. This usage more or less corresponds, I believe, to Gerald Edelman's concept of "secondary" or reflective consciousness, which is counterposed to "primary" consciousness (in his writings from the 1987 *Neural Darwinism* to the 2006 *Second Nature: Brain Science and Human Knowledge*). Primary consciousness denotes the wakefulness which characterizes the neural system of many subhuman species (and in this sense, as Mark Solms has suggested, in his 2013 paper,

Freud's "id" is conscious). I adopt the term "lived experience" to cover the adventures of self-consciousness, and I take psychoanalysis to be the healing science of lived experience. Lived experience is the subject matter of free-associative praxis, but cannot be said to be its "subject," since lived experience is crafted from forces that are otherwise than the apparently authorial "I"—this is the central discovery of Freud's Copernican revolution.

3 This appraisal is from his 1931 "Preface to the Third (Revised) English Edition" of *The Interpretation of Dreams*.

4 This is the wellspring of nostalgia as it has affected the discipline of psychoanalysis. A rudimentary discussion of this was offered in my 1995 polemic on the future of psychoanalysis.

5 See my 2015 paper on this topic.

6 As will become evident, this book moves against the current vogue for "phenomenological psychoanalysis." This trend is exemplified by writings such as Gunnar Karlsson's recent text, *Psychoanalysis in a New Light*, which is most interesting. It is preceded by a range of efforts (distinct from Binswanger's *Daseinanalyse*), including investigations by eminent researchers such as Eugène Minkowski and Henri Ey. Contemporarily, George Atwood and Robert Stolorow continue to advocate for a certain sort of "phenomenological" or intersubjective approach to psychoanalysis.

7 Georg Groddeck's 1923 *The Book of the It* indeed offers a valuable "take" on the experience of self-consciousness as invaded by a foreign intruder. I follow Laplanche's opinion that it is curious how Freud adopted (and acknowledged) Groddeck's term in his 1923 *Das Ich und das Es*, even while deviating from Groddeck's emphasis on foreign intrusion (the "It" as the interior nonidenticality of the "I"), by conceptualizing the "Es" ("It" or "Id" in its Latinized and technized translation in the *Standard Edition*) as the biological center of psychic life that is more or less exterior to the "ego organization." It should be noted here that Freud's 1933 slogan, *Wo Es War, Soll Ich Werden* ("Where It was, should I become"), which the Strachey translation renders tendentiously as "Where Id Was, There Ego Shall Be," was preceded by Groddeck's 1923 fomula, *Wir werden von unserem Es gelebt* ("We are lived by our It"), which drew from Nietzsche's *It thinks me*.

8 As has been my custom in earlier writings (for example, on meditation), I capitalize "Love" to distinguish it from the common usage of "love," which denotes certain forms of affectionate attachment. In this book, capitalized Love intimates a momentum that can be tied to the mythematic reality of libidinality. This is the Love to which the notion of *Ahimsa* alludes, at least in the expanded sense of praxis as developed by Mohandas Gandhi among many others.

9 The idea of casting oneself into the fire—with the accompanying notion that one will thereby be reworked, remolded, and recast by the Holy Spirit—is familiar across many traditions of mystical writing, perhaps most notably in Sufism. The allusions are deliberate here, for there is something about the psychoanalytic trajectory, as a surrendering of the certainties and securities of self-consciousness to the flow of free-associative discourse, that intimates a mystical process. This will be discussed further in what follows.

10 Keats's notion is well discussed in Li Ou's *Keats and Negative Capability*. Most strikingly, in his letter of 21 December 1817, Keats describes this as requiring an individual to be "capable of being in uncertainties, mysteries, doubts, without any irritable reaching after fact and reason." This notion of a sort of anti-foundational openness is, I believe, crucial to understanding the distinctiveness of psychoanalysis—and its differentiation from therapeutics. Importantly, this opinion is shared by Wilfred Bion in his indispensable texts.

11 Notably, this "still small voice of calm" (the hymnal riff given by John Greenleaf Whittier in 1872 to the phrase from the Third Book of Kings) was a call to passionate action. However, in this context, passionate action would include both contemplative retreat and what Heidegger would have called the *Destruktion* of idols. It might be noted that

Bollas writes of psychoanalysis as a mode of meditation, whereas I tend to think that contemplation might be the more accurate term.

12 Much of what follows owes to the writings of Louis Breger, Henri Ellenberger, Peter Gay, Eric Kandel, Darian Leader, Adam Phillips, Carl Schorske, Samuel Weber, and Eli Zaretsky.

13 Jones's three-volume text has, of course, achieved the status of being the "official biography," which is in many ways regrettable. Jones can well be supplemented, if not entirely supplanted, not only by Ellenberger and Breger, but also by works such as Adam Phillips's *Becoming Freud.* George Makari's *Revolution in Mind* and *Questions for Freud* by Nicholas Rand and Maria Torok also offer some useful perspectives. Mikkel Borch-Jacobsen and Sonu Shamdasani's 2012 *Freud Files* raises some critical issues which cannot be overlooked (as does Borch-Jacobsen's earlier work, *The Freudian Subject*).

14 The extensive debates and controversies surrounding and succeeding Foucauldian discourse analysis and his genealogical methods need not be detailed here. At this juncture, I will merely deploy the term "masterdiscourse," drawing loosely, but in a way that serves this book, from Foucault's *The Order of Things* and his subsequent *The Archaeology of Knowledge*, as well as from notions of hegemony derived from the writings of Antonio Gramsci.

15 The influential philosopher, Karl Löwith, in his *From Hegel to Nietzsche*, judges Kierkegaard and Marx as Hegel's two great successors and his assessment of Nietzsche is especially interesting in this context. Jon Mills' 2002 book provides an outstanding study of Hegel's "anticipation" of psychoanalysis.

16 Much of my understanding of Kierkegaard's response to the Hegelian apotheosis of what he called "Thought," owes to Mark Taylor's excellent texts. John Mullen's emphasis on the role of self-deception and cowardice in Kierkegaard's philosophy is also interesting.

17 It should be noted that Freud never references Kierkegaard in his published writings. In a letter to Abraham, dated 31 October 1914, he does mention Jaspers (misspelling the name as "Jasper"), who at that time was a junior member of the philosophy department at the University of Heidelberg (having graduated its medical school in 1908); the tone is disparaging as Freud complains that Binswanger "makes too much of Jasper." Freud's later letter to Binswanger, dated 20 August 1917, while not mentioning any philosophical works in particular, seems testily challenging. It contains the memorable lines: "I am uneasy about one thing. What are you proposing to do about the unconscious, or rather, how will you manage without the unconscious? Has the philosophical devil finally got you in his clutches? Reassure me."

18 This is not to slight some of the excellent scholarship of the so-called "Freudo–Marxist" literature with which this book is aligned. Victor Wolfenstein's *Psychoanalytic-Marxism* provides one of the better surveys of this field, in which there is a quite extensive literature.

19 This somewhat ambiguous attitude toward Nietzsche is also well exemplified by Freud's letter to Lothar Bickel of 28 June 1931 (cited in Gay's *Freud: A Life for our Time*), in which he writes: "Hence I have rejected the study of Nietzsche although—no, because—it was plain that I would find insights in him very similar to psychoanalytic ones."

20 Andreas-Salomé's 1894 study of Nietzsche is still most interesting. See also the most helpful discussions in Daniel Chappelle's *Nietzsche and Psychoanalysis*, Ronald Lehrer's *Nietszche's Presence in Freud's Life and Thought*, and Wolfenstein's *Inside/Outside Nietzsche.* It might be noted that Richard Sterba reports that Freud once remarked, in one of his private Wednesday meetings, "he who wants to be original as a psychoanalyst should not have read Nietzsche." Sterba concludes that "many of Freud's psychological findings had been expressed in an *aperçu* form in Nietzsche's writings."

21 This is Kandel's summation in his excellent *The Age of Insight.*

22 In his 2012 essay, Georg Northoff offers a rather different taxonomy of perspectives on the unconscious, but one which—in line with the writings of most "neuro-

psychoanalysts"—significantly understates the significance of Freud's unconscious as a discovery of the constitution of self-consciousness as repressive. See also Northoff's *Neuropsychoanalysis in Practice.*

23 "Consilience" seems to be the battlecry of the current vogue for "neuropsychoanalysis," as exemplified by the journal of that title and by seminal texts such as those by Solms and Colin Turnbull.

24 Some of these issues are discussed by the contributors to José Carlos Calich and Helmut Hinz's 2007 anthology.

25 It can readily be demonstrated that Freud was markedly confused and ambivalent about the relevance of neuroscience to psychoanalysis. As is well known, prior to the writing of his 1895 "psychology for neurologists" (which he abandoned as soon as he had completed it), Freud published over two hundred neurological papers (Freud, 1877–1895). For the subsequent four decades, he is quite ambiguous about the relationship—actual or potential—between psychoanalytic discourse and the investigation of brain activity. For example, in 1914, he recommended that we "remember that all our preliminary formulations about psychological events will one day be based on [*auf den Boden*] organic transformations," which is a comparatively weak claim in that it does not necessarily imply that knowledge of organic events could or should take prescriptive priority over psychoanalytic praxis. However, six years later, he argued that "shortcomings in our description would probably disappear if, instead of psychological terms, we could use physiological or chemical ones," which is a far stronger claim, implying that physical explanations should take prescriptive priority over, and might eventually replace, psychological ones (thus, his metapsychology would dissolve into neuroscience). However, yet another six years later, in 1926, he appears to reverse his position by arguing that the material construction of the mental apparatus (*aus welchem Material er gebaut ist*) "is not a subject of psychological interest—psychology can be as indifferent to it as, for instance, optics can be to the question of whether the walls of the telescope are made of metal or cardboard," which elaborates his 1915 discussion of the explanatory *hiatus* between psychology and biology. All these considerations will need to be rethought in terms of the mythematic reality of libidinality, as discussed in this book (and in my 2015 paper).

26 Just as Freud was inclined to credit Nietzsche and Schitzler with anticipating, or discovering by other methods, the findings of psychoanalysis, he was also inclined to discern psychoanalytic themes in the classic literature. Ellenberger notes how Freud referred to the Greek tragedians and Shakespeare as his "masters," and indeed he quoted them frequently in his writings. The philosopher Giovanni Papini reports that Freud said to him: "In psychoanalysis you may find fused together though changed into scientific jargon, the three greatest literary schools of the 19th century: Heine, Zola and Mallarmé and united in me under the patronage of my old master, Goethe."

27 In his essay on Freud's Vienna, Bruno Bettelheim offers some interesting observations about the extent and quality of preoccupations with death that characterized Freud's environment, as well as the way in which ideas about the conjunction of death and sexuality were being explored at that time. Jean-Bertrand Pontalis's essay "On Death-Work," in his 1977 *Frontiers in Psychoanalysis*, presents some interesting ideas on this topic.

28 Useful discussions of modernism are provided by Theodor Adorno's *Minima Moralia* and, more recently, by Marshall Berman's *All that is Solid Melts into Air.*

29 Useful discussions of Freud's relationship with Judaism include not only Ellenberger's history, but also the discussions by David Bakan, by Dennis Klein, and by David Meghnagi.

30 There is a substantial literature discussing and critiquing Freud's use of archeological images, and it is perhaps unnecessary here to itemize salient references. In their provocatively excellent, albeit heavily Lacanian, *Knowing Nothing, Staying Stupid*, Dany Nobus and Malcolm Quinn point to some of the more conspicuous difficulties, for example with Freud's 1930 invitation for us to understand psychic entities by imagining

a Rome in which all historical epochs coexist and nothing has disappeared. This feat is, of course, more or less impossible, but perhaps the problematic invitation serves to emphasize to us the extent to which we cannot model thoughts and wishes as existing in space, only in a matrix of multiple temporalities.

31 This memorable phrase is actually part of a more nuanced sentence in a letter dated 25 March 1917 to Karl Abraham (pp. 346–347 of their *Complete Correspondence*). The full sentence reads: "You are right to point out that the enumeration in my last paper is bound to create the impression that I claim my place alongside Copernicus and Darwin. However, I did not wish to relinquish an interesting idea just because of that semblance, and therefore at any rate put Schopenhauer in the foreground." Freud has actually compared his discoveries to those of Copernicus both in his 1917 essay, "A Difficulty in the Path of Psychoanalysis," and in his 1917 *Introductory Lectures*.

32 This is one of the strengths of those—led in the anglophone world by Bollas—who have gone beyond Freud's advocacy of evenly suspended or free-floating attention on the part of the psychoanalyst, in order to argue for the significance of the practitioner's "reveries." Among Bollas's other texts, see 1999 *The Mystery of Things*. Also important in this context are several of the books by Thomas Ogden.

33 What follows is discussed in greater detail in my *Psychoanalysis and the Postmodern Impulse*—I stand by the arguments in that book, despite the perhaps excessively "postmodern optimism" that flavors their presentation.

34 "Analytico-referential" is the term used by Timothy Reiss and seems more or less equivalent to the generic "logical-empiricism" used by Gerard Radnitzky and others to designate "analytic" approaches to knowledge. The relevant label in German is *analytische Wissenschaftstheorie*, covering a range of "analytic" philosophies such as Popperianism, ordinary-language philosophy, formalism, and even pragmatism. For the purposes of this book, analytic-referential incorporates other common descriptors such as positivist, rationalist, and so forth.

35 *Différance* is, of course, Derrida's most famous neologism, in use even before the publication of *Writing and Difference*. See also Gilles Deleuze's *Difference and Repetition*, as well as the work of Alain Badiou and, less recently, Jean Baudrillard. François Laruelle's books are also especially helpful.

36 This quote is from Laplanche's essay "A Short Treatise on the Unconscious." These issues are also presented in his 1981 *Problématiques IV*, his 1987 *New Foundations*, and his 1993 *La Fourvoiement Biologisant de la Sexualité chez Freud* (translated as *The Temptation of Biology*), and the series of essays collected in *Freud and the 'Sexual.'*

37 Laplanche's theory of the "fundamental anthropological situation" is well discussed in his essays in *Freud and the 'Sexual,'* in his 1993 essay, "Seduction, Persecution, Revelation" (in his *Essays on Otherness*), and in his *Seduction, Translation, Drives*. Also interesting in this context is the discussion by Philippe Van Haute and Tomas Geyskens in their *Confusion of Tongues: The Primacy of Sexuality in Freud, Ferenczi, and Laplanche*. Wladimir Granoff's *Lacan, Ferenczi et Freud* also contributes, in a somewhat different vein, to this issue.

38 These processes of imposition or implanting are what Laplanche terms the fundamental anthropological situation—which he, perhaps misleadingly, considers a primary, inevitable, and universal mode of "seduction."

39 Some of the implications of this shift have been discussed in Bettelheim's *Freud and Man's Soul* as well as in my 1984 work, *Psychic Reality and Psychoanalytic Knowing*. The preference of the Strachey translators for technical, scientistic terminology that is more distant from lived experience has, of course, worsened this issue for anglophone readers. See also Darius Ornston's *Translating Freud*.

40 The term "analysand," bequeathed us by Sándor Ferenczi, has gained popularity, but I do not use it. The virtue of the term is indeed that it differentiates psychoanalytic treatments from medical procedures; for in psychoanalysis, the patient is more than fully participatory, whereas in most allopathic treatments he or she is merely the physical object of a manipulative procedure (as I like to quip, the allopathic patient is more or

less a cadaver that happens to be still alive). However, the defect of Ferenczi's neologism is that it encourages a denial of the issue of suffering. Given the derivation from the Latinate root, *patio*, meaning "I suffer," the patient is the one who suffers and this needs to be kept in focus. Psychoanalysis is not an undertaking to be engaged out of intellectual curiosity or merely for the purposes of training. With some slight humor, I would point out that no one "in their right mind" would undertake a sustained commitment to free-associative discourse. We only enter psychoanalysis because we know, or at least sense, that we are suffering and that "all that seems to be the case" is not necessarily so.

41 It may be noted that, writing to Fliess on 14 November 1897 (while in the intensity of his own self-interrogation), Freud himself states that "true self-analysis is impossible." The necessity of the presence of a psychoanalyst is discussed further in Chapter 11.

42 In his 1918 essay "From the history of an infantile neurosis," he had written quite adamantly that "one cannot reproduce the results of a psychoanalytic treatment in a way that is convincing or valid. Exhaustive protocols, recordings or transcripts, do not help at all, and their preparation is ruled out by the nature of the treatment" (this is my translation of: "Es hat sich bekanntlich kein Weg gefunden, um die aus der Analyse resultierende Überzeugung in der Wiedergabe derselben irgendwie unterzubringen. Erschöpfende protokollarische Aufnahmen der Vorgänge in den Analysenstunden würden sicherlich nichts dazu leisten; ihre Anfertigung ist auch durch die Technik der Behandlung ausgeschlossen").

43 The critical challenges of a discipline that is transmitted via a succession of intimate relationships (from Training Analyst to Candidate) need not be elaborated here. Psychoanalysis has been understandably criticized for its commitment to discipleship and the complexities that it entails: oedipal dynamics with the twin issues of identification or disidentification (compliance or rebellion) on the side of the trainee, and narcissism, as well as orthodoxy, on the side of the psychoanalyst. In short, all the problematic renditions of the Hegelian master/slave relationship have plagued the discipline from its earliest days. Surely this must, in some measure, account for the rivalry and rancor that so regularly occurs within and between training institutes, as well as the proclivities toward what can only—in a tragically paradoxical fashion—be termed "psychoanalytic fanaticism," as well as fundamentalism, if not fascism. See, for example, the diversity of discussions by Grosskurth in 1991, Schwartz in 1999, Reeder in 2004, Zaretsky in 2004, Kirsner in 2009, and Robles in 2010. For a discipline that is essentially about a discourse that opens itself to what is other and otherwise, it is remarkable, indeed appalling, how little independent thinking has occurred in the field. Perhaps one should be charitable about this: It must surely be acknowledged that the mandate of critical reflection on one's own theoretical and clinical allegiances is profoundly challenging for at least three reasons. First, these complex processes of identification (counter-identification or disidentification), which inevitably occur in the personal treatment that is indubitably necessary for training, cannot but constitute an obstruction to the development of independent critical thinking in the context of a fully-fledged professional identity, although this should not be, I believe, an insuperable obstacle. Second, the inherent challenge of psychoanalytic—or, for that matter, responsible psychotherapeutic—engagement requires the practitioner not only to tolerate but actually to cultivate authentically a high degree of uncertainty, of not-knowing, and indeed of methodically unknowing that which appears assuredly known. Thus, especially in the beginning phases of a psychoanalytic life, there is an understandable, but regrettable, tendency for practitioners to attach themselves, explicitly and sometimes almost desperately, to a particular theoretical framework that seems to "make sense" of their interactions with the patient; whereas seasoned practitioners, in the later phases of our careers, become all too inclined to imagine that we have "seen cases like this before," which suggests an accumulative reliance on implicit (and therefore uncritically held) theoretical models, as well as a potential constriction of openness to the unique character of each treatment. Third, the practitioner's narcissism also steers him or her

away from questioning, in a necessarily radical manner, the conditions of what we call "healing." It is all too easy for practitioners to slide into the supposition that the healer is already healed, that only the patient needs healing, and that questions concerning the fundamental characteristics of healing can be set aside presumptively. In psychotherapy, the practitioner's expertise may encourage the reassuring notion that he or she is more "developmentally mature" or more "socially adapted" than the patient. Indeed, from a psychotherapeutic standpoint (but not from a psychoanalytic one), this may have some sort of validity. However, unctuous beliefs about maturation and adaptation derail the idiographic labor of freeing the patient psychoanalytically. Rather, they tacitly presume the nature of the social "reality" toward which the patient is to mature adaptively and thus turn treatment into a benign (or not so benign) process of ideological transmission, as is discussed in this book.

44 I coin the term "workplay" to describe the discourse of patient and psychoanalyst. It is hoped that the term conveys the character of psychoanalytic discourse as both playing and working, yet also undermining the distinction. Bollas and others prefer the term "playwork," which I have rejected—without any disrespect for Bollas's fascinating writings—for no better reason than that it connotes, for me, the whimsy of kindergarten rather than the suffering that is at issue in psychoanalysis. However, it is possible that it also indicates a significant difference in emphasis between Bollas and myself. I think some of the ideas at issue here have—at least for me—been influenced by the Russian formalist tradition of cultural and literary criticism, starting perhaps with the writings of Viktor Shklovsky, whose notion of "enstrangement" (*ostranenie*, sometimes translated as "defamiliarization") is discussed in this book with the suggestion that free-associative discourse serves to make the familiar strange and to refuse to allow the alien to be unfamiliar. Also important for psychoanalysis are the writings of Mikhail Bakhtin, not only his ethical decentering of Kantian philosophy in *Toward a Philosophy of the Act*, and his writings on unfinalizability and polyphony—as well as the carnivalesque—but also the critique of Saussurean linguistics, formalism, and structuralism outlined in *Speech Acts and Other Late Essays*.

45 Of central interest in this book, this raises, of course, the question of interpretation: What gets interpreted in a psychoanalytic treatment if not meanings that are "in" the unconscious (and what, if any, is the role of insight in the changes to psychic life that are effected by psychoanalysis)? There are basically five, potentially mixable, approaches to such questions. (1) There is a variety of determinist answers: For example, interpretation serves to recover memories, by lifting amnesia, and thus to reconstruct a narrative that corresponds, somewhat accurately, with the patient's *real* history, thereby allowing the ego organization greater mastery over compulsive repetitiousness. This position implies an "unconscious" that can, by dint of psychoanalytic labors, be represented. (2) By contrast, there is a variety of hermeneutic answers: For example, interpretation serves to establish a coherent narrative by creatively filling in the gaps in memory (being less concerned whether what is remembered "really happened") and thus constructs a history that allows the ego organization to move forward with greater mastery. This position also implies an "unconscious" that could be represented, even if by a sort of double registration. It might be noted here that Freud, at various points, adopts both reconstructive and constructive attitudes toward interpretation. (3) Then there is a diverse collection of answers that pivot less on history and more on either the interpretation of "unconscious phantasies" in the here-and-now of the transference–countertransference engagement or the interpretation of here-and-now events in the intersubjective/interpersonal/relational development of the patient–practitioner dyad. Notoriously, these positions frequently seem to use the term "unconscious" for material that is actually preconscious and thus representable. (4) Another answer, exemplified in the writings of Paul Gray, Fred Busch, and others, is that interpretation should always be directed to an alleviation of the patient's resistances to reflection and self-analysis; for reasons that will be made clear later in this book, I am skeptical of this opinion, and of the notion of the "unconscious" that might be implied by a perspective that seems to assume that "all that

is the case" lies within the purview of the ego organization. (5) The answer to be given paramount attention in this text is that the psychoanalyst's interpretations and noninterpretive interventions serve to diminish or dissolve the patient's resistances to free-associating. As will be discussed, this answer emphasizes the libidinality of "bodilyness" of the free-associative process as an opening to the repressed unconscious—the significance of free-associative discourse as a workplaying along the repression barrier. This will be explained further in subsequent chapters. Useful discussions of some of these issues are to be found in Laplanche's 1993 essay, "Interpretation between Determinism and Hermeneutics," his 1994 sequel, "Psychoanalysis as Anti-Hermeneutics," and elsewhere. It should also be noted that another more sophisticated explanation of the effects of interpretation (coming principally from contemporary French thinking), which could, at a stretch, be considered a variant of the first position, is that an interpretation is a matter of *après coup* (or *Nachträglichkeit*) in that it reorganizes or reforms what has preceded it, and thus perhaps opens the way for further free-associating. On this issue, see, among others, Donnet's *The Analyzing Situation*.

46 As will be discussed in what follows, the "thing-presentation" is an enigmatic message or impulse of meaningfulness that cannot be captured, translated, or transfixed within representationality. It comprises a hidden meaning that always exceeds the arrival at interpretations, and in this manner is untranslatable. Yet the enigmatic and extraordinary energy of "thing-presentations" is itself the force that demands that psychoanalysis moves from one establishment of representational meaning to the next, indicting the supposed adequacy and deconstructing the sufficiency of whatever representational meaning has preceded its momentum. It is thus an embodied trace that resists every interpretive attempt to fixate or finalize its meaning. I touched on this centrally important issue in my 2015 paper for the 49th Congress of the International Psychoanalytic Association in Boston.

47 Preliminary discussions of this material were offered in my 1991 paper "Semiotics and its 'Other,'" and in the 2013 book, *What is Psychoanalysis?*

48 A Chinese and a Jewish gentleman were sitting next to each other on a train journey. They engage in lively conversation, joking and laughing together. Eventually, the Jewish man observes, "You know, it's wonderful how well we're getting along, especially when you consider Pearl Harbor." His new friend retorts, "What do you mean? Pearl Harbor! The Chinese had nothing to do with Pearl Harbor; that was the Japanese." The Jewish man responds, "Chinese, Japanese . . . what's the difference?" There is a pause in the conversation. "You are right, though," muses the Chinese man, "it is remarkable how well we are getting along, especially when you consider the sinking of the *Titanic*." The Jewish guy splutters, "What do you mean? The sinking of the *Titanic*! The Jews had nothing to do with the sinking of the *Titanic*." To this, the other interjects, "Well, you know, Greenberg, Goldberg, Iceberg . . . what's the difference?"

49 A discussion of this material was offered in my 1993 book *Psychoanalysis and the Postmodern Impulse* and is there rendered in somewhat different detail from what is here presented.

50 Much hinges on what I am, provisionally, calling the "as if" quality of this "root proposition." It may be noted that this echoes Freud's interest in Hans Vaihinger's 1911 *Philosophie des Als Ob*, which was a neoKantian development of Jeremy Bentham's "theory of fictions" and is often considered an important text on the utility of fictions as well as the human propensity toward self-deception. Bentham's ideas are discussed in Charles K. Ogden's *Bentham's Theory of Fictions* and in Frank Kermode's *The Sense of an Ending*.

51 Although such colloquialisms are inevitable in common clinical parlance, it must quickly be emphasized that the notion of "off/on track" mistakenly implies a singular trajectory of discourse (which is *not* what occurs in psychoanalysis). The term is used here merely to illustrate a certain aspect of the dialectic of deceptions that routinely occurs in the transference and countertransference. Similarly, in acknowledgment of a line of debate stimulated by Edward Glover's paper on "inexact interpretation," it must be questioned in what sense an interpretation can be "correct" or "incorrect."

52 While the idea that psychoanalysis ever involves the decoding of conscious enunciations for some other-than-conscious meaning must be contested, one cannot but recall here Bertram Lewin's 1948 paper in which he argues that phrases such as "I am thinking of nothing" or "I am blank" are frequently to be taken as allusions to the vulva that might appear as if ablated in comparison to the protuberant male genital. Such decodings are often of interest, but must not be mistaken for the method of psychoanalysis.

53 "To stir up the underworld" is Freud's 1927 translation, found in a letter of 30 January 1927 to Werner Achelis, of the phrase, *Acheronta movebo* (more literally "I will move the underworld"). It forms the second phrase of the epigraph to *Die Traumdeutung* (which was completed in 1899 and published early 1900). The full epigraph reads *Flectere si nequeo superos, Acheronta movebo*, which James Strachey translated as: "If I cannot bend the Higher Powers, I will move the Infernal Regions." Freud clearly liked the quotation (as is evident from his correspondence with Fliess), mentioning that he used it under the influence of Ferdinand Lassalle, the socialist–communist philosopher and activist who was Freud's contemporary. The line is given to Juno by Virgil in the *Aeneid*, with which Freud was fully familiar. The Acheron was the infernal river of pain, one of the five rivers of the underworld in Greek mythology, which is described in Homeric poems as the River of Hades. Interestingly, Plato in the *Phaedo* claimed to locate it beneath the earth in desert places (i.e. places desperately in need of water, but deprived of it), flowing in a contrary direction to Oceanus, the greatest river in the world. Aristophanes and Euripides both describe Acheron as a disgusting swamp.

54 See note 45 above.

55 At this juncture, I will suggest that in the everyday workplay engaged together by the patient and the psychoanalyst, several different types of discourse invariably co-occur. A "pure psychoanalysis," involving only free-associative speaking and listening with all the inevitable resistances to this praxis that must be interpretively addressed, is not usually—probably never—feasible. So inevitably, there are also educative and therapeutic procedures—including the formulation of interpretive insights, which I am designating "psychoanalytically informed" or "psychoanalytically oriented" therapy and not psychoanalysis per se. In every psychoanalysis, there are also times of friendly conversation, for whatever else transpires, the patient and the practitioner are embarked on a journey that involves, in the most profound way, a certain sort of friendship. I will return to these issues in later chapters.

56 I am aware that the term "treatment," when applied to psychoanalysis, is controversial in that for many commentators it implies a therapeutic procedure which invariably embarks with goals as to its desired outcome. I will retain the term, but do not accept this implication. Rather, in this book, "treatment" will merely refer to a way of treating whatever phenomena present themselves. The term "method" has similar problematic connotations, which need not be explored in detail here; suffice it to add that the "take" on psychoanalysis advanced in this book is quite aligned with Paul Feyerabend's 1975 and 1978 critique of universal methodological rules (as well as recent writings about nonphilosophy developed by Laruelle). For this reason I decline to refer to free-associative method as a methodology (method-*ology*) since to attribute logic to its method is to deny the powerful way in which psychoanalysis subverts the logic and rhetoric of "making sense."

57 This was addressed in my 2015 paper presented at the 49th Congress of the International Psychoanalytic Association.

58 Freud would have been familiar with William James's *Principles of Psychology* of 1890 (and the "Briefer Course" of 1892), with its discussion of consciousness as movement. It is less clear to me whether he knew James's later essays, such as the 1904 "Does Consciousness Exist?"

59 However, this is not to suggest that the analogy of striptease is entirely irrelevant to the considerations presented in this book, because—as will shortly be discussed—the process of surrendering oneself into the flow of free-associative discourse engages and connects the patient and the psychoanalyst in an essentially erotic momentum. Here

one might recall Roland Barthes's essay on this genre of dance, emphasizing as it does the devices which serve to deflect away from the sexual content of the unveiling. Perhaps more pertinently, one might consider the genre of transvestite striptease, in which the excitement crescendos toward the denouement. As the "woman" progresses toward the removal of her panties, she seems to flirt and tantalize her audience with the question, *Is there or is there not a penis hiding there?* Leaving aside a very necessary critique of the phallocentricity of this question (although it is certainly pertinent to the preoccupations of my female patient), it is evident here how profoundly the "dialectic" (to use a term that is very alive, but perhaps overburdened) or workplay of presence/absence (perhaps better expressed as absence–presence–absence) operates through the concatenation of associations. In a different way, this is clearly pertinent to the preoccupations of my male patient, for whom loss in terms of patricide/filicide (or rejection and abandonment, to use more sanitized terminology) and the tropes of deathfulness are evident.

60 In the 1890s, Freud began with the distinction between "thought-reality" and "external-reality," which continues in the *Interpretation of Dreams* where the former is also referred to as "psychic reality"—a distinction elaborated in the writings of 1913 and 1914. Thus, in his 1914 *History*, Freud writes that "psychic reality (*psychische Realität*) must be taken into account alongside practical reality" (*praktischen Realität*, which in 1916 Jones rather misleadingly translated as "actual reality"). In Freud's 1900 publication, externality is also referred to as "material reality" (a concept elaborated between 1913 and 1919), which in the 1913 *Totem and Taboo* is also called "historical reality" to cover the temporality of factual or material events as contrasted with the pluritemporality of the psyche. In short, the psychic versus material twofold nature of reality is expounded in the period prior to the First World War, the period of praxis, and the material has to refer not only to the external reality of things outside the organism, but also to the reality of neural and other organic or somatic events. Whether the discovery of "drive" implies that a third "register" of reality has to be added to the contrast between material and psychic reality (as will be discussed in Chapter 9).

61 Green, in his interview for Gregorio Kohon's 1999 anthology, *The Dead Mother: The Work of André Green*, expresses it in this way: "In the preconscious you have words and thoughts, but in the unconscious you are not supposed to have words and thoughts, you only have thing-presentations. This is something that for us is very important . . ."

62 Laplanche argues this forcefully—for example, "there are *no ideas in the unconscious*" (*New Foundations for Psychoanalysis*), and it is the "untranslatable that I term the unconscious, untranslatable but endlessly retranslated" (*Seduction, Translation, Drives*). For Green's articulation of this point, see previous note.

63 In this respect, Green's 1974 critique of the way in which Kleinianism routinely confuses the unconscious with the deeply preconscious has merit, and has not, in my opinion, been adequately answered by theorists in this lineage. I discuss this in my recent paper "Seven Questions for Kleinian Psychology."

64 The notion of the narratological imperative was discussed extensively in my *Psychoanalysis and the Postmodern Impulse* (especially pp. 170–175). As will become apparent in the course of this book, I find reading Derrida's writings crucially important for understanding the effects of free-associative praxis on the domain of representationality.

65 Following Ilka Quindeau's outstanding book, *Seduction and Desire: The Psychoanalytic Theory of Sexuality since Freud*, I use drive and desire more or less interchangeably, and will most often now refer to drive-desire.

66 The Lacanians have correctly alerted us to the way in which a certain sort of meaningfulness can become attached to signifiers that might appear irrelevant to the text—psychoanalysis becomes, as has been said, the "discipline of the detail." This sort of apparently capricious attachment has been well discussed by Serge Leclaire, from his participation in the now notorious 1960 Symposium of Bonneval (see Jeffrey Mehlman's *French Freud*) to his 1968 *Psychoanalyzing: On the Order of the Unconscious and the Practice of the Letter*. From his practice, Bollas (in *China on the Mind*) briefly gives the example

of a patient telling a story that involved a shoe, where the "sonic effect of the signifier" was to *shoo*! My example of *bar-bar-bar* or *b-b-b* will be discussed in what follows. However, in the Lacanian perspective, the way in which seemingly irrelevant signifiers come to express a certain sort of meaningfulness seems shorn of its erotic or energetic implication—for example, Leclaire writes that the "erotogenic body" is always a symbolic or represented body. This is an example of the distance between an orthodox Lacanian position and that advanced by Green or Laplanche (and by this book). There is also an interesting question here of other ways of approaching psychoanalytic method, such as those of Donald Winnicott (for example, in *Playing and Reality*), who seems to have favored presentation over representation (the performative aspects of communication over the constative), or Masud Khan (in *The Privacy of the Self*), who favored poetic forms of enunciation. While these may have connections with Lacanian method (as Bollas suggests), and in particular Lacan's way of listening to the detail of the "word" as a sound that may take priority over the sense of the phrase in which it is used, I am skeptical of these connections. In this regard, note my critique, later in this book, of those who erroneously equate free-associative discourse with active imagination or uncensorious story-telling.

67 The connections between death and sexuality, paternity and filicide/patricide have been explored quite extensively, with convincing reference to mythologies (Laius and Oedipus, Abraham and Isaac, Shiva and Ganesha, and, most controversially, God and Yeshua of Nazareth). In relation to the journeys of masculinity, see my 2009 paper on the Ganesha myth, as well as my more recent paper, "Fathering and the Consolidation of Masculinity: Notes on the Paternal Function in Andrey Zvyagintsev's *The Return (2015)*."

68 I do not intend a bad pun, but far more needs to be said (but will be bypassed here) about the oceanic feeling, first designated as such in Romain Rolland's 1927 letter to Freud, and interpreted in Freud's *Civilization and its Discontents* as bliss experienced at the breast. This is well discussed in William Parsons' *The Enigma of the Oceanic Feeling: Revisioning the Psychoanalytic Theory of Mysticism*.

69 This is brilliantly discussed by Derrida in his essay on resistances (in his 1996 *Resistances of Psychoanalysis*). The other works of Derrida that must be consulted in this regard include *Of Grammatology, Dissemination, Glas*, and, of course, *The Postcard*, as well as the later *Archive Fever: A Freudian Impression*.

70 Such matters are recently discussed in, for example, William Meissner's *The Therapeutic Alliance;* Jeremy Safran and Christopher Muran's *Negotiating the Therapeutic Alliance*, and, in a radically different vein, Donnet's *The Analyzing Situation*. Highly influential presentations on this topic have been those by Leo Stone and Ralph Greenson. Despite the tendency of some psychoanalysts to disparage Sándor Ferenczi's contributions (and understandably to have reservations about some of his more ill-advised clinical decisions), his thinking on empathy and activity need to be seriously considered. Especially valuable, in my opinion, is his advocacy of the psychoanalytic relationship as characterized by tenderness and passion (on these issues, the texts by Arnold Rachman, by Martin Stanton, and by André Haynal, are particularly useful, as are Ferenczi's two volumes of *Contributions*). Interpersonal and relational theorists—such as Lewis Aron and others—have done much to remedy the image of a dispassionate or emotionally disengaged practitioner who observes, infers, and ministers to the "data" provided by a speaking "object," the patient. However, the insistence on a "two-person" model of psychoanalytic treatment—as much as it rectifies the model of a white-coated scientist dealing objectivistically with the dehumanized phenomena of the patient—often seems to drift into an equal-and-opposite depiction of dyadic interaction that fails to understand the necessary lopsidedness of psychoanalytic discourse in opening the realm of the repressed. For example, consider Aron's interesting 1996 book, *A Meeting of Minds*, which emphasizes mutuality to the point of missing the significance of lopsidedness.

71 As indicated, Chapter 11 will discuss the role of the psychoanalyst. At this juncture, it needs to be said that many psychoanalysts, in the name of "maintaining boundaries,"

forget the necessity of friendship in the psychoanalytic relationship. The issue of boundaries (along with abstinence, neutrality, and lopsidedness) is indeed essential, but not a reason to forego the importance of friendship. On this issue, see my 2012 paper, "Boundaries and Intimacies: Ethics and the (Re)Performance of "The Law" in Psychoanalysis."

72 My thinking about friendship has been greatly influenced by Derrida's *The Politics of Friendship*. For competent refutations of the longstanding assumptions that a friendship can only be between equals, see essays by Amélie Rorty and Marilyn Friedman. Other useful discussions of friendship are provided by Daniel Hruschka, Mark Vernon, and in Michael Pakaluk's anthology. A useful discussion of the threefold characteristics of freedom, safety, and intimacy is provided by Adam Limentani's *Between Freud and Klein*.

73 This important argument that has been made, for example, by as diverse a group of commentators as Kurt Eissler, Lewis Brandt, Patrick Mahony, Riccardo Steiner, Guy Thompson, Lee Rather, and Axel Hoffer. Also important here are the writings of free association mentioned in note 1 above.

74 "Join in the conversation" (*mitzusprechen*) is the phrase Freud used as early as in his 1893 account of the way in which Frälein Elisabeth von R's painful legs would participate in the treatment discourse. The phrase is used again in 1918 with reference to the Wolfman's bowel movements. Given the nature of the repressed unconscious, as will be shortly elaborated, this openness to bodily expressions during the psychoanalytic session is vitally important. In my 2013 paper, "Free-associating with the Bodymind," I have described ways that I facilitate my own and the patient's capacity to listen to the voicing of our embodied experiences and I will return to this topic in subsequent chapters.

75 I write "some sort of textual analysis" because, of course, there are many ways to undertake such an analysis. The formulation of the "root propositions" in the two examples given in the preceding chapter are comparatively "pure" in that I would argue they are close to the manifest material (in the terminology of recent literature on "technique," these formulations are "experience-near"). However, much of the interpretive insight offered to patients in "psychoanalytically informed" or "psychoanalytically oriented" therapy is—for better or for worse—less "pure." For example, there are three major interpretive grids (for want of a more felicitous expression) by which many therapists listen to their patients and formulate their interpretations. First, the ego psychological or structural-functional therapist, greatly influenced by Robert Wälder's 1930 paper on multiple function, interprets every position in a free-associative chain as the ego organization's compromise formation in relation to the conflicting forces of id, superego, and reality; Scott Dowling's anthology, as well as papers by Sandor Abend, Dale Boesky, Charles Brenner, and Arnold Rothstein (to mention only a few) illustrate this theoretical approach. Second, the contemporary Kleinians use the vicissitudes of transference and countertransference to interpret the patient's "unconscious phantasies" in terms of the shifting between paranoid–schizoid and depressive–reparative positions; this therapeutic technique with its interpretive grid is illustrated by Ron Britton, John Steiner, Irma Brenman Pick, and Isca Salzberger-Wittenberg (again, to mention only a few). Third, today's interpersonal, intersubjective, and relational theories of psychotherapeutic technique interpret by means of a variety of what might loosely be characterized as a "me–you" interpretive grid, which owe less to Martin Buber's 1923 *Ich und Du*, and more to the various writings of Harry Stack Sullivan, infused with contributions from object-relations theory (e.g. William Ronald Fairbairn, Donald Winnicott), self-psychology (e.g. Heinz Kohut, Arnold Goldberg), as well as a notably diverse group of pioneers including Franz Alexander, Thomas French, Erich Fromm, Freda Fromm-Reichman, Karen Horney, René Laforgue, Otto Rank, Harald Schultz-Hencke, and Clara Thompson; contemporary examples of this approach are to be found in the works of Lewis Aron, Darlene Bregman Ehrenberg, Stephen Mitchell, and Paul Wachtel.

76 Heraclitus used the term *logos* for the central and centralizing principle of order and knowledge. Subsequently—for example, as developed by Ludwig Klages in his 1929 *Der Geist als Widersacher der Seele*), it comes to mean "the word" as the supreme ground and center of a system that enables us to know a world—a logocentric metaphysics. It is *the* representation of representationality (like a Platonic ideal form), an irreducibly original object that makes possible for us the presence of the world. Note here how logocentrism privileges presence and identity (absence is not-presence, difference is not-identity). Later, the term *phallocentrism* was coined to indicate the privileging of the masculine in the construction of representational meanings, and thus the difficulty or impossibility of thinking outside masculinist discourse. This is discourse that makes the one hierarchically superior to the other in the structure of binary oppositions (female as not-male and thus subordinate to male, and so forth). This led Derrida to develop the neologism *phallogocentrism*, the phallus as logos. As I have explored elsewhere, the phallus can be considered the primary mark by which meaning (identity versus difference) is created out of formlessness, and it is only "owned by" or *is* the abstract locus of the Symbolic Father. Thus, no actual father figure is the symbolic father, but in our fantasies–phantasies we may make this confusion, just as the penis can be mistaken as indicative of the phallus (an error that seems endemic to psychoanalytic thinking about "phallic" functioning). Importantly, no one "has," or can speak from the locus of, the phallus (none of us can say exactly what we mean, and mean only that), so in relation to this locus we are all—male and female—"castrated." Lacan discusses some of these aspects in his "The Significance of the Phallus" (in his *Écrits*). Unlike actual fathers, the Symbolic Father can neither be killed nor mourned, although "He" is memorialized as the Eternal One ("G") in every synagogue, cathedral, church, and mosque. It is also referenced by every shrine to Shiva's lingam (Shiva being the "god of gods"), which emblematizes the originary mark creating difference out of the formlessness of Shakti's energies, which are not unlike the Platonic *khôra* (in the *Timaeus*) or maternal receptacle that is the milieu of all meaningfulness (in the *Torah*, this is "the unformed void, with darkness over the surface of the deep and a wind from God sweeping over the water"). In relation to psychoanalysis, a primary reference on these issues is Derrida's essay, "Freud and the Scene of Writing," in *Writing and Difference* (as well as *Of Grammatology* and "Plato's Pharmacy" in *Dissemination*). Also important are the provocative discussions by Kristeva, Irigaray, Hélène Cixous and Catherine Clément (*The Newly Born Woman*), as well as by Judith Butler (*Gender Trouble, Bodies that Matter*, and particularly her essay on the "lesbian phallus").

77 See note 66 above.

78 Useful reading on this topic is Laplanche's 1993–2006 essays, "The Temptation of Biology: Freud's Theories of Sexuality with Biologism and Biology," as well as Green's 1973 *The Fabric of Affect in the Psychoanalytic Disourse*, several of the essays in his 1972–1986 *On Private Madness*, and the 1995 *La Causalité Psychique*.

79 It is not my intention to review this literature but, ever since Freud's writing, there have been innumerable studies of the "unconscious" that have nothing to do with the repressiveness of self-consciousness. Many of these claim to have achieved a rapprochement between Freud's psychology and cognitivist experimentation. The 2006 anthology edited by Ran Hassin, James Uleman and John Bargh covers some of the best cognitivist research on this topic with almost no reference to Freud's discoveries or to psychoanalysis in general (although a review on the back cover blithely announces that "the Freudian view of an infantile, primitive unconscious has proved to be far too limited"). An effort at "convergence" between experimentalist investigation and psychoanalytic ideas is better exemplified in the 1996 work by Howard Shevrin and his colleagues. Finally, it must be added that confusion over the notion of the unconscious is egregiously evident within the discipline of psychoanalysis—the term is so often used descriptively. Even within the rigors of Kleinianism, to give a further example, it is unclear whether usage of the term "unconscious phantasy" (see Isaacs's 1948 paper, as well as more contemporary discussions), has much to do with the

repressiveness of self-consciousness. Rather, the case can be made (by Green in 1974, for instance) that Kleinian technique addresses only matters that are deeply preconscious. This is discussed in my recent paper which questions some of the tenets of Kleinian psychology.

80 See note 65 above.

81 The *reality* of libidinality may well be, in some sense, *mythematic* (a term I have adopted specifically to explicate this issue) but is nonetheless essential to our understanding of the human condition. My recent paper (2014), "On the Mythematic Reality of Libidinality as a Subtle Energy System," elaborates this somewhat.

82 In this matter and in relation to the crucial importance of distinguishing the notion of drive from that of instinct, there is surely no more competent exegete of the implications of Freud's discoveries than Laplanche. The binding force of "lifefulness" (*Lebenstrieb*) connotes investment (*Besetzung*) of energy in representations, whereas the unbinding force of "deathfulness" (*Todestrieb*) connotes the disinvestment or dissipation of energy. See note 238 below.

83 Much of what follows was covered in three of my recent papers: (1) "On the Mythematic Reality of Libidinality as a Subtle Energy System: Notes on Vitalism, Mechanism, and Emergence in Psychoanalytic Thinking"; (2) "A Practitioner's Notes on Free-Associative Method as Existential Praxis"; and (3) "Critical Notes on the Neuro-Evolutionary Archeology of Affective Systems."

84 I write that it is the *ostensible* reason because there seems strong reason to believe that it is an aspect of the general resistance to free-associative praxis. This will be discussed in Chapter 12. It is, of course, also an aspect of the prevailing ideology that insists that, for a discourse to be scientific, it must be objectivistic (in the manner of logical–empiricist or positivist–naturalistic investigations).

85 As Laplanche put it in his 2001 essay "Countercurrent" (published in *Freud and the 'Sexual'*), the method of psychoanalysis (he writes "rationality within psychoanalysis") has "nothing to learn from the sciences of physical nature." This is not to say that Laplanche thinks psychoanalysis has anything to learn from the "sciences of human nature," as is evident from his 1994 essay "Psychoanalysis as anti-hermeneutics." Earlier in the same essay (and already partially quoted in my text), Laplanche writes that "psychoanalysis is first of all an absolutely new exploratory procedure, which reveals a *domain of being* (the 'processes of the soul') to which barely anything else gave access . . . Freud's *invention* is thus the invention of a method; his *discovery* is the unconscious—real, separate, and not immanent within the conscious." As should be clear, I am strongly in alignment with this viewpoint, with the intent of understanding what it might mean to explore a "domain of being" that is neither that of representationality, nor that of neural circuitry. This will be discussed further in what follows.

86 Karlsson's 2004 *Psychoanalysis in a New Light* is one of the best recent critiques of neuropsychoanalytic enterprise, although there remains more to be said given the escalating fashion for the alleged consilience between psychoanalysis and neuroscience. My main issue of criticsm with this enterprise is the reckless way in which issues of translatability (or nontranslatability) between modes of discourse is typically treated, and also the regular tendency to collapse the notion of drive-desire into concepts of biological mechanism (neural circuitry, innate reflexes, hormonal effusions, and other neurophysiological phenomena). Some of these issues are taken up in my—sadly rather unproductive—debate with Solms in a 2015 issue of *Psychoanalytic Review*.

87 To suggest that psychic energy or libidinality are mythematic notions-for-praxis might seem to be a denial of their reality, but this is not the case, as I explain in what follows. Although differing from Laplanche in my use of the terminology of myth, I am substantially in agreement with him when, in *Seduction, Translation, Drives*, he writes that "the drive is therefore neither a mythical entity, nor a biological force, nor a borderline concept. It is the impact on the individual and on the ego (*le moi*) of the constant internal stimulation exercised by the repressed thing-(re)presentations" (italics omitted).

88 See Kolakowski's 1972 essay *The Presence of Myth* for a competent exposition of a theme that has been multiply explored.
89 Examples of this are to be found in Damasio's 2000 and 2013 books, as well as LeDoux's 2003 text. Catherine Malabou, in her *What Should We Do With Our Brain?*, and in her later work with Adrian Johnson, discusses these issues, as does, in a very different mode, Thomas Nagel, both in his *The View from Nowhere* and in his 2012 essay, which is provocatively subtitled *Why the Materialist neo-Darwinian Conception of Nature is Almost Certainly False*. Some of these issues are further discussed in my 2014 paper "On the Mythematic Reality of Libidinality as a Subtle Energy System."
90 Freud's attitudes toward the possibility of telepathic communication occur in several of his published writings, in which he generally tends to downplay the extent of his conviction in the reality of telepathy. His letter to Ernest Jones of 7 March 1926 is particularly interesting in that he indicates that he has had telepathic experiences which "have attained such convincing power over me that diplomatic considerations [have] to be relinquished." But curiously—and it would seem, entirely illogically—Freud then proceeds to reassure Jones that his "acceptance of telepathy is [his] own affair" and that "the subject of telepathy is not related to *psychoanalysis*." Moreover, in terms of his assumption of the endogenous/exogenous distinction, it also seems curious that, while he could believe in thoughts as a subtle form of "energy" mysteriously moving from one individual to another, he does not seem to entertain the possibility that subtle energies in general might not be monadologically contained within the boundaries of the individual bodymind.
91 Expositions of some of these teachings from the Sanātana Dharma tradition can be found in Krishnachandra Bhattacharyya's *Studies in Philosophy*, Georg Feuerstein's *The Yoga Tradition*, and David White's *Yoga in Practice*. Poola Tirupati Raju's *Structural Depths of Indian Thought* also remains valuable.
92 General discussions of the notion of praxis are provided in Richard Bernstein's *Praxis and Action* and in Nicholas Lobkowicz's *Theory and Practice*. An example of fashionable usage of the term, ignoring any distinction between the notions of "praxis" and "practice," would be William Meissner's 1991 article in *Psychoanalytic Inquiry*.
93 This is found notably in Aristotle's *Nicomachean Ethics* and *Eudamion Ethics*, and is well discussed in Hannah Arendt's *The Human Condition*.
94 The retreat specifically from sexuality has been more comprehensively discussed in Green's *The Chains of Eros* and in Arthur Efron's *The Sexual Body*, as well as in my *What is Psychoanalysis?*
95 Relevant reviews are provided by Robert Plomin and his coauthors, as well as in *How Genes Influence Behavior* by Jonathan Flint, Ralph Greenspan, and Kenneth Kendler.
96 This is classically discussed in Niko Tinbergen's *The Study of Instinct* and Konrad Lorenz's *The Foundations of Ethology*. This lineage of research is also well presented in Richard Burkhardt's *Patterns of Behavior*.
97 The distinction between imposed or implanted messages and the possibility that such impulses also emerge from within the infant is debated in a most interesting exchange between Daniel Widlöcher and Laplanche. Although the crucial issue seems to be emphasized by Laplanche—namely, the subjection of the infant to the enigmatic messages that are imposed upon it from the caretaker's unconscious—the other issues emphasized by Widlöcher cannot be discounted. Indeed, these processes are not mutually exclusive and both might be operative. The debate is presented in Widlöcher's 2001 anthology.
98 Althusser discusses this in his *Lenin and Philosophy*. See also Butler's excellent essay *The Psychic Life of Power*, which parallels much of Laplanche's thinking, albeit with a different approach and genre (also important in this context is Butler's *Giving an Account of Oneself*).
99 It can, of course, be argued that the difference between *repression* (in which a representation is exiled from the purview of self-consciousness or its preconscious substrate and decomposed as a "thing-presentation") and *primal repression* (in which drive-desire energies emerge propped on the biological mechanisms in the formation of the earliest internal images or ideas, and affected greatly by the imposition or implantation

of enigmatic messages from outside the organism) is such that different terms should be employed. This is the significance of debates around Freud's occasional use of terms such as *ablehnen* (to fend off), *aufheben* (to abolish), *verleugnen* (to disavow), and *verwerfen* (to foreclose or repudiate). The last term emerged in Édouard Pichon's 1928 article on negation and was the subject of a debate in the 1920s between Freud and Laforgue over the processes of scotomization. Lacan then elaborates the notion in relation to his theory of psychosis (found in the *Écrits* and elsewhere). These matters are discussed in Élisabeth Roudinesco's *Lacan* and more recently by commentators such as Annick Ohayon and Alain de Mijolla.

100 The distinction between word-representations and "thing-presentations" will be further developed later. As I indicated previously, Freud makes a similar distinction in his 1895 *Entwurf* and in the 1900 *Traumdeutung* (with the discussion of the dream's "unfathomable navel"), but perhaps more explicitly in the 1905 book on jokes. It is developed as part of a more elaborate metapsychological formulation in the 1915 paper on the unconscious and the 1917 paper on mourning and melancholia, after which Freud seems to have dropped the notion as if it were inconvenient to his grander efforts to construct an objectivistic model of the "mental apparatus."

101 There is a disagreement here between Laplanche and Green. Green—as discussed in his 1997 book and elsewhere—seems to feel that Laplanche overemphasizes the *Trieb/Instinkt* distinction and, in so doing, underestimates the impact of biological functions and mechanisms on the movement and force of drives. Laplanche is indeed clear about the dangers of understanding drives as biological. This is particularly explicit in his 1993 book, which discusses how psychoanalysis has gone astray or been misdirected with theories that biologize the drives and sexuality. But Green seems to take this to mean that, in this respect, Laplanche merely returns to Lacan, making the entire psychoanalytic field about signification and excluding material reality. However, the problem I find in Green's position is that, in reasserting the proximity of drives and their material substrate, it might be implied that drives and the biological operations on which they depend are intertranslatable modes of discourse (Laplanche's emphasis on the imposition of enigmatic signifiers effectively precludes such translatability). Green does effectively address this implication in his 1995 book. I am unable to arbitrate between Laplanche and Green on this point because—in the manner of an old joke—I have a sense that both are correct. More importantly, I am entirely unclear whether this is a difference of theoretical emphasis that would have an impact on psychoanalytic praxis—the most significant issue, in my opinion, and it is an issue on which Laplanche and Green seem to agree, at least up to a point, is that *Triebe* are a different order of discourse from their material substrate in neural circuitry and hormonal operations (*Instinkte*), and that these orders of discourse are not intertranslatable. My exchange with Solms in 2015 emphasizes the significance (in terms of the nontranslatability between different modes of discourse) of accepting empirical reduction while rejecting the possibility of logical reduction.

102 As I will elaborate, the term "elective" is not used to suggest that it is chosen by an agent, but rather to emphasize how it is acquired through lived experience (initiated from outside the organism by an entity so radically "other" that it is experienced as, and indeed is, "otherwise"). One might also suggest that this relation between the corporeal and the psychical is inherently somewhat capricious.

103 On this issue and on the issue of how drives become aggressive, I think Rapaport's writing remains useful, despite the fact that he did not make much of the critical difference between *Trieb* and *Instinkt.*

104 "Nipple-me-suck-pleasure" constitutes what Piaget, in his 1966 text with Bärbel Inhelder, would call a sensori-motor schema, which is the most basic of cognitive structures.

105 In addition to Laplanche's writings on repression as a failure of translation, this is well discussed in Green's *The Chains of Eros.*

106 A criticism that Green makes, which seems to have some validity, is that in his preoccupation with the *Trieb/Instinkt* distinction and the formation of the unconscious through the processes of primal repression, Laplanche effectively diminishes the significance of oedipal complexities as an organizing principle of the psyche. What should not be underestimated here is the role of the incest taboo (which, very loosely speaking, might be thought of as an *Instinkt*) in the formation of the "repression barrier" via the processes of what is called the oedipal complex.

107 This is my translation of *die Verdrängungslehre ist nun der Grundpfeiler, auf dem das Gebäude der Psychoanalyse ruht.* I have discussed in my 2013 book why *Grundpfeiler* should be rendered as "coordinate" rather than the more common "cornerstone." I also think it misleading to characterize psychoanalysis as a "building" (*Gebäude*), which implies a theoretical edifice, rather than as a praxis.

108 See my 2012 paper, "Boundaries and Intimacies: Ethics and the (Re)Performance of 'The Law' in Psychoanalysis."

109 Strictly speaking, there is no "encounter" with the incest taboo, and the taboo cannot depend on someone wielding the paternal function by actually reprimanding or threatening the child (although this does, of course, occur and the role of male caregivers in facilitating the child's separation from the maternal caregiver is well documented). As indicated in Chapter 2, Freud's intellectual milieu was considerably interested in the incest taboo, both in its evident universality and in the variability of its specific interpretations between cultures. In this book, I am not going to review the various explanations for this taboo, except to note that the taboo is not only directed toward consanguineous sexual partners (most decisively mother–son, mother–daughter, father–son, father–daughter, and also fraternally–sororally), but also toward those with whom one has lived in close domestic proximity during the first few years of life (as described by the Westermarck effect). In many respects, the Lacanian explanation that the taboo arises with, and is essentially an effect of, the individual's induction into language convinces me. However, of great interest are the speculations of anthropologists such as Peter Wilson as to how human culture "jumped" into existence with the concurrent institution of the social father, the establishment of the incest taboo, and the advent of language as a symbolization (as distinct from a signaling) system. However, what remains wholly unclear is whether the incest taboo requires the operation of symbolic language systems or vice versa. For the purposes of this book, I intend to consider the taboo to be "hard-wired," as if a modal action pattern or *Instinkt* (which, of course, does not mean that it cannot be overridden with inevitably disastrous consequences) that the Oedipus complex follows from, leans on, or is propped upon.

110 As Laplanche and Pontalis remind us, Freud wrote to Fliess as early as 6 December 1896 that he was working on the assumption that psychic reality comes into being by processes in which "the material present in the form of memory-traces being subjected from time to time to a *rearrangement* in accordance with fresh circumstances—to a *retranscription*." These authors show that Freud's notion of *Nachträglichkeit* is quite precise and characterized as follows: "(a) It is not lived experience in general that undergoes a deferred revision but, specifically, whatever it has been impossible in the first instance to incorporate fully into a meaningful context. The traumatic event is the epitome of such unassimilated experience. (b) Deferred revision is occasioned by events and situations, or by an organic maturation, which allow the subject to gain access to a new level of meaning and to rework his earlier interpretations. (c) Human sexuality, with the peculiar unevenness of its temporal development, provides an eminently suitable field for the phenomenon of deferred action." Crucial here, in our thinking about the relation or inevitably failed or failing retranscription of repressed "thing-presentations" into "word-representations" is Laplanche and Pontalis's writing on fantasy/phantasy (see also Pontalis's *Frontiers in Psychoanalysis*) and Green's discussion of how "fantasy binds libido to representations" in his 1983 essay "The Dead Mother."

111 What I have called the pluritemporality of time is, I believe, more or less equivalent to what Derrida and others in the contemporary French tradition call "the hetero-affection of time." Such issues have also been extensively discussed by Kristeva and others.

112 I will return to this point in the next chapter, because it pertains to the association between sexuality and the deathfulness of the self-conscious subject.

113 As indicated previously, Laplanche is perhaps the strongest proponent of this view. Differentiating himself from Laplanche, Green refers to drives as "metabiological"—and one wishes he had written more about the nonequivalence or untranslatability between biology and this "metabiological" realm.

114 In considering these issues, there is much to be learnt not only from the writings of Green and Laplanche, as well as Derrida, but also, in particular, from Samuel Weber's *The Legend of Freud*, and the contributions of Alan Bass, Jon Mills, and many others.

115 Emergentism was popular in the 20th century and is well discussed in papers to be found in Ansgar Beckermann, Hans Flohr, and Jaegwon Kim's anthology, *Emergence or Reduction?—Essays on the Prospects of Nonreductive Physicalism*, in Mark Bedau and Paul Humphreys' anthology, *Emergence: Contemporary Readings in Philosophy and Science,* and in the 2013 discussion by Antonella Corradini and Timothy O'Connor. On these issues, the work of Nagel (mentioned in note 89) is also excellent reading from a psychoanalytic standpoint.

116 Harald Atmanspacher and Wolfgang Fach have recently provided a discussion of the Pauli-Jung material, which is published under the title *Atom and Archetype: The Pauli-Jung Letters, 1932–1958*. The interpretation of Baruch Spinoza's position as a double-aspect monist comes mostly from the second part of his 1677 *Ethics*, about which Antonio Damasio's 2003 book has some interesting commentary. Solms and Turnbull's *The Brain and the Inner World* offers an influential statement of a widespread neuropsychoanalytic viewpoint. Donald Davidson's "anomalous monism," which is propounded in his *Essays on Actions and Events*, follows Spinoza in arguing for ontological monism (mind and matter are composed on one substance) combined with "conceptual dualism," meaning that mind and matter require different modes of explanation.

117 This position has been variously argued by Ernst Mach in his *The Analysis of Sensations*, by Richard Avenarius in his 1891 text, by William James in his *Essays in Radical Empiricism*, and by Bertrand Russell in some of his writings from 1921 onwards. It is also the position taken by some more contemporary philosophers, such as Kenneth Sayre.

118 Laplanche's 1993 essay, "A Short Treatise on the Unconscious" (reprinted in *Essays on Otherness*), and his 2003 paper, "Three Meanings of the Term 'Unconscious' in the General Theory of Seduction" (reprinted in *Freud and the 'Sexual'*), are especially interesting. For examples of how varied and antipsychoanalytically the term is now employed, Morris Eagle's survey of the current state of empirical evidence for processes and mechanisms that are other-than-conscious is very competent. The 2006 anthology by Ran Hassin, James Uleman, and John Bargh illustrates the magnitude of misunderstandings about psychoanalysis on the part of many cognitive scientists.

119 "Sexification" is a concept that I discussed, in a rather journalistic fashion, in my *Sexual Health and Erotic Freedom*, in which "sexuality" proliferates on the surface of cultural life (think here of media advertising, popular literature, the increasing availability, and diversity of "porn" on the Internet and elsewhere) and, at the same time, underlying fears of sexuality do not diminish (think here of the frequency of contemporary "sex acts" that actually entail an avoidance of the intensity of sensuality and orgasmicity) and indeed reactions against freedom of sexual expression intensify (think here of the crusades of the religious rightists, the rise in hate crimes against sexual minorities, the "war against sex" as a platform on which many politicians ascend to power. My argument has been that both directions of this phenomenon (a variety of forms of sex-obsessiveness and a variety of forms of sex-phobia) are born of underlying fearfulness about sexuality itself.

120 In this regard, Green's 1995 paper "Has Sexuality anything to do with Psychoanalysis?" is especially useful. Since the 1990s, there has been a slight revival of interest in the

erotic body within the psychoanalytic literature. Consider, for example, McDougall's 1989 *Theaters of the Body* and 1995 *The Many Faces of Eros*, as well as the writings of Robert Stoller. For psychosomatics, Marilia Aisenstein and Elsa Rappoport de Aisemberg's 2010 anthology *Psychosomatics Today: A Psychoanalytic Perspective* (in which Green has a paper) is excellent.

121 Although my views differ slightly from each of them, this chapter has been influenced not only by the writings of Laplanche and Green, but also by those of Joyce McDougall and Robert Stoller. It must be added that neither McDougall nor Stoller develop the *Trieb/Instinkt* distinction, which is disappointing. For example, McDougall, whose work on psychosomatics as well as her *The Many Faces of Eros* are so richly useful (and the latter text replete with interesting vignettes), descends to writing about "assuming our predestined anatomical destiny" in occasional references that are as misleading as they are tangential to her wealth of clinical insight. I also want to mention, with great appreciation, Arthur Efon's 1985 monograph, the extensive publications of Alphonso Lingis, as well as the works of Wilhelm Reich. My reading of the literature on "bodymind psychotherapy" (which is well reviewed by Michael Heller and also discussed in my *The Emergence of Somatic Psychology and Bodymind Therapy*) has also influenced my thinking significantly.

122 For reasons explained in my 2013 essay "Sensuality, Sexuality, and the Eroticism of Slowness," I write of fucking (and shitting), rather than more delicate, but highly ambiguous terms such as "sexual intercourse."

123 This quote is from his 2000 essay "Sexuality and Attachment," which is reprinted in *Freud and the 'Sexual.'* In the same collection, Laplanche's essay titled "Drive and Instinct" contains the following statement of the same crucial issue: "precisely those things that we think we know are, in fact, complicated by both the cultural and by infantile sexuality! What psychoanalysis teaches us—which seems utterly foreign—is that in man the sexuality of intersubjective origin [he means that which is acquired through the "fundamental anthropological situation" in which Caregivers impose enigmatic messages upon the Infant], that is, drive sexuality, *the sexuality that is acquired comes before the sexuality that is innate;* [with regard to puberty] *drive comes before instinct*, fantasy comes before function; and when the sexual instinct arrives, the seat is already occupied."

124 See especially Laplanche and Pontalis's 1968 paper "Fantasy and the Origins of Sexuality," which offers one compelling account of this issue.

125 The use of the term "unconsciously" in this sentence is descriptive. Such fantasies actually occur as preconscious and deeply preconscious, animated by the persistence and insistence of psychic energy that has been shaped by infantile and childhood experiences and that has been repressed. As Freud would appreciate, it is interesting how slang and jokes, as well as vulgar literature, about intercourse often betray what may be occurring beneath the superficial appearance of a "normal sex act." For example, in relation to my specific example of pissing on (or in) one's partner or being pissed on, it seems noteworthy that Barry Humphries has his rude protagonist (the Australian "Barry McKenzie") yell back at an inept psychiatrist, who has just asked him if he is frightened of women, "You dirty bastard, are you inferring *I splash me boots in the ladies.*" Also noteworthy is George Orwell's admission that, during penile–vaginal intercourse, he worries that he might need to urinate (and he assumes that this worry is common among heterosexual men).

126 So much has been written about Freudian thinking as instigating the alleged "sexual revolution" in the North Atlantic countries that it does not bear review herein. A notable example of this debate would be Germaine Greer's critique of D. H. Lawrence's not-so-revolutionary use of psychoanalysis for a masculinist thesis. However, Reich's 1936 *The Sexual Revolution* is still well worth reading.

127 I do not wish to belabor this point, which is nevertheless of crucial importance, but if one abolishes the distinction between drive and instinct (for the moment I will retain the English terms), it would seem that one interesting and perhaps vital distinction

between humans and the animal kingdom is erased. For example, if you watch lions mate, it seems rather evident that they are just "doing their instinctual thing" (she is hormonally in heat, exuding distinctive odors, he jumps on her and penetrates her, etc.). At no point do you get the impression that the sex act is influenced by their experiences at the maternal teat, or their rough-and-tumble play as youngsters. Rather, they have achieved physical adulthood and are instinctually programmed to copulate when the relevant triggering signals are activated. By contrast, for humans, copulation (the manner of initiating the act, the style of physical engagement, and the accompanying fantasies) is conditioned by a multitude of factors, of which the participants are not conscious, and which come under the rubric of "infantile sexuality" (feeding experiences with caregivers, experiences with shitting and toilet-training, the history of self-pleasuring and the attendant fantasies, the need to select partners who are satisfactorily disguised substitutes for the forbidden "primary love objects," and so forth). In other words, whereas instinctual activities may be wholly determined by the organism's biological constitution, the libidinal drive or desire (even though it leans-on biological functions and mechanisms) is never wholly determined by its physical sourcing, but rather is infused with varieties of meaningfulness that have been incorporated into the organism as a result of life experiences.

128 That practitioners avoid even inquiring into, let alone interrogating free associatively, the specifics of sexual activity is an assertion I am making (on the basis of hearing countless clinical presentations) that I doubt anyone is seriously going to contest. Nowadays, very few clinicians, even those who claim to be psychoanalytic, consider asking patients to free-associate to the memory of the fucking they reported (or didn't report) doing the previous night, and few, if any, understand the prime value of interrogating masturbatory fantasies. This is why I argued, in *Sexual Health and Erotic Freedom* (as a slight *homage* to pioneers such as Alfred Kinsey and Betty Dodson, with whom I otherwise have some disagreements) that being open about one's sexual inclinations is a revolutionary act; against this, a problematic notion of privacy has, unfortunately, returned to clinical discourse.

129 In terms of the 20th century's "sexual revolution" as "the revolution that wasn't," it is one thing to suggest that people were relieved of some of the worries about unwanted pregnancy and thus felt they had greater license to copulate, quite another to assert that the underlying fear of sexuality was thereby diminished. The latter, however welcome it might be, has definitely not been the result of this erstwhile "revolution" nor of the sexification of popular culture that has succeeded it.

130 David's *La bisexualité psychique* discusses the topic from a psychoanalytic standpoint at a time when there are still only a few psychoanalysts prepared to engage the issue seriously. Other interesting texts, although not psychoanalytic, include Santiago de la Iglesia Turiño's *Why Bisexuality makes us Human*, Steven Angelides's *History of Bisexuality*, and Erwin Haeberle's *Bisexualities*.

131 I believe I introduced the notion of our inherent *polysexuality* in my 2009 book (it is also deployed in my polemical essay, *Liberating Eros*), although it surfaced under François Peraldi's 1981 editorship. It is somewhat parallel to William Stayton's notion of "pansexualism," although the latter focuses more on the "object" of sexual activity (and says nothing about libidinality or drive). The term is picked up (without attribution) and developed in a slightly different fashion by Mark Blechner in his *Sex Changes*.

132 It is, of course, John Bowlby who led the movement to meld psychoanalysis with ethology, and thus gave rise to a lineage of object-relations theory as well as the current vogue for theories of attachment (e.g. Beatrice Beebe, Berry Brazelton, Virginia Demos, Martin Dornes, Joseph Lichtenberg, Hubert Montagner, Daniel Stern, René Zazzo, *et al.*), although in a sense these theoretical developments were anticipated by Ronald Fairbairn's emphasis on the object-seeking (as opposed to the libidinally activated) infant. However, it is unclear to what extent, in the long run, these

developments may have been as much a disservice to psychoanalytic thinking as a service to our clarity of theorizing (this is not to disparage the significance of some of the empirical research that has aided our ability to help caregivers bond with their infants). Bowlby failed to understand the significance of the distinction between *Trieb* and *Instinkt*, and thus ultimately cedes psychoanalysis to evolutionary biology. The problem recurs in much of what is written under the contemporary banner of "neuropsychoanalysis," including the contemporary writings on "the evolutionary archaeology of affective systems" by Jaak Panksepp; the failure to properly comprehend the role of *drives* in psychic life leads to excessive claims about the relevance of instinctual patterns (modal action patterns) that can perhaps be identified in the most ancient parts of our brain (for more on the overextension evolutionary biology in general, and of Panksepp's claims in particular, see my 2015 paper on "neuroevolutionary archaeology."

133 The assumption that all orders of discourse must be intertranslatable is patently false and hegemonic. Here I am in substantial agreement with Jane Flax and other commentators. It may be reasonable to assume that most propositions in the French language can be, at least approximatively, translated into the language of isiZulu or Iroquoian and vice versa. Even if the Chomskyan theory that all languages have a deep structure were to be disproved, the assumption is reasonable in that we assume some commonality to the functioning and the interests of culturally diverse members of the same species. In that sense, spoken languages are, so to speak, on an equal footing; even here, however, we need to be aware of the limits of translatability. However, it is an utter fallacy to take it as given that all modes of discourse must be intertranslatable. In fact, the fallacy invariably proves hegemonic in that one discourse is subordinated to the other in the name of "translation." The psychoanalytic revolution is, in this respect, the discovery that operating between the lawfulness of our biological nature and the lawfulness of our representationality is a discourse that is enigmatic and extraordinary. Libidinality is wild and mysterious, such that any effort at translation, in either direction, is so limited as for it to be more truthful to understand libidinality to be untranslatable.

134 The quote is from Green's *Chains of Eros*. Green does not use the term notion-for-praxis (which is my expression). Rather, he refers to libido as a "concept"—for reasons indicated earlier in my text, I think it is a mistake.

135 I use the term "catastrophe"—with the slightest illusion to the influential work of René Thom—to indicate a momentous set of events that dramatically changes the subsequent features of, in this case, the human organism.

136 It thus both connects with and must be differentiated from what has been written, for example by Adam Phillips, about flirtation.

137 Freud wrote this in a footnote to the 1920 edition of the *Three Essays on the Theory of Sexuality*. Three years later, in *Das Ich und das Es*, he argues that understanding the distinction between consciousness and the repressed is also such a shibboleth. There is no discrepancy between these statements because, without the incest taboo, there would be no repression (*eigentliche Verdrängung*) and no psychoanalytic unconscious. Given my appreciation for Laplanche's thinking, I find it curious that he seems to neglect the significance of the Oedipal complex, with its essential feature of the "encounter" with the incest taboo. In his writings, it is overshadowed by his preoccupation with the "fundamental anthropological situation." This is an issue for which Green has criticized him.

138 This is not the place to explore the voluminous literature on the issues of the Oedipus complex raised by Asian, African, and other non-European cultures. Suffice it to say that much of this literature focuses misleadingly on variations of family constellations and child-raising patterns; it thus overlooks or underemphasizes the universal features of the child's "encounter" with incest taboo.

139 As indicated in a previous note, "encounter" is not the optimal term for the processes by which the child comes to recognize the forbiddenness of certain forms of erotic gratification.

140 Recall here, as discussed in previous chapters, the meaningful pulsing of *bar-bar-bar* or *b-b-b*, hinting, in an enigmatic and extraordinary fashion, at the tremors of deathfulness and sexuality *within* our system of representable meanings, yet not *of* the law and order of representationality (hence, untranslated and untranslatable).

141 There are so many methods covered by the field of somatic psychology and bodymind therapy that only some general remarks are possible here. The field is well reviewed in more detail and more comprehensively in Michael Heller's *Body Psychotherapy* than in my 2010 book (which was only intended as a brief introduction). Reich's work, particularly the 1933 *Character Analysis*, is seminal, as well as influential texts such as Kurt Goldstein's 1934 *The Organism*, and Ernest Schachtel's 1959 *Metamorphosis*. Also, I think the psychoanalytic writings of Robert Fliess in 1950s on erogeneity, libidinality, and the "body ego" are too infrequently referenced today. The field of somatic psychology has proliferated particularly since the 1960s. Here the work of just a few of the many individuals, who are currently influential in the Anglo-American sphere (i.e. leaving aside continental Europe and elsewhere), can be referenced (in alphabetical order): Susan Aposhyan, David Boadella, Malcolm Brown, Christine Caldwell, Bonnie Bainbridge Cohen, Eugene Gendlin, Anna Halprin, Charles Kelley, Ron Kurtz, Stephen Levine, Alexander Lowen, Arnold Mindell, Pat Ogden, Albert Pesso, John Pierrakos, Illana Rubenfeld (one text by each of these authors will be selected for inclusion in the references). In connection with these lineages and of particular interest to psychoanalysis is, as I just mentioned, Robert Fliess's work (Robert was son of Wilhelm, Freud's friend and interlocutor). William Cornell's papers, despite their allegiance to Eric Berne's techniques of transactional analysis, are very helpful reading for the psychoanalytic practitioner.

142 This literature on the yoga tradition is voluminous, but often popular rather than scholarly. A usefully comprehensive survey of the field is provided by Feuerstein's *The Yoga Tradition*. As is well known, Jung wrote on kundalini yoga, and Mircea Eliade provides a useful examination of yoga as a philosophy. Günter von Hummel's *Yoga and Psychoanalysis* attempts to connect Kirpal Singh's "laya-yoga" with Lacanian perspectives. The literature on psychoanalysis and meditation, particularly in the Buddhist tradition, is also voluminous, yet helpful to the extent that it is body-oriented. Anthony Molino's two anthologies provide helpful summaries of a portion of this literature. Reginald Ray introduces embodied meditation practices in the tantric tradition, in a way that I have found useful as reflected in my paper "Free-associating with the Bodymind." On the relation between psychoanalysis and oriental ways of approaching life, Bollas's writings are characteristically interesting; in this context, see in particular his 2013 *China on the Mind*. Also interesting in this regard is Irigaray's *Between East and West*.

143 By referring to the "empirical evidence" of this tradition, I am not implying that these doctrines follow an empiricist philosophy nor that their standards of evidence meet standards of logical–empiricist or positivist–naturalistic science. On the latter point, see my paper "Research in Body Psychotherapy." However, I am implying that the findings of this tradition are empirical in the sense that they emerge through concrete experiences of healing practices.

144 That the vicissitudes of transference and countertransference is as much an embodied experience as one that can be brought within the purview of reflection and representation (a point which needs further discussion) only serves to reinforce the importance of the ethic of the nonphysical intimacy, or "abstinent erotics," required for psychoanalytic treatment.

145 This is discussed in my paper "Free-associating with the Bodymind."

146 Two interesting and rather different discussions of some of these issues are offered by Jean-François Lyotard in his 1974 *Libidinal Economy*, and by Alphonso Lingis, both in his 1983 and 1985 books.

147 For example, the idea of recruiting complexity theories that describe the phenomena of nonlinear dynamic systems (and likewise some contemporary versions of field theory) also seems fraught with the ambition to tame a realm that is inherently disrup-

tive, rambunctious, and lawless. Although there is nothing about psychoanalysis in this volume (although there are contributions on psychopathology and psychotherapy), the anthology edited by Stephen Guastello, Matthijs Koopmans and David Pincus reviews the efforts to bring nonlinear dynamic systems theories into the orbit of psychology.

148 There is obviously much more that could be developed here, but it is beyond the scope of this book. Some understanding of the libidinization of hatred was explored well before Freud's time—for example, by William Hazlitt. As is clear, I do not see any reason to posit speculatively the operation of innate destructiveness or primal envy in the manner to which the Kleinians are committed. It seems quite possible that Hazlitt's 1823 essay "On the Pleasure of Hating" was familiar to Freud.

149 This is, of course, reminiscent of Max Stirner's 1845 idea of the self as "creative nothing," as well as other commentaries.

150 In their *Minutes of the Vienna Psychoanalytic Society* (Volume 1), Herman Nunberg and Ernst Federn report that Freud reiterated this theme on 30 January 1907, stating that "our cures are cures of love." The tone of this seems as if it might refer to something more profound than the rather pejorative notion of "transference cures."

151 Following my practice in earlier writings, I will distinguish "love" in the common sense of an affectionate attachment from "Love" (with the first letter in the upper case) as this opening of being-in-the-world to the process of its own truthfulness. The significance of this distinction will become evident in what follows.

152 The debate between Freud and Ferenczi—along with its peculiarities and improprieties—is now well documented. In recent years, under the burgeoning of interpersonal and relational approaches particularly in the United States, there has been a revival of interest in Ferenczi's techniques. The Freud–Ferenczi correspondence is illuminating, and the latter's views are well represented in his 1924 coauthored work with Rank, as well as the anthology edited by Michael Balint, *Final Contributions to the Problems and Methods of Psychoanalysis*. For useful discussions of the controversy over the so-called "Budapest School" of psychoanalysis, see André Haynal's *Disappearing and Reviving: Sándor Ferenczi in the history of psychoanalysis*, as well as his *Controversies in Psychoanalytic Method: From Freud and Ferenczi to Michael Balint*. The history of the school is addressed well by Judit Meszaros. Also interesting on the issues associated with Ferenczi's clinical methods are Martin Stanton's *Sándor Ferenczi: Reconsidering Active Intervention* and Arthur Rachman's *Sándor Ferenczi: Psychoanalyst of Tenderness and Passion*. For examples of the recent "Ferenczi revival," see Judit Szekacs-Weisz and Tom Keve's 2012 anthology, Lewis Aron and Adrienne Harris's 1993 anthology, or the contributions of Peter Rudnytsky and his colleagues. Jonathan Sklar's *Landscapes in the Dark* is also of great interest.

153 One simple and colloquial way to express this is that the psychoanalyst must always be able both to find something to like about the patient and to empathize with his or her plight, even when the patient is being ruthlessly and horribly exasperating. As I look back on those treatments that were not so successful, I recognize that my lapses in this capacity were always the source of the failures—that is, to be specific, the cases where my narcissism interfered. This is why, as I have written in previous essays, when psychoanalysis fails, it is invariably because of the psychoanalyst's narcissism.

154 In fact, the educative and therapeutic aspects of the relationship between patient and practitioner can easily serve to accommodate the psychoanalyst's resistances to performing psychoanalytically. Too frequently, treatments that are branded "psychoanalysis" are actually forms of psychoanalytically informed or psychoanalytically oriented therapy, and this is almost entirely a matter of the psychoanalyst's narcissism manifested as his or her resistances to psychoanalysis.

155 Perhaps it could be added that it is only a "good idea" if the patient has, in the course of the initial consultations, some sense of liking the psychoanalyst and of confidence in him or her. While the patient's initial impressions of the practitioner may be exceedingly misleading, a patient who embarks on a treatment with a practitioner toward whom he or she has no reactions "in the gut" is often setting up the treatment such that it will never become psychoanalytic.

156 What follows omits much that needs to be discussed. Perhaps it should be noted that I am in sympathy with those commentators (such as Brian Bird in his 1972 paper) who contend that transferential processes are both ubiquitous and yet uniquely addressed in psychoanalysis. Even now, over a century after Freud's writings on transference, there are still so many questions that need further exploration and exposition. Some of the major papers within the voluminous literature on transference have been judiciously collected in Robert Langs's *Classics in Psychoanalytic Technique* and also in Aaron Esman's *Essential Papers on Transference*.

157 The "gathering in" that routinely occurs as the treatment progresses is what is often called the development of the "transference neurosis"—a phenomenon in which it is often observed that the patient feels increasing destabilized within the psychoanalytic relationship, even while feeling more content with relations outside the treatment. As one patient expressed it, "when I started with you, I had all sorts of problems, but now, just two years later, I seem to be more at ease with all those issues and *my feelings for you have become the problem*"! The lopsidedness or asymmetry of psychoanalysis as a sort of "dialogical monologue" obviously contributes significantly to the way in which the transference neurosis develops.

158 Lacan's discussion of these terms is in the *Écrits* as well as *Séminaires I, II* and *XI*. Also useful is Lorenzo Chiesa's *Subjectivity and Otherness*, as well as the writings of Bruce Fink.

159 See in particular Lacan's *Séminaires* of 1954–1955 and of 1964 (as well as those of 1959–1960 and 1972–1973). See also Fink's writings and Dany Nobus and Malcolm Quinn's *Knowing Nothing, Staying Stupid*.

160 This is why the notion of *interpellation*, as given a preliminary discussion in Althusser's theory of the way in which the subject is constituted ideologically, is so useful. The thinking and speaking subject, the "I" of self-consciousness, is *hailed into being* by the enunciations of other subjects (who in turn are already ideologically constituted).

161 This notion was discussed in some detail in my *Psychoanalysis and the Postmodern Impulse*, but the relevant literature here is voluminous. The following are the main writings of Derrida on this topic: *Speech and Phenomena*, *Of Grammatology*, *Margins of Philosophy*, *Dissemination*, and *The Postcard*. Also important are the psychoanalytic writings of feminists such as Julia Kristeva and Luce Irigaray.

162 See note 76 above.

163 As expounded by Derrida, this is the *logos*, the totalizing or universalizing and centralizing metaphysics of an identitarian system, by which *being* comes to be represented semiotically. See note 76 above. Obviously, there is far more at stake here than can be accommodated in the brevity of this book.

164 In a certain sense, this is the hypocrisy, the pretension, of every exponent of ideology or priest. This would include every parent or educator (using "education" here in the sense of "schooling"), every politician or governor, and every therapist. In this connection, it should be noted that Freud, in his 1925 Preface to August Aichhorn's book, and again in his 1937 essay "Analysis Terminable and Interminable," referred to the three "impossible professions" as educating, governing, and healing. However, the inclusion of "healing" can only mean—the sense I am using the term in this book—therapy. "Psychoanalysis" would only be included if the practitioner assumes the authoritative position of the big-Other and declines the free-associative deconstruction of this phantasm—perhaps this is the position of mastery that Freud himself assumed increasingly as his movement developed and his writings became less revolutionary.

165 This is, I believe, the sense in which Freud, in his 1925 autobiographical study, wrote that the castration complex has "the profoundest significance in the formation of character" in both boys and girls. While the encounter with anatomical differences undoubtedly has major repercussions on the formation of everyone's personality, the acceptance—or more precisely the multiple strategies and tactics by which we refuse to accept—that the "I" is not the center of the meanings that comprise our being-in-the-world is, since it is the issue of our inherent fracturation, surely the mainspring of what defines who we are, the identities that are our "character."

166 In this sense, psychoanalysis is a discipline of humility and surrender to the *what is*, to which the flow of free-associative thinking and speaking opens us. To some, this might be considered its spiritual basis, as a dedication to the ethics of compassion, appreciation, and grace (of which surrender and humility are aspects). Even if one bypasses this issue of spirituality, there can be no question that psychoanalysis is inherently and essentially a method by which idols are challenged and debunked.

167 All this is well described in Laplanche's series of essays collected as *Freud and the 'Sexual.'*

168 The notion of the term "sacred" can be misleading. I use it here in a secular sense to denote all that is most precious about the human condition.

169 The specifics of this procedure are discussed in somewhat greater detail in my essay, "Free-associating with the Bodymind."

170 One might say that this is why the patient and the psychoanalyst appear with such regularity in the latent dream thoughts and wishes constitutive of each other's dreams. Freud indicated that the manifest content of the dreams of patients in psychoanalysis always make reference to the psychoanalyst; he did not explore more thoroughly how problematic it is for the treatment if the patient is not in some way featuring in the dreams of the psychoanalyst. What is typically the case when a patient enters treatment and begins to experience the seduction of the psychoanalyst, is that his or her dream life begins to open and become more accessible.

171 This is the sense in which Laplanche asserts that seduction is "the foundational process of being human."

172 We may note that Freud's reputed self-analysis actually had several interlocutors—Breuer, Fliess, Jung, and others—and, despite the heroic character of his efforts, his understanding of transferences and of the otherwise messages of his erotic embodiment seems to have been decidedly limited.

173 I add "figuratively" because, although self-analysis is not possible, it is well known that the processes of psychoanalysis can to some extent continue between sessions, during vacation breaks in the treatment, and for some time after termination. Obviously, the critically significant issue is the way in which the patient experiences the practitioner and may indeed hold the latter "in mind" as a presence even during times of literal absence.

174 Viviane Chetrit-Vatine's *The Ethical Seduction of the Analytic Situation* brilliantly brings together Levinas and Laplanche in an understanding of the feminine-maternal origins of the ethical function of the psychoanalyst. The writings of Kristeva and Irigaray are also indispensable in this regard. Simone de Beauvoir's *Ethics of Ambiguity* remains interesting in relation to the ethicality of psychoanalytic processes.

175 Levinas's work is extremely informative on these issues, from his 1948 *Time and the Other* through to his writings in the 1990s. John Llewelyn's *Emanuel Levinas: The Genealogy of Ethics* is also helpful. Sarah Harasym's anthology *Levinas and Lacan* also discusses these issues in a psychoanalytic context.

176 Strictly speaking, this is not entirely accurate. For reasons that are clear from my discussion of the way in which the patient's free-associative discourse must, to some extent, be spoken as if into a void, it is important that the patient not be able to see the psychoanalyst (although I believe it is important that the patient should have the freedom to turn his or her head in order to see the psychoanalyst's face, if he or she feels the need to do so). However, the psychoanalyst should, in my opinion, position his or her chair such that the patient's face is visible from behind and at an angle.

177 "Dreads the discourse of free association" may seem like an extreme way to state this issue, because typically (or at least for many patients) the "ego organization" will allow at least a few moments of free-association before a resistance intervenes. Dread is scarcely too strong a term for an activity that threatens the ego's organization; moreover, the "dread" is, of course, rarely experienced consciously.

178 These are resistance from the id, from the superego, and three additional types from the ego organization: That derived from repression, from transference resistance, and from the secondary gains accrued from conflict. Although this categorization may make

sense in the context of the structural–functional model promulgated in 1923 and 1926, it is utterly unclear what difference such theoretical propositions make to the way in which resistances are addressed in the psychoanalytic situation. Since it is "the ego" that orchestrates and organizes resistances, according to its own need to manage signal anxiety, it is "the ego" that must be addressed interpretively if resistances are to be modified or relinquished. Some of these issues are addressed in the articles collected by Donald Milman and George Goldman; see also Pietro Castelnuovo-Tedesco's interesting 1986 paper.

179 On the issue of the psychoanalyst's resistances, Michel Larivière's 1997 paper is interesting, as it is clear that there has been far too little consideration of this topic (despite the readiness with which commentators have identified Freud's resistances to his own process of discovery). Albeit with a different emphasis, Derrida's 1998 *Resistances of Psychoanalysis* remains indispensable reading. As will be discussed in the next section, perhaps the most pernicious and powerful of the resistances performed by psychoanalysts is their tenacity in holding on to theoretical constructs and the illusion-delusion that they are engaged in an objectivistic procedure in which a theoretical model will be applied to the "data" provided by the patient. Some of this was given preliminary discussion in my 1994 paper, "Critical Notes on the Psychoanalyst's Theorizing."

180 I discussed the crucial issue of the way in which the "fundamental rule," Freud's *Grundregel*, is communicated in my *What is Psychoanalysis?* Specifically, the command "*You must say everything that comes to mind*" (regardless of whether it seems disagreeable, unimportant, or nonsensical, as Freud elaborates in his 1938/1940 *Abriss*) seems too authoritarian and sets the patient up for failure, since the patient will invariably find the injunction impossible to follow fully (that is, every patient has substantial resistances to free-association). Modifying the requirement—for example, by saying "Please try to say everything that comes to mind" hardly alleviates the situation. A serious omission, of course, is "what comes to body" as discussed in my essay, "Free-associating with the Bodymind." In his 1913 paper, "On Beginning the Treatment," Freud offers an interesting extended version of his way of communicating the rule. My current practice is to say something like: "It is most helpful if you try to tell me everything that comes to mind or that occurs within your body, even if it seems irrelevant, even if it seems rude or is about me, and even if it is the sort of thing you would censor in ordinary conversation. I know it is difficult to say everything, so whenever you find yourself unwilling to speak about something that occurs to you or within you, it would be important that we discuss together why certain things might be difficult to say aloud to me."

181 In some significant measure, we again owe this shift to Anna Freud's elaboration of ego psychology. Consider the following example, which is modified from her 1936 text. How does the psychoanalyst respond when the patient says: "There is something on my mind, but I cannot talk about it." There was a tendency in the early days of psychoanalysis for the practitioner to respond either with silence or with something like: "You have to" or even "If I am going to be able to help you, you must tell me everything." A more effective way to address resistances always involves an understanding of, but not collusion with, the way in which the resistance seems to serve the "I" or "ego organization." For example, one might say something like: "I appreciate your telling me that there is something on your mind that you feel unable to tell me. [After all, the patient is cooperating with the practitioner by disclosing this]. I know this means that when you feel ready to tell me, you will do so. [Obviously, there is a slight, and perhaps unavoidable, pressure in this phrasing, but after all, the psychoanalyst must stand by the conviction that all disclosures are indeed safe.] In the meantime, can we discuss why it is that somethings feel as if they cannot be spoken of? [Here, obviously, the implication is that, whatever the content, such matters can be talked about.] Generally, such a considerate way of addressing the resistance—a way that implicitly acknowledges that the patient is protecting something from the imaginary dangers of being more free and forthright—prompts an alleviation, if not a complete dissolution,

of the resistance. At the very least, it effectively makes the resistance the focus for subsequent free-associative elaboration and interrogation.

182 Most practitioners have had patients who, under the guise of "associating," insist on recounting the entire course of events between sessions, and who, if confronted on this tendency, protest that it cannot be helped because this is indeed "what's coming to mind."

183 Interestingly, in his *Reminiscences*, Binswanger reports a session in which Freud chided him, telling him that he was making such good sense that it was uninteresting! This mode of resistance is unfortunately common with patients who see psychoanalysis as merely a matter of "making sense" of their personal history. In a more pronounced variant of this resistance, there can almost be an "as if" quality to the patient's "associating."

184 An instance of this would be a patient of mine who was inclined, almost after every few utterances, to exclaim "This is terrific stuff!"

185 Again, it is the extent to which genuine free association diverges, slightly but profoundly significantly, from procedures of active imagination or uncensored story-telling should be noted here.

186 Again, a preliminary discussion of this appears in my 1994 paper, "Critical Notes on the Psychoanalyst's Theorizing." It is also discussed in my 1984 and 1993 books. Also, on the impossibility of reporting "objectively" what occurs in a psychoanalytic session, see above.

187 Freud's organization of meetings—the "Psychological Wednesday Society" or "Wednesday Group" as it is better known—dates from 1902, although he had been hosting seminars and lectures for some years previously. The "Vienna Psychoanalytical Society" was constituted in 1908, and that year an international conference was held in Salzburg, the "First Congress for Freudian Psychology" (proposed by Jones and presided over by Jung). This is usually taken to be the founding of the IPA, although the organization was not formally established until 1910.

188 The history of differences and disagreements between Freud and Ferenczi—through the 1920s and until the latter's death in 1933—is in a category of its own, and certainly is not a simple instance of defection. The history is chronicled in Martin Stanton's *Sándor Freneczi: Reconsidering Active Intervention* and the story is also recounted and discussed in Arnold Rachman's 1997 text. Excellent discussions of some of the issues surrounding Ferenczi are provided in Haynal's books of 1988 and 2002. Also useful in this connection is Peter Rudnytsky's *Reading Psychoanalysis*.

189 Some aspects of this history are presented in Reuben Fine's *A History of Psychoanalysis* and in many other texts. The formulation of standards for psychoanalytic training, which was initiation under the leadership of Max Eitingon in the early 1920s, but never universally adopted, did little if anything to cohere the psychoanalytic movement theoretically.

190 Freud's wish to build a movement has been well documented by his various biographers, including Jones, and is given specific discussion—both apologetic and severely critical—in 1971 books by Paul Roazen and by François Roustang. The tension between his role as "master" of the movement and that of his role as scientific innovator is interestingly discussed in André Haynal's *Psychoanalysis and the Sciences*.

191 I believe Lacanianism does not escape this criticism. As argued in my 1984 book, the big-Other becomes the notion of a totality that effectively centers the human condition.

192 Adler's thinking is presented in his *Collected Clinical Works*, and there is a sizeable literature on Adler and his movement. Paul Stepansky's *In Freud's Shadow* is well regarded, and the historical issues are discussed in Jan Ehrenwald's *History* as well as Ellenberger's *Discovery of the Unconscious*.

193 Frankl's 1937 paper and his famous 1946 book are indicative of his commitment to a "height" psychology that assumes the integration, or potential integration, of the individual who faces the challenges or adversities of the surrounding world. Frankl's 1995 autobiographical work describes his contact with Freud and indicates how, prior

to joining the Adlerians, he has been rejected by Paul Federn for training in psychoanalysis. Interestingly, Timothy Pytell has also informed me that Frankl was mentored by the anti-Freudian Rudolf Allers, who was a conservative Catholic. Pytell's papers provide important information about Frankl's ideological commitments. Geoffrey Cocks's *Psychotherapy in the Third Reich* is a valuable source on the Göring Institute.

194 On the issue of the development of notions of selfhood through the modern era, Charles Taylor's *Sources of the self: The making of modern identity* is very useful.

195 It is interesting to note that, under the influence of his Jungian proclivities, Henry Murray used to argue that Herman Melville's 1851 *Moby Dick* comprises the most compelling testimony to an authentically American discovery of the "unconscious" in the Western canon. As early as the 1920s, Murray was active in teaching psychoanalytic theories, while advocating that their development be wrested away from the influence of Vienna. Some of this is indicated in his *Explorations in Personality*. The determination of American practitioners to distance themselves from the influence of Vienna is perhaps also evident in the way in which the American Psychoanalytic Association and the New York Psychoanalytic Institute, both founded in 1911, defied Freud's judgment by restricting access to training to those holding a medical qualification.

196 Sullivan's work and the extent of his influence are examined in Helen Swick Perry's *Psychiatrist of America* and elsewhere.

197 For example, Otto Fenichel's 1945 text, *The Psychoanalytic Theory of Neurosis*, which was for many years treated as a basic introduction to the field (particularly in the United States), praises Hartmann's "conflict-free sphere" and suggests that classic psychoanalysis was too preoccupied with mental conflict at the expense of a focus on adaptation. By the end of the 1930s, Fenichel had, like so many of the Viennese and Berlin trained psychoanalysts, relocated to the USA, which in part accounts for the influence of his work on the American ego psychological tradition.

198 The concept of normality and the tenet that "normal people" can be described and differentiated from those who are "pathological" is not only pre-Freudian in its tendentiousness (contesting, for example, Freud's trenchant arguments in 1905 which effectively abolished the normal/abnormal distinction), but is also inevitably and irredeemably saturated in ideological purposes. Hartmann's paper on the concept of health, which is effectively amplified by Anna Freud's last writings on the "psychology of normal development," never pauses to consider the character of the "reality" to which the individual is enjoined to adapt in the interests of his or her "maturation." Having assumed that there is a "conflict-free sphere" of ego functioning, it seems to follow that the more one's conduct is governed by the operations of this sphere, the more adapted and "normal" one will be. The circularity of such theorizing is stupendous (perhaps stupefying), as it never seems to occur to its proponents that social arrangements that are founded on internal contradictions (colloquially, a "sick" society) might succeed in the ideological production of subjects that function apparently without conflict in the context of these arrangements. The myth of apolitical healing underwrites the entire bourgeois enterprise of specifying normality so that those who do not adapt to the status quo can have their deviations subjected to appropriate treatment. Obviously, we owe much to Foucault and to many who have followed his lead in exposing the political implications of our concepts of "mental illness"—including commentators such as Jeff Weeks, Roy Porter, and David Ingleby. See also Paul Verhaeghe's *On Being Normal and Other Disorders* and Bollas's important writings on normopathy and the normotic.

199 Klein had been established in London since 1926, over a decade prior to the arrival of the Freud family. This chronology, and because of Klein's liaison with Jones (who had founded the British Psychoanalytical Society, which was originally called the London Psychoanalytical Society, in 1913), Kleinian perspectives, particularly on early development, prevailed in England even before Klein's later development of her ideas on schizoid mechanisms (as well as envy and gratitude, or guilt and reparation). The clash between the Kleinians and the Anna Freudians culminated in the so-called "Controversial Discussions" from 1941 to 1945, which have been well documented

by Pearl King and Riccardo Steiner, as well as extensively discussed in the subsequent literature.

200 Competent discussions of the independent group within the British Psychoanalytical Society are provided by the contributors to Gregorio Kohon's 1986 anthology, by Judith Hughes in her 1989 *Reshaping the Psychoanalytic Domain*, and by Eric Rayner's 1991 *The Independent Mind in British Psychoanalysis*.

201 Erikson, who arrived in the USA earlier in the 1930s, is often included in this list of ego psychological luminaries, although in many respects he can be more aptly categorized in the self/relational tradition. Another significant voice is that of Sterba. Despite being a Gentile, he fled Vienna in solidarity with Freud's "Wednesday Group" of which he was a member, making his new home in Detroit. He continued his allegiance to the ego psychological tradition (although thinking of his practice as "classical"), despite coming into conflict with the orthodoxy of the American Psychoanalytic Association, because of his advocacy of nonmedical training.

202 This is not to suggest some sort of harmonious and monolithic development of ego psychological thinking and the absence of power-mongering within the American Psychoanalytic Association. Douglas Kirsner's 2009 book amply describes and documents the tensions between different factions, and particularly those between New York, Boston, and Chicago. Also useful are the thoughtful essays collected in John Burnham's *After Freud Left*, as well as the two volumes of historical analysis by Nathan Hale.

203 Lacan's attack on ego psychology is to be found both in his *Écrits* and his *Four Fundamental Concepts of Psychoanalysis*, as well as several of the *Séminaires*. It is also discussed across three of Roudinesco's books. However, I think it can fairly be said that Lacan polemicizes the issue, by which I mean that he dismisses ego psychology and then leaves us to infer from his own theorizing details of the reasons for this trenchant dismissal.

204 Karlsson's 2004 work is one of the better attempts to meld psychoanalysis with Husserlian phenomenology, although significantly I believe he fails to give sufficient consideration to the notion of repression and to free-associative discourse as a derepressive praxis. My critique of phenomenology and of the various subjectivist renderings of psychoanalytic method is given a philosophical treatment in *Psychic Reality and Psychoanalytic Knowing*.

205 In Sterba's words, "therapeutic dissociation of the ego is a necessity if the analyst is to have the chance of winning over part of it to his side, conquering it, strengthening it by means of identification with himself and opposing it in the transference to those parts which have a cathexis of instinctual and defensive energy." Sterba's paper has been criticized by several commentators, including Mitchell in his 1995 *Hope and Dread in Psychoanalysis*. Not least of the issues here is that what motivates the patient to develop this "therapeutic ego-dissociation" depends on his or her gradual identification with the psychoanalyst's observing and interpreting functions through the transference; since such identifications can be fostered by fear as much as affection, this might be seen to raise an ethical problem. Moreover, since it is the patient's superego functioning (already an aspect of his or her functioning that has been differentiated out of the ego organization) that tends to impair the ego's ability to judge its own functioning in a balanced manner (generating what will later be called "adaptive compromise formations" between the demands of id impulses, reality factors, and superego stringencies), the patient's acquisition of an "analytic ego" is necessarily a transformation of both superego and ego components in line with the values represented by the person of the practitioner.

206 Ego psychology thus gained popularity in the USA for the same sort of ideological reasons that self/relational perspectives burgeoned in that culture. The more your ego is "conflict-free," then presumably the more your "conflict-free" ego is your "self"—comfortable in its own individualist sense of integrity, self-reliance, achievement, self-interest, and mastery. Even if these characteristics are illusional and delusional, they comprise the point at which self-interrogation ceases, leaving the subject a well-adapted participant in the culture of capitalism.

207 This distinction between the stasis of alienation and the kinesis of estrangement is discussed in my *Psychoanalysis and the Postmodern Impulse* and will be revisited in the final chapter.

208 The importance of the concept of sublimation—at least for those ego psychologists who continue to refer to the notion of drives—cannot be overestimated. How else is an ego psychologist to theorize a "mental apparatus" that begins life suffused by "id" impulses and yet develops a "conflict-free" sphere of functioning? Yet despite a sizeable literature on the topic, the concept remains extremely ambiguous—indeed, replete with internal contradictions. The history of the concept is well documented in Hans Loewald's 1988 work, and it may be noted that even Hartmann was dissatisfied with its lack of cogency, as is discussed in John Muller's 1999 paper, "Modes and Functions of Sublimation," and elsewhere.

209 The notion of alienation (in the broader social, rather than the inner psychological, sense) has been widely discussed, particularly in the Marxist literature. See, for example, the important works by authors such as Richard Schacht, István Mészáros, Bertell Ollman, Richard Schmitt, and Rahel Jaeggi. Issues concerning the embodied dimension of alienation are briefly discussed in the chapter on "Oppression and the Momentum of Liberation" in my 2010 book.

210 For reasons of brevity, in this book I am going to bypass the complex relationship between Bion's vitally significant work and the more orthodox Kleinian movement.

211 I am uncomfortably aware that this listing does not do justice to the developments of Kleinianism in South America, much of which cannot be easily accessed within the anglophone world.

212 Here one must acknowledge the important Kleinian distinction between a powerfully determinative *phantasy* that is necessarily "unconscious" and a *fantasy* that might be as whimsical as a conscious daydream or as impactful as a preconscious narrative. However, the Kleinian literature more frequently than not uses the term "unconscious" in a descriptive, rather than in the repressed sense, and hence these "unconscious phantasies" might actually be preconscious. This is discussed in Green's critique of Kleinianism—see previous note.

213 As I indicated, Klein also seems to hint, in her later writings, at an innate capacity for care or love—a concept that is somewhat better developed in neo-Kleinian writings and other object-relations formulations, such as Fairbairn's and Winnicott's. For a discussion of such matters, Ian Suttie's 1935 *The Origins of Love and Hate* is still interesting.

214 That the observation of infants is no basis for the promulgation of theories about psychic life after infancy has been ably argued by Peter Wolff (himself a seasoned researcher of behaviors in infancy) in 1996 and by Green in the Sandlers's 2000 anthology *Clinical and Observational Psychoanalytic Research*. In brief, the problem is that one can read into the behavior of infants all sorts of speculations about their psychic life. Thus, as I have suggested elsewhere, Esther Bick observes infants and finds a baby who seems to endorse Kleinian tenets, Margaret Mahler observes a baby more or less compatible with Hartmann's ego psychology, whereas Daniel Stern discovers a baby who seems to fit a Winnicottian description, Josph Lichtenberg's baby seems to favor a Kohutian model of development, Virginia Demos sees the baby in terms of a specific affect theory, and most recently Beatrice Beebe documents a baby who seems to conform to an intersubjectivist paradigm. This list of the speculative-baby-observing industry that is currently much in fashion could be multiplied.

215 By "active imagination," I mean techniques such as the visualization of images and narratives, as well as the expressive use of "automatic writing," dance, painting, sculpture, and so forth. Such techniques are described by Jung in his 1913–1916 and 1957–1961 writings. These ideas are amplified by Barbara Hannah in her 2001 *Encounters with the Soul*, by Anthony Stevens in his 1999 *On Jung*, and elsewhere—it seems unlikely that Jung himself recognized sufficiently the discrepancy between his advocacy of active imagination and his earlier 1904–1907 experimental work with associations. The controversial issues around this topic are briefly discussed in my "Free-

associating with the Bodymind, in which I wrote that "while there can be no question that expatiating on, as well as exploring fulsomely, the vistas and horizons of self-expression can be therapeutic, there is a critical difference between such ventures and the process of surrendering to the dispossessive momentum of the free-associating (given the way that this momentum temporally dislocates the subject, compromises its sense of solidity, and subverts its confidence in itself). To define this difference simplistically, the former constructs whereas the latter deconstructs. Self-expression remains in the orbit of the subject's epistemological appropriation and closure, preserving the solidity of the 'I–now–is' by keeping the subject within a unilinear temporality. By contrast, the free-associative process of dispossession and deconstruction jeopardizes the established being-in-the-world of self-consciousness, opening the 'I–now–is' to the truthfulness (by which I mean the force, trajectory, and momentum) of a movement in which it is disclosed as having been compromised by 'past-futures.' Although, on the level of appearances, this difference between self-expression and free-association may sometimes seem slight, it is always profoundly significant."

216 This view of facing the abyss is developed somewhat in my 1999 and 2004 papers.

217 Although there may be some important distinctions to be made between the notions of emancipation and liberation, I shall use these terms synonymously in this chapter. Despite their religious undertones, I find Enrique Dussel's *Philosophy of Liberation* and his *Politics of Liberation* useful, as well as any number of contemporary commentators, including the prolific Slavoj Žižek. Also, important to note here is that to call free-association a "method" may be stretching certain of the connotations of this term—see note 56 above.

218 In my 1993 book, this was discussed in terms of the "act of establishment," by which meanings are, so to speak, pinned down representationally or semiotically, by means of repetition.

219 Surely, living at the end-times of global capitalism when social arrangements are ubiquitously characterized by domination, exploitation, systemic violence, and the spectre of ecocide, the notion of "good citizenship" must be interrogated psychoanalytically as well as politically (which is not to suggest that a psychoanalytic inquiry is other than political). Sadly, the very organization of the "psychoanalytic movement" and the social position of many practitioners mitigates against such questioning.

220 This line of critique has been developed in many places; for instance, in the extensive political literature that cautions against reformism, classically exemplified by Rosa Luxemburg's 1899 critique ("Reform or Revolution") of Eduard Bernstein's revisionist perspective. Žižek's essays on violence also review the dilemmas inherent in this issue. As he expresses it, in the end-times of capitalism—today's global constellation—in which exploitative and oppressive sociopolitical formations unravel into an escalating momentum of genocide and ecocide, there is no clear solution and no self-evident "light at the end of the tunnel" because a critical analysis of the current human situation makes one aware that any such light might well "belong to a train crashing towards us."

221 This is surely why Freud consistently opposed the idea of psychosynthesis. "I shake my wise head over psychosynthesis," he wrote to Jung on 16 April 1909, reiterating these objections in his 1919 paper, "Lines of Advance in Psychoanalytic Therapy." However, he could not bring himself to see the conflict between the goals of therapy and the effects of psychoanalysis, even though this conflict is latently but acutely evident in his two 1937 essays.

222 In his 1997 paper, "Aims of the Psychoanalytic Process," Laplanche makes an argument very similar to mine, although with less overt emphasis on the process being that of free-association. Laplanche deftly begins his argument by quoting Freud's 1920 paper on female homosexuality, in which he writes that situations "such as a prospective homeowner ordering an architect to build him a villa according to his own tastes and specifications, or of a pious philanthropist commissioning an artist to paint a sacred picture in the corner of which is to be a portrait of himself worshipping, are fundamentally incompatible with the conditions of psychoanalysis." Laplanche calls "psychoanalysis"

undertaken with equivalent goals "made-to-order" or "ready-made," but he could just as well have such procedures "therapy." Interestingly, he briefly mentions the problem of the psychoanalysis of candidates-in-training, where all too easily the goal to produce a particular sort of personality comes to derail the psychoanalytic process.

223 A similar argument is ably presented by Todd Dean in a 2013 commentary. He marshals some comments made by Freud in his 1910 paper on "Wild Analysis," Lacan's 1953 manifesto, Siegfried Bernfeld memories of Freud's dismissive attitude toward "the authorities" of psychoanalytic pedagogy, Laplanche's *Essays on Otherness*, and some informal remarks by Darian Leader. Dean then reaches the following interesting conclusions: "psychoanalysis is not defined by its technique, but by its effects. To be clear, while we may not know what particular effects will be produced in any given case, we do know that there will be effects, as long as we use our knowledge to engage with the unknown and unknowable." Here, of course, I would emphasize that this knowledge is that of a method or praxis, rather than some speculative model of the functioning of the mental apparatus. Dean continues by suggesting that "we can even say something about what these effects will be: There will always be some element of surprise, of the new, in them; furthermore, they will be the consequence of analytic discourse, not of an arrival at a particular understanding. And they won't result from the application of a predetermined technique, regardless of that technique's expressed goals."

224 These matters were discussed more fully in my *The Emergence of Somatic Psychology and Bodymind Therapy*.

225 At the risk of unnecessary reiteration, let it be emphasized that psychoanalysis can have no set outcomes and does not even aspire to the pacification or elimination of those formations that the dubious discipline of psychopathology designates "symptoms." Of course, psychoanalytic treatment may well make sense of symptoms, and thus have them lose their power over the subject, but this is definitely *not* equivalent to the goals that govern the labor of behavioral technicians, for whom the removal of symptoms and the installation of a "good citizen" is the be all and end all of their tricks. As psychoanalysts know—or should know—symptom removal can always do "more harm than good" to the patient, precisely because there is a deeply implicated relationship between the suffering of the individual psyche and the reality of oppressive and exploitive sociocultural arrangements within which the individual is constituted and then conducts his or her life. This relationship is, of course, a matter to which Marie Langer (in her paper "Psicoanálisis sin Divan") and others have tried to draw our attention. There is a sense in which Kierkegaard was correct when, in 1849, he argued that the first task is to "identify the sickness," but this is seriously incorrect if one assumes that the sickness is primarily a matter of the individual.

226 This paraphrases what Freud argued in his 1910 paper on "Wild Analysis" (which does "more harm to the cause of psychoanalysis than to individual patients"). The clinician, a physician who is the subject of Freud's criticism, had given a young, sexually dissatisfied divorcée a piece of advice, consisting of three options, that, in the context of that historical epoch and social class, would have been scandalous: "return to your husband, take a lover, or pleasure yourself." Freud does not condone the practice of issuing advice, but also suggests that its *effect* may be psychoanalytically helpful, in that it compels the woman to face and to listen to the "real cause" of her problem. That is, the very scandalousness of the advice, coming from the authority of a physician, has the effect of spontaneously unsettling the patient (since none of the alternatives were acceptable to her). This effect might be, in some limited sense, psychoanalytic, although it is only a sort of "one-time" deconstructive intervention and lacks the ongoing processive commitment that free-associative method necessarily entails. Some of these ideas are well discussed in Dean's 2013 article, who also refers to Phillips's apt comment in 2002 that Freud was "curiously unforthcoming" about the procedures or "rules" of psychoanalytic engagement. It is also unquestionably true that Freud, despite his support for the Max Eitingon's prescriptions formulated in the 1920s for training

in psychoanalysis, was quite dismissive of the authoritarianism of psychoanalytic pedagogy.

227 Again, I must express my appreciation to Dean's article for alerting me to Charles Olson's wonderful poem, "The Kingfishers," which includes a Maoist aphorism that is very pertinent to psychoanalysis: *nous devons, nous lever et agir!* ("we must stand up and act," which is obviously a sequel to Marx's injunction that "Philosophers have hitherto only interpreted the world in various ways; the point is to change it"). I fully realize that, at least superficially, this might seem to contrast or contradict what was argued at the beginning of this chapter about the pitfalls of any therapeutic imperative to *do something* in the face of suffering. The crux of this difference is exactly the profound divergence between the liberatory effects of psychoanalysis as a praxis and the ambition to achieve certain outcomes that characterizes therapeutic practice.

228 This was discussed at somewhat more length in my *Psychoanalysis and the Postmodern Impulse*. See also Badiou's important writings.

229 See Adorno's writings on negative dialectics and the associated publications of the Frankfurt School, particularly Max Horkheimer, Walter Benjamin, and Herbert Marcuse. Of this group, it is, of course, Marcuse who attended most directly to psychoanalysis; see his *Eros and Civilization* as well as *One-Dimensional Man*, and the collection of writings recently edited by Douglas Kellner and Clayton Pierce.

230 Although it is unclear whether William Morris intended the irony of his 1890 title, utopian visions become "News from Nowhere." Although much scholarship has been devoted to analyzing why the great communist vision failed, we cannot skirt around the fact that it failed and that we now, living in the end-times of global capitalism, have no clear vision of alternative arrangements—a point made repetitively, in recent years, by Žižek and many others.

231 I believe this is what Lacan is trying to convey when, in his *Écrits*, he writes that the patient "begins the analysis by speaking about himself without speaking to you or by speaking to you without speaking about himself. When he can speak to you about himself, the analysis will be over." Interestingly, Lacan also speaks of the end of psychoanalysis as coming-to-terms with one's own mortality. Dylan Evans's *Dictionary* discusses several different ways in which Lacan addresses the issues of termination.

232 This is surely reminiscent, among many other sources, of Thomas Mann's distinctively psychoanalytic insight, spoken by Hans Castorp in the *Magic Mountain*, published in 1924: "The body, love, death . . . these three are only one. For the body is sickness and voluptuousness, and it is this that causes death, yes, they are carnal both of them, love and death, and that is their terror and their great magic!" For a riff on the capitalized notion of Love, see my *Liberating Eros* and related publications.

233 Heidegger, in trying to culminate and restart two-and-a-half millennia of Western philosophizing, warns us against the term *Geist*—from the 1927 *Being and Time* through to his more psychoanalytically resonant writings of the 1950s and 1960s. Yet *spirit* remains a beguiling term. Consider the notion of libidinality in connection with the Kena Upanishad: "Who sends the mind to wander afar? Who first drives life to start on its journey? Who impels us to utter these words? What cannot be spoken with words, but that whereby words are spoken, know that alone to be Brahman, the Spirit; and not what people here adore. What cannot be thought with the mind, but that whereby the mind can think, know that alone to be Brahman, the Spirit; and not what people here adore. If you think you know Brahman, the Spirit, then surely you do not" (the Sanskrit author of the Upanishads is anonymous—this quotation is adapted from three translations). From a very different tradition, we might also consider the lines in William Wordsworth's "Tintern Abbey," written in 1798: "and in the mind of man—a motion and a spirit, that impels all thinking things, all objects of all thought, and rolls through all things." In the context of the idea that psychic energy is a movement of presencing-and-absencing (which will be mentioned again shortly), it is interesting to note that, in the *Gospel of Thomas*, Yeshuah indicates that the "evidence" of the Spirit within us is "motion and rest."

234 In future, we must consider, and correct with psychoanalytic understanding, what the discipline of economics has traditionally failed to comprehend—namely, the inner significance of an entire range of acts that are sacrificial, or that appear sacrificial—from Marcel Mauss's work on gifts and gift economies, to Georges Bataille's and René Girard's various writings on sacrifice and self-sacrifice, and to Irigaray's more recent psychoanalytic work on feminine social formations and the infrastructure of female economies that are founded on unremunerated nurturing.

235 The significance of "keeping thinking erotic" is discussed by Alan Bass and Don Moss in their 2012 commentary. The independent thinking of these two practitioners is consistently refreshing, and I am particularly appreciative of Bass's *Difference and Disavowal* and his *Interpretation and Difference*.

236 As Freud expresses it in the Interpretation of Dreams: "mindestens eine Stelle, an welcher er unergründlich ist, gleichsam einen Nabel, durch den er mit dem Unerkannten zusammenhängt" ("at least one place at which it is unfathomable, like a navel, a passage through which it is connected to the unknown").

237 This is reported in Sterba's *Reminiscences* and perhaps less directly in the Nunberg and Federn's *Minutes of the Vienna Psychoanalytic Society*.

238 This interpretation of what Freud may have intended, in the writing of *Beyond the Pleasure Principle*, trenchantly repudiates the idea that *Todestrieb* is to be equated with a destructive-aggressive motive (Weiss, Klein), or with an end-of-life motive to die (Federn); closer is Jones's notion of *aphanisis* as the fading-of-desire, discussed by Lacan in his seminar on female sexuality. Rather, what is impressive are the inchoate insights of Spielrein's 1912 paper, "Die Destruktion als Ursache des Werdens," which suggest how creative and destructive (in the entropic sense) are inextricably entwined in life's every act. Freud's 1920 essay acknowledges Spielrein's paper, but perhaps he was more influenced by it than he readily knew or admitted. The writings of Maurice Blanchot and Derrida on death remain indispensable; Lingis's *Deathbound Subjectivity* is also profoundly helpful as are the writings of David Wood. See also the Lacanian writings of Richard Boothby. Franco de Masi's *Making Death Thinkable* provides a different approach to the topic.

239 This somewhat parallels Green's discussion (in "The Dead Mother"), which is notably ambivalent about representationality. In his terms, the very thing that makes the individual's passion viable, which is its representation, is also that which gives the lie to representationality. In his paper "Taking Aims: André Green and the Pragmatics of Passion," Phillips discusses how Green treats the "positive role" of unbinding and indicates how *Lebenstriebe* and *Todestriebe* are, in a sense, not exclusively antagonistic, but often collaborative in so far as unbinding leads the way to a more fruitful and creative rebinding.

240 In his discussion of Freud's assertion that every text has an "unfathomable navel," Derrida suggests that, even after exhaustive textual analysis, texts remain enigmatic, pointing to the *omphalos*, the unknown and unknowable "navel" of the world. We might question whether Derrida might equally have allegorized this "navel" as the formless *yoni* (epitomizing Shakti energy) that contains and makes possible the mark of difference that is effected by the Shiva *lingam*.

REFERENCES

Adler, A. W. (1898–1937). *The Collected Clinical Works of Alfred Adler* (12 vols, edited by H. T. Stein). Bellingham, WA: The Alfred Adler Institute of Northwest Washington, 2005.

Adorno, T. W. (1951). *Minima Moralia: Reflections from Damaged Life*. Brooklyn, NY: Verso.

—— (1964). *The Jargon of Authenticity*. London: Routledge, 2002.

—— (1965–1966). *Lectures on Negative Dialectics: Fragments of a Lecture Course 1965/1966* (edited by R. Tiedemann, translated by R. Livingstone). Cambridge: Polity Press, 2008.

—— (1966). *Negative Dialectics* (translated by E. B. Ashton). New York: Seabury.

Aisenstein, M. & Rappoport de Aisemberg, E. (eds, 2010). *Psychosomatics Today: A Psychoanalytic Perspective*. London: Karnac Books.

Alexander, F. G. (1921–1961). *The Scope of Psychoanalysis, 1921–1961: Selected Papers*. New York: Basic Books, 1961.

—— (1946). *Psychoanalytic Psychotherapy: Principles and Application* (with T. M. French and others). Lincoln, NE: University of Nebraska Press, 1980.

Alford, C. F. (1989). *Melanie Klein and Critical Social Theory: An Account of Politics, Art, and Reason Based on her Psychoanalytic Theory*. New Haven, CT: Yale University Press, 2001.

—— (1998). Melanie Klein and the nature of good and evil. In: P. Marcus & A. Rosenberg (eds), *Psychoanalytic Versions of the Human Condition: Philosophies of Life and their Impact on Practice*. New York: New York University Press, pp.118–139.

Althusser, L. (1971). *Lenin and Philosophy and Other Essays*. New York: Monthly Review Press, 2001.

Andreas-Salomé, L. (1894). *Nietzsche* (edited and translated by S. Mandel). Champaign, IL: University of Illinois Press, 2001.

—— (*c.* 1930–1937). *Looking Back: Memoirs* (edited by E. Pfeiffer in 1951 & 1973, translated by B. Mitchell). Emeryville, CA: Marlowe, 1995.

Anon. (*c.* 800 BCE). Kena Upanishad. In: *The Ten Principal Upanishads* (translated by Shree Purohit Swāmi & W. B. Yeats). London: Faber & Faber, 1937. [Also in *The Principal Upanishads* (translated by Swāmi Nikhilananda). Mineola, NY: Dover, 2003. And in: *The Upanishads* (translated by E. Easwaran). Tomales, CA: Nilgiri Press, 1987.]

Anzieu, D. (1975). *Freud's Self-analysis* (translated by Peter Graham). London: Hogarth Press.

—— (1985). *The Skin Ego: A Psychoanalytic Approach to the Self* (translated by Chris Turner). New Haven, CT: Yale University Press, 1989.

—— (ed., 1987). *Psychic Envelopes* (translated by D. Briggs). London: Karnac Books, 1990.
—— & Tarrab, G. (1990). *A Skin for Thought: Interviews with Gilbert Tarrab on the Interface of Psychology and Psychoanalysis*. London: Karnac Books.
Aposhyan, S. (2004). *Body–mind Psychotherapy: Principles, Techniques, and Practical Applications*. New York: W. W. Norton.
Arendt, H. (1958). *The Human Condition* (2nd edn). Chicago: University of Chicago Press.
Aristotle (*c.* 364–322 BCE). *The Complete Works of Aristotle* (2 vols, edited by J. Barnes). Princeton, NJ: Princeton University Press,1984.
Arlow, J. A. & Brenner, C. (1964). *Psychoanalytic Concepts and the Structural Theory*. New York: International Universities Press.
—— (2001). *A Meeting of Minds: Mutuality in Psychoanalysis*. New York: Routledge.
—— & Harris, A. (eds, 1999–2011). *Relational Psychoanalysis* (5 vols). London: Routledge.
—— & Harris, A. (eds, 1993). *The Legacy of Sándor Ferenczi*. London: Routledge.
Aron, L. (1996). *A Meeting of Minds: Mutuality in Psychoanalysis*. London: Routledge.
Aron, L. & Harris, A. (eds., 1993). *Relational Psychoanalysis*. London: Routledge.
Assagioli, R. G. (1965). *Psychosynthesis: A Collection of Basic Writings*. Amherst, MA: Synthesis Center, 2000.
Atwood, G. E. & Stolorow, R. D. (1984). *Structures of Subjectivity: Explorations in Psychoanalytic Phenomenology and Contextualism*. London: Routledge.
Auden, W. H. (1939). *In Memory of Sigmund Freud: Collected Poems*. New York: Random House, 1976, pp. 215–218.
Austin, J. L. (1955). *How to do Things with Words: The William James Lectures Delivered at Harvard University in 1955* (edited by J. O. Urmson & M. Sbisà). Oxford: Clarendon Press.
Avenarius, R. (1891). *Der Menschliche Weltbegriff* (4th edn). Leipzig, Germany: Reisland, 1927.
Bachelard, G. (1934). *The New Scientific Spirit* (translated by A. Goldhammer). Boston, MA: Beacon Press, 1984.
—— (1938). *The Formation of the Scientific Mind* (translated by M. McAllester Jones). Bolton: Clinamen, 2002.
—— (1940). *The Philosophy of No: A Philosophy of the New Scientific Mind* (translated by G. C. Waterson). New York: Orion, 1968.
Bachofen, J. J. (1861). *Myth, Religion, and Mother Right* (translated by R. Manheim). Princeton, NJ: Princeton University Press, 1992.
Bacon, F. (1597–1625). *The Essays* (edited by J. Pitcher). London: Penguin, 1986.
—— (1620). *The New Organon* (edited by L. Jardine & M. Silverthorne). Cambridge: Cambridge University Press, 2000.
Badiou, A. (1982). *The Theory of the Subject* (translated by B. Bosteels). London: Continuum, 2009.
Bakan, D. (2004). *Sigmund Freud and the Jewish Mystical Tradition*. Mineola, NY: Dover.
Bakhtin, M. M. (1919–1921). *Toward a Philosophy of the Act* (translated by V. Liapunov). Austin, TX: University of Texas Press, 1993.
—— (1970–1975). *Speech Genres and Other Late Essays* (translated by V. W. McGee). Austin, TX: University of Texas Press, 1986.
Barratt, B. B. (1984). *Psychic Reality and Psychoanalytic Knowing*. Hillsdale, NJ: Analytic Press.
—— (1991). Semiotics and its "other": Notes on the psychoanalytic unconscious. In: B. E. Litowitz & P. S. Epstein (eds), *Semiotic Perspectives on Clinical Theory and Practice: Medicine, Neuropsychiatry and Psychoanalysis*. Berlin: Mouton de Gruyter, 127–156.
—— (1993). *Psychoanalysis and the Postmodern Impulse: Knowing and Being since Freud's Psychology*. Baltimore, MD: Johns Hopkins University Press.
—— (1994). Critical notes on the psychoanalyst's theorizing. *Journal of the American Psychoanlytic Association*, 42, 697–725.

—— (1995). Psychoanalysis and the future: Postmodern impulses versus the nostalgia for certainties. In: S. R. Friedlander (ed.), *Confronting the Challenges to Psychoanalysis: Collected Papers from the Fifth Annual Conference of the International Federation for Psychoanalytic Education*. Knoxville, TN: International Federation for Psychoanalytic Education, 177–185.

—— (1999). Cracks: On castration, death and laughter. In: J. Barron (ed.), *Humor and Psyche*. New Haven, CT: Yale University Press, 57–67.

—— (2004). Desire and death in the constitution of I-ness. In: J. Reppen, J. Tucker & M. A. Schulman (eds). *Way Beyond Freud: Postmodern Psychoanalysis Observed*. London: Open Gate Press, 264–279.

—— (2005). *Sexual Health and Erotic Freedom*. Philadelphia, PA: Xlibris/Random House.

—— (2006). *What is Tantric Practice?* Philadelphia, PA: Xlibris/Random House.

—— (2009). *Liberating Eros*. Philadelphia, PA: Xlibris/Random House.

—— (2009). Ganesha's lessons for psychoanalysis: Notes on fathers and sons, sexuality and death. *Psychoanalysis, Culture and Society*, 14, 317–336.

—— (2010). *The Emergence of Somatic Psychology and Bodymind Therapy*. Basingstoke: Palgrave Macmillan.

—— (2012). Boundaries and intimacies: Ethics and the (re)performance of The Law in psychoanalysis. *International Forum of Psychoanalysis*, 24, 204–215. First published 1 October as DOI: 10.1080/0803706X.2012.714907.

—— (2013). Free-associating with the bodymind. *International Forum of Psychoanalysis*, 22, 161–175. First published 21 January as DOI:10.1080/0803706X.2012.729860.

—— (2013). *What is Psychoanalysis? 100 years after Freud's Secret Committee*. London: Routledge.

—— (2013). Sensuality, sexuality, and the eroticism of slowness. In: *The Culture of the Slow* (edited by N. Obaldiston). Basingstoke: Palgrave Macmillan, 136–153.

—— (2014). A practitioner's notes on free-associative method as existential praxis. *International Forum of Psychoanalysis*, 23, 195–208. Published 26 March as iFirst 10.1080/0803706X.894255.

—— (2015). On the mythematic reality of libidinality as a subtle energy system: Notes on vitalism, mechanism, and emergence in psychoanalytic thinking. *Psychoanalytic Psychology*, 32, 626–644. Published on 27 January 2014 as iFirst 10.1037/a0034973.

—— (2015). Critical notes on the neuro-evolutionary archaeology of affective systems. *Psychoanalytic Review*, 102, 183–208.

—— (2015). Rejoinder to Solms' response to Critical notes on the neuro-evolutionary archaeology of affective systems. *Psychoanalytic Review*, 102, 221–227.

—— (2015). Fathering and the consolidation of masculinity: Notes on the paternal function in Andrey Zvaginstsev's The Return. *Psychoanalytic Review*, 102, 347–364.

—— (2015). Opening to the Otherwise: Today's Unconscious and the Necessity of Free-Association for Psychoanalytic Praxis. *International Journal of Psychoanalysis*, Paper read at the 49th Congress of the International Psychoanalytic Association in Boston, MA.

—— (in press). Seven questions for Kleinian psychology. *Psychoanalytic Psychology*, in press.

Barthes, R. (1955). Striptease. In: *A Barthes Reader* (edited by S. Sontag). New York: Hill & Wang, 1982, 85–88.

Bass, A. (2000). *Difference and Disavowal: The Trauma of Eros*. Palo Alto, CA: Stanford University Press.

—— (2006). *Interpretation and Difference: The Strangeness of Care*. Palo Alto, CA: Stanford University Press.

—— & Moss, D. (2012). On keeping thought erotic: Some problems in contemporary theory and practice. *Division for Psychoanalytic Psychology Review: A Quarterly Psychoanalytic Forum*, 6, 29–33.

Bataille, G. (1927–1939). *Visions of Excess: Selected Writings, 1927–1939* (edited and translated by A. Stoekl). Minneapolis, MN: University of Minnesota Press, 1985.

—— (1949). *The Accursed Share* (3 vols, translated by R. Hurley). New York: Zone Books, 1988–1991.

Baudrillard, J. (1983). *Fatal Strategies* (translated by P. Beitchman & W. G. J. Niesluchowski). New York: Semiotext(e), 2008.

—(1987). *The Ecstasy of Communication* (translated by B. Schütze & C. Schütze). New York: Semiotext(e), 2012.

—— (1992). *The Illusion of the End* (translated by C. Turner). Standford, CA: Stanford University Press, 1994.

—— (2008). *Radical Alterity* (translated by M. Guillaume & A. Hodges). New York: Semiotext(e), 2008.

Beauvoir, S. de (1947). *The Ethics of Ambiguity* (translated by D. Frechtman). New York: Citadel.

—— (1949). *The Second Sex* (translated by C. Borde & S. Malovany-Chevallier). New York: Vintage.

Beckermann, A., Flohr, H. & Kim, J. (eds, 1992). *Emergence or Reduction? Essays on the Prospects of Nonreductive Physicalism*. Berlin: Mouton de Gruyter.

Bedau, M. A. & Humphreys, P. (eds, 2008). *Emergence: Contemporary Readings in Philosophy and Science*. Cambridge, MA: Bradford Books.

Beebe, B. & Lachmann, F. M. (2005). *Infant Research and Adult Treatment: Co-constructing Interactions*. London: Routledge.

Benjamin, W. (1913–1940). *Walter Benjamin: Selected Writings* (4 volumes). Cambridge: Belknap Press.

Bergson, H-L. (1907). *Creative Evolution* (translated by A. Mitchell). Scotts Valley, CA: CreateSpace (Palgrave Macmillan), 2011.

Berlin, I. (1969). *Four Essays on Liberty*. Oxford: Oxford University Press.

Berman, M. (1982). *All that is Solid Melts into Air: The Experience of Modernity*. New York: Simon & Schuster.

Bernfeld, S. (1962). On psychoanalytic training. *Psychoanalytic Quarterly*, 31, 453–482.

Bernstein, R. J. (1971). *Praxis and Action: Contemporary Philosophies of Human Activity*. Philadelphia, PA: University of Pennsylvania Press.

Bettelheim, B. (1956–1989). *Freud's Vienna and Other Essays*. New York: Vintage, 1989.

—— (1983). *Freud and Man's Soul: An Important Re-interpretation of Freudian Theory*. New York: Vintage.

Bhattacharyya, K. (1907–1936). *Studies in Philosophy* (edited by G. Bhattacharyya, 3rd edn). Delhi: Motilal Banarsidass, 2008.

Bick, E. (1968). The experience of the skin in early object-relations. In: Harris, M. & Bick, E. (eds). *The Tavistock Model: Papers on Child Development and Psychoanalytic Training* (revised edn). London: Karnac Books, 133–138.

Binswanger, L. (1930). *Dream and Existence* (with an Introduction by M. Foucault, edited by K. Hoeller). Amherst, NY: Humanities Press, 1993.

—— (1957). *Sigmund Freud: Reminiscences of a Friendship*, translated by N. Guterman. New York: Grune & Stratton.

Bion, W. R. (1962). *Learning from Experience*. London: William Heinemann.

—— (1963). *Elements of Psychoanalysis*. London: William Heinemann.

—— (1965). *Transformations*. London: William Heinemann.

Bird, B. (1972). Notes on transference: Universal phenomenon and hardest part of analysis. *Journal of the American Psychoanalytic Association*, 20, 267–301.

Blanchot, M. (1948). *Death Sentence* (translated by L. Davis). Barrytown, NY: Station Hill of Barrytown Press, 1998.

—— (1994). The instant of my death. In: M. Blanchot & J. Derrida, *The Instant of My Death /Demeure: Fiction and Testimony* (translated by E. Rottenberg). Palo Alto, CA: Stanford University Press, 2000.

—— (2002). *A Voice from Elsewhere* (translated by C. Mandell). Albany, NY: State University of New York Press, 2007.

Blechner, M. J. (2009). *Sex Changes: Transformations in Society and Psychoanalysis*. London: Routledge.

Blumgart, L. (1916). Abstracts from the "Jahrbuch für psychoanalytische und psychopathologische Forschungen." *Psychoanalytic Review*, 3, 90–114.

Boadella, D. (1987). *Lifestreams: An Introduction to Biosynthesis*. London: Routledge, Kegan & Paul.

Boesky, D. (1991). Conflict, compromise formation, and structural theory. In: S. Dowling (ed.), *Conflict and Compromise: Therapeutic Implications*. New York: International Universities Press.

Bollas, C. (1999). *The Mystery of Things*. London: Routledge.

—— (2002). *Free Association (Ideas in Psychoanalysis)*. Cambridge: Icon Books.

—— (2007). *The Freudian Moment*. London: Karnac Books.

—— (2009). *The Evocative Object World*. London: Routledge.

—— (2009). *The Infinite Question*. London: Routledge.

—— (2013). *China on the Mind*. London: Routledge.

Boothby, R. (1991). *Death and Desire: Psychoanalytic Theory in Lacan's Return to Freud*. London: Routledge.

—— (2001. *Freud as Philosopher: Metapsychology after Lacan*. London: Routledge.

Borch-Jacobsen, M. (1982). *The Freudian Subject* (translated by Catherine Porter). Stanford, CA: Stanford University Press, 1988.

—— & Shamdasani, S. (2012). *The Freud Files: An Inquiry into the History of Psychoanalysis*. Cambridge: Cambridge University Press.

Bowlby, J. (1969–1980). *Attachment and Loss* (3 vols). New York: Basic Books.

Brandt, L. W. (1977). Psychoanalyse versus psychoanalysis: Traduttore, traditore. *Psyche–Zeitschrift für Psychoanalyse*, 31, 1045–1051.

Brazelton, T. B. & Cramer, B. G. (1991). *The Earliest Relationship: Parents, Infants, and the Drama of Early Attachment*. Cambridge, MA: De Capo.

Breger, L. (2000). *Freud: Darkness in the Midst of Vision*. New York: Wiley.

Brenner, C. (1994). The mind as conflict and compromise formation. *Journal of Clinical Psychoanalysis*, 3, 473–488.

Brentano, F. (1874). *Psychology from an Empirical Standpoint* (translated by A. Rancurrello, D. Terrell, & L. McAlister). London: Routledge & Kegan Paul, 1973.

Britton, R. (1998). *Belief and Imagination: Explorations in Psychoanalysis*. London: Routledge.

Brown, M. (1989). *The Healing Touch: An Introduction to Organismic Psychotherapy*. Mendocino, CA: LifeRhythm.

Buber, M. (1923). *I and Thou* (translated by W. Kauffman). New York: Hesperides Press, 2006.

Burkhardt, R. W. (2005). *Patterns of Behavior: Konrad Lorenz, Niko Tinbergen, and the Founding of Ethology*. Chicago: University of Chicago Press.

Burnham, J. (ed., 2012). *After Freud Left: A Century of Psychoanalysis in America*. Chicago: University of Chicago Press.

Busch, F. (1995). *The Ego at the Center of Clinical Technique*. Northvale, NJ: Jason Aronson.

—— (2013). *Creating a Psychoanalytic Mind: A Psychoanalytic Method and Theory*. London: Routledge.

Butler, J. P. (1990). *Gender Trouble: Feminism and the Subversion of Identity*. London: Routledge, 2006.

—— (1993). *Bodies that Matter: On the Discursive Limits of Sex*. London: Routledge, 2011.

—— (1993). The lesbian phallus and the morphological imaginary. In: S. Salih (ed., with J. Butler), *The Judith Butler Reader*. Oxford: Blackwell, 138–180.

—— (1997). *The Psychic Life of Power: Theories in Subjection*. Palo Alto, CA: Stanford University Press.

—— (2005). *Giving an Account of Oneself* (4th edn). New York: Fordham University Press.

Caldwell, C. (1996). *Getting our Bodies back: Recovery, Healing, and Transformation through Body-centered Psychotherapy*. Boston, MA: Shambhala.

Calich, J. C. & Hinz, H. (eds, 2007). *The Unconscious: Further Reflections*. London: International Psychoanalytical Association.

Canguilhem, G. (1943/1966). *The Normal and the Pathological* (translated by C. R. Fawcett & R. S. Cohen). New York: Zone Books, 1991.

—— (1952). *Knowledge of Life* (translated by S. Geroulanos & D. Ginsberg). New York: Fordham University Press, 2008.

—— (1977). *Ideology and Rationality in the History of the Life Sciences* (translated by A. Goldhammer). Cambridge, MA: MIT Press, 1988.

—— (1994). *A Vital Rationalist: Selected Writings from Georges Canguilhem* (translated by A. Goldhammer). New York: Zone Books.

Castelnuovo-Tedesco, P. (1986). Fear of changes as a source of resistance in analysis. *Annual of Psychoanalysis*, 14, 259–272.

Chapelle, D. (1993). *Nietzsche and Psychoanalysis*. Albany, NY: State University of New York Press.

Chetrit-Vatine, V. (2012). *The Ethical Seduction of the Analytic Situation: The Feminine-Maternal Origins of Responsibility for the Other* (translated by A. Weller). London: Karnac Books, 2014.

Chiesa, L. (2007). *Subjectivity and Otherness: A Philosophical Reading of Lacan*. Cambridge, MA: MIT Press.

Cieszkowsi, A. (1838–1848). *Selected Writings of August Cieszkowski* (translated by A. Liebich). Cambridge: Cambridge University Press, 2010.

Cixous, H. & Clément, C. (1975). *Newly Born Woman* (translated by B. Wing). Minneapolis, MN: University of Minnesota Press, 1986.

Clark, R. W. (1980). *Freud: The Man and the Cause*. New York: Random House.

Cocks, G. (1997). *Psychotherapy in the Third Reich: The Göring Institute* (2nd revised edn). New Brunswick, NJ: Transaction.

Cohen, B. B. (1994). *Sensing, Feeling and Action: The Experiential Anatomy of Body–Mind Centering* (2nd edn). Toronto: Contact Editions, 2008.

Comte, A. (1848). *A General View of Positivism*. Charleston, SC: Nabu Press, 2011.

Cooley, C. H. (1902). *Human Nature and the Social Order*. New York: Charles Scribner's Sons, 1922.

Copernicus, N. (1543). *On the Revolutions of Heavenly Spheres* (translated by C. G. Wallis). Amherst, NY: Prometheus Books, 1995.

Cornell, W. F. (2008). *Explorations in Transactional Analysis: The Meech Lake Papers*. Pleasanton, CA: TA Press.

Corradini, A. & O'Connor, T. (2013). *Emergence in Science and Philosophy*. London: Routledge.

Damasio, A. R. (2000). *The Feeling of What Happens*. San Diego, CA: Harcourt.

—— (2003). *Looking for Spinoza: Joy, Sorrow, and the Feeling Brain*. Boston, MA: Mariner.

—— (2013). *Self Comes to Mind: Constructing the Conscious Brain*. New York: Vintage.
David, C. (1992). *La Bisexualité Psychique*. Paris: Payot.
Davidson, D. (2001). *Essays on Actions and Events* (2nd edn). Oxford: Oxford University Press.
Dean, J. T. (2013). "What does not change" – Technique and effects in psychoanalysis. *Division Review: A Quarterly Forum* (of Division 39, The Division for Psychoanalysis of the American Psychoanalytic Association), 7 (Spring), 20–26.
Deleuze, G. (1966). *Bergsonism* (translated by H. Tomlinson & B. Habberjam). New York: Zone Books.
—— (1968). *Difference and Repetition* (translated by P. Patton). New York: Columbia University Press, 1994.
Demos, E. V. (1985). The elusive infant. *Psychoanalytic Inquiry*, 5, 553–568.
—— (2016). *Development, Motivation, and the work of Silvan Tomkins*. London: Routledge.
Derrida, J. (1967). *Writing and Difference* (translated by A. Bass). Chicago: University of Chicago Press, 1978.
—— (1967). *Speech and Phenomena: And Other essays on Husserl's Theory of Signs* (translated by D. B. Allison). Evanston, IL: Northwestern University Press, 1973.
—— (1967). *Of Grammatology* (2nd edn, translated by G. C. Spivak). Baltimore, MD: Johns Hopkins University Press, 1998.
—— (1972). *Margins of Philosophy* (translated by A. Bass). Chicago: Chicago University Press, 1982.
—— (1972). *Dissemination* (translated by B. Johnson). Chicago: University of Chicago Press, 1983.
—— (1974). *Glas* (translated by J. P. Leavey & R. Rand). Lincoln, NE: University of Nebraska Press, 1986.
—— (1975). *The Postcard: From Socrates to Freud and Beyond* (translated by A. Bass). Chicago: University of Chicago Press, 1987.
—— (1993). *The Gift of Death* (translated by D. Wills). Chicago: University of Chicago Press, 1996.
—— (1994). *The Politics of Friendship* (translated by G. Collins). London: Verso, 2005.
—— (1995). *Archive Fever: A Freudian Impression* (translated by E. Prenowitz). Chicago: University of Chicago Press, 1996.
—— (1996). *Resistances of Psychoanalysis* (translated by P. Kamuf, P-A Brault, & M. Naas). Stanford, CA: Stanford University Press, 1998.
Dewey, J. (1934). *Art as Experience*. New York: Penguin Perigree, 2005.
Donnet, J-L. (2005). *The Analyzing Situation* (translated by A. Weller). London: Karnac Books, 2009.
Dornes, M. (2002). *Psychanalyse et Psychologie du Première Age*. Paris, France: Presses Universitaires de France.
Dowling, S. (ed., 1991). *Conflict and Compromise: Therapeutic Implications*. New York: International Universities Press.
Durkheim, E. (1898). La prohibition de l'inceste. *L'Année Sociologique*, 1, 1–70.
Dussel, E. (1977). *Philosophy of Liberation* (translated by A. Martinez & C. Morkovsky). Eugene, OR: Wipf & Stock, 2003.
—— (2011). *Politics of Liberation: A Critical Global History* (translated by T. Cooper). Norwich: SCM Press.
Eagle, M. (2013). Assessing evidence for the unconscious. Paper given at the Annual Rapaport-Klein Study Group. Stockbridge, MA: Austen Riggs Center.
Eddington, A. S. (1928). *The Nature of the Physical World*. London: Macmillan.
Edelman, G. M. (1987). *Neural Darwinism: The Theory of Neuronal Group Selection*. New York: Basic Books.

—— (1990). *The Remembered Present: A Biological Theory of Consciousness*. New York: Basic Books.
—— (1992). *Bright Air, Brilliant Fire: On the Matter of Mind*. New York: Basic Books.
—— (2004). *Wider than the Sky: The Phenomenal Gift of Consciousness*. New Haven, CT: Yale University Press.
——— (2006). *Second Nature: Brain Science and Human Knowledge*. New Haven, CT: Yale University Press.
Efron, A. (1985). The sexual body: An interdisciplinary perspective. Special issue of *Journal of Mind and Behavior*, 6 (1 & 2).
Ehrenberg, D. B. (1992). *The Intimate Edge: Extending the Reach of Psychoanalytic Interaction*. New York: W.W. Norton.
Ehrenwald, J. (1991). *The History of Psychotherapy*. Northvale, NJ: Jason Aronson.
Eissler, K. R. (1975). Die Rolle des freien Einfalls in zwei biographischen Arbeiten über Freud. *Psyche–Zeitschrift für Psychoanalyse*, 29, 1096–118.
Eliade, M. (1954). *Yoga: Immortality and Freedom* (translated by W. R. Trask). Princeton, NJ: Princeton University Press, 1970.
Ellenberger, H. (1970). *The Discovery of the Unconscious: The History and Evolution of Dynamic Psychiatry*. New York: Basic Books.
Ellis, H. (1905). *Sexual Selection in Man: Studies in the Psychology of Sex*, Vol. 4. Charleston, SC: Qontro Classic, 2010.
Engels, F. (1884). *The Origin of the Family, Private Property and the State*. London: Penguin Classics, 2010.
Erikson, E. H. (1950–1987). *The Erik Erikson Reader* (edited by R. Coles). New York: W. W. Norton.
—— (1959). *Identity and the Life Cycle*. New York: Norton, 1994.
Esman, A. (ed., 1990). *Essential Papers on Transference*. New York: New York University Press.
Etchegoyen, H. (1991). *The Fundamentals of Psychoanalytic Technique*. London: Karnac Books.
Ey, H. (1968). *Consciousness: A Phenomenological Study of Being Conscious and Becoming Conscious* (translated by J. H. Flodstrom). Bloomington, IN: Indiana University Press, 1978.
Evans, D. (1996). *An Introductory Dictionary of Lacanian Pychoanalysis*. London: Routledge.
Fairbairn, W. R. D. (1931–1964). *From Instinct to Self: Selected Papers of W. R. D. Fairbairn* (2 vols, edited by D. E. Scharff & E. F. Birtles). Northvale, NJ: Jason Aronson, 1994.
—— (1952). *Psychoanalytic Studies of Personality*. London: Routledge, 1994.
Federn, P. (1934). The awakening of the ego in dreams. *International Journal of Psychoanalysis*, 15, 296–301.
—— (1936). Zur Unterscheidung des gesunden und krankhaften Narcissmus. *Imago*, 22, 5–38.
Fenichel, O. (1945). *The Psychoanalytic Theory of Neuroses* (3 vols). New York: Norton, 1995.
Ferenczi, S. (1916). *Sex in Psychoanalysis: Contributions to Psychoanalysis* (translated by E. Jones). Mineola, NY: Dover Publications, 1956. (The original title was *Contributions to Psychoanalysis*, with a later edition being titled *First contributions to psychoanalysis*.)
—— (1926–1933). *Final Contributions to the Problems and Methods of Psychoanalysis* (edited by M. Balint). London: Hogarth Press, 1955.
—— & Rank, O. (1924). *The Development of Psychoanalysis*. New York: International Universities Press, 1986.
Feuerstein, G. (1998). *The Yoga Tradition: Its History, Literature, Philosophy and Practice*. Prescott, AZ: Hohm Press.
Feyerabend, P. (1975). *Against Method*. London: Verso, 2010.
—— (1978). *Science in a Free Society*. London: Verso, 1982.
—— (1996). *The Tyranny of Science*. Cambridge: Polity Press.
Fine, R. (1979). *A History of Psychoanalysis*. New York: Columbia University Press.

Fink, B. (1996). *The Lacanian Subject.* Princeton, NJ: Princeton University Press.
—— (1997). *A Clinical Introduction to Lacanian Psychoanalysis: Theory and Technique.* Cambridge, MA: Harvard University Press.
—— (2007). *Fundamentals of Psychoanalytic Technique: A Lacanian Approach for Practitioners.* New York: W. W. Norton.
—— (2014). *Against Understanding* (2 vols). London: Routledge.
Flax, J. (1992). *Thinking Fragments: Psychoanalysis, Feminism, and Postmodernism in the Contemporary West.* Berkeley, CA: University of California Press.
—— (2012). *Disputed Subjects: Essays on Psychoanalysis, Politics and Philosophy.* Hove: Routledge.
Fliess, R. (1956). *Erogeneity and Libido: Addenda to the Theory of the Psychosexual Development of the Human.* New York: International Universities Press.
—— (1961). *Ego and Body Ego: Contributions to their Psychoanalytic Psychology.* New York: Schulte.
Flint, J., Greenspan, R. J. & Kendler, K. S. (2010). *How Genes Influence Behavior.* Oxford: Oxford University Press.
Foucault, M. (1961). *Madness and Civilization* (translated by R. Howard). New York: Random House, 1965.
—— (1961). *History of Madness* (edited by J. Khalfa, translated by J. Murphy). London: Routledge, 2006.
—— (1966). *The Order of Things: An Archaeology of the Human Sciences* (translated by A. S. London). New York: Pantheon, 1970.
—— (1969–1971). *The Archeology of Knowledge* (translated by A. M. Sheridan Smith). New York: Pantheon, 1972.
Frankl, V. (1937). Zur geistigen problematik der psychotherapies On the mental/spiritual problem of psychotherapies. *Zentralblatt für Psychotherapie,* 10, 33–45.
—— (1946). *Man's Search for Meaning: An Introduction to Logotherapy.* New York: Simon & Schuster, 1984.
—— (1995). *Was nicht in meinen Büchern steht.* What was not said in my books. Munich, Germany: Quintessenz.
French, T. M. (1946). *Psychoanalytic Psychotherapy: Principles and Application* (with F. G. Alexander and others). Lincoln, NE: University of Nebraska Press, 1980.
Freud, A. (1936). *The Ego and the Mechanisms of Defense.* London: Karnac Books, 1993.
—— (1936–1980). *The Writings of Anna Freud* (8 vols). New York: International Universities Press.
—— (1980). *Psychoanalytic Psychology of Normal Development* (Vol. 8 of *The Writings of Anna Freud*). New York: International Universities Press.
Freud, S. (1877–1895). *The Complete Neuroscientific Works of Sigmund Freud* (4 vols, edited by M. Solms). New York: Norton, in press.
—— (1892). Draft K. The neuroses of defence. *Standard Edition,* 1, 220–229. (This document is a precursor to the 1896 publication of "Further remarks on the neuropsychoses of defence.")
—— (1893). Studien über Hysterie: Krankengeschichten. *Gesammelte Werke,* 1, 99–251. (Translated as: Frälein Elisabeth von R – Case histories from studies on hysteria. *Standard Edition,* 2, 135–181.)
—— (1893). Zur Psychotherapie der Hysterie. *Gesammelte Werke,* 1, 252–312. [Translated as: The psychotherapy of hysteria – From Studies on hysteria. *Standard Edition,* 2, 253–305.]
—— (1894). Draft E. How anxiety operates. *Standard Edition,* 1, 189–195. (This document is a precursor to the 1894 publication of "On the grounds for detaching a particular syndrome from neurasthenia under the description 'Anxiety Neurosis.")

—— (1894). Über die Berechtigung, von der Neurasthenie einen Bestimmten Symptomen-Komplex als 'Angstneurose' Abzutrennen. *Gesammelte Werke*, 1, 315–342. (Translated as: On the grounds for detaching a particular syndrome from neurasthenia under the description 'Anxiety Neurosis.' *Standard Edition*, 3, 85–115.)

—— (1895). Entwurf einer Psychologie. In: M. Bonaparte, A. Freud & E. Kris (eds) *Aus den Anfängen der Psychoanalyse*, London: Imago, 1950, 371–466. (Translated as: Project for a scientific psychology. *Standard Edition*, 1, 295–397.)

—— (1896). Weitere Bemerkungen über die Abwehrneuropsychosen. *Gesammelte Werke*, 1, 379–403. (Translated as: Further remark on the neuropsychoses of defence. *Standard Edition*, 3, 157–185.)

—— (1900). Die Traumdeutung. *Gesammelte Werke*, 2–3, 1–642. (Translated as: The interpretation of dreams. *Standard Edition*, 4–5, 1–627.)

—— (1901). Über den Traum. *Gesammelte Werke*, 2–3, 645–700. (Translated as: On dreams. *Standard Edition*, 5, 633–686.)

—— (1905). Drie Abhandlungen zur Sexualtheorie. *Gesammelte Werke*, 5, 29–145. (Translated as: Three essays on the theory of sexuality.*Standard Edition*, 7, 130–243.)

—— (1905). Der Witz und seine Beziehung zum Unbewussten. *Gesammelte Werke*, 6, 1–285. (Translated as: Jokes and their relation to the unconscious. *Standard Edition*, 8, 1–247.)

—— (1910) Über Psychoanalyse. *Gesammelte Werke*, 8, 3–60. (Translated as: Five lectures on psychoanalysis. *Standard Edition*, 11, 1–56.)

—— (1910). Über 'Wilde' Psychoanalyse. *Gesammelte Werke*, 8, 118–125. (Translated as: 'Wild' psychoanalysis. *Standard Edition*, 11, 219–230.)

—— (1910). Eine Kindheitserinnerung des Leonardo da Vinci. *Gesammelte Werke*, 8, 128–211. (Translated as: Leonardo da Vinci and a memory of his childhood. *Standard Edition*, 11, 57–138.)

—— (1911). Letter to Ludwig Binswanger, 10 September. In: L. Binswanger, *Sigmund Freud: Reminiscences of a Friendship* (translated by N. Guterman). New York: Grune & Stratton, 1957, pp. 32–33.

—— (1913). Das Interesse an der Psychoanalyse. *Gesammelte Werke*, 8, 390–420. (Translated as: The claims of psychoanalysis to scientific interest. *Standard Edition*, 13, 165–190.)

—— (1913). Zur Einleitung der Behandlung. *Gesammelte Werke*, 8, 454–478. (Translated as: On beginning the treatment. *Standard Edition*, 12, 121–144.)

—— (1914). Zure Geschichte der Psychoanalystishen Bewung. *Gesammelte Werke*, 10, 44–113. (Translated as: On the history of the psychoanalytic movement. *Standard Edition*, 14, 7–66.)

—— (1914). Zur Einführung des Narzissmus. *Gesammelte Werke*, 10, 138–170. (Translated as: On narcissism: An introduction. *Standard Edition*, 14, 67–102.)

—— (1915). Trieb und Triebschicksale. *Gesammelte Werke*, 10, 210–232. (Translated as: Instincts and their vicissitudes. *Standard Edition*, 14, 109–140.)

—— (1915). Die Verdrängung. *Gesammelte Werke*, 10, 248–261. (Translated as: Repression. *Standard Edition*, 14, 146–158.)

—— (1915) Das Unbewusste. *Gesammelte Werke*, 10, 264–303. (Translated as: The unconscious. *Standard Edition*, 14, 166–204.)

—— (1915/1916–1917). Vorlesungen zur Einfürung in die Psychoanalys, *Gesammelte Werke*, 11. (Translated as: Introductory lectures on psychoanalysis. *Standard Edition*, 15 & 16.)

—— (1917). Metapsychologische Ergänzung Zur Traumlehre. *Gesammelte Werke*, 10, 412–416. (Translated as: A metapsychological supplement to the theory of dreams. *Standard Edition*, 14, 217–235.)

—— (1917). Trauer und Melancholie. *Gesammelte Werke*, 10, 428–446. (Translated as: Mourning and melancholia. *Standard Edition*, 14, 243–258.)

—— (1917). Eine Schwierikeit der Psychoanalyse. *Gesammelte Werke*, 12, 3–12. (Translated as: A difficulty in the path of psychoanalysis. *Standard Edition*, 17, 135–144.)

—— (1918). Aus der Geschichte einer Infantilen Neurose. *Gesammelte Werke*, 12, 29–157. (Translated as: From the history of an infantile neurosis. *Standard Edition*, 17, 1–124.)

—— (1919). Wege der Psychoanalytischen Therapie. *Gesammelte Werke*, 12, 183–194. (Translated as: Lines of advance in psychoanalytic therapy. *Standard Edition*, 17, 157–168.)

—— (1920). Jenseits des Lustprinzips. *Gesammelte Werke*, 13, 3–69. (Translated as: Beyond the pleasure principle. *Standard Edition*, 18, 1–64.)

—— (1920). Über die Psychogenese eines Falles von Weiblicher Homosexualität. *Gesammelte Werke*, 12, 271–302. (Translated as: The psychogenesis of a case of homosexuality in a woman. *Standard Edition*, 18, 147–172.)

—— (1923). Das Ich und das Es. *Gesammelte Werke*, 13, 237–289. (Translated as: The ego and the id. *Standard Edition*, 19, 12–66.)

—— (1923). "Psychoanalyse" und "Libidotheorie." *Gesammelte Werke*, 13, 211–233. (Translated as: Two encyclopedia articles. *Standard Edition*, 18, 235–259.)

—— (1925). Die Verneinung. *Gesammelte Werke*, 14, 11–15. (Translated as: Negation. *Standard Edition*, 19, 235–239.)

—— (1925). Notiz über den 'Wunderblock.' *Gesammelte Werke*, 14, 3–8. (Translated as: A note upon the 'mystic writing-pad.' *Standard Edition*, 19, 225–232.)

—— (1925). Selbstdarstellung. *Gesammelte Werke*, 14, 33–96. (Translated as: An autobiographical study. *Standard Edition*, 20, 7–74.)

—— (1925). Geleitwort zu Aichhorn's "Verwahrloste Jugend." *Gesammelte Werke*, 14, 565–567. (Translated as: Preface to Aichhorn's "Wayward Youth." *Standard Edition*, 19, 271–276.)

—— (1926). Hemmung, symptom und angst. *Gesammelte Werke*, 14, 113–205. (Translated as: Inhibitions, symptoms and anxiety. *Standard Edition*, 20, 75–176.)

—— (1929–1939). *The Diary of Sigmund Freud*, 1929–1939 (translated by M. Molner). London: Macmillan, 1992.

—— (1930). Das Unbehagen in der Kultur. *Gesammelte Werke*, 14, 421–506. (Translated as: Civilization and its discontents. *Standard Edition*, 21, 57–146.)

—— (1931). Preface to the third (revised) English edition of "The Interpretation of Dreams." *Standard Edition*, 4, xxxi.

—— (1933). Neue Folge der Vorlesungen zur Einführung in die psychoanalyse. *Gesammelte Werke*, 15. (Translated as: New introductory lectures on psychoanalysis. *Standard Edition*, 22, 5–182.)

—— (1937). Die endliche und die unendliche Analyse. *Gesammelte Werke*, 16, 59–99. (Translated as: Analysis terminable and interminable. *Standard Edition*, 23, 209–254.)

—— (1937). Konstruktionen in der Analyse. *Gesammelte Werke*, 16, 43–56. (Translated as: Constructions in analysis. *Standard Edition*, 23, 257–269.)

—— (1938/1940). Abriss der Psychoanalyse. *Gesammelte Werke*, 17, 67–138. (Translated as: An outline of psychoanalysis. *Standard Edition*, 23, 144–207.)

—— & Abraham, K. (1907–1925). *The Complete Correspondence of Sigmund Freud and Karl Abraham, 1907–1925* (translated by C. Schwarzacher). London: Karnac Books, 2002.

—— & Binswanger, L. (1908–1938). *The Sigmund Freud – Ludwig Binswanger Correspondence, 1908–1938* (edited and translated by G. Fichtner). New York: Other Press.

—— & Fliess, W. (1887–1904). *The Complete Letters of Sigmund Freud to Wilhelm Fliess, 1887–1904* (edited and translated by J. M. Masson). Cambridge, MA: Belknap Press, 1986.

—— & Jones, E. (1908–1939). *The Complete Correspondence of Sigmund Freud and Ernest Jones* (edited by R. A. Paskauskas). Cambridge, MA: Belnap Press, 1995.

Friedman, M. (1993). Feminism and modern friendship: Dislocating the community. In: N. K. Badhwar (ed.), *Friendship: A Philosophical Reader*. Ithaca, NY: Cornell University Press, pp. 285–302.

Fromm, E. S. (1942). *Fear of Freedom*. London: Routledge, 1984.

—— (1951). *The Forgotten Language: An Introduction to the Understanding of Dreams, Fairy Tales, and Myths*. New York: Henry Holt, 1976.

—— (1970). *The Crisis of Psychoanalysis*. New York: Holt, Rinehart & Winston.

—— (1976). *To Have or To Be*. New York: Continuum, 1997.

Fromm-Reichman, F. (1960). *Principles of Intensive Psychotherapy*. Chicago: University of Chicago Press.

Galatzer-Levy, R. M. (1976). Psychic energy: A historical perspective. *Annual of Psychoanalysis*, 4, 41–61.

Gay, P. (1987). *A Godless Jew*. New Haven, CT: Yale University Press.

—— (2002). *Schnitzler's Century: The Making of Middle-class Culture 1815–1914*. New York: W. W. Norton.

—— (2006). *Freud: A Life for our Time*. New York: W. W. Norton.

Gendlin, E. T. (1997). *Experiencing and the Creation of Meaning: A Philosophical and Psychological Approach to the Subjective*. Evanston, IL: Northwestern University Press.

Girard, R. (2003). *Sacrifice* (translated by M. Pattillo & D. Dawson). Lansing, MI: Michigan State University Press.

Glover, E. (1931). The therapeutic effect of inexact interpretation: A contribution to the theory of suggestion. *International Journal of Psychoanalysis*, 12, 397–411.

Goldberg, A. I. (1978). *The Psychology of the Self: A Casebook*. New York: International Universities Press.

—— (1988). *A Fresh Look at Psychoanalysis: The View from Self Psychology*. Hillsdale, NJ: Analytic Press.

—— (1999). *Being of Two Minds: The Vertical Split in Psychoanalysis and Psychotherapy*. London: Routledge.

Goldstein, K. (1934). *The Organism*. New York: Zone Books.

Gramsci, A. (1914–1926). *Gramsci: Pre-prison Writings* (edited by R. Bellamy, translated by V. Cox). London: Cambridge University Press.

—— (1926–1934). *Prison Notebooks* (3 vols, translated by J. A. Buttigieg). New York: Columbia University Press, 2010.

Granoff, W. (2001). *Lacan, Ferenczi et Freud*. Paris: Gallimard.

Gray, P. (1994). *The Ego and Analysis of Defense*. Northvale, NJ: Jason Aronson.

Green, A. (1973). *The Fabric of Affect in the Psychoanalytic Discourse* (translated by A. Sheridan). London: Routledge, 1999. *L'Affect*. Paris: Presses Universitaire de France.

—— (1974). Surface analysis, deep analysis (The role of the preconscious in psychoanalytical technique). *International Review of Psychoanalysis*, 1, 415–423. (Reprinted in *On Private Madness*. Madison, CT: International Universities Press, 1986.)

—— (1972–1986). *On Private Madness*. Madison, CT: International Universities Press.

—— (1983). The dead mother. In: *On Private Madness*. Madison, CT: International Universities Press, 142–173.

—— (1983). *Life Narcissism, Death Narcissism* (translated by A. Weller). London: Free Association, 2001.

—— (1993). *The Work of the Negative* (translated by A. Weller). London: Free Association Books, 1999.

—— (1995). *La Causalité Psychique*. Paris: Odile Jacob.

—— (1995). Has sexuality anything to do with psychoanalysis? *International Journal of Psychoanalysis*, 76, 871–883.
—— (1995). An interview with André Green. *New Formations*, 26, 15–35.
—— (1997). *The Chains of Eros: The Sexual in Psychoanalysis* (translated by L. Thurston). London: Rebus Press, 2000.
—— (2000). *La Diachronie en Psychanalyse*. Paris: Éditions de Minuit.
—— (2000). The central phobic position: A new formulation of the free association method. *International Journal of Psychoanalysis*, 81, 429–451.
—— (2002). *Time in Psychoanalysis: Some Contradictory Aspects* (translated by A. Weller). London: Free Association Books.
—— (2002). *Psychoanalysis: A Paradigm for Clinical Thinking* (translated by A. Weller). London: Free Association Books.
—— (2002). *Key Ideas for a Contemporary Psychoanalysis: Misrecognition and Recognition of the Unconscious* (translated by A. Weller). London: Routledge, 2005.
—— (2005). *Psychoanalysis: A Paradigm for Clinical Thinking* (translated by A. Weller). London: Free Association Books.
—— (2011). *Illusions and Disillusions of Psychoanalytic Work* (translated by A. Weller). London: Karnac Books.
Greenberg, J. & Mitchell, S. A. (1983). *Object Relations in Psychoanalytic Theory*. Cambridge, MA: Harvard University Press.
Greenson, R. R. (1967). *The Technique and Practice of Psychoanalysis*. New York: International Universities Press.
Greer, G. (1970). *The Female Eunuch*. New York: Harper, 2006.
Groddeck, G. (1923). *The Book of the It* (translated by V. M. E. Collins). London: Vision Press, 1979.
Gross, O. (1901–1920). *Ausgewählte Texte 1901–1920 (herausgegeben von L. L. Madison)*. Hamilton, NY: Mindpiece Publishing, 2008.
Grosskurth, P. (1991). *The Secret Ring: Freud's Inner Circle and the Politics of Psychoanalysis*. Cambridge, MA: Addison-Wesley.
Guastello, S. J., Koopmans, M. & Pincus, D. (2011). *Chaos and Complexity in Psychology: The Theory of Nonlinear Dynamical Systems*. Cambridge: Cambridge University Press.
Habermas, J. (1968). *Knowledge and Human Interests* (translated by J. J. Shapiro). London: Heinemann, 1972.
Haeberle, E. J. & Gindorf, R. (eds, 1998). *Bisexualities*. London: Continuum.
Hale, N. G. (1971). *Freud and the Americans: The Beginnings of Psychoanalysis in the United States, 1876–1917*. Oxford: Oxford University Press.
—— (1995). *The Rise and Crisis of Psychoanalysis in the United States: Freud and the Americans, 1917–1985*. London: Oxford University Press.
—— & Heller, J. B. (eds, 1971). *James Jackson Putnam and Psychoanalysis: Letters between Putnam and Sigmund Freud, Ernest Jones, William James, Sándor Ferenczi, Morton Prince, 1877–1917*. Cambridge, MA: Harvard University Press.
Halprin, D. (2008). *The Expressive Body in Life, art, and Therapy: Working with Movement, Metaphor and Meaning*. Philadephia, PA: Jessica Kingsley.
Hannah, B. (2001). *Encounters with the Soul: Active Imagination as Developed by C. G. Jung*. Brooklyn, NY: Chiron.
Harasym, S. (ed., 1998). *Levinas and Lacan: The Missed Encounter*. Albany, NY: State University of New York Press.
Hartmann, E. v. (1869). *Philosophy of the Unconscious: Speculative Results According to the Inductive Method of Physical Science* (translated by W. C. Coupland). Charleston, SC: Nabu Press, 2010.

Hartmann, H. (1927–1959). *Essays on Ego Psychology: Selected Problems in Psychoanalytic Theory*. New York: International Universities Press, 1965.

—— (1939). *Ego Psychology and the Problem of Adaptation* (translated by D. Rapaport). New York: International Universities Press, 1964.

—— (1939). Psychoanalysis and the concept of health. *International Journal of Psychoanalysis*, 20, 308–321.

Hassin, R. R., Uleman, J. S. & Bargh, J. A. (eds, 2006). *The New Unconscious*. Oxford: Oxford University Press.

Haute, P. V. & Geyskens, T. (2004). *Confusion of Tongues: The Primacy of Sexuality in Freud, Ferenczi, and Laplanche*. New York: Other Press.

Haynal, A. (1988). *Controversies in Psychoanalytic Method: From Freud and Ferenczi to Michael Balint* (translated by J. E. King). New York: New York University Press, 1990.

—— (1993). *Psychoanalysis and the Sciences: Epistemology-History* (translated by E. Holder). Berkeley, CA: University of California Press.

—— (2002). *Disappearing and Reviving: Sándor Ferenczi in the History of Psychoanalysis*. London: Karnac Books.

Hazlitt, W. (1823). *On the Pleasure of Hating*. New York: Digireads, 2010.

Hegel, G. W. F. (1807). *Phenomenology of Spirit* (translated by A. V. Miller). London: Allen & Unwin, 1969.

—— (1817–1830). *Philosophy of Mind* (translated by W. Wallace). Oxford: Oxford University Press, 1971.

Heidegger, M. (1927). *Being and Time* (translated by J. Macquarrie & E. Robinson). New York: Harper & Row, 1962.

—— (1950–1960). *Poetry, Language, Thought* (translated by A. Hofstadter). New York: Harper & Row, 1971.

—— (1959). *Discourse on Thinking* (translated by J. M. Anderson & E. H. Freund). New York: Harper & Row, 1966.

—— (1959). *On the Way to Language* (translated by P. Hertz & J. Stambaugh). New York: Harper & Row, 1971.

—— (1969). *On Time and Being* (edited and translated by J. Stambaugh). New York: Harper & Row, 1972.

Heller, M. C. (2012). *Body Psychotherapy: History, Concepts, and Methods* (translated by M. Duclos). New York: W. W. Norton.

Heraclitus of Ephesus (*c.* 500 BCE). *Fragments* (translated by B. Haxton). London: Penguin.

Herbart, J. F. (1824–1825). *Psychologie als Wissenschaft*. Charlston, SC: Nabu, 2013.

Hess, M. (1837). *The Holy History of Mankind and Other Writings* (edited and translated by S. Avineri). Cambridge: Cambridge University Press, 2004.

Hirschfeld, M. (1933). *Men and Women: The World Journey of a Sexologist*. New York: AMS Press, 1974.

Hoffer, A. & Youngren, V. R. (2004). Is free association still at the core of psychoanalysis? *International Journal of Psychoanalysis*, 85, 1489–1492.

Horkheimer, M. (1967). *Critique of Instrumental Reason*. London: Continuum International, 1983.

—— & Adorno, T. W. (1944). *Dialectic of Enlightenment* (translated by E. Jephcott). Standord, CA: Stanford University Press, 2007.

—— (1937). *The Neurotic Personality of our Time*. New York: W. W. Norton, 1994.

Hruschka, D. J. (2010). *Friendship: Development, Ecology, and Evolution of a Relationship*. Berkeley, CA: University of California Press.

Hughes, J. M. (1989). *Reshaping the Psychoanalytic Domain: The Work of Melanie Klein, W. R. D. Fairbairn, and D. W. Winnicott*. Berkeley, CA: University of California Press.

Hume, D. (1748). *An Enquiry Concerning Human Understanding* (edited by E. Steinberg). Indianapolis, IN: Hackett, 1993.

Hummel, G. v. (2011). *Yoga and Psychoanalysis.* Stoughton, WI: Books on Demand.

Humphries, B. (1988). *The Complete Barry McKenzie* (illustrated by Nicholas Garland). London: Methuen.

Husserl, E. (1904–1911). *The Phenomenology of Internal Time Consciousness* (translated by J. S. Churchill). Bloomington, IN: Indiana University Press, 1964.

Ingleby, D. (ed., 2004). *Critical Psychiatry: The Politics of Mental Health* (2nd edn). London: Free Association Books.

Irigaray, L. (1974). *Speculum of the Other Woman* (translated by G. C. Gill). Ithaca, NY: Cornell University Press, 1985.

—— (1977). *This Sex which is Not One* (translated by C. Porter). Ithaca, NY: Cornell University Press, 1985.

—— (1982). *Elemental Passions* (translated by J. Collie & J. Still). London: Routledge, 1992.

—— (1984). *An Ethics of Sexual Difference* (translated by C. Burke and G. C. Gill). Ithaca, NY: Cornell University Press, 1993.

—— (1985). *To Speak is Never Neutral* (translated by G. Schwab). New York, NY: Continuum, 2002.

—— (1990). *Je, tu, nous: Toward a Culture of Difference.* New York: Routledge, 1993.

(1994). *To Be Two* (translated by M. M. Rhodes & M. F. Cocito-Monoc). New York: Continuum, 2001.

—— (1999). *Between East and West: From Singularity to Community* (translated by S. Pluháček). New York: Columbia University Press, 2003.

—— (2002). *The Way of Love* (translated by H. Bostic & S. Pluháček). New York: Continuum.

—— (2008). *Sharing the World.* New York: Continuum.

—— (2012). *In the Beginning, She Was.* London: Bloomsbury Academic.

Isaacs, S. (1948). The nature and function of phantasy. *International Journal of Psychoanalysis*, 29, 73–97.

Izenberg, G. N. (1976). *The Existentialist Critique of Freud: The Crisis of Autonomy.* Princeton, NJ: Princeton University Press.

Jablonski, N. G. (2008). *Skin: A Natural History.* Berkeley, CA: University of California Press.

Jacobsen, K. (2009). *Freud's Foes: Psychoanalysis, Science, and Resistance.* Lanham, MD: Rowan & Littlefield.

Jacobus, M. (2006). *The Poetics of Psychoanalysis: In the Wake of Klein.* Oxford: Oxford University Press.

Jacoby, R. (1975). *Social Amnesia: A Critique of Contemporary Psychology.* Boston, MA: Beacon Press.

Jaeggi, R. (2014). *Alienation* (translated by F. Neuhouser & A. E. Smith). New York: Columbia University Press.

Jakobson, R. & Halle, M. (1956). *Fundamentals of Language.* The Hague, Netherlands: Mouton.

James, W. (1878–1899). *William James: Writings, 1878–1899* (edited by G. E. Myers). New York: Library of America, 1992.

—— (1902–1910). *William James: Writings, 1902–1910* (edited by B. Kuklick). New York: Library of America, 1987.

—— (1912). *Essays in Radical Empiricism.* Lincoln, NE: University of Nebraska Press, 1996.

Johnston, A. & Malabou, C. (2013). *Self and Emotional Life: Philosophy, Psychoanalysis, and Neuroscience.* New York: Columbia University Press.

Jones, E. (1910–1935). *Papers on Psychoanalysis.* Boston, MA: Beacon Press, 1961.

—— (1927). The early development of female sexuality. *International Journal of Psychoanalysis*, 8, 459–472.

—— (1929). Fear, guilt and hate. *International Journal of Psychoanalysis*, 10, 383–397.

—— (1953–1957). *The Life and Work of Sigmund Freud* (3 vols). New York: Basic Books, 1981.

Jung, C. G. (1904–1907). *Studies in Word Association* (translated by M. D. Eder). Seattle, WA: Amazon/Kindle, 2012.

—(1912). *Wandlungen und Symbole der Libido* [Transformation and Symbolism of the Libido]. Published as *Psychology of the unconscious: A Study of the Transformations and Symbolisms of the Libido – A Contribution to the History of the Evolution of Thought* (translated by B. M. Hinkle). London: Kegan Paul Trench Trubner.

—— (1913–1916). *Jung on Active Imagination* (edited by J. Chodorow). Princeton, NJ: Princeton University Press, 1997.

—— (1932). *The Psychology of Kundalini Yoga* (edited by S. Shamdasani). Princeton, NJ: Princeton University Press.

—— (1957–1961). *Memories, Dreams, Reflections* (edited by A. Jaffe; translated by R. Winston & C. Winston). New York: Vintage.

Kandel, E. R. (2012). *The Age of Insight: The Quest to Understand the Unconscious in Art, Mind, and Brain, from Vienna 1900 to the Present*. New York: Random House.

Karlsson, G. (2004). *Psychoanalysis in a New Light*. Cambridge: Cambridge University Press, 2010.

Kaufmann, W. A. (1950). *Nietzsche: Philosopher, Psychologist, Anti-Christ*. Princeton, NJ: Princeton University Press, 1975.

Keats, J. (1899). *The Complete Poetical Works and Letters of John Keats* (Cambridge edn). Boston, MA: Houghton Mifflin.

Kelley, C. R. (2004). *Lifeforce: The Creative Process in Man and Nature*. Victoria, BC: Trafford Press.

Kellner, D. & Pierce, C. (eds, 2011). *Herbert Marcuse: Philosophy, Psychoanalysis and Emancipation (Collected Papers of Herbert Marcuse, Vol. 5)*. London: Routledge.

Kermode, F. (1967). *The Sense of an Ending: Studies in the Theory of Fiction* (with a new epilogue). Oxford: Oxford University Press, 2000.

Khan, M. (1974). *The Privacy of the Self*. London: Karnac Books, 1996.

Kierkegaard, S. (1843). *Either/Or: Kierkegaard's Writings, Vols 3 & 4* (translated by E. H. Hong & H. V. Hong). Princeton, NJ: Princeton University Press, 1987.

—— (1843). *Fear and trembling/Repetition: Kierkegaard's Writings, Vol. 6* (translated by E. H. Hong & H. V. Hong). Princeton, NJ: Princeton University Press, 1983.

—— (1843–1844). *Eighteen Upbuilding Discourses: Kierkegaard's Writing, Vol. 5* (translated by E. H. Hong & H. V. Hong). Princeton, NJ: Princeton University Press, 1992.

—— (1844). *The Concept of Anxiety – A Simple Psychologically Orienting Deliberation on the Dogmatic Issue of Hereditary Sin: Kierkegaard's Writings, Vol. 12.1* (translated by R. Thomte & A. B. Anderson). Princeton, NJ: Princeton University Press, 1981.

—— (1846). *Concluding Unscientific Postscript to Philosophical Fragments: Kierkegaard's Writings, Vol. 12* (translated by E. H. Hong & H. V. Hong). Princeton, NJ: Princeton University Press, 1992.

—— (1849). *The Sickness unto Death* (edited by H. V. Hong & E. H. Hong). Princeton, NJ: Princeton University Press, 1983.

King, P. H. M. & Steiner, R. (1992). *The Freud/Klein Controversies in the British Psychoanalytic Society, 1941–1945*. London: Routledge.

Kirsner, D. (2009). *Unfree Associations: Inside Psychoanalytic Institutes*. Lanham, MD: Jason Aronson.

Klages, L. (1929). *Der Geist als Widersacher der Seele*. Bonn: Bouvier Verlag.

Klein, D. B. (1987). *Jewish Origins of the Psychoanalytic Movement*. Chicago: University of Chicago Press.

Klein, M. (1921–1960). *The Writings of Melanie Klein* (4 vols). London: Hogarth.

—— (1952). On the criteria for the termination of an analysis. *Psychoanalytic Quarterly*, 21, 270.

—— (1960). On mental health. *British Journal of Medical Psychology*, 33, 237–241.

—— (1964). Love, guilt and reparation. In: M. Klein & J. Riviere, *Love, Hate and Reparation*. New York: Norton, 57–119.

Kohon, G. (ed., 1986). *The British School of Psychoanalysis: The Independent Tradition*. London: Free Association Books.

—— (ed., 1999). *The Dead Mother: The Work of André Green*. London: Routledge.

Kohut, H. (1950–1981). *Selected Writings of Heinz Kohut* (4 vols, edited by P. Ornstein). London: Karnac Books.

—— (1971). *The Analysis of the Self*. New York: International Universities Press.

—— (1977). *The Restoration of the Self*. New York: International Universities Press.

—— (1978). *The Search for the Self* (edited by P. H. Ornstein). New York: International Universities Press.

—— (1980). *Advances in Self Psychology* (edited by A. Goldberg). New York: International Universities Press.

Kolakowski, L. (1972). *The Presence of Myth* (translated by A. Czerniawski). Chicago: University of Chicago Press, 1989.

—— (1988). *Metaphysical Horror*. New York: Basil Blackwell.

Korsch, K. (1923). *Marxism and Philosophy* (translated by F. Halliday). New York: Monthly Review Press.

Kosík, K. (1963). *Dialectics of the Concrete: A Study on Problems of Man and World* (Boston Studies in the Philosophy of Science, Vol. 52, edited by R. S. Cohen & M. W. Wartofsky). Dordrecht, Holland: D. Reidel, 1976.

Koyré, A. (1957). *From the Closed World to the Infinite Universe*. Radford, VA: Wilder, 2008.

Krafft-Ebing, R. F. v. (1886). *Psychopathia Sexualis* (translated by F. S. Klaf). New York: Arcade, 2011.

Kris, A. O. (1996). *Free Association: Methods and Process* (revised edn). London: Routledge.

Kristeva, J. (1974). *Revolution in Poetic Language* (translated by M. Waller). New York: Columbia University Press, 1984.

—— (1975). *The System and the Speaking Subject*. Lisse, Netherlands: Peter de Ridder.

—— (1977). *Polylogue*. Paris: Seuil. (Partially translated as *Desire in Language*.)

—— (1977). *Desire in Language* (translated by L. S. Roudiez). New York: Columbia University Press, 1980.

—— (1980). *Powers of Horror: An Essay on Abjection* (translated by L. S. Roudiez). New York: Columbia University Press, 1982.

—— (1987). *In the Beginning was Love: Psychoanalysis and Faith* (translated by A. Goldhammer). New York: Columbia University Press.

—— (1991). *Strangers to Ourselves* (translated by L. S. Roudiez). New York: Columbia University Press.

—— (1992). *Time and Sense: Proust and the Experience of Literature* (translated by R. Guberman). New York: Columbia University Press, 1998.

—— (1998). Experiencing the phallus as extraneous, or women's twofold Oedipus complex. *Parallax*, 4(3), 29–43.

—— (2010). *Hatred and Forgiveness* (translated by J. Herman). New York: Columbia University Press.

Kuhn, T. S. (1962). *The Structure of Scientific Revolutions* (3rd edn). Chicago: University of Chicago Press, 1996.

Kurtz, R. (2007). *Body-centered Psychotherapy*. Mendocino, CA: LifeRhythm.

Labriola, A. (1907). *Essays on the Materialist Conception of History*. Chicago: C. H. Kerr.

Lacan, J. (1953). The function and field of speech and language in psychoanalysis. In: *Écrits: The First Complete Edition in English* (translated by B. Fink). New York: Norton, 2005.

—— (1953–1954). *Le séminaire, livre I: Les écrits techniques de Freud*. Paris: Seuil, 1975. (Translated as: *The seminars of Jacques Lacan, Book I: Freud's Papers on Technique, 1953–1954* (translated by J. Forrester). New York: Norton, 1988.)

—— (1954–1955). *Le Séminaire, Livre II: Le Moi Dans la Théorie de Freud et dans la Technique de la Psychanalyse*. Paris: Seuil, 1978. (Translated as: *The Seminars of Jacques Lacan, Book II: The Ego in Freud's Theory and in the Technique of Psychoanalysis, 1954–1955* (translated by S. Tomaselli). New York: Norton, 1988.)

——(1959–1960). *Le séminaire, livre VII: L'éthique de la psychanalyse*. Paris: Seuil, 1986.

—— (1964). *Le séminaire, livre XI: Les quatre concepts fondamentaux de la psychanalyse*. Paris: Seuil, 1973. (Translated as: *The Four Fundamental Concepts of Psychoanalysis* (translated by A. Sheridan). London: Hogarth, 1977.)

—— (1964–1980). *Feminine Sexuality: Jacques Lacan and the École Freudienne* (edited by J. Mitchell & J. Rose; translated by J. Rose). New York: Norton, 1983.

—— (1966). *Écrits*. Paris: Seuil. (Partially translated as: *Écrits: A Selection* (translated by A. Sheridan). London: Tavistock, 1977. Also translated as: *Ecrits: The First Complete Edition in English* (translated by B. Fink). New York: Norton, 2005.

—— (1972–1973). *Le Séminaire, Livre XX: Encore*. Paris: Seuil.

Laforgue, R. (1932). *Misère de l'homme Récit*. Paris: Denöel et Steele.

Laing, R. D. (1960). *The Divided Self: An Existential Study in Sanity and Madness*. London: Penguin.

Langer, M. (1985). Psicoanálisis sin divan. Paper presented to Cuba's Academy of Sciences. (Translated as: Psychoanalysis without the couch. *Free Associations*, 15, 60–66. Also discussed in: M. Langer (1981). *From Vienna to Managua: Journey of a Psychoanalyst* (translated by M. Hooks). London: Free Association Books, 1989.)

Langs, R. J. (ed., 1977). *Classics in Psychoanalytic Technique* (revised edition). Northvale, NJ: Jason Aronson.

Laplanche, J. (1970). *Life and Death in Psychoanalysis* (translated by J. Mehlman). Baltimore, MD: Johns Hopkins University Press, 1985.

—— (1981). *Problématiques IV: L'inconscient et le ça*. Paris: Presses Universitaires de France.

—— (1987). *New Foundations for Psychoanalysis* (translated by D. Macey). Oxford: Basil Blackwell, 1989.

—— (1992–1993). *Essays on Otherness* (edited by J. Fletcher). Abingdon: Routledge, 1999.

—— (1992). The unfinished Copernican revolution (translated by L. Thurston). In: *Essays on Otherness*. Abingdon: Routledge, 1999, 52–83.

—— (1992). *Seduction, Translation, Drives* (edited by J. Fletcher & M. Stanton; translated by M. Stanton). London, UK: Institute of Contemporary Arts.

—— (1993). *A Short Treatise on the Unconscious* (translated by L.Thurston). In: *Essays on Otherness*. Abingdon: Routledge, 1999, 84–116.

—— (1993). Interpretation between determinism and hermeneutics: A restatement of the problem (translated by P. Slotkin). In: *Essays on Otherness*. Abingdon: Routledge, 1999, 138–165.

—— (1993). *La fourvoiement biologisant de la sexualité chez Freud*. Paris: Synthélabo. (Reissued in 2006; translated in 2015.)

—— (1994). Psychoanalysis as anti-hermeneutics. *Radical Philosophy*, 79.
—— (1997). Aims of the psychoanalytic process. *Journal of European Psychoanalysis*, 5 (Spring–Fall).
—— (2000–2006). *Freud and the 'Sexual' – Essays 2000–2006* (translated by J. Fletcher, J. House, & N. Ray). New York: International Psychoanalytic Books, 2011.
—— (2006). *The Temptation of Biology: Freud's Theories of Sexuality with Biologism and Biology* (translated by D. Nicholson-Smith). New York: The Unconscious in Translation.
—— & Pontalis, J-B. (1968). Fantasy and the origins of sexuality. *International Journal of Psychoanalysis*, 49, 1–18.
—— & —— (1974). *The Language of Psychoanalysis* (translated by D. Nicholson-Smith). New York: W. W. Norton.
Larivière, M. (1997). The analyst's resistance to analysis. *Psychoanalytic Quarterly*, 17, 535–548.
Laruelle, F. (1986). *Philosophies of Difference: A Critical Introduction to Non-philosophy* (translated by R. Gangle). London: Continuum International, 2010.
—— (1996). *Principles of Non-philosophy* (translated by A. P. Smith & N. Rubczak). London: Bloomsbury Academic, 2013.
Lawrence, D. H. (1921–1922). *Psychoanalysis and the Unconscious and Fantasia of the Unconscious.* Mineola, NY: Dover, 2005.
Leader, D. (2000). *Freud's Footnotes*. London: Faber & Faber.
Leclaire, S. (1968). *Psychoanalyzing: On the Order of the Unconscious and the Practice of the Letter* (translated by P. Kamuf). Stanford, CA: Stanford University Press, 1998.
Lecourt, D. (1975). *Marxism and Epistemology: Bachelard, Canguilhem and Foucault*. London: New Left Books, 1975.
—— (2001). *La Philosophie des Sciences (Que sais-je?)*. Paris: Presses Universitaire de France.
LeDoux, J. E. (2003). *The Synaptic Self: How our Brains Become Who We Are* (2nd edn). New York: Penguin.
Lefebvre, H. (1966). *The Sociology of Marx* (translated by N. Guterman). New York: Columbia University Press, 1982.
Lehrer, R. (1994). *Nietzsche's Presence in Freud's Life and Thought: On the Origins of a Psychology of Dynamic Unconscious Mental Functioning*. Albany, NY: State University of New York Press.
Leopardi, G. (1817–1837). *Thoughts* (translated by J.G. Nichols). London: Hesperus Press, 2002.
Levinas, E. (1947). *Time and the Other* (translated by R. A. Cohen). Pittsburgh, PA: Duquesne University Press.
—— (1961). *Totality and Infinity: An Essay on Exteriority* (translated by A. Lingis). Pittsburgh, PA: Duquesne University Press.
—— (1974). *Otherwise than Being, or Beyond Essence* (translated by A. Lingis). The Hague, Netherlands: Martinus Nijhoff.
—— (1995). *Alterity and Transcendence* (translated by M. B. Smith). New York: Columbia University Press, 2000.
Levine, P. A. (2010). *In an Unspoken Voice: How the Body Releases Trauma and Restores Goodness.* Berkeley, CA: North Atlantic Books.
Lévi-Strauss, C. (1949). The problem of incest. In: *The Elementary Structures of Kinship* (edited and translated by R. Needham),12–28. Boston, MA: Beacon Press, 1971.
Lewin, B. D. (1948). The nature of reality, the meaning of nothing, with an addendum on concentration. *Psychoanalytic Quarterly, 17,* 524–526.
Lichtenberg, J. D. (1991). *Psychoanalysis and Infant Research*. London: Routledge.
Limentani, A. (1989). *Between Freud and Klein: The Psychoanalytic Quest for Knowledge and Truth.* London: Free Association Books.

Lingis, A. (1983). *Excesses: Eros and Culture*. Albany: State University of New York.
—— (1985). *Libido: The French Existentialist Theories*. Bloomington, IN: Indiana University Press.
—— (1989). *Deathbound Subjectivity*. Bloomington, IN: Indiana University Press.
Llewelyn, J. (1995). *Emanuel Levinas: The Genealogy of Ethics*. London: Routledge.
Lobkowicz, N. (1967). *Theory and Practice: History of a Concept from Aristotle to Marx*. Notre Dame, IN: University of Notre Dame Press.
Loewald, H. W. (1978). *Psychoanalysis and the history of the individual*. New Haven, CT: Yale University Press.
Lorenz, K. Z. (1982). *The Foundations of Ethology: The Principal Ideas and Discoveries in Animal Behavior*. New York: Simon & Schuster.
Lowen, A. (1975). *Bioenergetics*. New York: Coward, McCann & Geoghegan.
Löwith, K. (1964). *From Hegel to Nietzsche: The Revolution in Nineteenth Century Thought* (translated by D. E. Green). New York: Columbia University Press, 1991.
Lukács, G. (1919–1923). *History and Class Consciousness: Studies in Marxist Dialectics* (translated by R. Livingstone). Cambridge, MA: MIT Press, 1971.
Luxemburg, R. (1899). *Reform or Revolution and Other Writings*. New York: Dover, 2006.
Lyotard, J-F. (1974). *Libidinal Economy* (translated by I. H. Grant). Bloomington, IN: Indiana University Press, 1993.
McDougall, J. (1978). *Plea for a Measure of Abnormality*. New York: International Universities Press, 1980.
—— (1989). *Theaters of the Body*. New York: W. W. Norton.
—— (1995). *The Many Faces of Eros: A Psychoanalytic Exploration of Human Sexuality*. New York: W. W. Norton
McLennan, J. F. (1865/1876). *Studies in Ancient History: Comprising a reprint of primitive marriage*. Charleston, SC: Nabu Press, 2010.
Mach, E. (1886/1897). *The Analysis of Sensations and the Relation of the Physical to the Psychical* (5th edn, translated by C. M. Williams). New York: Dover, 1959. (Reproduced by Forgotten Books (Hong Kong), 2012.)
Mahler, M. S., Pine, F. & Bergmann, A. (2000). *The Psychological Birth of the Human Infant: Symbiosis and Individuation*. New York: Basic Books.
Maine, H. S. (1875). *The Early History of Institutions*. London: John Murray.
Makari, G. (2008). *Revolution in Mind: The Creation of Psychoanalysis*. New York: Harper Perennial.
Malabou, C. (2004). *What Should We Do with our Brain?* (translated by S. Rand). New York: Fordham University Press, 2008.
—— (2007). *The New Wounded: From Neurosis to Brain Damage* (translated by S. Miller). New York: Fordham University Press.
Mann, T. (1924). *The Magic Mountain* (translated by H. T. Lowe-Porter). New York: Vintage, 1969.
Mao Tse-tung (1937). On praxis. In: *Selected Works of Mao Tse-tung*, 1, 295–309. Beijing, China: Foreign Languages Press.
Marcuse, H. (1955). *Eros and Civilization: A Philosophical Inquiry into Freud*. London: Allen Lane, 1969.
—— (1964). *One-dimensional Man: Studies in the Ideology of Advanced Industrial Society*. Boston, MA: Beacon Press, 1991.
Marković, M. (1974). *From Affluence to Praxis: Philosophy and Social Criticism*. Ann Arbor, MI: University of Michigan Press.

—— & Petrović, G. (eds, 1965–1974). *Praxis: Yugoslav Essays in the Philosophy and Methodology of the Social Sciences* (Boston Studies in the Philosophy of Science, Vol. 36, edited by R. S. Cohen & M. W. Wartofsky). Dordrecht, Holland: D. Reidel, 1979.

Marx, K. (1844). Economic and philosophical manuscripts. In: L. D. Easton & K. H. Guddat (eds), *Writings of the Young Marx on Philosophy and Society*. Cambridge, MA: Hackett, 283–360.

—— (1845). Theses on Feuerbach. In: L. D. Easton & K. H. Guddat (eds), *Writings of the Young Marx on Philosophy and Society*. Cambridge, MA: Hackett, 400–402.

—— (1847). The poverty of philosophy. In: L. D. Easton & K. H. Guddat (eds), *Writings of the Young Marx on Philosophy and Society*. Cambridge, MA: Hackett, 474–496.

—— (1859). *A Contribution to the Critique of Political Economy*. Central, Hong Kong: Forgotten Books, 2012.

—— (1867). *Capital* (unabridged edition, edited by F. Engels). New York: International Publishers, 1967.

Masi, F. de (2004). *Making Death Thinkable: A Psychoanalytic Contribution to the Problem of the Transience of Life* (translated by P. Antinucci). London: Free Association Books.

Mauss, M. (1924). *The Gift: The Form and Reason for Exchange in Archaic Societies* (translated by W. D. Halls). New York: W. W. Norton, 2000.

Mead, G. H. (1934). *Mind, Self, and Society from the Standpoint of a Social Behaviorist* (edited by C. W. Morris). Chicago: University of Chicago Press, 1967.

Meghnagi, D. (ed., 1993). *Freud and Judaism*. London: Karnac Books.

Mehlman, J. (ed., 1976). *French Freud: Structural Studies in Psychoanalysis*. New Haven, CT: Yale University Press.

Meissner, W. (1991). A decade of psychoanalytic praxis. *Psychoanalytic Inquiry*, 11, 30–64.

—— (1996). *The Therapeutic Alliance*. New Haven, CT: Yale University Press.

Meltzer, D. (1978). *The Kleinian Development* (3 vols reissued in one). London: Karnac Books, 2008.

Mészáros, I. (1970). *Marx's Theory of Alienation*. London: Merlin Press, 2006.

Meszaros, J. (2013). *Ferenczi and Beyond: Exile of the Budapest School and Solidarity in the Psychoanalytic Movement During the Nazi Years*. London: Karnac Books.

Meyerson, E. (1908). *Identity and Reality* (translated by K. Loewenberg). Mineola, NY: Dover, 1962.

—— (1921). *Explanation in the Sciences* (translated by M-A. Sipfle & D. A. Sipfle). Boston Studies in the History and Philosophy of Science, 128. New York: Springer, 1991.

Mijolla, A. de (2010). *Freud et la France, 1885–1945*. Paris: Presses Universitaires de France.

Mill, J. S. (1859). *On Liberty* (edited by C. V. Shields). New York: Macmillan, 1956.

Mills J. (2002). *The Unconscious Abyss: Hegel's Anticipation of Psychoanalysis*. Albany, NY: State University of New York Press.

—— (2010). *Origins: On the Genesis of Psychic Reality*. Montreal: McGill-Queen's University Press.

Milman, D. S. & Goldman, G. D. (eds, 1986). *Techniques of Working with Resistance*. Northvale, NJ: Jason Aronson.

Mindell, A. (2001). *Working with the Dreaming Body*. Chicago: Lao Tse Press.

Minkowski, E. (1933). *Lived Time: Phenomenological and Psychopathological Studies* (translated by N. Metsel). Evanston, IL: Northwestern University Press, 1970.

Mitchell, S. A. (1995). *Hope and Dread in Psychoanalysis*. New York: Basic Books.

—— & Aron, L. (eds, 1999). *Relational Perspectives in Psychoanalysis: The Emergence of a Tradition*. Hillsdale, NJ: Analytic Press.

Molino, A. (ed., 1999). *The Couch and the Tree: Dialogues in Psychoanalysis and Buddhism*. New York: North Point Press.

—— (ed., 2013). *Crossroads in Psychoanalysis, Buddhism, and Mindfulness: The Word and the Breath*. Northvale, NJ: Jason Aronson.

Montagner, H. (1988). *L'Attachement: Les Débuts de la Tendresse*. Paris: Stock.

Morris, W. (1890). *News from Nowhere, and Other Writings*. London: Penguin Classics.

Mullen, J. D. (1995). *Kierkegaard's Philosophy: Self-deception and Cowardice in the Present Age*. Lanham, MD: University Press of America.

Muller, J. P. (1999). Modes and functions of sublimation. *Annual of Psychoanalysis*, 26, 103–125.

Murray, H. A. (1938). *Explorations in Personality*. New York: Oxford University Press.

Nagel, T. (1986). *The View from Nowhere*. New York: Oxford University Press.

—— (2013). *Mind and Cosmos: Why the Materialist Neo-Darwinian Conceptions of Nature is Almost Certainly False*. New York: Oxford University Press.

Nietzsche, F. (1881). *The Dawn: Thoughts on the Presumptions of Morality* (translated by B. Smith). Stanford, CA: Stanford University Press, 2011.

—— (1882). *The Gay Science: With a Prelude in Rhymes and an Appendix of Songs* (translated by W. Kaufmann). New York: Vintage, 1974.

—— (1883–1885). *Thus Spoke Zarathustra: A Book for Everyone and No One* (translated by R. J. Hollingdale). London: Penguin Classics, 1961.

—— (1886). *Beyond Good and Evil: Prelude to a Philosophy of the Future* (translated by W. Kaufmann). New York: Vintage, 1989.

—— (1887–1888). *On the Genealogy of Morals and Ecce Homo* (translated by W. Kaufmann). New York: Vintage, 1989.

—— (1888). *The Anti-Christ*. New York: Soho Press, 2010.

Nobus, D. & Quinn, M. (2005). *Knowing Nothing, Staying Stupid: Elements for a Psychoanalytic Epistemology*. London: Routledge.

Northoff, G. (2011). *Neuropsychoanalysis in Practice: Brain, Self and Objects*. Oxford: Oxford University Press.

—— (2012). What is the unconscious? A novel taxonomy of psychoanalytic, psychological, neuroscientific, and philosophical concepts. In: A. Fotopoulou, D. Pfaff & M. A. Conway (eds), *From the Couch to the Lab: Trends in Psychodynamic Neuroscience*. Oxford: Oxford University Press, 266–281.

Nunberg, H. (1931). The synthetic function of the ego. *International Journal of Psychoanalysis*, 12, 123–140.

—— (1932). *Principles of Psychoanalysis: Their Application to the Neuroses*. New York: International Universities Press, 1979.

—— & Federn, E. (1906–1918). *Minutes of the Vienna Psychoanalytic Society* (4 vols). New York: International Universities Press, 1962–1974.

Ogden, C. K. (1959). *Bentham's Theory of Fictions*. Lanham, MD: Littlefield Adams.

Ogden, P., Minton, K. & Pain, C. (2006). *Trauma and the Body: A Sensorimotor Approach to Psychotherapy*. New York: W. W. Norton.

Ogden, T. H. (1998). *Reverie and Interpretation: Sensing Something Human*. Lanham, MD: Jason Aronson.

—— (2001). *Conversations at the Frontier of Dreaming*. Lanham, MD: Jason Aronson.

—— (2005). *The Art of Psychoanalysis: Dreaming Undreamt Dreams and Interrupted Cries*. London: Routledge.

—— (2008). *Rediscovering Psychoanalysis: Thinking and Dreaming, Learning and Forgetting*. London: Routledge.

Ohayon, A. (2006). *Psychologie et Psychanalyse en France: L'impossible Rencontre, 1919–1969*. Paris: Éditions la Découverte.

Ollman, B. (1977). *Alienation: Marx's Conception of Man in Capitalist Society*. Cambridge: Cambridge University Press, 1977.

Olson, C. (1949). The kingfishers. In: *C. Olson, Selected Poems of Charles Olson* (edited by R. Creeley). Berkeley, CA: University of California Press, 1993.

Orange, D., Atwood, G. E. & Stolorow, R. D. (1997). *Working Intersubjectively: Contextualism in Psychoanalytic Practice*. Hillsdale, NJ: Analytic Press.

Ornston, D. G. (ed., 1992). *Translating Freud*. New Haven, CT: Yale University Press.

Orwell, G. (1920–1950). *The Collected Essays, Journalism and Letters of George Orwell* (4 vols). London: Harcourt Penguin, 1971.

Ou, L. (2009). *Keats and Negative Capability*. London: Continuum International.

Pakaluk, M. (ed., 1991). *Other Selves: Philosophers on Friendship*. Indianapolis, IN: Hackett.

Panksepp, J. & Biven, L. (2012). *The Archaeology of Mind: Neuroevolutionary Origins of Human Emotions*. New York: W.W. Norton.

Papini, G. (1969). A visit to Freud. *Review of Existential Psychology and Psychiatry*, 9(2), 130–134.

Parsons, W. B. (1999). *The Enigma of the Oceanic Feeling: Revisioning the Psychoanalytic Theory of Mysticism*. Oxford: Oxford University Press.

Pauli, W. & Jung, C. G. (1932–1958). *Atom and Archetype: The Pauli-Jung Letters, 1932–1958* (edited by C. A. Meier, translated by D. Roscoe). Princeton, NJ: Princeton University Press.

Peirce, C. S. (1931–1958). *Collected Papers of Charles Sanders Peirce* (8 vols, edited by C. Hartshorne, P. Weiss, & A. W. Burks). Cambridge, MA: Harvard University Press.

Peraldi, F. (ed., 1981). *Polysexuality* (special issue of Semiotexte, 4–1). New York: Columbia University Press.

Perry, H. S. (1982). *Psychiatrist of America: The Life of Harry Stack Sullivan*. Cambridge, MA: Belknap Press.

Pesso, A. (1984–2012). *Presentations and Lectures by Albert Pesso on Pesos Boyden System of Psychomotor Therapy*. Seattle, WA: Amazon Digital Services, 2013.

Phillips, A. (1994). *On Flirtation*. London: Faber & Faber.

—— (1999). Taking aims: André Green and the pragmatics of passion. In: G. Kohon (ed.), *The Dead Mother: The Work of André Green*. London: Routledge, 163–172.

—— (2002). Introduction. In: S. Freud, *Wild Analysis* (edited by A. Phillips). London: Penguin.

—— (2014). *Becoming Freud: The Making of a Psychoanalyst*. New Haven, CT: Yale University Press.

Piaget, J. & Inhelder, B. (1966). *The Psychology of the Child* (translated by H. Weaver). New York: Basic Books, 2000.

Pick, I. B. (1985). Working in the countertransference. *International Journal of Psychoanalysis*, 66, 157–166.

Pierrakos, J. (1990). *Core Energetics: Developing the Capacity to Love and Heal*. Mendocino, CA: LifeRythm.

Plato (*c*. 365 BCE). *Phaedo* (translated by D. Gallop). New York: Oxford University Press, 2009.

—— (*c*. 360 BCE). *The Theaetetus of Plato* (translated by M. J. Levett). Cambridge, MA: Hackett, 1990.

—— (*c*. 355 BCE). *Plato: Timaeus* (translated by P. Kalkavage). Bemidji, MN: Focus, 2001.

Plomin, R., DeFries, J. C., Knopik, V. S. & Neiderhiser, J. M. (2012). *Behavioral Genetics* (6th edn). London: Worth.

Pontalis, J-B. (1977). *Frontiers in Psychoanalysis: Between the Dream and Psychic Pain* (translated by C. Cullen & P. Cullen). London: Hogarth Press, 1981.Porter, R. (1987). *A Social History of Madness: The World Through the Eyes of the Insane*. New York: Plume.

—— (2003). *Madness: A Brief History*. Oxford: Oxford University Press.

Pribram, K. H. & Gill, M. M. (1976). *Freud's 'Project' Reassessed: Preface to Contemporary Cognitive Theory and Neuropsychology*. New York: Basic Books.

Pytell, T. (2001). The genesis of Viktor Frankl's third Viennese school of psychotherapy. *Psychoanalytic Review*, 88, 312–334.

—— (2006). Transcending the angel beast: Viktor Frankl and the American humanistic movement. *Psychoanalytic Psychology*, 23, 490–503.

—— (2007). Extreme experience, psychological insight, and holocaust perception: Reflections on Bettelheim and Frankl. *Psychoanalytic Psychology*, 24, 641–657.

Quindeau, I. (2013). *Seduction and Desire: The Psychoanalytic Theory of Sexuality since Freud* (translated by J. Bendix). London: Karnac Books.

Rachman, A. W. (1997). *Sándor Ferenczi: The Psychoanalyst of Tenderness and Passion*. New York: Jason Aronson.

Radnitzky, G. (1970). *Contemporary Schools of Metascience* (2nd revised edn). Atlantic Highlands, NJ: Humanities Press.

Raju, P. T. (1985). *Structural Depths of Indian Thought*. Delhi: South Asian Publishers.

Rand, N. & Torok, M. (1997). *Questions for Freud: The Secret History of Psychoanalysis*. Cambridge, MA: Harvard University Press.

Rank, O. (1929–1931). *Will Therapy*. New York: Norton, 1978.

—— (1932). *Psychology and the Soul: A Study of the Origin, Conceptual Evolution, and Nature of the Soul* (translated by G. C. Richter & E. J. Lieberman). Baltimore, MD: Johns Hopkins University Press.

Rapaport, D. (1996). *The Collected Papers of David Rapaport* (edited by M. M. Gill). New York: Jason Aronson.

Rather, L. (2001). Collaborating with the unconscious other: The analysand's capacity for creative thinking. *International Journal of Psychoanalysis*, 82, 515–531.

Ray, R. A. (2008). *Touching Enlightenment: Finding Realization in the Body*. Boulder, CO: Sounds True.

Rayner, E. (1991). *The Independent Mind in British Psychoanalysis*. Lanham, MD: Jason Aronson.

Reeder, J. (2004). *Love and Hate in Psychoanalytical Institutions: The Dilemma of a Profession*. New York: Other Press.

Reich, W. (1927). *Genitality in the Theory and Therapy of the Neuroses* (translated from *The Function of the Orgasm* by P. Schmitz, edited by M. Higgins & C. M. Raphael). New York: Farrar Straus Giroux.

—— (1927–1953). *Selected Writings: An Introduction to Orgonomy*. New York: Farrar, Straus and Cudahy, 1960.

—— (1933). *Character Analysis* (translated by T. P. Wolfe). London: Vision Press, 1950.

—— (1936). *The Sexual Revolution: Toward a Self-governing Character Structure* (translated by T. P. Wolfe). London: Vision Press, 1951.

Reichenbach, K. v. (1852–1856). *Odic Force* (translated by F. D. O'Byrne). Whitefish, MT: Kessinger, 2003.

Reik, T. (1936). *Surprise and the Psychoanalyst: On the Conjecture and Comprehension of Unconscious Processes* (translated by M. M. Green). London: Routledge, 2014.

—— (1948). *Listening with the Third Ear: The Inner Experience of a Psychoanalyst*. New York: Farrar, Straus & Giroux, 1983.

Reiss, T. J. (1988). *The Uncertainty of Analysis: Problems in Truth, Meaning, and Culture*. Ithaca, NY: Cornell University Press.

Ricoeur, P. (1965). *Freud and Philosophy: An Essay on Interpretation* (translated by D. Savage). New Haven, CT: Yale University Press, 1970.

Roazen, P. (1971). *Freud and his Followers*. Cambridge, MA: Da Capo Press, 1992.

Robles, M. U. (2010). *Fanaticism in Psychoanalysis: Upheavals in the Institutions*. London: Karnac Books, 2013.

Rolland, R. (1927). Letter to Sigmund Freud, December 5th, 1927. In: *Un beau visage à tous sens: Choix de letters de Romain Rolland (1866–1944)*. Paris: Albin Michel, 264–266.

Rorty, A. O. (1993). The historicity of psychological attitudes: Love is not love which alters not when it alteration finds. In: N. K. Badhwar (ed)., *Friendship: A Philosophical Reader*. Ithaca, NY: Cornell University Press, 73–90.

Rothstein, A. (2005). Compromise formation theory: An intersubjective dimension. *Psychoanalytic Dialogues*, 15, 415–431.

Roudinesco, E. (1986). *Jacques Lacan & Co. – A History of Psychoanalysis in France, 1925–1985* (translated by J. Mehlman). Chicago: Chicago University Press, 1990.

—— (1993). *Jacques Lacan: Outline of a Life, History of a System of Thought* (translated by B. Bray). New York: Columbia University Press, 1997.

—— (2011). *Lacan: In Spite of Everything* (translated by G. Elliott). London: Verso, 2014.

Roustang, F. (1971). *Dire Mastery: Discipleship from Freud to Lacan* (translated by N. Lukacher). Baltimore, MD: Johns Hopkins University Press, 1975.

Rubenfeld, I. (2001). *The Listening Hand: How to Combine Bodywork, Intuition and Psychotherapy to Release Emotions and Heal the Pain*. London: Piatkus Books.

Rubin, G. (1975). The traffic in women: Notes toward a political economy of sex. In: R. Reiter (ed.), *Toward an Anthropology of Women*. New York: Monthly Review Press, 157–210.

Rudnytsky, P. L. (2003). *Reading Psychoanalysis: Freud, Rank, Ferenczi, Groddeck*. Ithaca, NY: Cornell University Press.

——, Bokay, A. & Giampieri-Deutsch, P. (eds, 2000). *Ferenczi's Turn in Psychoanalysis*. New York: New York University Press.

Ruitenbeek, H. M. (ed., 1973). *Freud as We Knew Him*. Detroit, MI: Wayne State University Press.

Russell, B. (1921). *The Analysis of Mind*. London: Allen & Unwin,1978.

—— (1927). *An Outline of Philosophy*. London: Allen & Unwin, 1979.

—(1956). *Portraits from Memory*. London: Allen & Unwin.

Safran, J. D. & Muran, J. C. (eds, 2003). *Negotiating the Therapeutic Alliance: A Relational Treatment Guide*. New York: Guildford Press.

Salzberger-Wittenberg, I. (1973). *Psychoanalytic Insight and Relationships: A Kleinian Approach*. London: Routledge.

Sandler, J., Sandler, A-M. & Davies, R. (eds, 2000). *Clinical and Observational Psychoanalytic Research: Roots of A Controversy*. London: Karnac Books.

Santayana, G. (1905–1906). *The Life of Reason, or the Phases of Human Progress* (2 vols). Toronto: University of Toronto Press.

Sartre, J-P. (1943). *Being and Nothingness: An Essay on Phenomenological Ontology* (translated by H. E. Barnes). New York: Washington Square Press, 1993.

—— (1947–1957). *Essays in Existentialism* (edited by W. Baskin). Secaucus, NJ: Citadel Press.

—— (1960). *Search for a Method* (translated by H. E. Barnes). New York: Vintage, 1968.

—— (1960). *Critique of Dialectical Reason* (translated by A. Sheridan-Smith). London: Verso, 1976.

Saussure, F. de (1906–1911). *Course in General Linguistics* (edited by C. S. Bailey & A. Sechehaye, translated by W. Baskin). New York: McGraw-Hill, 1966.

Sayre, K. (1976). *Cybernetics and the Philosophy of Mind*. Atlantic Highlands, NJ: Humanities Press.

Schacht, R. (1970). *Alienation*. New York: Doubleday.

Schachtel, E. G. (1959). *Metamorphosis: On the Development of Affect, Perception, Attention, and Memory*. New York: Basic Books.

Schelling, F. W. J. (1797). *First Outline of a System of the Philosophy of Nature* (translated by K. R. Peterson). Albany, NY: State University of New York, 2004.

—— (1800). *System of Transcendental Idealism* (translated by P. L. Heath). Charlottesville, VA: University of Virginia Press, 1993.

Schmitt, R. (2002). *Alienation and Freedom*. Boulder, CO: Westview Press.

Schnitzler, A. (1897). *Round Dance and Other Plays* (edited by R. Robertson, translated by J. M. Q. Davies). Oxford: Oxford University Press, 2009.

Schopenhauer, A. (1818/1844). *The World as Will and Representation* (2 vols, translated by E. F. J. Payne). Mineola, NY: Dover, 1966.

Schorske, C. (1980). *Fin-de-siècle Vienna: Politics and Culture*. New York: Vintage.

Schultz-Hencke, H. (1940). *Der gehemmte Mensch: Entwurf eines Lehrbuches der Neo-Psychoanalyse*. Stuttgart: Thieme, 1989.

Schütz, A. (1967). *Phenomenology of the Social World* (translated by G. Walsh & F. Lehnert). Evanston, Il: Northwestern University Press.

Schwartz, J. (1999). *Cassandra's Daughter: A History of Psychoanalysis*. New York: Viking.

Segal, H. (1973). *Introduction to the Work of Melanie Klein*. London: Karnac Books, 1988.

Shevrin, H., Bond, J. A., Brakel, L. A. W., Hertel, R. K., & Williams, W. J. (1996). *Conscious and Unconscious Processes: Psychodynamic, Cognitive, and Neurophysiological Convergences*. New York: Guilford Press.

Shklovsky, V. (1917). Art as device. In: *Theory of Prose* (translated by B. Sher). Champagne, IL: Dalkey Archive, 1990, 1–14.

Silberer, H. (1914). *Hidden Symbolism in Alchemy and the Occult Arts: Understanding Mysticism and its Symbolism* (translated by S. E. Jelliffe). Scotts Valley, CA: CreateSpace, 2009.

Sklar, J. (2011). *Landscapes of the Dark: History, Trauma and Psychoanalysis*. London: Karnac Books.

Solms, M. (2013). The conscious id. *Neuropsychoanalysis*, 15, 5–19. London: Karnac Books, 3–86.

—— (2015). Reply to Barratt's "Critical notes on the neuro-evolutionary archaeology of affective systems." *Psychoanalytic Review*, 102, 209–219.

—— & Turnbull, O. (2011). *The Brain and the Inner World: An Introduction to the Neuroscience of Subjective Experience* (updated edition). London: Karnac Books.

Spielrein, S. (1912). Die Destruktion als Ursache des Werdens. *Jahrbuch für psychoanalytische und psychopathologische Forschungen*, 4, 465–503. (Translated as: Destruction as the cause of coming into being. *Journal of Analytical Psychology*, 39, 155–186. Also translated as: Destruction as cause of becoming. *Psychoanalysis and Contemporary Thought*, 18, 85–118.)

Spillius, E. B., Milton, J., Garvey, P., Couve, C. & Steiner, D. (2011). *The New Dictionary of Kleinian Thought*. London: Routledge.

Spinoza, B. (1677). *Ethics* (translated by E. Curley). London: Penguin, 2005.

Stanton, M. (1991). *Sándor Ferenczi: Reconsidering Active Intervention*. New York: Jason Aronson.

Stayton, W. R. (1980). A theory of sexual orientation. *Topics in Clinical Nursing*, 1(4), 1–7. Cited in Francoeur, R. T., Cornog, M., Perper, T., & Scherzer, N. A. (eds, 1995). *The Complete Dictionary of Sexology* (new expanded edition). New York: Continuum.

Steiner, J. (1994). Patient-centered and analyst-centered interpretations: Some implications of containment and the countertransference. *Psychoanalytic Inquiry*, 14, 406–422.

Steiner, R. (1987). A worldwide international trade mark of genuineness? Some observations on the history of the English translation of the work of Sigmund Freud, focusing mainly on his technical terms. *International Review of Psychoanalysis*, 14, 33–102.
—— (ed., 2003). *Unconscious Phantasy*. London: Karnac Books.
Stekel, W. (1911–1927). *Twelve Essays on Sex and Psychoanalysis* (edited and translated by S. A. Tannenbaum). New York: Critic and Guide.
—— (1922–1926). *Patterns of Psychosexual Infantilism: Disorders of the Instincts and the Emotions* (edited and translated by E. A. Gutheil). New York: Grove Press.
Stepansky, P. E. (1983). *In Freud's Shadow: Adler in Context*. Hillsdale, NJ: Analytic Press.
Sterba, R. F. (1982). *Reminiscences of a Viennese Psychoanalyst*. Detroit, MI: Wayne State University Press.
—— (1934). The fate of the ego in analytic therapy. *International Journal of Psychoanalysis*, 15, 117–126.
Stern, D. B., Mann, C., Kantor, S. & Schlesinger, G. (eds, 1995). *Pioneers of Interpersonal Psychoanalysis*. London: Routledge.
Stern, D. N. (2000). *The Interpersonal World of the Infant: A View from Psychoanalysis and Developmental Psychology*. New York: Basic Books.
Stevens, A. (1999). *On Jung*. Princeton, NJ: Princeton University Press.
Stirner, M. (1845). *The Ego and His Own: The Case of the Individual Against Authority* (translated by S. T. Byington, edited by J. J. Martin). Mineola, NY: Dover, 2005.
Stoller, R. (1968). *Sex and Gender*. London: Karnac Books, 1984.
—— (1975). *Perversion: The Erotic Form of Hatred*. London: Karnac Books, 1986.
—— (1985). *Presentations of Gender*. New Haven, CT: Yale University Press.
—— (1992). *Observing the Erotic Imagination*. New Haven, CT: Yale University Press.
—— (1993). *Porn: Myths for the Twentieth Century*. New Haven, CT: Yale University Press.
—— (2005). *Sweet Dreams, Erotic Plots*. London: Karnac Books.
Stone, L. (1977). *The Psychoanalytic Situation: An Examination of its Development and Essential Nature*. New York: International Universities Press.
Sullivan, H. S. (1947). *Conceptions of Modern Psychiatry*. New York: Norton, 1966.
—— (1953). *The Interpersonal Theory of Psychiatry*. London: Routledge, 2003.
—— (1953–1956). *The Collected Works of Harry Stack Sullivan* (2 vols). New York: W. W. Norton, 1956.
Suttie, I. D. (1935). *The Origins of Love and Hate*. London: Free Association Books, 1999.
Suzuki, D. T. (1932). *The Lankāvatāra Sūtra: A Mahāyāna Text* (compiled 350–400 CE). Boulder, CO: Prajña Press, 1978.
Szekacs-Weisz, J. & Keve, T. (eds, 2012). *Ferenczi for Our Time: Theory and Practice*. London: Karnac Books.
Taylor, C. M. (1989). *Sources of the Self: The Making of Modern Identity*. Cambridge, MA: Harvard University Press.
Taylor, M. C. (1975). *Kierkegaard's Pseudonymous Authorship: A Study of Time and the Self*. Princeton, NJ: Princeton University Press.
—— (1980). *Sources of the Self: The Making of Modern Identity*. New York: Fordham University Press, 2000.
Thomas, St. (*c.* 40 CE). *The Gospel of Thomas: Hidden Sayings of Jesus* (translated by M. Meyer). San Francisco, CA: HarperSanFrancisco, 1992.
Thompson, C. M. (1951). *Psychoanalysis: Evolution and Development*. Piscataway, NJ: Transaction, 2002.
Thompson, M. G. (1998). The fundamental rule of psychoanalysis. *Psychoanalytic Review*, 85, 697–715.

Tinbergen, N. (1951). *The Study of Instinct*. Oxford: Clarendon Press.

Torah (ND). *Torah: The Five Books of Moses*. Philadelphia, PA: Jewish Publication Society of America, 1962.

Torsti-Hagman, M. (2003). *Harvesting Free Association* (translated by E. Valle & K. Jalas). London: Free Association.

Turiño, S. de la (2010). *Why Bisexuality Makes us Human: The Biological Significance of Homosexuality*. Raleigh, NC: Lulu.

Vaidyanathan, T. G. & Kripal, J. J. (1999). *Vishnu on Freud's Desk: A Reader in Psychoanalysis and Hinduism*. Delhi: Oxford University Press.

Vaihinger, H. (1911/1925). *The Philosophy of 'As If' – A System of the Theoretical, Practical and Religious Fictions of Mankind* (translated by C. K. Ogden). Eastford, CT: Martino, 2009.

Verhaeghe, P. (2004). *On Being Normal and Other Disorders: A Manual for Clinical Psychodiagnostics* (translated by S. Jottkandt). New York: Other Press.

Vernon, M. (2010). *The Meaning of Friendship*. London: Palgrave Macmillan.

Virgil, P. M. (29–19 BCE). *The Aeneid* (translated by R. Fagles). New York: Viking Penguin, 2006.

Wälder, R. (1930). *Das Prinzip der Mehrfachen Funktion: Bemerkungen zur Überdeterminierung," Internationale Zeitschrift für Psychoanalyse*, 16, 286–300. (Translated in 1936 as: The principle of multiple function: Observations on over-determination. *Psychoanalytic Quarterly*, 5, 45–62.)

Weber, S. (1978). *Return to Freud: Jacques Lacan's Dislocation of Psychoanalysis* (translated by M. Levine). Cambridge: Cambridge University Press.

—— (1982). *The Legend of Freud*. Minneapolis, MN: University of Minnesota Press.

Weeks, J. (1985). *Sexuality and its Discontents: Meanings, Myths and Modern Sexualities*. London: Routledge.

Weiss, E. (1935). Todestrieb und Masochismus. *Imago*, 21, 396.

—— (1957). A comparative study of psychoanalytical ego concepts. *International Journal of Psychoanalysis*, 38, 209–222.

Westermarck, E. (1891). *The History of Human Marriage*. Charleston, SC: Nabu Press, 2010.

White, D. G. (ed., 2011). *Yoga in Practice*. Princeton, NJ: Princeton University Press.

Widlöcher, D. (2001). *Infantile Sexuality and Attachment – Sexualité infantile et attachement* (translated by S. Fairfield). New York: Other Press.

Wilson, P. J. (1983). *Man, the Promising Primate: The Conditions of Human Evolution* (2nd edn). New Haven, CT: Yale University Press.

—— (1991). *The Domestication of the Human Species*. New Haven, CT: Yale University Press.

Winnicott, D. W. (1965). *The Family and Individual Development*. London: Tavistock.

—— (1965). *The Maturational Processes and the Facilitating Environment: Studies in the Theory of Emotional Development*. London: Karnac Books, 1996.

—— (1968). *Collected Papers: Through Paediatrics to Psychoanalysis*. London: Tavistock.

—— (1971). *Playing and Reality*. London: Tavistock.

Wittgenstein, L. (1945–1949). *Philosophical Investigations* (translated by G. E. M. Anscombe). New York: Macmillan, 1968.

Wolfenstein, E. V. (1993). *Psychoanalytic-Marxism: Groundwork*. London: Free Association Books.

—— (2000). *Inside/Outside Nietszche: Psychoanalytic Explorations*. Ithaca, NY: Cornell University Press.

Wolff, P. H. (1966). *The Causes, Controls, and Organization of Behavior in the Neonate*. New York: International Universities Press.

—— (1996). The irrelevance of infant observations for psychoanalysis. *Journal of the American Psychoanalytic Association*, 44, 369–392.

—— (1996). Commentaries (on responses to Wolff's "The irrelevance of infant observations for psychoanalysis"). *Journal of the America Psychoanalytic Association*, 44, 464–474.

Wood, D. C. (1989). *The Deconstruction of Time*. Atlantic Highlands, NJ: Humanities Press International.

Wordsworth, W. (1798). Lines composed a few miles above Tintern Abbey. In: W. Wordsworth & S. T. Coleridge, *Lyrical Ballads* (edited by M. Schmidt). London: Penguin, 2007.

Zaretsky, E. (2004). *Secrets of the Soul: A Social and Cultural History of Psychoanalysis*. New York: Vintage.

Zazzo, R. (1977). *Psychologie de l'Enfant et Methode Genetique: Travaux et conferences*. Paris: Delachaux et Niestle.

—— (2009). *Les Jumeaux, le Couple et la Personne* (6th edn). Paris: Presses Universitaires de France.

Žižek, S. (2008). *Violence*. New York: Picador.

—— (2011). *Living in the End Times* (revised updated edn). London: Verso.

ACKNOWLEDGMENTS

There are many people to whom I wish to express my gratitude in relation to the writing of this essay. Some have actually read and commented on my writings, some are intellectual comrades and friends, some are simply individuals with whom I have in some way crossed paths and who have in some sense inspired and supported my thinking. There are too many to name, but those who must be explicitly mentioned are, in alphabetical order: Julia June Parker-Barratt, Maggie Boden, Christopher Bollas, Jacques Derrida (now deceased), Randy Ernest, Luce Irigaray, Sam Kimball, Julia Kristeva, Jerry Piven, Andrew Samuels, Ricky Schardt (now deceased), Tod Sloan, Barrie Ruth Straus (now deceased), Peter Wolff, Sue van Zyl. My indebtedness to the reading of the works of André Green and Jean Laplanche is evident by my dedication of this essay.

ABOUT THE AUTHOR

Born and raised in Europe, Barnaby B. Barratt was certified as an adult psychoanalyst by the American Psychoanalytic Association in 1991 and served as a Training Analyst with the Michigan Psychoanalytic Association for a decade before relocating to South Africa. He currently practices as a Training Analyst in Johannesburg, and is privileged to see ten patients a day in full psychoanalysis. He is also active as a Senior Research Fellow at the Wits Institute for Social and Economic Research at the University of Witwatersrand, and a member of both the *International Psychoanalytic Association* and the *International Federation of Psychoanalytic Societies*, as well as a Fellow of the *American Psychological Association*. Dr. Barratt received his first Ph.D. from Harvard University and is additionally qualified as a sexuality healer and somatic psychologist. He is strongly interested in Asian and African cultures, and is a longstanding activist for human rights and civil liberties.

INDEX

Printed in Dunstable, United Kingdom

79255174R00138